A Survey of Genesis Through the Lens of a Kingdom Scope

Volume One

By Sue Watkins

*Many Blessings,
Sue Watkins*

A Survey of Genesis Through the Lens of a Kingdom Scope (Volume One) Consolidated Edition

Copyright © 2020 by Sue Watkins.

All Rights Reserved.

Using brief quotations as a presentation for articles, books, or other material is permitted. Otherwise, it is not permissible to replicate, store in a retrieval system, or transmit in any form, by any means, electronic, mechanical, photocopy, recording, or any other excerpt of this work without the prior permission of the author.

Unless otherwise indicated, all Scriptures presented are from the text of The New King James Version, NKJV Copyright © 1982 Thomas Nelson, Inc., used by permission. All rights reserved worldwide. All Scripture quotations were retrieved using the One Touch Biblesoft Software. All Strong's reference numbers were taken from Biblesoft's New Exhaustive Strong's Numbers and Concordance with Expanded Greek-Hebrew Dictionary, Copyright © 1994, 2003, 2006, 2010 Biblesoft, Inc. and International Bible Translators, Inc., All rights reserved.

All emphases of Scripture are added by the author.

Printed in the United States of America

First Printing as a consolidated work: December 2021

MelekShalom Publishing

ISBN-9781089177265

Table of Contents

Author's Foreword v

DAY ONE

Introduction 1

Genesis One 5

Genesis Two 41

Genesis Three 69

Genesis Four 89

Genesis Five 97

DAY TWO

Genesis Six 103

Genesis Seven 123

Genesis Eight 129

Genesis Nine 133

Genesis Ten 143

Genesis Eleven 153

DAY THREE

Genesis Twelve 169

Genesis Thirteen 185

Genesis Fourteen 191

Genesis Fifteen 201

Genesis Sixteen 213

Genesis Seventeen 217

Genesis Eighteen 229

Genesis Nineteen 237

Genesis Twenty 245

Genesis Twenty-One 251

Genesis Twenty-Two 257

Genesis Twenty-Three 267

Genesis Twenty-Four 275

Source Material 285

Glossary 287

Author's Foreword

My primary intent when structuring this study was to expose the design God put into place in ages past. Concurrent with the building of His kingdom, God is directing humanity toward eternal righteousness. He is doing so purposefully, so all of Creation might dwell together. But somewhere in human history, the simplicity of that message was mislaid.

When a student of any work lacks understanding of intent, interpretation becomes based on assumption, and fallacy occurs. Although the Protestant Bible is a compilation of sixty-six books penned by forty authors over an expanse of two millennia, it is the story of Yahweh-Yeshua's dominion. Beginning with *Genesis* and going through to the final amen of *Revelation*, that theme doesn't deviate; it proclaims the Melchizedek Kingdom is and always shall be!

The basic understanding that the Holy Spirit is the source of each biblical scroll supports the idea that the kingdom in the making is Divine. Humans penned the words while mindful of those of their period and culture. However, since the words originated in the spiritual realm, they are not bound by time. These ancient writings are still relevant today. Although their history is crucial, knowing the past doesn't change the objective. Each book in our Bible was written to point mankind to Yeshua and his kingdom – the Kingdom of Righteousness.

Yeshua is the King of Righteousness – and Yahweh is the God of Righteousness. Their message to mankind, the Bible, reveals how their work in establishing their kingdom began and how it shall continue until the kingdom is established. *Genesis* is the introduction to that revelation. It's a primer, sort of a codex to unlock the Bible's remaining books and the mysteries they hold. This discovery came to me over thirty years ago after receiving a series of connecting dreams. Those dreams prodded me and pulled me into the book of *Genesis*. After a year of study, usually daily and for hours on end, unavoidable circumstances forced me to put aside my research. I boxed my notes and shelved them in the back of a closet. The study was stored but not forgotten.

Over the ensuing years, I would open my favorite Bible and read my handwritten marginal notes. The longing for answers remained, but day-to-day living kept me busy, leaving no time for intensive study.

Then in 2009 Holy Spirit interrupted my life again. He whispered, *"Return to your Hebraic roots."* My response was, *"I'm not Jewish."* But when no further instruction came, it dawned upon me Holy Spirit was directing me to return to my study of *Genesis*. Still, I hesitated. So, Holy Spirit arranged several unusual encounters. The details are not relevant. However, afterward, I knew *Genesis* was the goal. Before long, the research pivoted around a single notion: Adam was a king! Not sure why that thought amazed me, but it did, and as I pressed into that concept, a fabulous mosaic came together, and I saw the design – God's plan. Then finally, I realized *Genesis* is merely the beginning of *Revelation*.

Much of what is shared in this writing, I believe, was purposefully hidden in plain view. Timing is the key. You see, I am confident God hid *Genesis* for a time such as this – that *Revelation* might be discovered "anew" by those alive at the end of the present age.

If you have not studied *Genesis* and have relied on others for your understanding of Creation, then this work will, in all probability, shock you. If you have listened exclusively to mainstream Bible teachers, this work shall produce a new realization of "reality."

While this study began years ago, the understanding I now possess primarily came in the last ten years. In all honesty, God used others to influence my thinking. Thankfully through them, I have been pulled from a quagmire of religious dogma. Even so, the revelation I present to you was not gained by another. It came to me here a little and there a little. Scripture shall be given to support all my conclusions. If I can't prove my suppositions, I shall say so.

Some used of God to influence my thinking have passed on to their reward. Still, many linger in the land of the living. To them all, I owe a debt of gratitude. They are all Truth-Seekers, and as such, have endured much in the pursuit of verity. To each, I thank you – to do so sufficiently is impossible.

Nonetheless, you have my eternal gratitude. I thank all who write, produce videos, podcasts, and the like. Thank you for sharing your part of revelatory truth!

Oh yes! Before I forget, I dedicate this book to my friends and family who have hung in there. You know who you are!

Sue Watkins

DAY ONE

2 Peter 3:8

But, beloved, do not forget this one thing, that with the Lord, one day is as a thousand years and a thousand years as one day.

Introduction

A bible is merely a collection of similar works combined for a single purpose. Before there was the Holy Bible, there were individual scrolls grouped and classified as the *Torah* (the teachings given by Moses), the *Nevi'im* (the scrolls of the Prophets), and the *Ketuvim* (the writings of Daniel and others). Most were penned in Hebrew, except for certain sections of Daniel and Ezra's scrolls, composed in Aramaic.

In 450 B.C.E., the Second Temple priests combined all the sacred scrolls into a single collective work called the *Tanakh,* an acronym for **T**orah, **N**evi'im, and **K**etuvim. Since that conception, very few changes have been made to the Hebrew Bible.

About a hundred years later, in the third century B.C., the *Tanakh* was translated from Hebrew into Koine Greek. That, of course, was after Alexander the Great conquered the known world and Greek replaced Aramaic as the world's universal language. That new Greek Bible was called the Septuagint and was made available to all who could afford the purchase price, making it the first Bible for the common man.

During this same time, the scribes of the Second Temple began adding more texts to the Septuagint. Principally they added the scrolls commonly called the Apocrypha. That led to the casting aside of the Hebrew *Tanakh* almost entirely. Thereby causing the Septuagint to be the primary bible being read in Judea.

Actually, by the third century B.C.E., the average Jew neither read nor spoke Hebrew. Greek and Aramaic were the common languages of the known world, including Judea. Hebrew was rarely spoken outside of the Jerusalem Temple; its priests and rabbis read the Hebrew texts, in addition to the Septuagint, but they were the exception.

The Septuagint, still in use in the first century A.D., was the Bible Jesus and his disciples read. Hence, it was the bible of the early Christian Church.[1] In the 1600s, the English-speaking world was finally given a bible, the King James Bible of 1611.[2] The history is convoluted; nonetheless, the King James Bible was primarily translated from the Masoretic Texts, including the fourteen books of the Apocrypha. However, the King James Bible also added the newly compiled Greek "New Testament."

Even though today's *Tanakh* is presented using classical Hebrew, many of the words are considered outdated, just as is the original English of the KJV. However, most of the original scrolls of the *Tanakh* were not written in "script" Hebrew. Instead, they were penned in Paleo-Hebrew. Hebrew, written in script form, did not begin until the Jews were taken into Babylonian captivity, circa 560 B.C. Thus, most of the Old Testament scrolls were initially Paleo in form.

Additionally, we note that before the Tower of Babel fell, humans communicated via a common language. I propose to you that the common language of the ancients who built Nimrod's tower was Hebrew. For the simple reason, I'm convinced the language spoken in the spirit realm is Hebrew.

Hebrew is a Semitic language, which Academia claims was derived from expressions having more ancient

---

[1] https://www.conservapedia.com/Bible#Books of the Bible, retrieved 10/21/2019
[2] https://www.history.com/topics/religion/bible, retrieved 10/21/2019

origins than the nation of Israel. That is partially true, but not entirely. Not if we consider Adam the source of the people who would become Israel.

When God dispersed the builders at Babel, they corrupted the speech handed down from Adam. The academic world bases its claim on the fact that the artifacts from the Euphrates River Valley pre-date those of the Holy Land. But to my thinking, there is a flaw in that theory; it fails to account for the antediluvian era. Scripture, in my opinion, supports the notion that the culture established by Adam pre-existed that of the Sumerians. But that's another argument for another writing.

Since it is written that Adam communed with God daily, they communicated by some means, one familiar to both. Therefore, it is reasonable to believe Adam continued to speak the language he learned in Eden even after leaving the Garden. Consequently, I hold, Adam thought in Hebrew and spoke as he thought. Continuing with that reasoning, Noah spoke Hebrew because Adam did. Therefore, everyone who exited the ark spoke Hebrew. Consequently, it's a reasonable assumption that the builders of the Tower of Babel spoke Hebrew until the tower fell.

And the Lord God said: Open his mouth and his ears, that he may hear and speak with his mouth, with the language which has been revealed; for it had ceased from the mouths of all the children of men from the day of the overthrow (of Babel). And I opened his mouth, and his ears and his lips, and I began to speak with him in Hebrew in the tongue of the creation. And he took the books of his fathers, and these were written in Hebrew, and he transcribed them, and he began from henceforth to study them, and I made known to him that which he could not (understand), and he studied them during the six rainy months.[3]

So, you can readily understand the problem: Paleo Hebrew to script Hebrew. From the *Tanakh* to the Septuagint, translation errors have occurred. However, it is possible to overcome translation errors or biases by understanding that *"Scripture is given by inspiration of God, and is profitable for doctrine, for reproof, for correction, for instruction in righteousness, that the man of God may be complete, thoroughly equipped for every good work"* 2 Timothy 3:16-17. How? By studying the Scriptures as a whole. That is why we begin with *Genesis* and compare it to the "end" we find in *Revelation*.

The term *genesis* is Greek. Its root, *genos*, means race, birth, descent, and as *genesis* suggests, "the bringing forth of a generation." Typically, it denotes nativity, or the origin of a person, or a thing.

The scribes who converted the *B'reshiyth*[4] scroll into the Septuagint named its first book *Genesis* because they believed Moses' purpose was to record the lineage of those who descended from Abraham. The *B'reshiyth* scroll was indeed a history of a family that became a nation, yet it was more.

B'reshiyth loosely translates as "in the beginning." However, in its extended use, *b'reshiyth* also hints at the origins of mankind. Those origins were a creative act; procreation came later.[5] As you will soon discover, there was more to that "beginning" than just recording a family's lineage.

---

3 Charles, R.H. *The Book of Jubilees* (Kindle Locations 881-885) Kindle Edition (emphasis added).
4 The original name of the Torah's first scroll.
5 https://www.etymonline.com/word/genesis, retrieved 10/21/2019

Some will readily debate as to whether every word of the Holy Bible should be taken literally. Regarding that argument, we note Ezekiel 17:1-3, *"The word of the LORD came to me: 'Son of man, set forth an allegory and tell the house of Israel a parable.'"* Hence, let me state this clearly as possible - God's commands are literal. However, often He delivers those commands using figurative terms. Exodus 19:3-6 provides a perfect illustration - *"This is what you are to say to the house of Jacob and what you are to tell the people of Israel 'You yourselves have seen what I did to Egypt, and how **I carried you on eagles' wings and brought you to myself**. Now, if you obey me fully and keep my covenant, then out of all nations, you will be my treasured possession. Although the whole earth is mine, you will be for me a kingdom of priests and a holy nation.' These are the words you are to speak to the Israelites"* (emphasis added).

The previous verses from Exodus demonstrate Yahweh speaking literally and, at the same time, figuratively. Did God bring the Israelites out of Egypt on the wings of eagles, literally? No! The term "eagles' wings" is an ancient idiom meaning "exit swiftly." And indeed, the Israelites exited Egypt swiftly, doing so overnight (see Exodus 14).

Yahweh spoke to the patriarchs in terms they understood, often employing metaphors or picturesque language. In other words, the authors of the ancient scrolls used words to create visualizations that were culturally understood.

To further explain, let's play a word game. Say dog aloud and then look away from the page. What did you mentally picture when you looked away? Was it a dog or the letters that spell dog? Chances are you saw the letters, but whichever, your mental picture was nonspecific. Now say aloud, "black dog." Next, "barking black dog." Then "big angry black dog, barking." The picture formed in your mind changed with each added word for the simple reason that your intellect developed whatever aspect each word contributed to the image. Your imagination triggered the effect of both seeing and hearing. This illustration exemplifies the way Moses wrote *Genesis,* although with terms that were familiar to his readers.

Letter	Name	Numeric Value	Meaning	Paleo	Latin Equivalent
א	Aleph	1	Ox		A
ב	Bet	2	House		B
ג	Gimel	3	Lift up		G
ד	Dalet	4	Door		D
ה	Hei	5	Behold		H
ו	Vav	6	Nail		V
ז	Zayin	7	Weapon		Z
ח	Chet	8	Fence		CH
ט	Tet	9	Surround		T
י	Yod	10	Arm/Work		Y
כ	Kaf	20,500	Palm/Open		K
ל	Lamed	30	Staff/Control		L
מ	Mem	40,600	Water/Chaos		M
נ	Nun	50,700	Seed		N
ס	Samekh	60	Support		S
ע	Ayin	70	Eye/To see		
פ	Pey	80,800	Mouth/Word		P
צ	Tsade	90,900	Man/Desire		TS
ק	Qof	100	Behind		K
ר	Resh	200	Head Person		R
ש	Shin	300	Eat/Consume		SH
ת	Tav	400	Mark/Covenant		T

Genesis One

Genesis 1:1, "In the beginning, God created the heavens and the earth."

◀ **Genesis 1:1** ▶

776 [e]	853 [e]	8064 [e]	853 [e]	430 [e]	1254 [e]	7225 [e]
hā·'ā·reṣ.	wə·'êṯ	haš·šā·ma·yim	'êṯ	'ĕ·lō·hîm;	bā·rā	bə·rê·šîṯ
הָאָֽרֶץ׃	וְאֵ֥ת	הַשָּׁמַ֖יִם	אֵ֥ת	אֱלֹהִ֑ים	בָּרָ֣א	בְּרֵאשִׁ֖ית 1
the earth	and	the heavens	-	God	created	In the beginning

The above is a snapshot of the Interlinear Bible. Notice there are three versions: English, Hebrew, and transliterated Hebrew. The reference number over each word links to Strong's Exhaustive Concordance and Lexicons. If you have never used an Interlinear Bible as a study tool, I encourage you to begin to do so. In the footnote below is the web address of Bible Hub.[6] It's free - all you need is access to the internet.

Now look back at the chart of Hebrew letters. Note each letter has a Paleo symbol as well as a numeric value. That symbol is called a pictograph, and it is a representation of a linguistic concept. These ancient symbols add nuances to script Hebrew and complement the straightforward approach to interpretation. Explaining how this works in depth is beyond the scope of our study. Still, it's essential to recognize every letter was placed in the Bible purposefully. And for that reason, we must give each stroke of the pen its due consideration.

Using the Interlinear Bible, reading right to left, the transliterated Hebrew is *b'reshiyth* (in the beginning) *bara* (created) *Elohim* (God) *et h'shamayim* (the heavens) *vav'* (and) *et ha'erets* (the earth). Seven words in Hebrew – ten in English.

So, let's repeat Genesis 1:1 beginning with Hebrew, which I present left to right for the ease of your reading: *B'reshiyth bara Elohim et h'shamayim v' et ha'erets.* Then in English: "In the beginning, God created the heavens and the earth." Perhaps you noted there is a Hebrew word not translated into English – "*et?*" We shall return to that word momentarily, but first, notice the '*vav*' (the emboldened *v*' that follows *h'shamayim*).

Applying the rules of Hebrew syntax, a *vav* often serves as a conjunction. Naturally, someone decided Moses placed that particular *vav* in the sentence to do just that – to be conjunctive. The problem is I'm not convinced that was Moses' intent.

---

6 https://biblehub.com/interlinear/genesis/1.htm, retrieved 10/23/2019

Revelation 21:1, *"Now I saw a new heaven and a new earth, for the first heaven and the first earth had passed away."*

Most Christians think of terrestrials as humans and celestials as angels. Therefore, each exists in different realms. Suppose we define "realm" as a sphere of influence or even a territory, then yes. In that case, terrestrials and celestials exist in different realms. Suppose we define a "realm" as a kingdom. In that case, It's my belief that when God created "in the beginning," that was true then as well. Essentially, I propose Moses used the *vav* to imply heaven and earth were fastened together. In other words, that which God desired for the end, He created in the beginning.[7]

Now, let's focus on the two-letter word *"et."* Et or the *aleph-tav* cannot be translated into English. Teachers of Hebrew will say *"et"* is a preposition or perhaps an adverb. I have no argument with that explanation of *"et."* However, I shall contend throughout this study that Holy Spirit often meant the את for something more than a preposition or an adverb. The את marks, in fact, the ת *(tav)* means "the mark." The א *(aleph)* symbolizes the ox head, the symbol of strength, the crown of leadership. Thus, when the *Aleph-Tav* appear together, as in Genesis 1:1, something far more significant than grammatical structure is in play. These two Hebrew letters are telling us to look to the king – the Eternal King.

This insight "fell upon me" like a ton of bricks. Proverbs 25:2, *"It is the glory of God to conceal a thing: but the honor of kings is to search out a matter."* Prophet Isaiah wrote that God's words are given *"precept upon precept; line upon line; here a little, there a little."* This indicates we should think of Scripture as a mosaic of data points, which we are to assemble. Essentially as we would, a puzzle. Therefore, we shall adhere to Isaiah's principle and build on this concept together, line upon line throughout this study. So, we shall gather the pieces and rearrange them that we might see what God has concealed. For revelatory truth, the whole picture is required to *"present yourself approved by God; a worker who does not need to be ashamed, rightly dividing the word of truth,"* 2 Timothy 2:15.

According to Strong's OT #7225,[8] the first word of Genesis 1:1 is *re'shiyth* (pronounced ray-sheeth). The root of *re'shiyth* is *ro'sh*. *Ro'sh* means in the first place, whether of time, order, rank, specifically, a first fruit.

I'm sure you noticed; the Interlinear Bible has the first word of Genesis 1:1 as **b'reshiyth**. That means a *"bet"* was added to *re'shiyth*. Why? The *bet* (the second letter of the Hebrew alphabet) signifies the Creator's intent for plurality. What? Plurality? God wants to dwell with His Creation. He wants a family.

Isaiah 46:9-10, *"Remember the former things, those of long ago; I am God, and there is no other; I am God, and there is none like me. I make known the end from the beginning, from ancient times, what is still to come. I say: My purpose will stand, and I will do all that I please."*

Revelation 21:1-3, *"And I saw a new heaven and a new earth: for the first heaven and the first earth were passed away; and there was no more sea. And I John saw the holy city, new Jerusalem, coming down from God out of heaven, prepared as a bride*

---

7 The concept that heaven and earth were connected in the beginning is important. The premise that God formed a "single" creation – in a "singularity" event must be considered if we are to grasp that He has but one kingdom, one government.

8 All Strong's numeric references were taken from Biblesoft's New Exhaustive *Strong's Numbers and Concordance with Expanded Greek-Hebrew Dictionary*. Copyright © 1994, 2003, 2006 Biblesoft, Inc. and International Bible Translators, Inc.

adorned for her husband. And I heard a great voice out of heaven saying, 'Behold, the tabernacle of God is with men, and he will dwell with them, and they shall be his people, and God himself shall be with them, and be their God.'"

The Creator designed the beginning with the end in mind. At the end of this age, God will tabernacle with mankind forever and ever! That means: God and His righteous created beings will NOT have separate dwelling places. This is why Holy Spirit drew a "*bet*"[9] as the first letter of *Genesis*.

The *aleph* brings order; it denotes oneness and, thus, symbolizes the Godhead. When the *aleph* and *bet* are placed side by side, they form the word, אב – *Ab*, Father.

Father (Creator and Supreme God) expresses Himself as Yahweh. He also manifests, especially to humans, as Yeshua. Yahweh and Yeshua are one God, one Spirit, and together form "the" Divine Family of the Cosmos – Father, Son, and Spirit. They are the House of God. Yet, they desire more. Their plan from the beginning has been to merge with the righteous, thereby forming the Kingdom of Righteousness.

At the end of the current age, there shall be a marriage between Christ and the Righteous. If we substitute the word "merge" with "wed," the grand design for the Creation becomes more apparent. God desiring to "create" His own kind, planned for the transformation of humans. They are to be like Christ Jesus.

Exodus 19:5-6 was a proposal of marriage (a merger): *"Now, if you obey me fully and keep my covenant, then out of all nations, you will be my treasured possession* (this phrasing infers Yahweh is speaking to His wife/bride). *Although the whole earth is mine, you will be for me a kingdom of priests and a holy nation."*

Thousands of years later, the Creator would again propose. The second proposal was to the *ekklēsía* (the New Testament church). That proposal was the last marriage proposal God shall make. Yeshua asked his followers to come out of the world and become his. This final proposal from the Son (בן *ben*) of Man to mankind was also an expression of the Father's desire.

Please do not misunderstand what I am stating. I am not saying that the Father is the Son or the Son is the Father, but both are א (*aleph*); thus, both are the Creator. They are the first house, along with the pre-Adamic celestials. The second/final house that the Bible was written to is also the everlasting kingdom, which God is currently building.[10]

Everything began with אב - Yahweh as the *Aleph* and Yeshua as the *Bet*. Together they are "the" first house – *Abba's* House. But because the *bet* is the first letter placed in the Bible – Yeshua is the Head of *Abba's* House. Note that both אב (*Ab*) and בן (*ben*) contain a "*bet*." What are we to make of that? Simply, that Creation was "for" the Son – it began with Him and ends with Him!

Revelation 22:12-16, *"Behold, I am coming soon! My reward is with me, and I will give everyone according to what he has done. I am the* **Alpha and the Omega,** *the First and the Last, the Beginning and the End. Blessed are those who wash*

---

9 Please note from the chart of Hebrew letters that a *bet* equates with "house."
10 To be exact, God is not bringing mankind into His family to transform men into gods. God is adopting mankind to make them "children."

their robes, that they may have the right to the tree of life and may go through the gates into the city. Outside are the dogs, those who practice magic arts, the sexually immoral, the murderers, the idolaters, and everyone who loves and practices falsehood. I, Jesus, have sent my angel to give you this testimony for the churches. I am the Root and the Offspring of David and the bright Morning Star."

- Alpha = *Aleph*
- Omega = *Tav*

Yeshua clearly stated that he is the *Aleph-Tav*. He is the first and last letter of the Bible. If we note he is the "*bet*" of Genesis 1:1 and the *nun* in the "amen" of Revelation 22:21. Then he is the Son *(Bet-Nun)* who fulfills the desires of the Father *(Aleph-Bet)*. That is why, according to Ephesians 2:22 that we are *"in him, you too are being built together to become a dwelling in which God lives by his Spirit."*

Moses revealed Yeshua as the *Bet*. John saw him as the *Nun*. Through Yeshua, as the Son, we are transformed into a dwelling for God. All the words God has spoken *"is the Word"* and *"through him, all things were made."* The purpose of the word, given to mankind, was to make *"the Word flesh,"* that HE might make *"his dwelling among us."*

Before Adam, the cosmos was populated by an older species. Then the god of Chaos disrupted Divine Order. So, the Creator began again, doing so with Adam (as a new species). And again, after Adam sinned. And again, after the great flood. And again, after the Tower of Babel. And again, after Abraham's offspring went into Egypt. These "redo" were not mistakes of Creation; they were actually phases of the "grand" plan. Not at any time was the Creator caught off guard by either angelic or human acts.

Revelation 21:1 *"And I saw a new heaven and a new earth: for the first heaven and the first earth were passed away; and there was no more sea.* Did God intentionally organize two cosmic governments, one for the beginning and another for the end of the age? I think not. So, when we connect Genesis 1:1 with Revelation 21:1, we need to consider what John was saying passed away. The "what" is discovered by reading the adjoining phrase - *"there was no more sea."* There shall not be a sea in the age to come is exceptionally significant and explained when we understand the "sea" represents Chaos.

Let's turn back to the word *b'reshiyth*; additional examination is warranted. As indicated, "in the beginning" is typically expressed in Hebrew as *re'shiyth*. The root word is *reysh* and means "of the highest within an order. Yet, Moses chose to use a *bet* as the first letter because Moses was signaling that the dwelling of the highest order was maintained by covenant. What covenant? What order?

Psalms 110:4, *"The Lord has sworn and will not relent, 'You are a priest **forever** according to the **order** of Melchizedek,'"* (emphasis added). Rooted in this verse is the covenant between Father and Son.

"Order," as used in Psalms 110:4, is *dibrah*, the feminine version of *dabar*. It is possible to translate *dabar* and *dibrah* as "word" or "a spoken matter." But as noted, it was translated in this passage as "order." Order is defined by most dictionaries as "the arrangement or disposition of people or things with each other, according to a sequence, pattern, or method." "Order" is feminine, whereas "word" is masculine. And note what happens when we add the word "forever." Forever – *'owlam* means concealed, properly within or by eternity. Thus, Psalms 110:4 means, "Yahweh has sworn and will not relent. According to the "ordering" of Melchizedek, you (Yeshua) are a priest concealed from eternity to eternity." In other words, from the eternal past into the infinite future, Yeshua is the Melchizedek. But since the order is feminine, a bride is needed.

You see, Father God made a covenant with God the Son. Yeshua would inherit the Kingdom of Righteousness when the bride matured. The Groom, as Word, brings order, but the bride must express the Word! The Melchizedek Kingdom is governed by an "order" of kings and priests. The "head" of the Melchizedek Kingdom is Yeshua (he is King/High Priest). However, the body (the ruling citizens) of the Melchizedek Kingdom is the Bride of Christ. This understanding was concealed. It is now ready to be spoken! That which was hidden for the end-time is ready to be revealed by a prophetic bride!

𐤀𐤔𐤉𐤕 This pictographic presentation of *reshiyth* translates as "the head and strong leader consumes the hand (the deed) that separates (fences off)." Yeshua is the head of Yahweh's house. He is the "strong leader" who consumes the works of the adversarial system. He has fenced off the righteous from the works of chaos.

Isaiah 28:16, *"Therefore thus says the Lord God, 'Behold, I lay in Zion for a foundation, a stone, a tried stone, a precious cornerstone, a sure foundation…'"* This foundational stone of God's Temple is Jesus. Stone or *eben* in Hebrew representationally suggests "First Son."

Psalms 102:25, *"Of old have you laid the foundation of the earth: and the heavens are the work of your hands."*

Isaiah 48:13, *"Mine hand also hath laid the foundation of the earth, and my right hand hath spanned the heavens…."*

Matthew 25:34, *"Then shall the King say unto them on his right hand, 'Come, you blessed of my Father, inherit the kingdom prepared for you from the foundation of the world…'"*

Ephesians 3:14-19, *"For this cause, I bow my knees unto the Father of our Lord Jesus Christ, of whom the whole family in heaven and earth is named, that he would grant you, according to the riches of his glory, to be strengthened with might by his Spirit in the inner man; that Christ may dwell in your hearts by faith; that you, being rooted and grounded in love, may be able to comprehend with all saints what is the breadth, and length, and depth, and height; and to know the love of Christ, which passes knowledge, that you might be filled with all the fullness of God."*

Bara and *b'reshiyth* stem from the same root– *br* – house of the highest order. The word "*bara*" means to create by cutting. God, as the Creator *Elohiym*, cut Word from Himself to create. Essentially, God made a covenant with Himself. In other words, Yahweh covenanted with Yeshua to create.

Strong's OT#1254 defines *bara'* as a primitive root that means create; to cut. It is also true that only Yahweh is capable of *bara*. Only He can maintain an everlasting covenant. Through the Yahweh-Yeshua covenant, all life forms came into being and are held together. God did not create from "nothing." Instead, by the sound of His Word!

Many have speculated that the *elohim* of Genesis 1:1 was the "Divine Council." It wasn't. They are not

Creators. Yahweh's Divine Council is a collective body of superior beings. They are the *elohim* – "the gods from there." However, they are not allowed to create realms of existence. That exclusive privilege belongs to Yahweh. So, Yahweh is the *Elohiym* of Genesis 1:1.

Later in this writing, we shall dive deeper into the Divine Council and its role as we currently understand it. To do so now would muddy the waters (even more).

Elohim can be translated as: "gods of, or from, there."[11] Strong's OT #430 is '*elohim* (el-o-heem), the plural form of OT #433 *Eloah*. In the ordinary sense, *elohim* means gods (plural). When specifically used in the plural form, especially with "the" as a precedent article, *elohim* is almost always translated as *Elohim* to signify the Supreme God. Occasionally *elohim* supplies the needed deference to divine beings or simply serves as a needed superlative. In nearly all regards, *elohim* equates to *allah* [Aramaic] to denote the deities that came from the spirit world. The singular root of *elohim* is *el*. *El* can either be translated as a god or as Supreme God. When understood properly, *elohim* designates residency. By that, I mean *elohim* should be viewed as "those from the spirit world" when used in the collective sense.

The following verses explain further:

→ Leviticus 19:4, *"Turn you not unto idols, nor make to yourselves molten gods (elohim), I am the Lord your God (Elohim)."* In this instance, both the gods and Yahweh, as the Superior God, are referenced.

→ Deuteronomy 6:14, *"You shall not go after other gods (elohim), of the gods (elohim) of the people which are round about you…."* These two uses of *elohim* refer to the gods worshipped instead of Yahweh.

→ 1 Samuel 28:13, *"And the king said unto her, 'Be not afraid: for what saw thou?' And the woman said unto Saul, 'I saw gods (elohim) ascending out of the earth'"* The *elohim* of this verse refers to the spirits of the dead Nephilim.

The spirit world, of course, is unseen by humans. Hence it is thought that it has more spatial dimensions than the seen realm. In my opinion, that theory is flawed. Dimensional space does not vary throughout the universal order of existence. The difference between the seen and the unseen "worlds" is not the number of dimensions. Let me say this another way. Humans are flawed; they are incapable of perceiving all the spatial dimensions.

So far, our understanding of Genesis 1:1 (*b'reshiyth bara elohim* את *ha-shamayim* ו את *ha-erets*) – is - When *Elohiym*[12] created (He) formed the את heavens and the את earth (the entire cosmos). The "when" should be clear. God created the existence of the cosmos before Genesis 1:2 occurred.

While the Bible is not explicit concerning details, enough information is shared to know a rebellion occurred. Apparently, that rebellion began when certain members of the Divine Council wanted more power, and chaos resulted. Before Genesis 1:1, or perhaps during the space of existence between Genesis 1:1 and 1:2, Chaos[13] sought to unseat the Godhead. To counter, Yahweh determined a new ordering was

---

11 Heiser, Michael S., *The Unseen Realm: Recovering the Supernatural Worldview of the Bible* (Kindle Locations 454-455). Lexham Press. Kindle Edition
12 In this writing Elohiym refers to Yahweh as the Supreme God and Judge.

needed. Essentially, the new order placed a new "ruler" over the divine government. *'Erets* (the sphere that would later be known to humans as earth) was assigned as the seat for the new government, or perhaps more likely, it was merely redesigned. Anyway, from that point onward, the Eternal Melchizedek was set to rule over Yahweh's kingdom, forever and ever.

Allow me to reiterate that Yahweh functions per the rules of righteousness. My apologies for being repetitive. However, we all must learn to think in spiritual terms. Yahweh is the God of Righteousness, the source of ALL righteousness. His kingdom is the Kingdom of Righteousness, and the king of that kingdom is the King of Righteousness (Melchizedek).

Psalms 89:14, *"Righteousness and justice are the foundation of your throne, love and faithfulness go before you."*

Yahweh, the Supreme God, the Creator, sits as the Judge over the Divine Council. However, as previously stated, at some point in the ancient past, a rebellion occurred. I feel confident it started within the Divine Council. A new "order" or arrangement for the government of Yahweh's kingdom was mandated. According to Scripture, by the end of this age, that new order shall fully rest upon the shoulders of the Eternal Melchizedek.

So, according to *bara elohim*, God cut a covenant with Himself since only He could fulfill the covenant's stipulations. That covenant determined "WHO" would govern the cosmos. Cosmos is a Greek word that means the orderly system that exists within all things.

In addition to viewing *Genesis* as the restoration of order, be mindful that Moses was not writing a discourse on creationism versus Darwinism. *Genesis* was written for the benefit of the Israelites after the exodus from Egypt. Although Moses had led the Israelites out of Egypt, Egypt was still in their thinking. They built a golden calf and sacrificed to it while Moses negotiated their marriage to the Creator of the Cosmos. By the way, Egypt in biblical symbolism represents a sin-tainted world.

Moses did not deny the existence of other deities. Instead, he presented the case for Hebrew exceptionalism and gave a record of the beginnings of the Kingdom of Yahweh. The same kingdom (government) which the Israelites were to fashion once they occupied the Promised Land.

Revelation 1:8, *"I am the Alpha (Aleph) and the Omega (Tav)," says the Lord God, "who is, and who was, and who is to come, the Almighty."*

Revelation 21:6, *"He said to me: 'It is done. I am the Alpha and the Omega, the Beginning, and the End.'"*

Revelation 22:12-13, *"Behold, I am coming soon! My reward is with me, and I will give it to everyone according to what he has done. I am the Alpha and the Omega, the First and the Last, the Beginning and the End."*

Hebrews 1:1-4, *"God, who at sundry times and in differing manners spoke in time past unto the fathers by the prophets, has in these last days spoken unto us by his Son, whom he hath appointed heir of all things, by whom also he made the worlds; who*

---

13 Chaos is personified deliberately. Chaos is the seven-headed dragon of Revelation 13, and the fourth beast of Daniel 7:7.

being the brightness of his glory, and the express image of his person, and upholding all things by the word of his power, when he had by himself purged our sins, sat down on the right hand of the Majesty on high being made so much better than the angels, as he hath by inheritance obtained a more excellent name than they."

John 1:1-3 *"In the beginning was the Word, and the Word was with God, and the Word was God. He was with God in the beginning. Through him, all things were made; without him, nothing was made that has been made."*

Hebrew 1:5-13, *"For to which of the angels did God ever say, 'You are my Son, today I have become your Father?' Or again, 'I will be his Father, and he will be my Son?' And again, when God brings his firstborn into the world, he says, 'Let all God's angels worship him.' In speaking of the angels, he says, He makes his angels winds, his servants as flames of fire.' But about the Son, he says, 'Your throne, O God, will last forever and ever, and righteousness will be the scepter of your kingdom. You have loved righteousness and hated wickedness; therefore, God, your God, has set you above your companions by anointing you with the oil of joy.' He also says, 'In the beginning, O Lord, you laid the foundations of the earth, and the heavens are the work of your hands. They will perish, but you remain; they will all wear out like a garment. You will roll them up like a robe; like a garment, they will be changed. But you remain the same, and your years will never end.' To which of the angels did God ever say, "Sit at my right hand until I make your enemies a footstool for your feet?"'*

"I am the Aleph and Tav," as an idiom means "I am the 'a' and the 'z,'" - *"the first and the last."* Or to state more precisely, "I am the beginning, the commencement to the outermost, which is the end...."[14]

Earth kings have always believed their power and authority came from God (gods). Concerning Adam, this was unquestionably true. The *aleph* represented his divine commission as *'erets* first king, and the *tav* signified the authority of the covenant that gave purpose to his life. Hence, for as long as he lived, Adam was the king over all earthly kings. Adam represented Yahweh, and because he did, he was qualified to use the *Aleph-Tav* as his royal emblem, the seal exclusively associated with the Kingdom of Righteousness. As Paleo-Hebrew markings, *Aleph-Tav* ✝📯 pictures the "covenant of a strong leader," who is the King of kings.

Yet, Yeshua told John the Revelator that he "is" the *Aleph-Tav*. In the truest sense, Adam represented Yeshua. Yeshua was given his Divine "commission" before Adam was created. That clearly indicates Yeshua was the King of kings before Adam. So, indeed Yeshua is the *Aleph* (the first), and since he is eternal, he is the last; therefore, the *Tav*.

Adam's act of disobedience caused him to fail as a righteous representative. Yeshua was obedient to Yahweh, even to death. That obedience qualified him to be the King of Righteousness. The reality is Yeshua went to the Cross as the sacrificial Lamb of God because it was required of him. Apostle Paul wrote because Yeshua died and rose again, he was granted all authority. So, the *Aleph* belongs to Yeshua not because he is God but because he fulfilled his Divine commission. Essentially, it was the Cross that afforded Yeshua the *Tav* – the power of "the" Overcomer of Death. He then is the Eternal Melchizedek, the Eternal King of Righteousness. Yeshua, alone, deserves the *Aleph-Tav* as his royal insignia.

Initially, the *Aleph* was drawn as the head of an ox 📯 to represent strength, leadership, and power. Whereas

---

14 https://www.cepher.net/on-the-aleph-tahv.aspx, retrieved 10/22/2019

the original *Tav* resembled ✝ or x (a tilted cross) and symbolized covenant as a joining together of perfection. Over time, *Aleph-Tav* became an idiom expressing the embodiment of all righteousness. Yeshua is righteousness personified - the first and the last - which commences and completes the First and Second House of Yahweh. In this writing, the second house, which is presently being built, is what I shall refer to as the Melchizedek Kingdom. The *Aleph-Tav* is its emblem, denoting the Melchizedekian Order.

1 Peter 1:20, *"He was chosen before the creation of the world but was revealed in these last times for your sake."*

Verse Two

> Genesis 1:2 – *'Erets* became formless; void; darkness fell upon the abyss, (then) Divine Spirit passed-over faces (in) the waters (author's rendering).

Genesis 1:1-2 is a preamble to the remaining verses of Chapter One. Verses one and two introduce Father God as the Architect, God the Son as the Builder, and Spirit God as the Supervisor-in-Charge, and their plan to overcome the works of Chaos by building the Melchizedek Kingdom. In other words, these first two verses supply the rationale for "re-structuring" the government of the cosmos.

Mayim translates as waters (plural). *Mayim* is also used in a singular sense occasionally. Such as water. Additionally, verse two does not read 'the' Spirit, nor 'a' Spirit, but *Ruach Elohiym*. Which informs the reader that "Spirit" *Elohiym* hovered above the waters. *Ruach* can also mean the breath of life or the wind of movement; thus, it would also be correct to render the verse "the Breath of Life passed over the sea of chaos." Which perhaps, paints a picture of Holy Spirit moving over the "faces" held captive in the sea. Or perhaps, the faces that comprised the sea of Chaos. But if it was the latter, why did *Ruach Elohiym* hover?

A fallen god, Chaos, cast out of Yahweh's Holy Place, fell, forming an abyss. He rose up to become a roaring sea covering the field of Yahweh. As vile darkness, this dragon rose from the deep, spread out like treacherous waters, covering the face, the whole of *'erets*! Seeing into the future, Spirit God, concerned for the faces held captive by Chaos' deception, assessed the situation. Then said, *"Let there be Light!"* Thus, the hovering afforded assessment of the situation.

Chaos entered *'erets,* causing it to become void, empty, dark, and flooded with water. Nothing might have existed before Genesis 1:1. However, Genesis 1:2 clearly describes more than an incomplete Earth. It portrays a state of distress in *'erets*.[15] *"Erets* was formless and distorted. The text utilizes two descriptive words: *tohu* (confused and empty) and *bohu* (uninhabitable). These two strongly suggest *'erets* was previously inhabited. If that was the case, it is highly likely that Eden, as a cosmic mountain, was connected to *'erets* before Genesis 1:2. And for that reason, the Creator restructured *'erets,* making it His field for His expected harvest.

---

[15] *'Erets* is Hebrew and translated often as earth, world, land, ground. Symbolically, *'erets* is the middle domain existing between heaven and hell. Spiritually, it is the field where humans are harvested.

Choshek (Hebrew for darkness) is Strong's OT #2822 (kho-shek). *Choshek* is both literal and figurative and often portrayed with "death."

Tehowm[16] (Hebrew for "the deep"), Strong's OT #8415 (teh-home), is defined as an abyss (a surging mass of water). Still, the ancients considered the abyss more than the source of the seas or subterranean waters. As indicated, *tehowm* parallels in meaning with the Greek word abyss, thus suggesting a subterranean region "under" *'erets*. The ancients theorized "*tehowm*" was **under** *'erets*, not **in**.

This abyss was intended for (assigned to) the fallen rebellious spirits to inhabit. It could not support human life since it was thought to be as far below *'erets* as heaven is above. Still, it would become the realm or domain that the souls of dead humans were escorted to in their afterlife. I hesitate to say it was "hell," but that's the general idea.

Now, note the following from Isaiah 60:2, *"For, behold, the darkness* (choshek) *shall cover the earth, and gross darkness* (araphel) *the people…."*

Apostle Paul expressed a similar thought: *"And you he has quickened; you who were **dead in trespasses and sins**. Where in time past you walked according to the course of this world, according to the **prince of the power of the air**, the spirit that now works in the children of disobedience…."* Ephesians 2:1-2 (emphasis added).

Paul wrote *archon*, and the translators, prince. Paul penned *xxousias* which was translated as power. The implication is that this *archon* functions with superior force as the prince over the "government" of the air. He rules in the breathable atmosphere (the *aeros of 'erets*). His superior strength (influence) over humans is strong because he is a fallen god possessed with a maniacal desire to destroy mankind by provoking them to commit evil.

Whereas Genesis 1:1 introduces the Superior God who creates, Genesis 1:2 introduces the concept of Chaos,[17] as a god who deceives. Consequently, the text depicts the ongoing cosmic war by juxtaposing its commanders. Or we could say Genesis 1:1 introduces Yahweh-Yeshua, and Genesis 1:2 makes known their adversaries, darkness, and death.

Paniym (faces) is the plural of *paneh*. *Paneh* describes the portion of the face that turns or looks. In other words, someone's facial appearance. That there were *paniym* in the waters – suggests the faces belonged to humans, caught in the cosmic sea of chaos.

Bohu means empty or void. *Bohu* is used only three times in Scripture. All three times are in conjunction with *tohu*.

1) Genesis 1:2, *"And the earth was **without form**, and **void**; and darkness was upon the face of the deep. And the*

---

16 *Tĕhôm*, usually translated "the deep," occurs in Gen 1:2 as a designation of the primeval sea and is frequently used in the OT to denote the cosmic →sea (*Yam*) – Dictionary of Deities and Demons in the Bible.

17 *Drakōn* is the Greek word (Latin draco) which is used in LXX (33 occurrences), NT and Pseudepigrapha for a large monster which often appears as opponent of God or his people. It is often related to the sea and can be identified or associated with a snake (→Serpent). In the NT, the word only appears in Revelation (13 occurrences) – *Dictionary of Deities and Demons in the Bible*.

Spirit of God moved upon the face of the waters."

2) Isaiah 34:11, *"But the cormorant and the bittern shall possess it; the owl also and the raven shall dwell in it: and he shall stretch out upon it the line of* **confusion***, and the stones of* **emptiness***."*

3) Jeremiah 4:23, *"I beheld the earth, and, lo, it was* **without form, and void;** *and the heavens, and they had no light."*

Conclusion: *Tohu* and *bohu* work in tandem, and together, they spew forth chaos and confusion. Confusion is a twisting of truth, deception, evil at work. 1 Corinthians 14:33, *"For God is not the author of confusion…."*

The KJV and the NIV translated *hayah* as "was," and I totally disagree with their rendering. *Hayah*[18] (haw-yaw) means to exist by "come to pass," to become. Earth **became** empty and void.

Ruach Elohiym – the BREATH (or the Life Force of God Supreme) hovered over the faces held captive by confusion (dark waters).

Moved – *rachaph (raw-kahf)* – means to flutter. In other words, Holy Spirit fluttered his wings and separated the people from Chaos as He breathed upon them. He passed over the waters and spoke the Word of God to those He saw there. He witnessed to them that they might hear and, consequently, be set free. That, my friend, was Earth's first Passover!

Deuteronomy 32:11-12, *"As an eagle stirs up her nest, flutters* (rachaph) *over her young, spreads abroad her wings, takes them, bears them on her wings, so the Lord alone did lead him, and there was no strange god with him."*

Isaiah 60:1-2, *"Arise, shine; for your light has come! And the glory of the Lord is risen upon you. For behold, the darkness shall cover the earth, and deep darkness the people; but the Lord will arise over you, and His glory will be seen upon you."*

Genesis 1:2 paints a picture of a loving God, Holy Spirit, like a dove, fluttering over the captives held in the chaotic sea of deception. And gives reason for why God created (re-created).

In summarization, before examining the six days of Creation, let's recap Genesis 1:1-2. As previously stated, these two verses supply the reason for the acts of creation that began with Genesis 1:3. However, they are more. They introduce the entire Bible and could be paraphrased as "At the beginning of all things, God created the cosmos. The earth became uninhabitable and empty, and in the abyss was darkness. The Spirit of God hovered over the faces of the waters…"

The keywords introduce God (*Elohiym*), *'erets,* darkness (Chaos), Holy Spirit. Additionally, we see the love of God toward the future species, mankind. Knowing the end from the beginning, "Light" was birth from compassion, *"for God so loved the world, He gave His only Son."*

Day One

---

[18] Strong's OT #1961 *hayah* (haw-yaw); a primitive root [compare OT #1933]; to exist, i.e., be or become, come to pass (always emphatic, and not a mere copula or auxiliary).

Genesis 1:3–5, *"And God said, 'Let there be light,' and there was light. And God saw the light, that it was good, and God divided the light from the darkness. And God called the light Day, and the darkness he called Night. And the evening and the morning were the first day."*

Light, in Hebrew, is *owr* (aleph-vav-resh). The pictograph of *owr* 𐤀𐤅𐤓 symbolizes a strong leader connected to "the head." In other words, Yeshua, linked to Yahweh, is "a strong leader" and "the Light of the World," revealing righteousness.

John 8:12, *"When Jesus spoke again to the people, he said, 'I am the light of the world. Whoever follows me will never walk in darkness but will have the light of life.'"*

James 1:17, *"Every good gift and every perfect gift is from above, and cometh down from the Father of lights, with whom is no variableness, neither shadow of turning."*

The verb in Genesis 1:3 is "said." God spoke, and it was so. Day One was an immediate response to Holy Spirit's hovering. *"So shall my word be that goes forth out of my mouth: it shall not return unto me void, but it shall accomplish that which I please, and it shall prosper in the thing whereto I sent it."* Isaiah 55:11.

Scripture is clear that there was a cosmic rebellion against the authority of the Creator. What is not clear is when it began and how many were involved. We know, also from Scripture, that rebellion is ongoing. It shall not be eradicated until the end of the current age.

Please note my meaning is eliminated until the end of the age. The rebellion is already defeated. It was defeated in Genesis 1:3. However, Yahweh uses His adversaries as footstools.

Some believe that evil began in the Garden of Eden. Sin had to exist before, or the serpent's intent when speaking to Eve that she would "know good and evil" had no substance.

It is possible creation began with verse three, that nothing existed before Day One other than primordial elements. It's more likely, Yahweh was re-creating. In my opinion, of these two scenarios, the latter, because of Scripture, is more sustainable.

Analyzing Day One, from the perspective that a governmental rebellion occurred in a pre-Adamic civilization, Yahweh's immediate reaction would be to secure the kingdom. Isn't that what happened in verse three? God dispelled the enemy with a single command. *"For thus said the Lord that created the heavens; God Himself that formed the earth and made it; He hath established it,* **He created it not in vain***, and* **He formed it to be inhabited***,"* Isaiah 45:18 (emphasis added).

Yahweh did not directly respond to Chaos – but commanded the Light to BE. He did so with one word - *Y'hiy* - EXIST!

1 John 1:5, *"This then is the message which we have heard of Him, and declare unto you, that God is light, and* **in Him is no darkness** *at all"* (emphasis added). By speaking to light, the Creator proclaimed His Son, Yeshua, as the

Eternal King. The pictograph of *y'hiy* depicts a hand extended on both sides of the word "Behold." So, I suggest that the command for light to "exist" was essentially, "Behold the hands that extend from eternity to eternity on the CROSS!"

Exodus 6:6-7, *"Therefore, say to the Israelites: 'I am the LORD, and I will bring you out from under the yoke of the Egyptians. I will free you from being slaves to them, and I **will redeem you with an outstretched arm** and with mighty acts of judgment. I will take you as my own people, and I will be your God"* (emphasis added).

The Hebrew *yod* is an arm or a hand extended as to reach outward.[19] Did God shine "light" on the Cross on Day One? The answer is yes – more ways than one!

'Erets was uninhabitable. It became an empty wasteland. That suggests the darkness within *'erets* was not natural. Instead, it was triggered. Indeed, there was physical darkness covering *'erets*. However, the imagery presented in the language insinuates that the darkness was unnatural. Unnatural in the sense that "it" somehow attempted to prohibit light from "being."

So, let's again analyze what we know. First, the Creator created heaven and earth. Note, no mention is made of the underworld, hell.[20] Yet, there are three spheres of existence. Heaven, Earth, and Hell. Or better yet, let's use Hebrew: 1) *Shamayim,* 2) *'Erets,* 3) *Sheol.* Only *'erets* is perceived by human sensory awareness; the other two are invisible to humans because both *Shamayim* and *Sheol* are spiritual. *'Erets,* as perceived by mankind, is material, although I submit that *'erets* is also a part of the spiritual realm.

Okay, now if the Creator did not create the underworld, who did? Perhaps the fallen gods of darkness and death? And consider this: Was *'erets* an integral part of the spiritual realm before re-created? Was it previously inhabited by a civilization of non-terrestrials? If so, what caused the planet to become empty and void? Was it the darkness or the water covering its surface? Or was the latter an effect of the former?

The Bible attests angelic beings existed before mankind. Of course, angels[21] are not only ancient, they are non-terrestrial. Also, they have a civilization, an orderly society. In fact, they have a hierarchy of government, which became the pattern for human civilization.

That raises another question: Did the sun, moon, and stars exist before Genesis 1:3? There is no reason to believe they did not. Actually, logic suggests they did. So, if the sun existed, why was there no light?

My reason for taking you down this rabbit trail is simply this: Genesis was not written to prove science. The language is spiritual, and the truth of Genesis 1 is spiritually discerned. To understand the imagery, we need to ask: From where did the *choshek* (darkness) come? I suggest "he" fell – through the *'erets* – into the underworld creating "*Sheol*." Hence, *'erets* became empty and void of original intent.

We also note that the imagery of Genesis 1 alludes to the pre-Exodus condition of the Hebrews, primarily

---

19 https://hebrew4christians.com/Grammar/Unit_One/Aleph-Bet/Yod/yod.html, retrieved 10/22/2019
20 The term hell is used because it is the one most familiar.
21 Angel is another term that is misused but used to introduce this concept since it is the one most familiar.

regarding the ten plagues. Exodus 10:21 states that the darkness *(choshek)* *"which could be felt"* covered *"all the land of Egypt"* so that *"they saw not one another."* Yet, that darkness did not breach Goshen (Exodus 10:23). The darkness of that plague was beyond natural yet constrained by God, made to exist only in Egypt and not in Goshen.

'Arphel and *choshek* are not the same. *Choshek* is thick darkness that is void of light. It is often described as tangible darkness. *Choshek* is frequently personified by such adverbial phrases as "reached out" or "it grabbed." Also note, *choshek* typically manifests in conjunction with death. Repeatedly in Scripture, darkness is accompanied by death to suggest spiritual activity. *'Arphel*, though translated as darkness, occurs when a light source is obscured. For instance, sunset. Whenever the sun falls below the horizon, it is difficult to see for the simple reason the horizon covers the sun.

Was the darkness of Genesis 1:2, Satan? Well, yes, in that it was adversarial. While on this subject, we should establish the following: The adversary "are many." Satan is another term that is misused. The word satan was derived from the Hebrew, *ha'SaaTaan,* which translates into English as "the adversary." It is a legal term analogous to "prosecuting attorney."

Isaiah 60:1-2, "**Arise, shine** for your light is come, and the glory of the Lord is **risen** upon you. For, behold, the darkness shall cover the earth, and gross darkness the people: but the Lord shall **arise** upon you, and His glory shall be seen upon you..." (The author's rendering.)

"Risen" and "arise" are translated from the same Hebrew word: *zarach* (illuminate). Yahweh instructed Isaiah to command the people to arise and shine. This imagery portrays Holy Spirit zapping the people with beams of light, commanding them, "Arise! Shine!" Or, using modern-day vernacular - "Get up and reside in the light, live in your light, your portion of light! You are illuminated, so go and be the lights of the world."

The "gross darkness" of the Isaiah 60 text is *'arphel*. *'Arphel* accompanies the *choshek*. *'Arphel* hides or conceals truth as an effect of *choshek*. In other words, *'arphel* is the consequence of *choshek*.

In Genesis 1:2, Holy Spirit moved over the waters and fluttered his wings. He breathed (blew) on the faces, illumination. He shone the light of Yeshua upon the lost and dying souls of humanity. This had the effect of pulling them from deception into revelation. (It is no coincidence the Bible begins with Genesis and ends with Revelation.)

No wonder John wrote: *"In the beginning was the Word and the Word was with God, and the Word was God. He was in the beginning with God. All things were made through Him, and without Him, nothing was made that was made. In Him was life, and the life was the light of men. And the light shines in the darkness, and the darkness did not comprehend it."*[22]

> *Genesis 1: 4-5 "And God saw the light, that it was good: and God divided the light from the darkness. And God called the light Day, and the darkness he called Night. And the evening and the morning were the first day."*

---

22 John 1:1-5

The light was good, *towb*. *Towb*, as defined by Strong's OT #2895, is an adjective. Only occasionally is it used as a noun. However, when used as an adverb, it is translated as "well."

God divided the light from the dark by adding a Door to the House. (Divide is *badal*.) Yeshua, as the Door to the Kingdom, protects the righteous from evil. Since a door functions as a barrier, evil must have permission to touch the righteous. The light of Day One "divided" the righteous from the unrighteous.

Yowm (day) is defined by Strong's OT#3117, and interestingly, while *yowm* is translated as day, it also refers to an era of time. Most often, *yowm* denotes a space of time such as "the day of" or "on that day." Spelled *yod-vav-mem*, and pictographically as ᴍYᴧ represents an extended hand securing the waters.

Night (*layil*) is defined by Strong's OT#3915 as a twisting. Light waves react differently when the atmosphere becomes dense due to the absence of bright light. Darkness affects light by refracting it; it twists away. God's light, however, was good. It stopped the twisting and weaving of deception. So, when God beheld the good that was accomplished by the Light, He announced his approval and therein decreed LIGHT better than the dark. That decree separated the two forces, thus drawing a clear distinction between their individual characteristics. Fundamentally, God placed a boundary about the night, which functions as the dimension known as time.

Its uncertain time was measured, before the decree of Genesis 1:4-5, as we measure it today. To understand my conclusion, note that after the evening and morning of Day Six, "evening" is never again mentioned. In other words, darkness ceased with the completion of Day Six, which explains why Revelation 22:5 proclaims there shall be *"…no more night."* When we get to Day Four, we see that time is measured (governed) by the sun's rotation. Hence, on Day One, concerning the physical matter, God removed the obstruction of darkness, which was perhaps, a thick cloud cover. That act, in turn, caused the sun's light to shine on the planet. But not until Day Four did God assign a timing (or limit) of the rotations of all luminary bodies.

Day Seven had no evening, which infers that the adversarial system is limited to six days. Then night (darkness) shall be no more. 2 Peter 3:8, *"But, beloved, do not forget this one thing, that with the Lord one day is as a thousand years and a thousand years as one day."*

Time is better understood when we realize it is relative to the speed of light. Time slows as space shrinks toward its origin. At the point where space begins (the event of "singularity"), time is eternal. The further one moves from the impact of singularity, the faster time moves. That is a convoluted way of saying that at the point of origin, time stops.

The science of physical matter posits that spacetime fuses spatial dimensions into time. And theorizes that there are at least eleven spatial dimensions. Human perception is limited to four.

Ephesians 3:18, *"May be able to comprehend with all saints what is the breadth* (time), **and length, and depth, and height***…"* (emphasis added). The ancients knew there were four dimensions to space before Einstein did. They also knew that God is Light – the source of light. (He is the source of the singularity.) Matter consists of His light and His sound. That explains, to the best of my ability, how it is that all dimensions co-exist in sync. How they came together to form the universe surrounding our planet, Earth, is beyond the scope of this teaching and my intellect. But they did, and I contend Genesis 1:1 is when it was all positioned. Then at some point before Genesis 1:2, chaos disrupted God's orderly arrangement. Thus, making Genesis 1:3 necessary.

One more quick note concerning *aleph* א. It has a numeric value of one but is formed by three strokes of the pen. Those strokes are *yod-vav-yod*. The upper *yod* is separated from the lower *yod* by a *vav* positioned in a crosswise manner. And note that the lower *yod* points downward. One God with two arms extended (Yahweh's and Yeshua's). One Arm remained in the unseen realm, and the other came down. The Arm who came down was separated from the other by the work of the *vav* (the Cross)!

- The value of the *yod* is ten; the value of the *vav* is six.
- The *vav* represents a hook and the *yod* a hand or an extended arm.
- Biblical numerology refers to ten as divine order, whereas six represents humanity.
- The *aleph* demonstrates God's grace toward mankind.

Representationally, on Day One, the Light (Yeshua) went to the Cross, extended his arms, and thereby reestablish the perfection of Yahweh's Divine order. This cannot be made up, not to this degree of perfection!

Day Two

> Genesis 1:6-8, *"And God said, 'let there be a firmament in the midst of the waters, and let it divide the waters from the waters.' And God made the firmament and divided the waters which were under the firmament from the waters which were above the firmament: and it was so. And God called the firmament Heaven. And the evening and the morning were the second day."*

The keywords of Day Two:
- *Amar* – Strong's OT#559 (aw-mar) is a primitive root that translates as to say; to answer; to appoint; to command; to call; to communicate.
- *Hayah* – Strong's OT#1961 (haw-yaw) is a primitive root that means to exist. That is, to be or to become; to come to pass (always emphatic and not a mere copula or auxiliary).
- *Raqiya'* - Strong's OT#7549 (raw-kee'-ah) this spelling is merely a more extended version of *raqa*. Both mean an expanse such as the firmament. (Firmament is an old English word that refers to the sky that arches above the planet.) *Raqa* is the visible arch over *'erets*. Principally, it is the atmosphere that extends from the earth's surface upward to the stratosphere.
- *Tavek* - Strong's OT#8432 (taw'-vek) means to sever, to bisect, and by implication to place in the center.
- *Badal* – Strong's OT#914 (baw-dal) translates as to divide in various senses, literally or figuratively, to separate; distinguish; differ; et cetera.

- *Mayim* – Strong's OT#4325 (mah'-yim) is the dual of a primitive noun that is most often used in a singular sense, for example, water rather than waters.
- *Asah* - Strong's OT#6213 (aw-saw) as "to do" a thing or to make a thing in the broadest sense, and the most comprehensive application; to accomplish, advance, or appoint a thing.

Essentially, *Elohiym* appointed a layer of sky between the waters, thereby dividing the waters of *'erets* from those extending beyond the upper atmosphere. After examining the Hebrew text closely, I believe God added another layer of extra-dimensional space. If my hypothesis is correct, then Day Two was when God prepared the cosmos for the inevitable consequence of Adam's sin.

The *raqiya* separated the physical from the spiritual, in my opinion. I hold that Day Two separated the third heaven from the second heaven, which, in my opinion, is within *'erets*. Dividing the waters caused the "firmament" to function as a barrier – the second heaven.

Basically, what I am saying is Day Two placed a barrier between the spiritual and what would become the physical. There were no "seen" or "unseen" dimensions of space at that point. So, figuratively, God merely commanded a separation to exist between the fallen and the righteous. He spoke a command, and the firmament snapped into position. God called the firmament "heaven" or *shamayim* (the upper waters).

"Call" in Hebrew is *qara'* and defined by Strong's OT#7121 (kaw-raw) as a primitive root representing the idea of accosting a person when calling out to them. It can also mean to adequately address them by their name. So, in other words, God called out to the existing righteous of His domain and commanded them to assemble, becoming a boundary.

Shamayim, according to Strong's OT#8064 (shaw-mah'-yim), is the plural form of *shameh* (shaw-meh). *Shameh* means to be lofty, as is the sky is aloft from the earth's surface. On the technical side, *shamayim* is the multiple stratums, including the visible arch where clouds move. It extends to the space beyond the sun, moon, and stars. Principally, it is a catch-all word that means everything above *'erets* surface. The Septuagint used *steroma* rather than firmament. *Steroma* translates as heavenly vaults.

Another view of this would be to say Day Two created "the" atmosphere. That is when God decided that a separation should exist between heaven and earth. And that the waters of heaven must be separated from those of *'erets*.

Raqiya infers a pounding of the earth as a sign of passion. Could it be when God parted the waters to expand space, He hammered *'erets*? What an image! Of course, that image is only visible when reading the Hebrew text. Additionally, there is another meaning in the root of *raqa* (Strong's OT#7554). It means to overlay with thin sheets of metal. Wow! These metaphors are striking and require a great deal of thought to decipher. Perhaps, Yahweh placed a sound barrier about the second heaven (those metaphorical thin sheets of metal). Maybe He desired the sounds emitting from there to be "tinny?"

The third heaven is Yahweh's abode (see 2 Corinthians 12:2). The second heaven is the atmosphere above *'erets*, and the first is the sky over *'erets*. The *"prince of the power of the air"* roams the second heaven looking for "whom" he may devour (see Ephesians 2:2). It's not my intent to imply that God pounded the earth. Nor to say that tin is floating around somewhere in outer space. Instead, the visual I hope to leave you with is the Creator fenced off the adversaries. Thus, making it more difficult for the deception of the adversaries to "stick" to the *'erets*.

These verses also marked the *raqiya* as *Aleph-Tav*. *And God made the* את *firmament… And God called the firmament Heaven* – please note God did not name the firmament *raqiya* – he called it *shamayim*, that is an important distinction. The celestial space (outer space) containing the sun, moon, and stars is *raqiya*.

A Midrash story explains that *shamayim* is a contraction of two words, *sham* plus *mayim*. The two words were joined to establish the concept, "true water is from there." (That makes perfect sense when we recall that water symbolizes words, and *mayim* is Hebrew for water. Hence, *shamayim* are lofty waters.)

Day Three

> Genesis 1:9-13, *"Then God said, 'Let the waters **under** the heavens be gathered together into **one place**, and let the dry land appear,' and it was so. And God called the dry land **Earth ('erets),** and the gathering together of the waters He called **Seas**. And God saw that it was **good**. Then God said, 'Let the earth bring forth grass, the herb that yields **seed**, and the fruit tree that yields fruit according to **its kind**, whose **seed is in itself, on the earth**,' and it was so. And the earth brought forth grass, the herb that yields seed according to its kind, and the tree that yields fruit, whose seed is according to its kind. And God saw that it was **good**. So, the evening and the morning were **the third day***" (emphasis added).

In this first chapter of *Genesis,* God spoke on ten different occasions. Each time was a decree. According to biblical numerology, ten represents the perfection of the Divine, symbolizing that order exists. *'Amar* (said), as defined previously, means to appoint. In other words, there is more than vocalization happening with *'amar*. The emphasis is on tone, implying the command is forcefully issued. Since Yahweh commanded a different decree each of the ten times, His instructions for establishing systematic order were progressive. Each command added a new element for the benefit of mankind and ultimately for the kingdom.

- God spoke to light.
- God spoke to the firmament.
- God spoke to the waters under the firmament.
- God spoke to the earth to bring forth seed (to be fruitful).
- God spoke to the firmament and brought forth order within the celestial sky.
- God spoke to the waters to bring forth life.

- God spoke to the earth to bring forth living creatures.
- God spoke to the Divine Council and then created man.
- God spoke to the man and assigned dominion.
- God spoke again to man, instructing him what was suitable for meat (meat, as used in this context, equates with rest).

We note that on Day Three, God commanded the waters under the heavens to amass. Scientifically speaking, from that moment onward, Earth was a biosphere, having both land and sea.

- Day One – light – released revelation – the Word.
- Day Two – atmosphere (oxygen) – the breath of Holy Spirit.
- Day Three – the land (soil) came forth as a medium for what was next, which was seed.

We should discuss these three steps for a moment. They are like the redemptive process, which is most often referred to as salvation. A person must first realize they need a savior, that they are lost and dying without God. Therefore, step one is a revelation. Step two Holy Spirit breathes upon the individual, giving them the desire to know Yeshua as Lord. Step three is the receiving of Yeshua into their heart.

Figuratively, "the soil of the soul" is the heart, and the seed is God's Word.

Matthew 13:11-39, *"He replied, 'The knowledge of the secrets of the kingdom of heaven has been given to you, but not to them… though seeing, they do not see; though hearing, they do not hear or understand… when anyone hears the message about the kingdom and does not understand it, the evil one comes and snatches away what was sown in his heart… the one who sowed the good seed is the Son of Man. The field is the world, and the good seed stands for the sons of the kingdom. The weeds are the sons of the evil one, and the enemy who sows them is the devil. The harvest is the end of the age, and the harvesters are angels."*

Yahweh assembled, **under** the firmament (heaven), the waters on the surface of the planet. Note the word "under." It is *tachath* and defined by Strong's OT#8478 (takh'-ath) as being at the bottom, depressed beneath. *Tachath* is used as an adverb with the "firmament." Thus, the waters beneath the upper firmament were commanded to submit to the "higher" element, suggesting *'erets* and the "seas" were commanded to bow before heaven. Hence, the sea (chaos) was subjugated on Day Three. Though the adversarial gods were defeated, they did not yet know it. In fact, they have yet to submit. Which is the hidden message of Day Three. Yahweh was hiding His Seed from the adversary, but no one knew.

Let's briefly discuss the adversarial system, populated by fallen gods and their minions, for they are ancient, having existed in the eternal past. These entities were once superior, but after they were separated from Holy Spirit, they became inferior, no longer having access to the Spirit of Wisdom. Self-focused, dependent upon themselves, they are driven by lust, greed, and pride. Make no mistake, they are powerful; nevertheless, they are defeated. Yet, they haven't been forced to submit to their demise. Once, they were privy to the Throne of the Almighty. Now they are forced to listen "in" as Yahweh communicates with mankind. They spy. Even so, we mustn't think it strange they understand Yahweh's words or that they act upon them, usually before mankind.

Psalms 95:5, *"The sea is his, for he made it, and his hands formed the dry land."* Translation: He appointed the sea its boundaries but shaped the dry land as a potter shapes a receptacle.

Proverbs 8:28-31, *"…when he established the clouds above and fixed securely the fountains of the deep, when he **gave the sea its boundary** so the waters would not overstep his command, and when he marked out the foundations of the earth. Then I was the craftsman at his side. I was filled with delight day after day, rejoicing always in his presence, rejoicing in his whole world and delighting in mankind"* (emphasis added).

Psalms 104:2-3, *"He wraps himself in light as with a garment; he stretches out the heavens like a tent **and lays the beams of his upper chambers on their waters.**"* (The floor of His lofty chambers is like the flow of His Divine words – they support all His endeavors.)

Jeremiah 5:22, *"Should you not fear me?" declares the LORD. "Should you not tremble in my presence? I made the sand a boundary for the sea, an everlasting barrier it cannot cross. The waves may roll, but they cannot prevail; they may roar, but they cannot cross it."* (Translation: "I established the Seed of Abraham like sand, to hold back the sea.")

Jonah 1:9, *"He answered, 'I am a* **Hebrew, and I worship the LORD, the God of heaven, who made (appointed)** *the sea* **and** *the land"* (emphasis added).

'Erets (Earth), spelled *aleph-resh-tsade,* is a field, the cosmic field of Yahweh. It is where He plants His Seed. The *"tsade"* within the spelling of *'erets* symbolizes a harvest. Matthew 9:37-38, *"Then he said to his disciples, 'The harvest is plentiful, but the workers are few. Ask the Lord of the harvest, therefore, to send out workers into his harvest field.'"*

God called the dry land *'erets,* and the amassed waters were called seas or *yamiym*. And then God saw that it was good. What was good? The separation between water and land was good.

Y*amiym* in Hebrew is the plural of *yam*. In pictographic form ᴡᴡᴧ⊣ *(yam)* implies that the hand of chaos is at work. No wonder the sea typifies chaos!

Daniel 7:2-3, *"Daniel said: 'In my vision at night I looked, and there before me were the four winds of heaven **churning up the great sea. Four great beasts, each different from the others, came up out of the sea**'"* (emphasis added).

Once the waters were amassed in one place, and the *erets* manifested, that was good.

> *"And said Elohiym – bring forth from the earth, grass herbs yielding seed, trees, fruit-bearing fruit after his kind, whose seed be in the earth – and it was so."*

'Erets was dry once the waters were amassed, but the seed God planted did not manifest as vegetation, not immediately. Genesis 1:12 clearly states that the *'erets* brought forth grass and herb yielding seed after his kind, and the tree yielding fruit, whose seed was, after **his** kind… yes, you read that right. The text does not

read **its** kind – but "his" kind. So, to be clear, "*And said Elohiym – to the earth.*" Yahweh spoke to *'erets* to bring forth grass, herbs yielding **seed,** trees having **fruit** (or seed) after "His" kind – and it was so. But also note that while the seed went into the soil, yet there were no mature plants. Fully-grown plants did not manifest in *'erets*, the field on Day Three, but later, after Day Six.

"Dry land" or *yabbashah* (Strong's OT#3004) is translated as ashamed, confused, or disappointed. *Yabbashah* (dry land) and *'erets* (the field) must not be viewed as the same. So, the land where God planted seed was not *yabbashah* but was *'erets*. In other words, the seed was not planted in the dry ground but in a field void of chaotic water. This matters because the metaphoric language reveals the mercy of God.

While I cannot say that Moses was refuting Egyptian cosmology in how he wrote this chapter. Nonetheless, he used language that should have produced that effect.

Egypt's chief god-controlled darkness. That god worked his mischief alongside another who ruled over water. Those two were among the high-ranking gods of the larger divine assembly of the Egyptian pantheon. In my estimation, Moses was essentially saying, "No, folks. You have been lied to. Yahweh alone controls light, the dark, the seas, and the land – for they are His."

What Moses did, by writing both figuratively and literally, was to foreshadow the works of Yeshua. That you might "see" my point, please note the symbolic meaning of the following terms: tender grass, herbs, and trees. Trees, such as fruit-bearing trees, are representative of spiritual maturity. Grass represents the new convert, a baby Christian. The recent convert is a tender sprout having entered God's house through the door. Herbs are a little older; they have been abiding in the house yet aren't fruitful. Trees, on the other hand, are rooted and grounded; they are fruitful. Grass, herb, tree, all have seed and sprout; all are alive and growing. Metaphorically, they all belong to the Kingdom.

2 Kings 19:26, *"Therefore their inhabitants were of small power, they were dismayed and confounded; they were as the grass of the field, and as the green herb, as the grass on the housetops, and as corn blasted before it be grown up."* Green herbs have yet to produce mature seeds.

Isaiah 37:27, *"Therefore their inhabitants had little power; they were dismayed and confounded; they were as the grass of the field; and the green herb; as the grass on the housetops; and grain blighted before it is grown."*

Psalms 1:1-3, *"Blessed is the man that walks not in the counsel of the ungodly, nor stands in the way of sinners, nor sits in the seat of the scornful. But his delight is in the law of the Lord, and in his law does he meditate day and night. And he shall be like a tree planted by the rivers of water, that brings forth his fruit in his season; his leaf also shall not wither, and whatsoever he does shall prosper."*

- Strong's OT#1877 – grass - *deshe'* (deh'-sheh) a sprout; by analogy, grass.
- Strong's OT#6212 – herb - `*eseb* (eh'seb) stems from an unused root meaning glisten (or be green as grass or any tender shoot).
- Strong's OT#6086 – tree - `*ets* (ates) comes from a word that means to fasten or make firm, which is used to describe a tree because it is strong.

- Strong's OT#2233 *zera`* (zeh'-rah) is derived from *zara*. Basically, it means to sow; to plant; to conceive, both figuratively and literally. It is the seed of a fruit or plant; and can be viewed as posterity, a child.
- Strong's OT#6529 *periy* (per-ee') from *parah* and means to bear fruit and increase (literally or figuratively) the reward that arises from planting.
- Strong's OT#4327 *miyn* (meen) from an unused root meaning to portion out; a sort; more specifically – to form a species.

Day Three did not end with a lush green landscape. The land looked barren. However, help was on "his" way. God's Word was in the soil. Seed was "in" *'erets*, but before the seed could take root and mature as plants, there needed to be a Day Six. (If you are curious about my meaning, go ahead and read Genesis 2:5-7.)

Three is the ג *gimmel*. The third letter of the *Aleph-Bet*. Primarily, it means to be "lifted up." Genesis 22:4, *"Then on the third day Abraham lifted up his eyes and saw the place afar off."* Exodus 19:11, *"And be ready against the third day for the third day the Lord will come down in the sight of all the people upon mount Sinai."* Hosea 6:1-2, *"Come, and let us return unto the Lord: for he hath torn, and he will heal us; he hath smitten, and he will bind us up. After two days will he revive us: in the third day he will raise us up, and we shall live in his sight."* Acts 10:40, *"Peter speaking said: 'Him, God raised up the third day, and displayed him openly…'"*

During Day Three, God saw good twice. He blessed the day twice, which caused the day to be a day of divine fruitfulness and prosperity.

Day Four

> Genesis 1:14-19, *"And God said, 'Let there be lights in the firmament of the heaven to divide the day from the night; and let them be for signs, and for seasons, and for days, and years: And let them be for lights in the firmament of the heaven to give light upon the earth,' and it was so. And God made two את great lights; את the greater light to rule the day, and את the lesser light to rule the night: he made the stars also. And God set them in the firmament of the heaven to give light upon the earth, and to rule over the day and over the night, and to divide the light from the darkness, and God saw that it was good. And the evening and the morning were the fourth day."*

According to ancient texts, gateways exist between *Shamayim*, *'Erets*, and *Sheol*. Oddly enough, the *dalet*, the fourth Hebrew letter, was initially drawn to suggest just that, a doorway. John 10:9, Yeshua said, *"I am the door and by me, if any man enters in, he shall be saved and shall go in and out and find pasture."* So, essentially Day Four established a pathway, or doorway, between the field (the physical existence of mankind) and the cosmic mountain (the spiritual presence) of Yah. (This thought shall become more apparent as we continue into the remainder of this study.)

Day Four also established the organizational chart of Yeshua's kingdom. The sun (Son) was positioned as the governor to rule over the expanse of the universe (the cosmos). The moon and the stars were placed to function as the "lesser lights," which figuratively represents the army of heaven.

Obviously, light and darkness cannot co-exist; light is always the superior force, and thus, the dominant element. Day One granted the cosmos LIGHT (revealed that King Yeshua was to govern the cosmos). Additionally, it also restricted the dark (the adversarial system) to a specified timetable. Since Day One was the first occurrence of an evening and a morning, Day One established the division of "time" by dividing the night from the day. The earlier division should not be confused with the latter one of Day Four, which did not establish time but sectioned it into seasons or *mo'edim*. Basically, "time" needed to be organized. So, God marked His calendar with the *mo'edim* - the events that gave purpose:

- Seasons of celebration
- Appointments that gave Light governance

The "lights in the *raqia*" are separators; their purpose is to divide. And as said previously, *badal* means to divide. However, *badal* has several other meanings. The most applicable to this discussion is that these lights exhibit the difference between the night and the day. Not only do they mark time every 24 hours, but they also represent the "day" as everlasting and the night as temporary. The sun rises each day, yet the same is not true of the moon or stars. The moon has no light of its own, and the stars travel or seem to, from night to night.

Revelation 22:4-5, *"They will see his face, and his name will be on their foreheads. There will be no more night. They will not need the light of a lamp or the light of the sun, for the Lord God will give them light. And they will reign forever and ever."*

The sun illuminates the time called day, the moon and stars, the night, but far less brilliantly than the sun does the day. Day Four appointed the sun as the governor over the day and bound darkness to nighttime, for it must relinquish its reign with the sun's rising. Although the sun sets, it always rises again. Therefore, every day is a new message – God's mercies are renewed, morning by morning! The message of salvation is in the sky! Literally!

However, notice that God determined that the darkness would not have absolute reign over the time assigned as night. He positioned Lieutenant Governors for the night – the moon and the stars. *Elohiym* "made"- *'asah* -appointed **two** great lights.

- Two – Strong's OT#8147 *shenayim* (shen-ah'-yim) two or twofold.
- Great - Strong's OT#1419 *gadowl* (gaw-dole), also spelled *gadol* and means great in any sense, also means "the **elder**."
- Light - Strong's OT#3974 *ma'owr* (maw-ore') or *ma'or* (maw-ore') also (in plural) feminine *me'owrah* (meh-o-raw') or *meorah,* properly a luminous body or luminary.

Genesis 1:16 contains three *Aleph-Tavs,* and all are associated with the two great lights. The greater light, along with the lesser light, rules (*memshalah*) over the cosmos. These two great lights were marked *Aleph-Tav,* indicating they are Melchizedek in nature. Strong's OT#4475 (mem-shaw-law') defines *memshalah* as meaning "to rule realm(s)" and have dominion over governments. Thus, the two "great" lights were given the needed authority to rule.

We also note that the word moon is not in the original text. The literal translation from Hebrew is "lesser light." The greater or elder *Aleph-Tav* light was assigned the day; thus, he is the Lord of the Day. The lesser or the subservient *Aleph-Tav* light was told to govern the night. Since the night (dark) is allotted to the adversary, there is an additional message: the lesser light reflects; it is not a source of light. The bride is to overcome the adversary, not by her own light, but by Yeshua's. On that note, any illumination derived from the lesser light only occurs when that body is aligned with the more excellent light.

After positioning the more excellent light, and its companion, the stars were assigned to function as "*signs and for seasons; for days, and years.*" Meaning that the stars were told to send signals to note a change in seasons (*mo'edim*).

- Signs – Strong's OT#226 '*owth* (oth) a signal (literally or figuratively) a flag, beacon, monument, omen, prodigy, evidence, et cetera.
- Seasons – Strong's OT#4150 *mowed'* or *mo'ed* (mo-ade') an appointment; a fixed time or season, specifically a festival; conventionally a year; by implication, an assembly (convened for a definite purpose); technically a congregation; by extension, a place of meeting; also, a signal (as appointed beforehand).
- Day – Strong's OT#3117 *yowm* (yome) from an unused root meaning to be hot; a day (the warm hours) whether literal (from sunrise to sunset, or from one sunset to the next) or symbolic (a space of time defined by an associated term, which is often used as an adverb); an age, or era.
- Years – Strong's OT#8141 *shaneh* (shaw-neh') a year (as a revolution of time); a whole age.
- Night - Strong's OT#3915 *layil* (lah-yil) a twist (away from the light), night; figuratively, adversity; night as a season.

Day Four:
- Established omens to send a message
- Set the time of God's feasts
- Established seasons and periods of time
- Established the structure of the kingdom

There are five hidden messages in Day Four:
- The sun is the "elder" light, just as Yeshua is the bride's elder brother.
- The lesser light reflects the elder light just as the bride reflects the Groom.
- The greater *Aleph-Tav* light has dominion over the ages.
- The lesser *Aleph-Tav* light has dominion only during the time granted to the *layil*.
- The stars represent the spiritual princes of the unseen realm. They were appointed as the heavenly host and assigned to assist the greater light. They function as co-labors with the lesser light. (Please note, no star has permission to rule at any time, day, or night.)

Psalms 19:1-6, *"The heavens declare the glory of God; and the firmament shows his handiwork, day unto day* **utters speech,** *and night unto night shows knowledge. There is no speech nor language where their voice is not heard. Their line is gone out through all the earth, and their words to the end of the world. In them hath* **he set a tabernacle for the sun, which is as a bridegroom** *coming out of his chamber and rejoices as a strong man to run a race. His going forth is from the end of the heaven, and his circuit unto the ends of it: and there is nothing hid from the heat thereof"* (emphasis added).

The constellations serve as the sun's tabernacle (dwelling), which causes the universe itself to be God's personal handiwork. Outer space speaks (expresses knowledge). In other words, the stars are a covering for the sun, and they exist as a message. That message is what the ancients called the Mazzaroth. Mazzaroth means a garland of crowns. And note, God knows the number of stars that exist and has assigned each a name.

Psalms 147:4, *"He determines the number of the stars and calls them each by name."* Isaiah 40:26, *"Lift up your eyes on high, and behold who hath created these things that brings out their host by number:* **he calls them all by names by the greatness of his might,** *for that he is strong in power; not one fails"* (emphasis added).

Dr. Chuck Missler made an excellent study on this subject that he titled, *'Signs in the Heavens.'* The following is a quote taken from that work: "If we view the celestial skies as a sphere centered above us, there is a band at an angle – the ecliptic – through which the sun takes an apparent path over the course of the year. The ecliptic is divided into 12 sections according to the 12 months of the year, and each section has its own sign. These 12 constellations can be seen in a 360-degree turn of the heavens, along with the three additional constellations associated with each one. Close attention to the sun's path through these constellations offers a consistent means of keeping track of the months of the sidereal year."[23]

Psalms 19:1 paraphrased: The *shamayim* (heavens) declare God's glory (*kabowd*); his handiwork (*ma'aseh*) in the *raqia* (firmament). (Meaning that the weightiness of His splendor is found in the "art" of the sky.)

There is a story associated with each of the twelve primary constellations. When those twelve are assembled as one story, they build upon each other to create the Mazzaroth. The first story is of a virgin carrying an ear of wheat in one hand and a palm branch in the other. She, like the others, is best known by her Latin name, Virgo. Moving counterclockwise across the sky, we next see Libra the Scales. Then Scorpio the Scorpion; Sagittarius the Bowman; Capricornus the Goat; Aquarius the Waterman; Pisces the Fishes; Aries the Ram; Taurus the Bull; Gemini the Twins; Cancer the Crab, and the last, the twelfth constellation, is Leo the Lion.

- → The Virgin – foreshadows the virgin birth of the Promised Seed
- → The Scales – the Promised Seed will bring justice
- → The Scorpion – the Promised Seed will have a conflict with the serpent
- → The Archer – the Promised Seed will triumph
- → The Goat – the Promise Seed will be sacrificed
- → The Waterman – the Promised Seed will pour (living) waters upon the Earth

---

[23] *Signs in the Heavens*, Copyright 2014 by Chuck Missler, Published by Koinonia House, Koinonia Institute. Kindle Edition.

- → The Two Fishes – the Promised Seed will have two houses that shall become one
- → The Ram – the Lamb as the Promised Seed, will be slain, yet rise again
- → The Bull – the Promised Seed is the ruling Judge over the Great Assembly
- → The Twins – the Promised Seed shall have a bride
- → The Crab – the Promised Seed shall be the victor when the serpent's head is under his feet
- → The Lion – the Promised Seed is the everlasting King

The full, extended version of the Mazzaroth story is complex and detailed. So, what is given in this setting is the abridged version to underscore why God deliberately positioned every star. Of course, I've added a New Testament slant to my interpretation. Hopefully, I have given enough information that it is evident, God wrote the totality of His six-step plan in the Mazzaroth. If you are interested in knowing more about the Mazzaroth, I recommend the following three sources: *Anatomy of the Heavens* by John Klein; *The Gospel in the Stars* by Joseph Seiss; *The Witness of the Stars* by E.W. Bullinger.

Mo'ed is the singular form of *moedim*, which means set times, appointed times, the feasts of God. The feasts are:

- Passover
- Unleavened Bread
- Firstfruits
- Pentecost
- Trumpets
- Atonement
- Tabernacles

The advent of Yeshua's first coming fulfilled the first four feasts; the final three shall be celebrated at his return. Leviticus 23: 1-4, *"And the LORD spoke to Moses, saying, 'Speak to the children of Israel, and say to them: The feasts of the LORD, which you shall proclaim to be holy convocations, these are My feasts. These are the feasts of the LORD, holy convocations which you shall proclaim at their appointed times.'"*

Day Five

> Genesis 1:20-23, *"And Elohiym said, 'Let the waters bring forth abundantly the moving creature that has life, and fowl that may fly above the earth in the open firmament of heaven.' And Elohiym created great את (sea monsters) and every את living creature that moves, which the waters brought forth abundantly, after their kind, and every את winged fowl after his kind: and Elohiym saw that it was good. And Elohiym blessed them, saying, 'Be fruitful, and multiply, and fill the את waters in the seas, and let fowl multiply in the earth.' And the evening and the morning were the fifth day."*

Ezekiel 17:1-3, *"The word of the LORD came to me, 'Son of man, set forth an allegory and tell the house of Israel a parable.'"* Matthew 13:24, *"Jesus told them another parable…."* Psalms 49:4, *"I will incline mine ear to a parable."*

Psalms 78:1-2, *"Give ear, O my people, to my law: incline your ears to the words of my mouth. I will open my mouth in a parable: I will utter dark sayings of old…."*

Teaching by using parables is often a preferential way of communicating complex concepts. This is especially true if the teacher has a more encompassing grasp of an idea or situation than their audience. Hence, the teacher will give an illustration in terms that their student will understand. In many respects, this is how Holy Spirit designed the Bible. He inspired examples to teach humanity spiritual lessons. He did this purposefully. Through intelligent design, God provided at least two layers of meaning to every event recorded in Scripture. (The rabbis of the Second Temple would raise that number, proclaiming there are at least four layers in all Scripture.)

Mashal means parable. Strong's defines *mashal* OT#4912 as a pithy maxim, usually of symbolic nature, a simile presented as an adage, poem, or discourse. Note the spelling *mem-shin-lamed.* It creates a pictograph of  inferring that a parable requires chewing, like the chewing of bread. Soooo be prepared. Day Five will require chewing.

Genesis 1:20a *"And the Eternal One commanded the waters to swarm that they might bring forth living creatures, in an abundant measure…."*

Recall that waters, or *mayim,* equates to word. Yahweh's command made the waters swarm.

- Swarm – Strong's OT#8317 *sharats* (shaw-rats) means to wriggle, by implication to swarm or abound; to breed (bring forth, increase) abundantly (in abundance), creep.
- Living – Strong's OT #2416 *chay* (khah'-ee) alive; life (or living thing) whether literally or figuratively.
- Creatures – Strong's OT#5315 *nephesh* (neh'-fesh) a breathing creature, for example, an animal of (abstract) vitality; used very widely in a literal or figurative sense.

Genesis 1:20b, *"and fowl that may fly above the earth in the* **open** *firmament of heaven."*

When we amplify this verse, it reads that "the waters swarmed and in so doing brought forth living creatures. The kind of creatures that live in the water, and also those who fly about as "faces" in the firmament of *shamayim."* The original text doesn't read "open" but *paniym* (faces). That infers that the firmament was filled with faces. *"In the faces of the firmament…"* is the literal translation.

Given that the stars are analogous with spirit beings, then the faces in the firmament belong to spirit beings. We also note that both the *raqia* and the *shamayim* have a firmament. These "firmaments" could be viewed as barriers between the third and second heavens. My conclusion is that Day Five exposes the faces of the second heaven, whereas Day Four those of the Third Heaven.

Of course, in the literal sense, these verses refer to birds of the air. Yet, the symbolic parallel of the imagery is one of spirits traveling through the firmaments. Keep in mind that these can be either holy or rebellious.

Genesis 1:21a: "Yahweh created the great fish; the great creatures (the leviathan and the great dragon)."

Young's Literal Translation of this same verse: *"And God prepared the great monsters and every living creature that is creeping…."* Again, we are presented with a literal and figurative meaning.

Let's gather a few scriptures to build our understanding:
- Ezekiel 28:15, *"You were blameless in your ways **from the day you were created till wickedness was found** in you"* (emphasis added).
- Revelation 20:2-3, *"He seized **the dragon, that ancient serpent**, who is the devil, or Satan, and bound him for a thousand years"* (emphasis added).
- Isaiah 27:1, *"In that day the Lord with his sore and great and strong sword shall punish leviathan the **piercing serpent, even leviathan that crooked serpent and he shall slay the dragon that is in the sea**"* (emphasis added).
- Revelation 12:9, *"**The great dragon was hurled down, that ancient serpent** called the devil, or Satan, who leads the whole world astray. He was hurled to the earth, and his angels with him"* (emphasis added).
- Psalms 104: 24-26, *"O Lord, how manifold are your works! in wisdom have you made them all: the earth is full of your riches. So is this great and wide sea, wherein are things creeping innumerable, **both small and great beasts. There go the ships: there is that leviathan, whom you made to play therein**"* (emphasis added).

Sea-serpent in Hebrew is *taniyn* or *tanniym* (either spelling works). *Taniyn* can refer to a marine or a land-based creature such as sea-serpents, dragons, and the like. So, yes, God created the "creatures and monsters." Yet, in their original state, they were perfect without sin. Nevertheless, they, through their own design, filled themselves with wickedness.

Regarding the leviathan, *"On earth, there is nothing like him, which is made without fear. He beholds every high thing; he is king over all the children of pride,"* Job 41:33-34. Ezekiel 28:17, *"Your heart became proud on account of your beauty, and you corrupted your wisdom because of your splendor. So, I threw you to the earth; I made a spectacle of you before kings."* Isaiah 14:12,15, *"How you have fallen from heaven, O morning star, son of the dawn! You have been cast down to the earth, you who once laid low the nations!... You are brought down to the grave, to the depths of the pit (Sheol)."*

When first studying Day Five, I was puzzled at the implied idea that Yahweh made a covenant with the great sea monster of these verses. Note, Ezekiel 28:14, *"You were **anointed** as a guardian cherub, for so I ordained you."* And Job 41:4, *"Will he make a covenant with you? Will you take him as a servant forever?"* It then dawned upon me that Yahweh did not break covenant with the adversary; the adversary broke covenant with Yahweh when he attempted to be God. As a result, the adversary and his followers were banished from the kingdom and assigned to the outer darkness. So, before their banishment, they served the Most High. These rebellious gods were created as ministers, but they acted according to their will and "became" filled with iniquity. Therefore, we must never forget they revolted intentionally as sentient, intellectual free-will agents. They are responsible for the evil they propagate. That is why they are *Aleph-Tav* sea monsters. They are enemies of the *Aleph-Tav* system.

"And ELOHIYM created the את *great sea monsters, and every* את *living creature that moves, which the waters brought forth abundantly, after their kind, and* את *every winged fowl after his kind"* Genesis 1:21, The Cepher. [24]

There are some, not all, of the spirit realm who have wings. Exodus 25:20, *"And the cherubim shall stretch forth their* **wings** *on high, covering the mercy seat with their* **wings,** *and their faces shall look one to another; toward the mercy seat shall the faces of the cherubim be"* (emphasis added).

The waters brought forth the sea monsters and the winged fowl. Yes, the waters brought forth. The good guys wearing white hats, those of heaven's firmament, were from the waters above *'erets*. On the other hand, the hosts of the adversarial system, the subterranean creatures wearing black hats, are from the chaotic seas.

The winged fowl are "his kind" – they were created as divine, but when they fell into the waters of *'erets,* they brought forth after "their kind." This will make more sense when we begin to study Genesis 6. Additionally, we note that the waters from which the monsters came are not specified. They are of both, the waters from above the firmament and those below.

Genesis 1:20-23 positioned the adversarial sphere. They were "placed" in their domain on Day Five. Not as newly created beings but as pre-existing life-forms.

Day Four positioned Kingdom government, Day Five arranged the adversarial hosts.

"And Elohiym blessed them…." God did not bless the adversary but instead the fish and the birds. It was never Yahweh's intent for spirit beings to "multiply" or for them to abide in *'erets.*

Matthew 13:41, *"The Son of Man will send out his angels, and they will weed out of his kingdom everything that causes sin and all who do evil."*

Matthew 25:31, *"When the Son of Man comes in his glory, and all the angels with him, he will sit on his throne in heavenly glory."*

Matthew 26:53-54, *"Do you think I cannot call on my Father, and he will at once put at my disposal more than twelve legions of angels?"*

The fifth day is one of beholding, which is the proper meaning of the *hei*, the fifth Hebrew letter. With the beholding is revealing. Yahweh **beheld** His work, then commanded them: "Increase - and excel in whatsoever respect I have sent you that you may accomplish my word."

---

24 *Cepher*, Cepher Publishing Group, LLC

Day Six

Genesis 1:24-31, *"And God said, 'Let the earth bring forth the living creature after **his** kind, cattle, and creeping thing, and beast of the **earth** after **his** kind,' and it was so. And God made the beast of the earth after his kind, and cattle after his kind, and everything that creeps upon the **earth** after **his** kind, and God saw that it was good. And God said, **'Let us make man in our image, after our likeness** and let them have dominion over the fish of the sea, and over the fowl of the air, and over the cattle, and over all the earth, and over every creeping thing that creeps upon the earth.' So, **God created man in his own image**, in the image of God created he him; **male and female created he them**. And God blessed them, and God said unto them, 'Be fruitful, and multiply, and replenish the earth, and subdue it: and have **dominion** over the fish of the sea, and over the fowl of the air, and over every living thing that moves upon the earth.' And God said, 'Behold, I have given you every herb bearing seed, which is upon the face of all the earth, and every tree, in which is the fruit of a tree yielding seed; to you, **it shall be for meat**. And to every beast of the earth, and to every fowl of the air, and to everything that creeps upon the earth, wherein there is life, I have given every green herb for meat,' and it was so. And God saw everything that he had made, and behold, it was **very good**. And the evening and the morning were the sixth day"* (emphasis added).

We shall move through the sixth day, point by point but first, let's reassess the purpose of the previous five days.

- א – Day One – Light
- ב – Day Two - Atmosphere
- ג – Day Three – Seeding of the biosphere
- ד – Day Four – Ecliptic alignment
- ה – Day Five – Ecosystem

The preceding five days prepared the sixth to receive mankind. Each made the planet inhabitable, not for the previous inhabitants, but for a new species. Once again, Yahweh's field was harmonious, thus ready to be the seat of cosmic government. God purposefully waited until the environment was suitable, then created mankind. In other words, what restored the corrupted chaotic planet, echoed across the cosmos in preparation for a new order of government. First, recreate order, then position (install) the chosen king on the throne.

Yahweh began working on Day Six, not with the creation of mankind, but of Mammalia and Reptilia. Like Day Three, Day Six had two segments. The first brought forth land creatures, and the second portion of the day put into play the man who would "image" God. Recognizing that God's final creative act[25] was what completed the *genesis* of a new kingdom is vital.

---

25 To be clear, in my opinion Yahweh is still creating. This statement is regarding Genesis 1.

So, let's turn our attention to the "end game." What was Yahweh's goal? Was the ultimate goal the Cross; the salvation of mankind? Did God send Yeshua to the 'erets to die? Well, no and yes! Just as the intent of the six days was two-fold, so was the mission of Yeshua. He had to win the cosmic war and then be installed on the Eternal Throne of the Eternal Kingdom. The Cross was a means to that end!

We must trust, without any doubt, God knew the end before He began creating; He planned accordingly. Yahweh planned Yeshua's death, burial, and resurrection before the act of "re-creating" began.[26] Yeshua's resurrection guaranteed the final victory! The nails of the Cross – nailed the enemy to his coffin! However, it was Yeshua's resurrection that sealed the adversary's tomb eternally!

1 Corinthians 15:23, *"The last enemy that will be destroyed is death."* But before the enemy can be destroyed, the King must be seated, *"Sit at My right hand, till I make Your enemies Your footstool"* Psalms 110:1.

Adam was created to rule. However, Day Six was designed to reveal the OVERCOMER!

Precisely, Adam was given all the characteristics of the Eternal Melchizedek except for "eternal" life. He was created immortal but did not have everlasting life. The provision for everlasting life was why the Tree of Life was in Eden.

Adam was created in the image of God, but he was not a member of the Godhead. He, like all life forms, was made as a servant. The requirement of submitting to God is why Yeshua said in John 8:29, *"I do nothing of myself; but as my Father hath taught me, I speak these things."* This is another truth not to be overlooked: Yeshua is Divine but did not enter 'erets as God, instead "as" the second Adam.

Through the first Adam, God would introduce the Melchizedek monarchy to the cosmos. Only first *"...God said, 'Let the **earth bring forth the living creature after his kind**, cattle, and creeping things, **and beasts of the earth after his kind**,' and it was so"* Genesis 1:24 (emphasis added).

Terrestrial is an adjective that means "from the earth." Terrestrial refers to any living thing that dwells on the land. The proper use of this adjective supplies the distinction between the planet's soil and its water systems. So, in theory, Day Six brought forth terrestrials.

Regarding that observation, we note the phrasing of Genesis 1:24. The terrestrials (excluding man) were not formed by God's hands but by command. Yahweh instructed the 'erets to 'yatsa. 'Yatsa (Strong's OT#3318) means to bring forth.

God commanded 'erets to bring forth seed-bearing plants on Day Three, but on Day Six, 'erets was commanded to bring forth living creatures. That establishes a correlation between Day Three and Day Six, for these two days has the field ('erets) producing a "harvest" of "his" kind. Additionally, we note these two days are the only two doubly blessed.

Again, it is not my intention to get "wonky," but there was more happening in this process than science can

---

26 Revelation 13:8 Yeshua is the *"Lamb slain from the foundation of the world."*

explain. God was encoding a message to mankind before there was a man. That message can only be understood spiritually. These creatures created before mankind are *nephesh*. Strong's OT#5314 (neh'-fesh) states that a *nephesh* is any lower form of life that breathes air. Moses listed three:

1. Cattle - Strong's OT#929 *behemah* (be-hay-maw) derived from an unused root (meaning to be mute); thus, a dumb beast, especially any sizeable four-footed animal.
2. Creeping things – Strong's OT#7431 *remes* (reh'-mes) reptiles or any other rapidly moving animal.
3. Beasts – Strong's OT#2416 *chay* (khah'-ee) alive; hence, raw (flesh); fresh (plant, water, year), strong. As a noun, especially in the feminine singular and masculine plural sense, the word refers to life (or living) things, whether literal or figurative.

A *nephesh* breathes air and moves about because it is alive. And we note that the *nephesh* was to reproduce as "his" kind. Genesis 1:24-25, *"And Elohiym said, 'Let the* **earth** *('erets) bring forth the living creature after* **his** *kind, cattle, and creeping thing, and beast of the earth ('erets) after* **his** *kind,' and it was so. -- And Elohiym made (Aleph-Tav) beasts of the earth after* **his** *kind, and (Aleph-Tav) cattle after* **his** *kind, and (Aleph-Tav) everything that creeps upon the* **earth** *(adamah) after* **his** *kind, and Elohiym saw that it was good."* Verse 24 and 25 read the same except verse twenty-four is addressed to the *'erets*, and there is no *Aleph-Tavs*. Verse twenty-five applies the *Aleph-Tavs* and is addressed to the *'adamah*.

The *'adamah* differs from *'erets*. *'Erets* is the realm of human existence, designated explicitly unto the living. *'Adamah* is the surface layer of *'erets* and refers to the general redness of soil. The root of *'adamah* is *adam*, and *adam* means to show blood in the face (to be flushed). The land-based animals were to have blood, not because they were of the *adamah*, but instead as a similarity to mankind, for the offering of substitute blood. The distinction is that while they were sanctioned, they were not anointed to be joined to the *adamah* but to *'erets*. However, the "beasts of the field" equate with the Nephilim.

Despite widespread assumption, Adam's name was not given to draw attention to the clay (the soil) from which his body was formed but to distinguish him as a unique creation with blood.

Romans 9:21, *"Does not the potter have the right to make out of the same lump of clay some pottery for noble purposes and some for common use?"* Isaiah 64:8, *"Yet, O Yahweh, you are our Father. We are the clay; you are the potter; we are all the work of your hand."* Isaiah 29:15-16, *"Woe to those who go to great depths to hide their plans from the LORD, who do their work in darkness and think, 'Who sees us? Who will know?' You turn things upside down as if the potter were thought to be like the clay! Shall what be formed, say to him who formed it, 'He did not make me?' Can the pot say of the potter, 'He knows nothing?'"* Isaiah 45:9, *"Woe to him who quarrels with his Maker, to him who is but a potsherd among the potsherds on the ground. Does the clay say to the potter, 'What are you making?'"*

Terrestrials are pottery. This "image design" differentiates them from the celestials. Though, in my opinion, Holy Spirit was placing the attention upon blood, not on the vessel. This is why we note that *'erets* brought forth the non-human terrestrial creatures (verse 24). And also why verse 25 shows those creatures creeping upon the *adamah* into the territory of the *Aleph-Tav*.

The creatures of *'erets* were assigned to Adam, who was of the *adamah*. However, concerning the issue of "blood," is it not true that the blood within animals differs from that of mankind? So, allow me to rephrase this, so my point is clear. Adam was formed from the *adamah* by the hand of Yahweh. The creatures were formed by *'erets*. Both mankind and the creatures are similar in that they are terrestrial and have blood. But animals were not created to "show blood" – Adam was! And I think the "elder" civilization of celestials was caught off guard by this uniqueness.

Leviticus 17:11-12, *"For the life of the flesh is in the blood, and I have given it to you upon the altar to make atonement for your souls; for it is the blood that makes atonement for the soul."*

As a side note, celestials are not redeemed by Yeshua. However, it is safe to say that it is required of them to choose their master. Therefore, loyalty to Yahweh is what separates the holy from the rebellious. If a celestial remains loyal to Yahweh-Yeshua, they retain their "first estate." If not, *"the angels which kept not their first estate, but left their own habitation, he hath reserved in everlasting chains under darkness unto the judgment of the great day,"* Jude 6.

Concerning humanity - Romans 10:10 applies: *"For with the heart man believeth unto righteousness, and with the mouth, confession is made unto salvation."* Romans 8:29, *"For whom he did foreknow, he also did predetermine to be conformed to the image of his Son, that he might be the firstborn among many brethren."* 1 Corinthians 15:49, *"And as we have borne the image of the earthly, we shall also bear the image of the heavenly."* Colossians 1:14-15, *"In whom we have redemption through his blood, even the forgiveness of sins; who is the image of the invisible God; the firstborn of every creature."*

Hebrews 1:1-3, *"God, who at sundry times and in different manner spoke in time past unto the fathers by the prophets, has in these last days spoken unto us by his Son, whom he hath appointed heir of all things, by whom also he made the worlds; who being the brightness of his glory, and the express image of his person, and upholding all things by the word of his power, when he had by himself purged our sins, sat down on the right hand of the Majesty on high...."*

Genesis 1:26-27, *"And Elohiym said, 'Let us make man in our image, after our likeness: and let **them have dominion** over the fish of the sea, and over the fowl of the air, and over the cattle, and over all the earth, and over every creeping thing that creeps upon the earth.' So Elohiym created* את *man in his own image, in the image of Elohiym created he him; male and female created he them"* (emphasis added).

Once again, we find action in the "said." This is the eighth said of Genesis 1. Eight in biblical numerology signifies a new beginning, a resurrection. The eighth Hebrew letter is *chet*, which indicates a "cutting from" by fencing off and dividing. It signals an action that is intended to prevent the adversary from obtaining that which belongs to Yahweh. With this "eight," *Elohiym* said, "Let us make (appoint) man (who has blood) in our image (as our representative), our likeness (that he may function in like manner)."

Genesis 1:26 infers God was speaking in the plural sense. Obviously, then He was talking to someone other than Himself. With whom He conversed becomes evident with verse twenty-seven. God created an את

(*Aleph-Tav*) man. If Adam imaged an *Aleph-Tav*, then it was the originally *Aleph-Tav* to whom Yahweh spoke. Thus, Yahweh was speaking to Yeshua.

Adam was fashioned in God's OWN image, "created male and female."[27] God created man as *zaakaar—uwnqeebaah*. These Hebrew terms translate as "male-female," not man and woman. God marked Adam as *Aleph-Tav* before He put the man to sleep. In other words, before his side was opened, even before he was created, Adam was appointed Melchizedek. The majestic splendor of this concept points to the purpose of mankind, with the understanding that the Melchizedek must have a bride.

The bride is the helper who secures the inheritance. Adam, and Eve, foreshadowed Yeshua and his Bride. Everything that God brought forth during the six days of creation prophesied toward the end of the age. That said, I also want to be on record as saying God did not pre-program Adam to falter in his commitment. Albeit the all-knowing God knew Adam would sin. And for that reason, the end was "put" into the beginning. Every day of the creating process built a new level of revelation and another defeat to Chaos. Eve was hidden in Adam, just as the Bride of Christ was hidden within Yeshua.

The man's body came from the *adamah*. The physical material of Adam's body was of *'erets*. Yet, he was to represent the Divine. In his original state, Adam was divine in spirit but not "cosmic" in nature. Adam's glory was unique; he would not govern the cosmos but *'erets*. On the other hand, the cosmic Yeshua came to *'erets*, to gain control of *'erets*, that he might gain control of the Cosmos. *"And now, Father, glorify me in your presence with the glory I had with you* **before** *the world (cosmos) began,"* John 17:52 (emphasis added).

Yahweh manifested, grabbed a hand full of clay. Then as only Yahweh can do, He shaped the clay into a human body and added to it a program. One that would cause the lifeless body to function as His representative. Kissing the soulless body, Yahweh breathed into Adam, spirit (the spark of life).[28] (I'm convinced the Yahweh who did these things was the Eternal Melchizedek – the Divine One who the Second Temple Rabbis call the "second" Power of Heaven.)

Genesis 1:26 gave Adam dominion, made him "royalty," whereas verse twenty-seven made Adam a Melchizedek (the Regent of Righteousness). From the get-go, Adam was the "time-based" Melchizedek. He was appointed to reign for a delegated period. It was intended for Adam to rule until the time Yeshua's inheritance was made complete. That made Adam a regent king for the Melchizedek Kingdom.

We have been taught Yeshua was the substitute for humankind on the Cross. That is not precisely accurate. Scripture gives evidence that in the strictest sense, Adam and Yeshua exchanged places at the Cross. Yeshua came as the Eternal Melchizedek to pay Adam's penalty. But let us not leap too far ahead. The questions we need to ask at this point are, "If God knew Adam would sin, why didn't he just place Yeshua on the eternal throne, as the Eternal Melchizedek? Why bring forth Adam?" The answer is simple: Without Adam, you nor I would exist. God wanted us!

---

27 It is my opinion that Adam, when first fashioned, was not gender specific, only after Eve was formed was "he" solely male.
28 The understanding of a soul is important. But so is the understanding of spirit. Adam was, as are all humans, body, soul, and spirit.

Genesis 1:27 utilized the term *bara* three times:
1. God **created** the *Aleph-Tav* man.
2. God **created** him as a representative.
3. God **created** them.

Verse twenty-six has been interpreted as meaning God assigned the human species dominion. Nope! Disagree. The verse states that Adam was to have dominion. And to fully exercise his authority, he needed a helpmate. Hence, the regent king, Adam, and his bride, Eve, were not only unique; they were the "them," the ones to whom dominion was assigned. To be clear, humanity, as a species, was not given dominion. If anything, the human species was to "occupy" Yeshua's kingdom until he inherits all that was promised to him.

> Genesis 1: 28 *"And God blessed them, and God said unto them, "Be fruitful, and multiply, and replenish the את earth, and subdue it: and have dominion over the fish of the sea, and over the fowl of the air, and over every living thing that moves upon the earth."*

Dominion or *radah* (*resh-dalet-hei*) was given that they might prevail against the adversarial system. The emphasis of verse twenty-eight is placed upon the blessing. It was that blessing that enabled Adam, as the man and woman, to be fruitful. Because of that blessing, they had the needed ability to overcome any enemy. They had a God-given right to exercise control over everything that moved upon or against the field of *'erets*.

- God blessed (*barak*) - acknowledged their worth.
- God charged them to be fruitful and then imparted an ability to increase.
- God charged them to multiply and imparted an ability to increase with abundance.
- God charged them to replenish the earth by filling it with kingdom law.
- God charged them to subdue, to subjugate the activity of the adversarial kingdom in *'erets*.

> Genesis 1:29-31 *"And God said, 'Behold, I have given you every herb bearing seed, which is upon the face of all the earth, and every tree, in the which is the fruit of a tree yielding seed; to you, it shall be for meat. And to every beast of the earth, and to every fowl of the air, and to everything that creeps upon the earth, wherein there is life, I have given every green herb for meat,' and it was so. And God saw everything that he had made, and behold, it was very good. And the evening and the morning were the sixth day."*

'Eseb = herb. Strong's OT#612 translates *'eseb* as grasses or herbs. Adam and his bride were given *Aleph-Tav* herb to eat as meat, which meant they were only to consume herbs or plants containing seed. Seed denotes the ability to be fruitful, which is *zara zera*. This phrasing implies fruit that bears seed.

John 4:32 and 34, Jesus said, *"I have meat to eat that you know not of.... my meat is to do the will of him that sent me, and to finish his work."*

"And God saw everything that He had made." He beheld that it was **very** (*me'od*) good. To rephrase: God saw that everything made as *Aleph-Tav* - was good - wholly good.

The sixth letter of the Hebrew alphabet is the *vav*, which symbolizes a nail. Hence, this final day secured Yahweh's house against the adversary. And that is why when he was nailed to the Cross, Yeshua cried out, "It is finished!"

Hebrews 7:17, *"For it is declared: 'You are a priest forever, in the order of Melchizedek.'"*

Revelation 21:1-4, *"I saw a new heaven and a new earth, for the **first** heaven and the **first** earth had passed away, and there was no longer any sea. I saw the Holy City, the new Jerusalem, coming down out of heaven from God, prepared as a bride beautifully dressed for her husband. And I heard a loud voice from the throne saying, 'Now the dwelling of God is with men, and he will live with them. They will be his people, and God himself will be with them and be their God."* (emphasis added).

Protos is the Greek word used by John to describe the current earth and heaven; they are in *protos* status (first status). But after transformation, they shall fold together, connecting as one realm. *Protos* is often used as a prefix. In fact, it is the prefix of "prototype." So, "In the beginning," God created the prototype for what is to come. Then, the "existing" heaven and earth will "fold together" and form one existence, not that the earth would entirely pass away. The word he used was *aperchomai* (to go off and come back). Earth will be transformed. After the change, there will be no chaos or sea. And heaven and earth will once again be one, the cosmic mountain of Yah.

2 Peter 3:10, *"the day of the Lord will come as a thief in the night; in which the heavens shall pass away* (come near and go away) *with a great noise* (a whizzing noise), *and the elements* (the orderly arrangement of it) *shall melt* (be loosen) *with fervent heat* (consumed), *the earth also and the works* (the toiling) *that are therein shall be burned* (consumed) *up"* (author's amplification).

Revelation 21:22-27, *"I did not see a temple in the city, because the Lord God Almighty and the Lamb are its temple. The city does not need the sun or the moon to shine on it, for the glory of God gives it light, and the Lamb is its lamp. The nations will walk by its light, and the kings of the earth will bring their splendor into it. On no day will its gates ever be shut, for there will be no night there. The glory and honor of the nations will be brought into it. Nothing impure will ever enter it, nor will anyone who does what is shameful or deceitful, but only those whose names are written in the Lamb's book of life."*

Philippians 2:10-11, *"Therefore God exalted him to the highest place and gave him the name that is above every name, that at the name of Jesus every knee should bow, in heaven and on earth and under the earth, and every tongue confess that Jesus Christ is Lord, to the glory of God the Father."*

Genesis Two

Genesis 2:4 *"This is the **history of the heavens and the earth when they were created**, in the day that **Yahweh Elohiym** made the earth and the heavens"* (emphasis added).

1. Day One – Light
2. Day Two - Atmosphere
3. Day Three – Seeding of the biosphere
4. Day Four – Ecliptic alignment
5. Day Five – Ecosystem
6. Day Six – Terrestrial life
7. Day Seven – Shabbat

Although God is beyond human comprehension, we need to add to our understanding of who He is. Therefore, let's begin by examining God's name, Yahweh, given to Moses while standing before the burning bush in an Egyptian desert. As he listened to God, Moses realized the One who spoke was more than Israel's Supreme Deity; He was also the self-existent, eternal entity reigning over the cosmos, outranking all other gods.

Yod-hei-vav-hei (Strong's OT#3068), the name God gave to Moses when introducing Himself at the burning bush. After spending a fair amount of time researching the meaning of this name, the conclusion I reached was God's sacred name is *Yah*. But when at the burning bush, *Yah* added *hayah*, which was interpreted, *Yahweh*. Still, the Hebrew text indicates God said, "*Yah* exists" or "I, *Yah* exist."

Exodus 3:14, *"And God said unto Moses, 'I AM THAT I AM…'"* Essentially, "Tell them that *Yah* exists because I exist." These words were an emphatic directive spoken in a tone that states, "I exist, so say unto the sons of Israel that **eh'yah** sent me." Or "Say unto the sons of Israel, *Yah* exists, and He sent me." The pictographic symbols translate as - "I, *Yah*" "Exist." These pictures can also mean "the First extended life; secures life."

Yah is the *El Elyon* (God, God most high). As such, He is the ultimate power and authority of the cosmos – no matter who else exists, it is impossible for any to be greater than *Yah*. All power and control are His, and He doles out authority or might as He sees fit. *Yah* is ever-present - all-powerful – all-knowing. Omnipresent – Omnipotent – Omniscient. *Yah* will not submit to another. He cannot. Not and still hold all things together by the "power of His word."

It is possible to interpret Exodus 3:14 as "tell them that the FIRST exists! – That there is but one Chief God, and I am He! They exist, as the children of Abraham, Isaac, and Jacob, because I exist!" Exodus 3:15 could be stated as *"Say this… 'Yahweh, the God of your fathers, the God of Abraham, the God of Isaac, and the God of*

Jacob, has sent me.'"

1 John 4:12, *"No one has seen God at any time."* John 1:18, *"No one has seen God at any time. Only begotten God, who is in the bosom of the Father, He has declared him."* The literal translation of this verse reads, *"God no one has ever seen, only begotten God, who is in the bosom (heart) of the Father...."* The phrase "no one" is non-specific. Who is the "no one?" Did John mean no human, no entity of any species, but only Yeshua?

How could that be when the Bible pictures Yahweh interacting with mankind? Perhaps, the following explains. *"God, who at various times in various ways spoke in time past to the fathers by the prophets, has in these last days spoken to us by His Son, who He has appointed heir of all things, through whom He made the worlds* (aiōnas – the ages), *who being the brightness of His glory and the express image* (exact copy) *of His person, and upholding all things by the word of His power, when purged sin, sat down at the right hand of the Majesty on high, having become so much better than the angels, as He has by inheritance obtained a more excellent name than they"* Hebrews 1:1-4.

Acts 17:27-28, *"God did this so that men would seek him and perhaps reach out for him and find him, though he is not far from each one of us. 'For in him we live and move and have our being.' As some of your own poets have said, 'We are his offspring.'"*

Colossians 1:15-18, *"He* (Yeshua) *is the image of the invisible God, the firstborn over all creation. For by Him, all things were created that are in heaven and that are on earth, visible and invisible, whether thrones or dominions or principalities or powers. All things were created through Him and for Him. And He is before all things, and in Him, all things consist. And He is the head of the body, the church, who is the beginning, the firstborn from the dead, that in all things He may have the preeminence."*

Yeshua is God's image, an image that humans can comprehend in their current fallen state. The full measure of God's glory is invisible to humans. That is why Yeshua is God's message; he can be perceived. Even so, we exist in God due to His love, mercy, and grace toward humanity. But what do these things mean? Primarily, the Father reveals the Son, and the Son reveals the Father. But is God genuinely invisible? Or only invisible to fallen man? Regarding this, Jesus said to see him is to see the Father. He also said that God is Spirit, and they who worship Him must do so in spirit and in truth.

The pre-incarnate Messiah manifested in the Old Testament. He did so as the Second Power of Heaven, who was also called Yahweh. You see, Judaism, pre-Christianity, recognized that Yahweh on occasion appeared with Yahweh.[29] This makes sense when we understand mankind images Yeshua (the Eternal Melchizedek) while Yeshua images Yahweh.

I love the following quote of Dr. Michael Heiser; it's worth remembering, *"Yahweh is inherently distinct and superior to all other gods. Yahweh is an elohim (a god), but no other elohim (gods) are Yahweh...."*

One additional note while still on this subject. Exodus 6:2-3, *"God also said to Moses, 'I am the LORD (Yahweh).*

---

[29] An example of this is in Genesis 15 when a "smoking pot" appeared with a "burning torch." Another example is Daniel 7. Daniel sees the Son of Man (Yeshua) and the Ancient of Days (Yahweh) in the same vision.

I appeared to Abraham, to Isaac and to Jacob as God Almighty (El Shaddai), but by my name the LORD (Yahweh), **I did** *not make myself known to them."* However, there is a flaw with this translation. The original Hebrew text suggests God did not make a statement but asked a question, *"…but by my name, Yahweh,* **did I** *not make myself known to them?"* The notion that Abraham did not know the name of his God is flawed, especially since *El Shaddai* is not a name but an appellation.

Pythagoras, in the 6th B.C., defined the cosmos as the harmonious systematic universe. So, "universe" and "cosmos" can be used synonymously. John 18:36, *"Jesus answered, 'My kingdom is not of this* **world**. *If my kingdom were of this* **world**, *my servants would fight, so I should not be delivered to the Jews, but now my kingdom is not from here"* (emphasis added). Note the word, world. In the Greek texts, it was cosmos. Jesus was not saying his kingdom wasn't in the universe, but that the Roman system (order) was not under his sovereignty. Jesus clarified his statement. He said that if they stood in his court, his servants would remove those who were hostile.

When the New Testament was written, "cosmos" inferred any orderly arrangement. Therefore, there are two vital points Jesus made: 1) He has a kingdom. 2) The court (government) where he stood was not under his appointed authority.

Matthew 4:8-10, *"Again, the devil* (diábolos) *took Him up on an* **exceedingly high mountain** *and showed Him all the kingdoms* (basileías) *of the world* (cosmos) *and their glory. And he said to Him, 'All these things I will give You if You will fall down and worship me.' Then Jesus said to him, 'Away with you, Satan! For it is written, "You shall worship the Lord* (Yahweh) *your God, and Him only you shall serve"* (emphasis added).

First, note that Jesus was taken to an "exceedingly high mountain." We can only speculate to which mountain Jesus was taken. Mount Hermon is the highest mountain in Israel[30] and the most likely. If it was Mount Hermon, then Jesus was taken to the "stronghold" of the fallen gods. Mount Hermon is to the fallen realm what Mount Zion is to the Kingdom of Righteousness.

Jesus was shown the order of the adversary's kingdom, "its" glory. Matthew used the word cosmos, but in Luke's rendering of this event, he said Jesus was shown the *oikouménēs* (the terrain). Essentially, Jesus was offered the kingdoms (the territories) of *'erets* and beyond, all realms controlled by the adversarial system. This infers that between the time of Adam and the advent of the Messiah, *'erets* fell into the hands of the adversary. Even more, I think the adversary was offering the Messiah a false inheritance, which included the abyss.

How was that possible? The universe in its infancy was ordered. Therefore, the only available conclusion is that the universe fell out of order when the earth appeared chaotic and the abyss was formed.

Additionally, we note that the adversary, through deception, gained control over the systems governing

---

[30] Mount Hermon is sacred to the fallen realm. So, it is reasonable to think the adversary took Jesus to this mountain to show him the kingdoms under his control.

mankind, and Jesus came to recover what was stolen and redeem the dead from the abyss. Even more, he came to rescue dying humanity from the world's systems. In other words, Jesus came to pay the penalty Adam owed, thereby redeeming Adam and all of his offspring. But Jesus did not come to "rule" over the dead or control the world's false systems, which is what the adversary offered him at that time.

Ostensibly, the Divine Council was charged with maintaining justice throughout the cosmos. So, did they fail? Apparently so. At this point, I will speculate about my current understanding of the existing order, which is being done away with. You see, the government of God, the Creator, is organized like a pyramid. The Godhead is the apex; under God is the Royal Court, then the Divine Council. All created entities (gods) are assigned to serve Yahweh in one manner or another.[31]

To rephrase so all is clear, God (Yah the Father) and the King (Yahweh-Yeshua the Son) rule. Under them are the Divine Court (the princes) and the Divine Council (the gods). Or to say the same thing in another way, Yahweh (Father) is over the Divine Council, Yeshua (Son) heads the Divine Court.

The "sons of God" are princes and rule over cosmic principalities similar to the structure of an earthly kingdom. Princes, dukes, and earls are the court of an earthly throne. In comparison, in the realm of spirits, these rulers are *"principalities and powers in heavenly places."* Their number appears limited. However, the number of those who sit in the Divine Council as gods is seemingly vast. These entities transcend human perception. Yet, I don't think that was the Creator's original intent.

The Court and Council are comprised of Cherubim, Seraphim, Ophanim, Hayyot, and many others. I also believe that the members of the Court are a part of the Divine Council. Yet, the Court and Council are of varying species and include angels but are in no way exclusively angels. Angels and satans are job descriptions. Messengers and prosecuting attorneys, respectively. Abilities, capabilities in their society are dependent upon their "job" assignment. Just as it is in human civilization.

Isaiah 14:12-17, *"How has **Lucifer** (hêlēl), that rose in the morning, fallen from heaven! He that sent orders to all the nations is crushed to the earth. But thou saidst in thine heart, 'I will go up to heaven,* **I will set my throne above the stars of heaven: I will sit on a lofty mount, on the lofty mountains towards the north: I will go up above the clouds; I will be like the Most High.'** *But now* thou <u>shalt</u> go down *to hell* (Sheol)*, even to the foundations of the earth. They that see thee shall wonder at thee, and say, 'This is the man* (male creature) *that troubled the earth* ('erets)*, that made kings* (kingdoms) *to shake; that made the whole world* (tēbēl – the inhabitants) *desolate and destroyed its cities* (a guarded place)" (Greek-English Septuagint: Brenton Edition emphasis added).

For a moment, forget everything you know concerning Isaiah 14. The being who was addressed in this setting was not named Lucifer. Hêlēl is defined by Strong's OT#1966 as the morning star.

Earth's morning star is Venus. However, this term, "morning stars," is a symbolic epithet used in the Bible as a metaphor to signify the created sons of God. They are the princes of the royal court.

---

[31] The imagination of the Creator knows no limit. He has created a vast universe inhabited by a vast number of entities.

Venus is the second planet from the sun, and since it is a terrestrial planet, it is viewed as Earth's twin. As the brightest object in the sky, the ancients regarded it sacred.

The Romans named the star after one of their most important deities, Venus. However, the Greeks called this goddess Aphrodite; her male counterpart was Ares. The Canaanites worshipped her as Astarte, the Babylonians as Ishtar, and the Sumerians as Inanna. But note that this god/goddess is androgynous. In effect, the gods are genderfluid anthropomorphic shapeshifters. They manifest or present themselves in whatever form suit the moment. That is why Isaiah 14 is addressed to Enlil[32] but described as Venus.

Revelation 17:1-4, *"Come," he said, "I will show you the condemnation and punishment of the great prostitute who sits on many waters, with whom the kings of the earth committed sexual immorality and the earth's inhabitants got drunk with the wine of her immorality." So, he carried me away in the Spirit to a wilderness, and there I saw a woman sitting on a scarlet beast that was full of blasphemous names and had seven heads and ten horns."*[33] The "woman" sat (resided) on the beast. She was within the persona of the beast.

Revelation 22:16. *"I, Jesus, have sent My angel to testify to you these things in the churches. I am the Root and the Offspring of David, the Bright and Morning Star."* Comparing Isaiah 14:12 to Revelation 22:16 seems to be incongruous. But not so. You see, at some point in the ancient past, the Isaiah 14 character determined he deserved to be treated as the Son of *Yah*. He wanted to rise above all others in the Divine Court and Divine Council to be seated with God the Father as God the Son.[34] In other words, I think he wanted to be the Eternal King, to do away with Yeshua or replace him, at the very least, to be his equal.

Before my research for this study, I firmly believed that Isaiah 14 and Ezekiel 28 were directed to the same fallen god. However, I have since discovered those who argue they were not. Their primary premise is Ezekiel 28 connects to Eden.[35] In contrast, Isaiah 14, with the Mount of Congregation. They believe these two places don't equate. However, they do. Rather than going into a long explanation as to why I say they are the same, I offer this conclusion: Isaiah 14 is merely another view of the events of Revelation 12. The Isaiah 14 "god" is the "king" of the Babylonian system, the anti-Christ system. That indicates a competitive spirit rose in this entity, causing him to become the personification of pride and lust. To my thinking, he transformed from the bringer of "light" to become the bringer of "chaos." That would also make him the instigator of the rebellion that occurred in the pre-Adamic *'erets*. So, yes, *hêlēl* is the god of chaos and the entity described in Ezekiel 28.

Please understand, my understanding of these matters is fluid. So, when the Bible is not crystal clear, for me to say anything with absolute certainty is disingenuous. Nonetheless, as of this writing, I am convinced *'erets* (earth) existed before the occurrence of Genesis 1:2. I also believe the planet was the original "seat" of

---

[32] "*Helel* is equivalent phonetically to the Sumerian *Enlil* … and Akkadian *Illil* (or *Ellil*)" Hamp, Douglas. *Corrupting the Image 2: Hybrids, Hades, and the Mt Hermon Connection* (p. 9). Eskaton Media Group. Kindle Edition.
[33] The NET Bible®, Copyright © 1996-2006 by Biblical Studies Press, L.L.C., Dallas, Texas, www.bible.org. All rights reserved. Used by permission.
[34] Based on certain texts it is my opinion *"Helel"* is 'the elder' of Yah's Creation., Yeshua as God was not created.
[35] Eden is Yah's cosmic mountain, which places the Mount of Congregation in Eden. Eden existed before *'erets*.

Yah's cosmic mountain. The location of "Eden." And that "Eden" was created as an interdimensional sphere affording access to the entire cosmic system. I do not believe we live in a multi-verse reality but an interdimensional reality where the physical and spiritual co-exist. However, in the beginning, there was not a physical-spiritual separation. Nor shall there be when the current age is over.

Eden, the ancient pre-Adamic civilization, still exists, but in the spiritual domain. The Divine Council is responsible for justice in that domain, and the Divine Court rules and reigns. Scripture, per my opinion, indicates that the *hêlēl* was seated over the Divine Council as its reigning prince. If I'm correct, then his rebellion must have shaken the Divine Council to the core. Which explains why Yah appointed Yeshua the Melchizedek, the King of Righteousness - to restore order to the Divine Council.

While we are on this subject, I am persuaded that Earth and the other planets of our Solar System were inhabited before the rebellion. So, essentially, it was the Solar System that fell in disarray. Keep in mind there are galaxies beyond the Milky Way. ("In no way am I offering any opinion about anything that does not involve Earth," the author said sarcastically.)

Anyway, getting back on track by returning to the "history" of the generations of heaven and earth, *Elohiym* is the title we use to point to Yah as the Judge of the Judges. As the Ancient of Days, He sits as the Supreme God over all the "gods." Remember, the gods make up the Divine Council and the princes the Divine Court, and since the princes are also members of the Divine Council, they are gods. Therefore, essentially, the terms "gods and princes" are also job descriptions. The gods are the judges who decide whether justice prevails in the cosmos, whereas princes reign over territories. These princes were meant to rule righteously. And because these two positions differ, the authority and power associated with each vary.

After the rebellion, Yah determined to gift Yeshua the reign of all government. That meant the Court and the Council needed reordering. And that was when it was decided, though he is the Son, Yeshua must show absolute obedience to Yah. Essentially, before agreeing to Yah's plan, allowing Yeshua to sit on the Throne and govern them, the Divine Council demanded Yeshua prove himself worthy. In conjunction with establishing his throne, he had to do away with Chaos, forever and ever.

Ephesians 1:3-12, *"Blessed be the God and Father of our Lord Jesus Christ, who has blessed us with every spiritual blessing in the heavenly places in Christ, just as He chose us in Him before the foundation of the world, that we should be holy and without blame before Him in love,* **having predestined us to adoption as sons by Jesus Christ to Himself***, according to the good pleasure of His will, to the praise of the glory of His grace, by which He made us accepted in the Beloved. In Him we have redemption through His blood, the forgiveness of sins, according to the riches of His grace which He made to abound toward us in all wisdom and prudence, having made known to us the mystery of His will, according to His good pleasure which He purposed in Himself,* **that in the dispensation of the fullness of the times He might gather together in one all things in Christ, both which are in heaven and which are on earth — in Him***. In Him also we have obtained an inheritance, being predestined according to the purpose of Him who works all things according to the counsel of His will, that we who first trusted in Christ should be to the praise of His glory"* (emphasis added).

So, the reordering of the Court and Council meant some would be unseated, and others added. Adam was added, whereas the adversaries of Yah's plan were unseated.

Ephesians 3:9-12, *"...and to make all see what is the fellowship of the mystery, which **from the beginning of the ages has been hidden in God who created all things through Jesus Christ;** to the intent that now the manifold wisdom of God might be made known by the church to the principalities and powers in the heavenly places, according to the eternal purpose which He accomplished in Christ Jesus our Lord...."* (emphasis added).

Hebrews 5:6-11, *"You are a priest forever according to the order of Melchizedek," who, in the days of His flesh, when He had offered up prayers and supplications, with vehement cries and tears to Him who was able to save Him from death and was heard because of His godly fear, though He was a Son, yet **He learned obedience by the things which He suffered**. **And having been perfected**, He became the author of eternal salvation to all who obey Him, called by God as High Priest 'according to the order of Melchizedek,' of whom we have much to say, and hard to explain, since you have become dull of hearing"* (emphasis added).

Ephesians 1:22-23, *"And He put all things under His feet, and gave Him to be head over all things to the church, which is His body, the fullness of Him who fills all in all."*

So, to be clear, Yeshua was installed to rule over the Divine Court and the Divine Council after the rebellion. But he is not currently sitting as presiding King over the Divine Council because the final enemy must be dealt with. The last enemy is "death."

Revelation 12:3-4, *"And another sign appeared in heaven: behold, a great, fiery red dragon having seven heads and ten horns, and seven diadems on his heads."*

*"And war broke out in heaven: Michael and his angels fought with **the dragon**, and the dragon and his angels fought, but they did not prevail, nor was a place found for them in heaven any longer. So, the great dragon was cast out, that serpent of old called the Devil and Satan, who deceives the whole world; he was cast to the earth, and his angels were cast out with him,"* Revelation 12:7-9 (emphasis added). As of this writing, I believe it was this particular dragon who led the pre-Adamic rebellion. He is portrayed as a multiple-headed dragon because he is a system, the rebellious system.

Although *'erets* is a part of the cosmos, I don't think the Divine Council was given the "re-created" *'erets* to administer. Scripture indicates *'erets* was assigned to Adam, solely his to judge. Consequently, *'erets* was designated as belonging to the Melchizedek (Yeshua). The Council was to work with Adam by securing his words concerning *'erets*. My supposition is that they were to keep at bay the entities of the spirit realm from interfering with Adam's domain. Adam, nonetheless, was a qualified member of the Divine Council. To understand, let's return to John 18:36, *"Jesus answered, 'My kingdom is not of this world* (cosmos – meaning of this order).*"* Obviously, within the cosmos, there are two kingdoms in operation. Jesus' kingdom is the Melchizedek Kingdom, the Kingdom of Righteousness. The other kingdom is ruled by the adversaries (those who were in the Divine Council and were seated previously in the Divine Court).

There is only one Supreme God (Yah). His kingdom is the rightful kingdom; the other is not only "anti" Yahweh; it is illegal in all regards. Psalms 110:1, *"The Lord said to my Lord, 'Sit at My right hand, till I make your enemies your footstool.'"*

Daniel 7:9-10, *"I beheld till the thrones were cast down, and the Ancient of days did sit, whose garment was white as snow, and the hair of his head like the pure wool: his throne was like the fiery flame, and his wheels as burning fire. A fiery stream issued and came forth from before him: thousand, thousands ministered unto him, and ten thousand times ten thousand stood before him: the judgment was set, and the books were opened."*

Psalms 82:1 from the KJV, *"God stands in the congregation of the mighty; He judges among the gods...."* This same verse from the Dead Sea Scroll Bible:[36] *"God takes his stand in the divine council; he holds judgment among the gods."* Another translation is *"Elohim stands in the 'el' assembly and administers judgment among the elohim."*

Revelation 20:4, *"I saw thrones on which were seated those who had been given authority to judge."*

Psalms 89:7-8, *"In the council of the holy ones God is greatly feared; he is more awesome than all who surround him. O LORD God Almighty, who is like you? You are mighty, O LORD, and your faithfulness surrounds you."*

John 10:34-36, *"Is it not written in your Law, 'I have said you are gods' If he called them 'gods,' to whom the word of God came and the Scripture cannot be broken, what about the One the Father set apart as his very own and sent into the world?"*

Terms that equate with Divine Council:
- Elohim
- Heavenly Host
- Thrones
- Sons of God
- Judges
- Great assembly
- Holy ones
- Princes
- Lower-case "g" gods

For additional information regarding the Divine Council, I suggest the following two books by Dr. Michael Heiser: *Supernatural* and *The Unseen Realm*.

To my thinking, there is no more suitable term to denote the spirit kingdom of Yahweh than to call it the Kingdom of Righteousness. And regarding that kingdom, the New Testament book of Hebrews clarifies Yeshua is the Eternal Melchizedek. So, by instructing his disciples to pray, *"Your kingdom come. Your will be done on earth as it is in heaven,"*[37] Jesus was encouraging their understanding that the "Melchizedek Kingdom" needed to overtake *'erets*.

---

36 Abegg, M., Jr., Flint, P., & Ulrich, E. (1999). *The Dead Sea Scrolls Bible: The Oldest Known Bible Translated for the First Time into English* (Ps 82). New York: Harper One.
37 Luke 11:2

Yeshua came to the realm of *'erets* as the only Begotten Son of Father God. Any confusion surrounding the preceding sentence stems from a misunderstanding of what the phrase "only-begotten" means. Thus, we will examine the phrase first, from the Hebrew perspective, and then from the Greek.

Begotten in Hebrew is *yalad* (yaw-lad). Strong's OT#3205 states that it's from a primitive root that means to bear young, causatively to beget, medically to function as a midwife, and specifically, to show lineage.

"Only-begotten" is *monogenoús* in Greek. Strong's NT #3439 defines *monogenoús* as the only one born. (*Mono - genes* = sole [mono] race (genos])

Yeshua is a race or species unto himself! Yeshua is unique. He is one of a kind! Birth by Holy Spirit, his physical body came from God's DNA, not from pro-created human DNA. Yet, Yeshua was born of a woman as an infant. But praise God, He returned to the Father as a mature Son of Man!

Now I will go out on a limb and say Jesus was not 100% human and 100% God. Yeshua is and always shall be fully Divine. However, Yeshua entered a body created by WORD and took on the "likeness" of Adam as a new species (only begotten – *mono genos*). He walked upon the "field of *'erets*" as a human because he needed to show human lineage. Yet, Yeshua is the Promised Seed! Whose Seed? Yahweh's![38]

1 John 3:2, *"Beloved, now are we the sons of God, and it doth not yet appear what we shall be: but we know that, when he shall appear, we shall be like him; for we shall see him as he is."* 1 Corinthians 15:50, *"Now this I say, brethren, that flesh and blood cannot inherit the kingdom of God; nor does corruption inherit incorruption."*

1 Corinthians 15:49, *"And just as we have borne the likeness of the earthly man, so shall we bear the likeness of the man from heaven."* Yeshua came from the unseen spiritual realm as (or like) a man, yet he was not human. He came to create a new race! Double WOW!

He was not from Adam but was "the Son of Man." The term "son of man" translates as meaning "the builder of mankind!" As the Son of Man, he is the BUILDER of the NEW MAN – the one new man!

Let me repeat: Yeshua is unique - one of a kind. He came to transform humanity by making humankind into a new species. That new species is "his kind." The "new species" is to be conformed to his image, to be exactly like him. Therefore, all humans must be "born again."

To accomplish the task assigned, Yeshua needed the support of the most powerful system in the cosmos. In biblical terms, he was given the keys to the kingdom to establish God's righteous government. The government of God rests squarely upon Yeshua's shoulders. The keys to the Kingdom are HIS!

Isaiah 9:6, *"For unto us a child is born, unto us, a son is given,* **and the government shall be upon his shoulder,** *and his name shall be called Wonderful, Counsellor, the mighty God, the everlasting Father, the Prince of Peace"* (emphasis added).

Revelation 1:17-18, *"When I saw him, I fell at his feet as though dead. Then he placed his right hand on me and said: 'Do*

---

[38] This understanding will be developed progressively.

not be afraid. I am the First and the Last (Aleph-Tav) I am the Living One; I was dead, and behold I am alive forever and ever! **And I hold the keys of death and Hades**" (emphasis added).

Psalms 2:7-9, *"He said to me, 'You are my Son today I have become your Father. Ask of me, and I will make the nations your inheritance, the ends of the earth your possession. You will rule them with an iron scepter, and you will dash them to pieces like pottery.'"*

Psalms 110:4, *"The LORD (Yahweh) has sworn and will not change his mind,* **'You are a priest forever, in the order of Melchizedek**.*'"* (Transliterated - *kohen 'owlam 'al dibrah Maliki-Tsedeq*)

- *Kohen* – officiating priest
- *'Owlam* -concealed in eternity
- *Dibrah* – by reason of…
- *Malki-Tsedeq* Strong's OT#4442 (mal-kee-tseh'-dek) is formed by combining OT#4428 and OT#6664 and translates as "king of right."

"You are – the officiating priest, concealed in eternity, by the reason, that you are the rightful King."

Melchizedek was never a name but a title belonging to the king of the highest rank. The spelling of the word caused it to be a construct phrase. In Semitic languages, nouns can be positioned to modify another noun. In this case, *malki* modifies *tsedeq*. Yet, there is a problem adequately translating the term due to the *'yod* positioned between *malk* and *tsedeq*. The *yod* is a suffix to *malk,* which makes the construction of the phrase less than conclusive. The effect of the *yod* reconfigures "King Righteous" into "King my Righteous." In other words, my King is Righteous.

After researching this term at length, I concluded there was a reason these two words, *malki,* and *tsedeq,* were combined. I suspect Melchizedek was not a word until the Tower of Babel era, when it was meant to signify Noah as the rightful king, not Nimrod.

Most modern scholars translate Melchizedek as King of Righteousness, and that is perfectly understandable given the words of Hebrews 7:2 that state as much, *"First, his name means 'king of righteousness…'"* Even so, when one examines the etymology, the more accurate interpretation is the one presented.

The term Melchizedek appears only twice in the Old Testament. The first instance is found in Genesis 14 when the then Melchizedek met with Abraham. The second instance is the Psalms 110:4 verse.

Though Adam was assigned dominion, giving him the rank of a sovereign, he was a proxy, a regent King/High Priest. The argument I hear most often against this notion is that "Adam was not a king because he had no one to rule over." In other words, God needed a population of people for Adam to be a king. What nonsense! (Although, if I am truthful, I thought the same for many years.)

The characteristics of a Melchizedek:
- At any given time, only one Melchizedek can reign
- A Melchizedek is first a Firstborns

- They are chosen to serve after being deemed righteous by Yahweh
- They are not allowed to commit a dishonorable act
- The Melchizedek is both a king and a high priest
- They are first appointed, then anointed to serve
- The primary responsibility of the Melchizedek is to establish and maintain a relationship with Yahweh so *'erets,* as a domain, is accepted as righteous, which is the duty of High Priest
- The Melchizedek is also the Prophet of *'Erets*
- As the King of kings, he judges all matters concerning *'erets;* his word is final
- He is a member of the Divine Council

Terms analogous with the Melchizedek Kingdom:
- God's Kingdom
- The Kingdom of Heaven
- The Kingdom of Light
- God's House; temple; a dwelling place
- Church of the Firstborn(s)
- Righteous
- Zion
- One New Man
- Bride of Christ

→ 2 Samuel 5:7, *"Nevertheless, David captured the fortress of Zion, the City of David."*

→ 2 Kings 19:31, *"For out of Jerusalem will come a remnant, and out of Mount Zion a band of survivors the zeal of the LORD Almighty will accomplish this."*

→ Psalms 2:6, *"I have installed my King on Zion, my holy hill."*

→ Psalms 48:2, *"Beautiful for situation, the joy of the whole earth, is mount Zion, on the sides of the north, the city of the great King."*

Genesis 2:4-7, *"This is **the account** of the heavens and the earth when they were created. When the Yahweh Elohiym made the earth and the heavens and no shrub of the field had yet appeared on the earth, and no plant of the field had yet sprung up, for Yahweh Elohiym had not sent rain on the earth, and there was no (Aleph-Tav) man to work the ground, but streams came up from the earth and watered the (Aleph-Tav) whole surface of the ground the Yahweh Elohiym formed the (Aleph-Tav) man from the dust of the ground and breathed into his nostrils the breath of life, and the man became a living being. "This is the history of the heavens and the earth when they were cut out and created; when they entered into a covenant with Yahweh when he made them."*

The explanations I gave to open this chapter hopefully expand on the dynamic forces in the realm we call heaven. Moses put the work of creation on display in Genesis 2:4, then attributed the "birth" of them as the work of Yahweh. The term Moses used to connotate "birthing" is interesting. It is *towledah* (to-led-ah). *Towledah* translates as generations. *Towledah* also means the history of a family. However, the more frequent use of *towledah* refers to the activities of a midwife. In effect, Moses proclaimed, *"This was the birth record of the heavens and the earth when they were appointed covenant with Yahweh Elohiym."*

The KJV translated Genesis 2:4 as *"These are the generations of the heavens and of the earth when they were created,* **in the day** *that the Lord God made the earth and the heavens…."* The phrase "in the day" is anchored in *yom* (day). *Yom*, however, is not limited to a specified time; it can last anywhere from 24 hours to an era of time. Whether we agree or disagree about the six days of Genesis 1, each being a literal 24 hours, needs to be pushed aside. The core message of these verses was not about time. Instead, it was about the establishment of God's government.

Genesis 2:5, *"…and* **every plant of the field before** *it was in the earth, and every herb of the field* **before** *it grew for the Lord God had not caused it to rain upon the earth, and there was not a* **man** *to till the ground"* (emphasis added).

We have discussed this previously but let me say again, Day Three absolutely had to occur before Day Six. Yahweh established a "pattern" with days three and six. Genesis 2:5 outlines the pattern: Plant seed, water the soil, till, then harvest. The pattern occurs on the micro "individual" level as well as the macro "kingdom "level:

Micro:
- Evangelize - seed
- Prophesy - water
- Teach and Pastor until mature - till
- Harvest

Macro:
- Jesus seeded
- Holy Spirit watered
- The church tills
- The harvest is the end of the age

Matthew 13:37-43, *"He who sows the good seed is the Son of Man. The field is the world, the good seeds are the sons of the kingdom, but the tares are the sons of the wicked one. The enemy who sowed them is the devil, the harvest is the end of the age, and the reapers are the angels. Therefore, as the tares are gathered and burned in the fire, so it will be at the end of this age. The Son of Man will send out His angels, and they will gather out of His kingdom all things that offend and those who practice lawlessness and will cast them into the furnace of fire. There will be wailing and gnashing of teeth. Then the righteous will shine forth as the sun in the kingdom of their Father. He who has ears to hear, let him hear!"*

"Before" or *terem* is defined by Strong's OT#2962 as to interrupt or suspend. Wait a minute, Sue. Are you saying Yahweh paused the plants before they grew?

Yes - *"for Yahweh had not caused it to rain because there was no man to till the (Aleph-Tav) ground."*

The analogy of earth being God's field is prevalent throughout Scripture, and why the connection between Day Three and Day Six is so crucial to grasp. There cannot be a harvest until two additional conditions are met. 1): the soil must be well watered, and 2) then it must receive the "seed." Day Three prophesied to the harvest of Day Six. Day Three "seeded" *'erets,* but the seeds could not grow until "watered," and a man "tilled" the soil. And so, Yahweh suspended all growth until man was created.

Let's expand that concept. Humans grow or form according to assigned DNA. When a person submits to God and accepts Yeshua as their King, their DNA is "renewed" by Holy Spirit. Additionally, they must learn how to be righteous. That is, one must relearn how to live according to the law of Love. Which basically means the soil of the heart must be tilled.

By the way, "to till" is the same as to cultivate. When soil is cultivated, weeds are removed. Still, the soil must be broken apart to allow rain (water) retention and air penetration optimization.

- Rain is Strong's OT#4305 *matar* (maw-tar) means rain
- Till is Strong's OT#5647 *'abad* (aw-bad) means to work (as in any sense), but by implication, to serve, thus, to till
- Ground is Strong's OT#127 *'adamah* (ad-aw-maw) soil, which is typically red. (Remember? It shows "blood.")
- Mist – *'ade* – the pictograph of this word depicts God's Door

Genesis 2 explains that Yahweh had yet to send "rain." In this context, the image of rain is parallel with the outpouring of the Holy Spirit. Without Holy Spirit's anointing, no man is capable of tilling the *(Aleph-Tav) 'adamah.*

- → Joel 2:28-29, *"And it shall come to pass afterward that I will pour out My Spirit on all flesh; your sons and your daughters shall prophesy, your old men shall dream dreams, your young men shall see visions. And, on My menservants and on My maidservants, I will pour out My Spirit in those days."*
- → John 3:5-6, *"Jesus answered, 'I tell you the truth, no one can enter the kingdom of God unless he is born of water and the Spirit.'"*
- → John 4:10, *"Jesus answered her, 'If you knew the gift of God and who it is that asks you for a drink, you would have asked him, and he would have given you living water.'"*
- → John 4:13-14, *"Jesus answered, 'Everyone who drinks this water will be thirsty again, but whoever drinks the water I give him will never thirst. Indeed, the water I give him will become in him a spring of water welling up to eternal life.'"*
- → John 7:38-39, *"Whoever believes in me, as the Scripture has said, streams of living water will flow from within him.'"*
- → Acts 1:5, *"For John baptized with water, but in a few days, you will be baptized with the Holy Spirit."*

Rarely used today, "till" is an old English word that means to cultivate. In the Paleo-Hebrew, "till" translates as "see the house door." Holy Spirit causes mankind to see Yeshua, which equates with seeing the Truth.

Joel 2:28, *"I will pour out my Spirit on all people."* This prophecy foretold of Jesus' ascension when he would send Holy Spirit to reveal the way to salvation. But even before Joel wrote these words, Moses wrote about the *paniym* of the *'adamah* needing to be made moist and broken. In the moist broken soil of the heart, the word is planted.

Yahweh Elohiym formed the *(Aleph-Tav)* man from moist soil. Soil that the Holy Spirit had "watered and sanctified" as *'adamah*. Adam was created from sanctified soil. Otherwise, he would not have been *(Aleph-Tav)*.

> Genesis 2:1, *"Thus the heavens and the earth were finished, and all the host of them."*

Host or *tsaba* (tsaw-baw), as defined by Strong's OT#6635, is a mass of persons. The term is militaristic. *Tsaba* is a campaign, literally or figuratively. Consequently, it refers to the "massing" of people for the purpose of war. In other words, *tsaba* is the assembling of an army.

At no time during the six days of creating did God need assistance. Let's phrase that another way, at no time during the creating process did man assist God. God not only brought restoration – He did it alone!

Revelation 12:11, *"They overcame him* (the great dragon) *by the blood of the Lamb,* **and by the word of their testimony***...."* (Emphasis added). Jesus gave his blood; mankind merely witnessed his act!

> Genesis 2:1-3 *"Thus the heavens and the earth, and all the **host of them, were finished**. And on the **seventh** day, God ended His **work** which **He had done**, and He **rested** on the **seventh** day from all **His work** which **He had done**. Then God blessed the (Aleph-Tav) seventh day and sanctified it because in it He **rested** from all **His work** which God had **created** and **made**. This is the history of the heavens and the earth when they were **created**."*

Day Six finalized Yahweh's plan, whereas Day Seven acknowledged the strategy comprehensively finished. The heavens and earth were completed, the host of them assembled. Plain and straightforward, while it was yet the sixth day, God's work was complete. God did not wait until Day Seven and then cease to work. He stopped working on Day Six and celebrated Day Seven since nothing was left to accomplish.

Genesis 1:31 to 2:3 introduces a single thought: *"God saw all that he had made, and it was very good. And there was evening, and there* **was morning--the sixth day***. Thus, the heavens and the earth were completed in all their vast array. By the seventh day, God had finished the work he had been doing; so, on the seventh day, he rested from all his work. And God blessed the seventh day and made it holy because on it he rested from all the work of creating that he had done."*

God completed his work "the morning of the sixth day." Basically, the results were complete with the *boqer*, sunrise. *Boqer* translates as "morning," the arrival of the dawn, daybreak. Ancient rabbis taught that a *"yom"* (day) began at sunset; thus, with the evening. And evening ends with the sunrise, yet the day is not over until the next sunset.

John 9:4-5, *"As long as it is day, we must do the work of him who sent me. Night is coming when no one can work. While I am in the world, I am the light of the world."* Yahweh "worked" during the night and examined His work at sunrise. He then sealed all He had done by saying, "Hey, that's good! That is exceptionally good!"

Perhaps the reason Yahweh proclaimed His work exceptionally good was *"... **at dawn** on the first day of the week, Mary Magdalene and the other Mary went to look at the tomb. There was a violent earthquake, for an angel of the Lord came down from heaven and, going to the tomb, rolled back the stone and sat on it. His appearance was like lightning, and his clothes were white as snow. The guards were so afraid of him that they shook and became like dead men. The angel said to the women, 'Do not be afraid, for I know that you are looking for Jesus, who was crucified. He is not here; he has risen, just as he said. Come and see the place where he lay. Then go quickly and tell his disciples He has risen from the dead...'"* Matthew 28:1-7.

The seventh Hebrew letter is the *zayin* - a weapon. *Zayin* means to cut off; to harvest; to pierce. Thus, because the harvest is in the barn, the seventh day is a day of rest. Furthermore, the seventh day is the only day God sanctified as holy *(qâdâsh)*. Strong's OT#6942 (kaw-dash) defines *qâdâsh* as being from a primitive root that means cleaning, making, or perceiving, or observing, as ceremonially cleansed. *Qâdâsh* is typically translated as holy. The spelling of *qâdâsh* is interesting: *qof-dalet-shin*. The *qof* represents the last part of an arch (the end of a cycle), *dalet* is "door," and *shin* means "to consume or to destroy." *Qâdâsh* occurs when the door is shut against the Destroyer.

Ezekiel 20:20, *"And qâdâsh (set apart) my Shâbaths; and they shall be a sign between me and you, that you may know that I am Yahweh Elohiym."*

God rested on the seventh day *(Shâbath)*. Strong's OT#7673 (shaw-bath) defines *shâbath* as a repose; to desist from exertion, literally and figuratively. The pictograph ⊐ש of *Shâbath* portrays a destroyed adversarial system. The door of the house is shut and sealed, marked with the king's seal, which of course, is the *Aleph-Tav*. Thereby separating the righteous from the unrighteous.

Day Seven of Genesis foreshadows the millennial reign of Yeshua. *"And Elohiym blessed the (Aleph-Tav) the seventh day..."* - the seventh day belongs to the Melchizedek!

Revelation 20:1-4, *"Then I saw an angel coming down from heaven, having the key to the bottomless pit and a great chain in his hand. He laid hold of the dragon, that serpent of old, who is the Devil and Satan, and bound him for a thousand years; and he cast him into the bottomless pit, and shut him up, and set a seal on him so that he should deceive the nations no more till the thousand years were finished, and they lived and reigned with Christ for the thousand years."*

Hebrews 4:1-16 *"Therefore, since the promise of entering **his rest still stands**, let us be careful that none of you be found to have fallen short of it. For we also have had the gospel preached to us, just as they did, but the message they heard was of no value to them because those who heard did not combine it with faith. Now we who have believed enter that **rest**, just as God* *has said, 'So I declared on oath in my anger, "They shall never enter my **rest.**"' **And yet, his work has been finished since the creation of the world.** For somewhere, he has spoken about the seventh day in these words: 'And on the seventh day God **rested** from all his work.' And again, in the passage above, he says, 'They shall never enter my **rest.'** It still remains that some will enter that **rest, and those who formerly had the gospel preached to them did not go in because of their disobedience.** Therefore, God again set a certain day, calling it Today, when a long time later he spoke through David, as was said before: 'Today if you hear his voice, do not harden your hearts.' For if Joshua had given them **rest,** God would not have spoken later about another day. There remains, then, **a Sabbath-rest** for the people of God; for anyone who enters **God's rest also rests from his own work,** just as God did from his. Let us, therefore, make every effort to enter that **rest** so that no one will fall by following their example of disobedience. For the word of God is living and active. Sharper than any double-edged sword, it penetrates even to dividing soul and spirit, joints, and marrow; it judges the thoughts and attitudes of the heart. Nothing in all creation is hidden from God's sight. Everything is uncovered and laid bare before the eyes of him to whom we must give account. Therefore, since **we have a great high priest** who has gone through the heavens, **Jesus the Son of God,** let us hold firmly to the faith we profess. For we do not have a high priest who is unable to sympathize with our weaknesses, but we have one who has been tempted in every way, just as we are, yet he was without sin. Let us then approach the throne of grace with confidence so that we may receive mercy and find grace to help us in our time of need"* (emphasis added).

Shâbath rest is God's kind of rest. It's an indescribable peace knowing His work is finished. However, for us to possess His rest, we must have faith. "Rest" in Koine Greek is *katapausis* (kat-ap'-ow-sis). Strong's NT#2663 defines this type of rest as a repose, although accompanying the rest is a stance of abiding.

Abiding, in the Kingdom of the Melchizedek, should be "restful." The preceding passage from Hebrews contends those of the Exodus approached the Promised Land and failed to enter rest because they fell short by not understanding the gospel given by Moses. Moses preached a similar gospel to the one preached by Yeshua, which is: God's work is finished, and the kingdom is at hand (within grasp).

Cessation from human work does not make the *Shâbath* holy. *Shâbath* is followed by entering the rest Yahweh provided. Even though they experienced the miracles of Yahweh firsthand, the Israelites considered it impossible to take the land Yahweh promised. They failed to take into consideration the significance of *Shâbath*. Their lack of faith prevented them from entering the Promised Land. Yahweh considered that lack to be disobedience.

Now, as living humans, we have a physical body. We have emotions, and intellect and a self-directing will. But at the core of who we are as individuals is a spirit. The physical body is the only characteristic of these that sets mankind apart from other species. Those who we have previously termed spirit beings also have a body, an intellect, a self-directing will, and are capable of emotion.

The uniqueness of the human body comes from human DNA. DNA, or deoxyribonucleic acid, is the chemical inside living cells that instruct living organisms to grow and function. Personally, I think of DNA as the software that makes the hardware operate. But for the scientific nerds: DNA transmits the genetic instructions that cause living organisms to develop, function, and among other things, reproduce.[39]

Thus, deoxyribonucleic acid acts much like a storage bank for information, which causes the following sentence to be crucial in understanding the truth of human existence. "Information has rightly become known as the third fundamental, universal quantity."[40] The information in Adam's DNA came directly from the Creator. He programmed Adam human. From that unique DNA, the human species was developed, including Eve.

> "A DNA fiber is only about two-millionths of a millimeter thick so that it is barely visible with an electron microscope…. The amount of information is so immense in the case of human DNA that it would stretch from the North Pole to the equator if it were typed on paper, using standard letter sizes."[41]

Biology involves information that creates function. However, information is nonmaterial, not biological (physical). In other words, genetic information is passed forward as a process of purpose, not as a physical property. The information passed from generation to generation is a set of instructions that determines species. There are other factors that either work with or against human DNA to produce the next generation. Factors such as environmental issues, food, drugs, or exposure to toxins, just to name a few. These can be epigenetic, which will change the structure of DNA by altering how molecules bind to proteins. Structural changes may occur when genes are "messed with." Such as switching genes on when they should be off or vice versa.[42]

According to Scripture, before God breathed into Adam, every generation that has existed or will exist was planned and placed inside Adam's DNA. That thought is astonishing. Yahweh planned all contingencies of all generations. In fact, he numbered each generation. According to Acts 17:25-26, *"He gives to all life, breath, and all things. And He has made from one blood every nation of men to dwell on all the face of the earth and has determined their pre-appointed times and the boundaries of their dwellings…."* Essentially, God established a timetable for each generation. That means He planned a purpose for everyone, not just Adam. That's mind-boggling! God is so detailed He stipulated the boundaries of each generation, their time, and birth order. He even wrote those determinations in a book.

Though Adam was created in *'erets* from the physical materials of *'erets*, his spirit came from the Divine. Adam did not become a living being because he had a body. He became a living soul because of the quickening of the Spirit of Yahweh, which entered his body. Hence his first breath came from Yahweh.

Adam's life force (his spirit) was ignited by Yahweh, filling him (anointing him) with excellency to function as the regent king/high priest. However, no other being created or procreated has possessed a body as unique as Adam's.

Song 1:2, *"Let him kiss me with the kisses of his mouth: for his love is better than wine."*

---

[39] https://www.conservapedia.com/Deoxyribonucleic acid, retrieved October 24, 2019
[40] https://creation.com/information-science-and-biology retrieved September 22, 2021
[41] Dr. Werner Gitt, *In the Beginning was Information*, p 85.
[42] http://www.//alumni.duke.edu/magazine, retrieved October 24, 2019

Luke 1:35-36, *"The angel answered, 'The Holy Spirit will come upon you, and the power of the Most High will overshadow (rest) you. So, the holy one to be born will be called the Son of God."*

Adam was programmed to interact with the spirit realm, not just with the physical. In fact, he was formed to function as a liaison between the two.

> Genesis 2:8-17, *"Now Yahweh Elohiym **planted** a garden in the **east**, in **Eden**; and there he put the (Aleph-Tav) man he had formed. And Yahweh Elohiym made all kinds of trees grow out of the ground, trees that were pleasing to the eye and good for food. In the middle of the garden were the tree of life and the tree of the knowledge of good and evil. A river watering the (Aleph-Tav) garden flowed from Eden; from there, it was separated into four headwaters. The name of the first is the Pishon; it winds through the (Aleph-Tav) entire land of Havilah, where there is gold. The gold of that land is good; aromatic resin and onyx are also there. The name of the second river is the Gihon; it winds through the (Aleph-Tav) entire land of Cush. The name of the third river is the Tigris; it runs along the east side of Asshur. And the fourth river is the Euphrates. The Yahweh Elohiym took the (Aleph-Tav) man and put him in the Garden of Eden to work and take care of it. And the Yahweh Elohiym commanded the man, 'You are free to eat from any tree in the garden; but you must not eat from the tree of the knowledge of good and evil, for when you eat of it, you will surely die"* (emphasis added).

"To plant" is *nata'* in Hebrew. Strong's OT#5193 (naw-tah) defines *nata'* as to fit or fix a thing into position; specifically, as to plant; literally or figuratively, to fasten. God fastened his garden **into** Eden. The intriguing aspect of that notion is that the "garden" pre-existed. The garden lowered or dropped onto *'erets* and then fastened into the physical. Suppose we think of Eden as a cosmic city. The garden was the core of the city. It housed government buildings. The point is Eden was both physical and metaphysical.

Strong's OT#1588 defines a garden (*gan*) as a fenced-in area; surrounded by a hedge. Possibly we should view the "*gan*" as a small area, fenced-off from a more extensive region. That image would foreshadow Moses' Wilderness Tabernacle. Considering the garden in Tabernacle terms, the garden was Yahweh's Holy Place within the Great Assembly of the Divine Council. Whatever the case, it was a busy place with more activity than planting trees and maintaining flowers.

The "*gan*" was set apart, made distinct in the domain of *'erets*, as exclusively belonging to the Eternal Melchizedek. Which explains why Adam was given access, why it was his "abode," his palatial estate.

That the Bible describes the garden as fastened to the "east" substantiates this understanding. East is *qedem* (Strong's OT#6924 (keh'dem). *Qedem* also means in "the front" or at the "fore." It has a qualitative meaning that points toward the antiquity of a thing. Consequently, when used explicitly as an adverb, *qedem* refers to origin. That indicates that the "*gan*" was indeed ancient when it was fastened into the physical Eden. And why I make a distinction between the physical Eden and the cosmic Eden. The cosmic Eden and its *gan* existed in other dimensions but were "fasten" by a portal that was made to open into the physical, re-created *'erets*. Genesis 2:8 could possibly read, "Fasten, *Elohiym* Yahweh, a fenced-in place on the mountains of Eden from antiquity. There He placed the (*Aleph-Tav*) man after he was fashioned to purpose."

Moses uniquely spelled Eden with a *bet*.[43] The addition of the *bet* signaled Eden was a mountain. This peculiar spelling of Eden is used only twice in the Bible, Genesis 2:8 and Ezekiel 28:13-14 where it is stated, *"Thou hast been **in Eden the garden of God**..., thou was upon **the holy mountain of God**; thou hast walked up and down in the midst of the stones of fire"* (emphasis added).

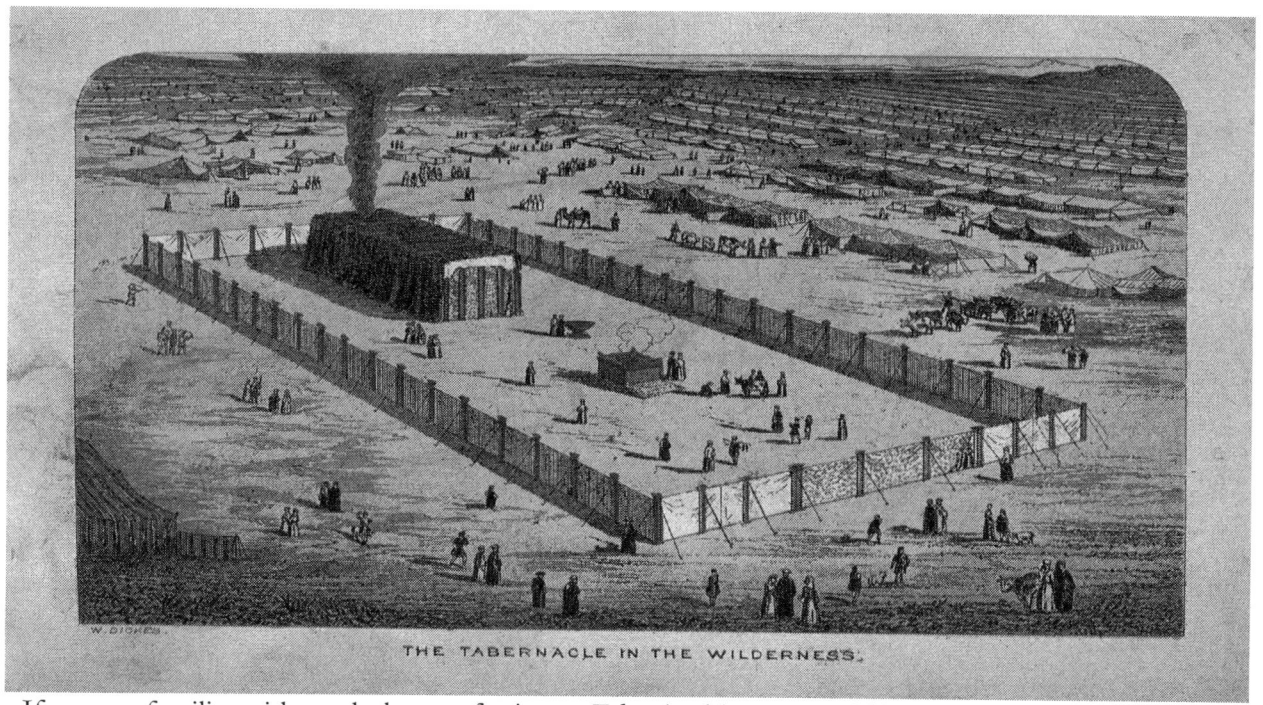

THE TABERNACLE IN THE WILDERNESS.

If you are familiar with mythology, referring to Eden in this way would be similar to saying it was like Mount Olympus, the mountain of Zeus. I am not saying that Yahweh and Zeus equate. Instead, offering an example of how the ancients viewed Eden. It was more than a geographic location on the map; it was a sphere of influence upon the universe. It was multi-dimensional, accessible to the spirit world and to Adam.

Additionally, that which it was, is what it shall be. That garden, in my opinion, was a "city not made with hands." And it housed an ancient civilization, yet to the physical eye, one not enhanced by spiritual sight, it was hills, trees, and plants. However, Eden was the gateway to the cosmos. And the place where Yahweh was worshipped. In other words, Yah's dwelling. Where He walked and talked with Adam daily. It was supernatural and natural all at the same time. There was no division of time or space within Eden or its garden, for they, too, like Adam, were perfect.

The sketch depicting the topographical features of Jerusalem reveals a *shin* that the ancients believed marked the land as Yahweh's. Notice that the left arm of the *shin* wraps around Mount Zion, which is the Mount of "righteousness," and the other around Mount Moriah, where Abraham placed Isaac on the altar.

---

43 The transliterated spelling is *b'ēdēn*.

Incidentally, there is speculation as to the true meaning of the term *El Shaddai*. What we know is that *el* is the Semitic term for god. So, the confusion lies with the true meaning of *Shaddai*. However, as I researched, a fascinating discovery came to my attention. It proclaimed that *El Shaddai* originally meant: "God of the Mountains!" Yahweh placed His name around those mountains to mark them as "the" Holy Place. They gave entrance into his Kingdom of Righteousness.

Har Tsiyyon (Zion) might have originally meant the "mountain of protection." Still, it came to relate to righteousness and everlasting life due to its association with King David. On the other hand, Moriah represents sacrifice and death because it was where Abraham sacrificed Isaac.

"There is some archaeological evidence to support the concept that the crucifixion of Jesus was on the summit of Mount Moriah, probably near the present-day Damascus Gate and the Garden Tomb. Meaning the crucifixion occurred at the same location as Abraham's offering of Isaac. God said, 'On the mount of the Lord it [the final offering for sin] will be provided.'"[44]

By the time of Jesus' first advent, Mount Moriah was known as Golgotha and associated with King David. A story is told, a legend of sorts, which proclaims David, after beheading Goliath, took his head to Moriah and buried it there. Afterward, the hill was referred to as *gulgōlet*, "the skull," or Golgotha in Latin.

Moriah means to be seen of Yah. Moriah (Golgotha) is the hill where Yeshua defeated the adversarial kingdom. Like King David, Yeshua slew a giant and buried its head on that hill when he defeated the "lord of death" on the Cross.

- King David ruled from Mount Zion.
- King Solomon's temple was built on Mount Moriah.
- → Genesis 22:2, "*And he said, 'Take now your son, your only son Isaac, whom you love, and go into the land of Moriah; and offer him there for a burnt offering upon one of the mountains which I will tell you of.'*"
- → 2 Chronicles 3:1, "*Then Solomon began to build the house of the Lord at Jerusalem in mount Moriah, where*

---

[44] *Mount Moriah, Site of the Temple Mount in Jerusalem,* by Lambert Dolphin http://www.templemount.org/moriah2.html, retrieved October 24, 2019

the Lord appeared unto David, his father, in the place that David had prepared in the threshing-floor of Ornan the Jebusite."

I suspect the Tree of Life was on Mount Zion, and the tree of knowledge, upon Mount Moriah.

- → Proverbs 11:30, *"The fruit of the righteous is a tree of life."*
- → Proverbs 15:4, *"A wholesome tongue is a tree of life: but perverseness therein is a breach in the spirit."*
- → Revelation 22:14, *"Blessed are they that do his commandments, that they may have right to the tree of life and may enter in through the gates into the city."*

Genesis 2:10-14: *"Now a river went out of Eden to water the (Aleph-Tav) garden, and from there it parted and became four river heads. The name of the first is **Pishon**; it is the one which skirts (or surrounds) the whole (Aleph-Tav) land of **Havilah**, where there is **gold**. And the gold of that land is good. **Bdellium and the onyx stone** are there. The name of the second river is **Gihon**; it is the one, which goes around the whole (Aleph-Tav) **land of Cush**. The name of the third river is **Hiddekel**; it is the one, which goes toward the **east of Assyria**. The fourth river is the **Euphrates**"* (emphasis added).

A river went out of Eden, the cosmic mountain, to water the (spiritual) garden. Moses did not provide the name of this river, only that it watered the garden. As I wondered about this, Revelation 22 came to mind. *"Then the angel showed me* **the river of the water of life, as clear as crystal, flowing from the throne of God** *and of the Lamb down the middle of the great street of the city"* (emphasis added). It then dawned upon me that we are not given the name because it is a spiritual flow from the throne of God. I also realized that the river parted at the base of the cosmic mountain of God to form four natural "physical" rivers. In other words, the spiritual "parted" or *parad*, divided into separate flows of revelation for the current age.

That same river appears again, in the age to come. Revelation 21:22-22:5, *"I did not see a temple in the city, because the Lord God Almighty and the Lamb are its temple. The city does not need the sun or the moon to shine on it, for the glory of God gives it light, and the Lamb is its lamp. The nations will walk by its light, and the kings of the earth will bring their splendor into it. On no day will its gates ever be shut, for there will be no night there. The glory and honor of the nations will be brought into it. Nothing impure will ever enter it, nor will anyone who does what is shameful or deceitful, but only those whose names are written in the Lamb's book of life.* **Then the angel showed me the river of the water of life, as clear as crystal, flowing from the throne of God and of the Lamb down the middle of the great street of the city.** *On each side of the river stood the tree of life, bearing twelve crops of fruit, yielding its fruit every month. And the leaves of the tree are for the healing of the nations. No longer will there be any curse. The throne of God and the Lamb will be in the city, and his servants will serve him. They will see his face, and his name will be on their foreheads. There will be no more night. They will not need the light of a lamp or the light of the sun, for the Lord God will give them light. And they will reign forever and ever"* (emphasis added).

These four rivers functioned as boundaries protecting Eden from illegal access. They were entranceways into Eden, or we could say to enter Eden, one had to cross a river. Yahweh always returns the righteous to Eden via revelation. When they return, they return as Hebrews. They "crossed over" from deception into Truth.

> Genesis 2:11-12, *"The name of the first is **Pishon**; it is the one which skirt (or surrounds) the whole land of **Havilah**, where there is **gold**. And the gold of that land is good. **Bdellium and the onyx stone** are there"* (emphasis added).

Pishon (Strong's OT#6376) means "to disperse." If the Pishon was a naturally flowing river, its true identity is questionable. Flavius Josephus said it was the Ganges. The Midrash purports it as the Nile. Others say it became a dry channel that runs the course of the mountains near Medina.

> Genesis 2:13, *"The name of the second river is Gihon; it is the one which goes around the whole land of Cush."*

The root of Gihon is *giyach*. Strong's OT#1518 states that *giyach* means to break forth with water, such as an unborn babe breaking forth from the womb. Thus, Gihon (Strong's OT#1521) points to a "breaking forth" like the birthing of a fetus from a mother's womb. According to jewishvirtuallibrary.com, the flow of this river reflects its name. The water flow was not steady but intermittent, varying with the year's seasons and annual precipitation. It was a siphon-type karst spring. *The Siege of Jerusalem: Crusade and Conquest* describes the Gihon River as a siphon (a spring-fed flow). The water collected underground and then siphoned to the surface whenever the underground streams filled to the brim. That natural occurring feature made it necessary to accumulate the river's water into a pool so that water would be available when the spring was not "gushing forth."

> Genesis 2:14a *"The name of the third river is Hiddekel; it is the one which goes toward the east of Assyria."*

River Hiddekel (Strong's OT#2313) was also known as the Tigris. Daniel received his vision outlining the power struggle between the kings of the north and the south while standing on the banks of the Tigris (Hiddekel). Daniel 10:4, *"And in the four and twentieth day of the first month, as I was by the side of the great river, which is Hiddekel."* Hiddekel is mentioned only twice in the Bible (Genesis 2:14 and Daniel 10:4). Hiddekel is Hebrew, whereas Tigris is Greek. The ancient Sumerian name for this same river was *Idigna* (swift or running water).

> Genesis 2:14b, *"The fourth river is the Euphrates..."*

Strong's OT#6578 defines "Euphrates" as to announce or declare a thing. The word "Euphrates" is Greek; the Hebrew name of this river is *Perat*, which means "to speak what is most important as a sign." Jeremiah 51:63, *"And it shall be, when you have made an end of reading this book, you shall bind a stone to it, and cast it into the midst of Euphrates."*

To sum up, these four rivers seem to symbolize revelation that flows from God's Throne by surrounding the righteous, then breaking forth into a swift flow that decrees His purpose. Do these rivers and the meaning of their names bear a greater significance than this? I honestly don't know. My inner sense is they do; they represent the flow of prophetic revelation that we have yet to unlock.

> Genesis 2:15-17, *"Then the Yahweh Elohim took the (Aleph-Tav)* **man and put him in the garden of Eden to tend and keep it.** *And the Yahweh Elohim commanded the man, saying, "Of every tree of the garden you may freely eat; but of the tree of the knowledge of good and evil you shall not eat, for in the day that you eat of it you shall surely die"* (emphasis added).

Adam was instructed to tend (*abad*) and keep (*shamar*) the garden. *Abad* and *shamar* always appear together. They represent the servitude expected of priests and the adherence demanded unto the word of God.

Numbers 3:5, *"And the Lord spoke to Moses, saying: 'Bring the tribe of Levi near, and present them before Aaron, the priest, that they may serve him. And they shall attend* (shamar) *to his needs and the needs of the whole congregation before the tabernacle of meeting, to do* (abad) *the work of the tabernacle. Also, they shall attend* (shamar) *to all the furnishings of the tabernacle of meeting, and to the needs of the children of Israel, to do* (abad) *the work of the tabernacle.'"*

1 Chronicles 23:32, ... *"and that they should attend* (shamar) *to the needs of the tabernacle of meeting, the needs of the holy place, and the needs of the sons of Aaron, their brethren in the work* (abad) *of the house of the Lord."*

Simply stated, Adam functioned as a priest in the Garden of Yahweh. God did not create Adam and then walk away. Scripture is clear; they communed daily. Yet, religion has removed the existence of the supernatural from our thinking.[45] So, what I am suggesting is that the garden of Eden was a fully operational cosmic city that accommodated the activities of an orderly society of sentient beings. And within that city, Yahweh held court and met with all His "created sons," including the *elohim*. Furthermore, I am suggesting that Eden was interdimensional. While it was geographically located in *'erets*, it extended beyond into the spiritual heavens.

The language of Genesis 2 indicates Adam was given priestly duties beyond the dominion handed to him to

---

[45] Supernatural – that of or relating to an order of existence beyond the visible observable universe, especially of or relating to God, a spirit, devil, or god.

rule *'erets*. Both strongly suggest he had a Melchizedek nature, which further suggests he sat with the Divine Council. And that as a created son of Yahweh, Adam interacted with his "older" brothers in the Throne Room of the Most High God.

We additionally support this notion of Eden being a vast cosmic city "whose builder and maker are God"[46] with the following from Revelation 21:15-18. Note how these verses describe the New Jerusalem. *"The angel who talked with me had a measuring rod of gold to measure the city, its gates, and its walls. The city was laid out like a square, as long as it was wide. He measured the city with the rod and found it to be 12,000 stadia in length (**about 1,400 miles**) and as **wide and high** as it is long. He measured its wall, and it was 144 cubits thick, by man's measurement, which the angel was using. The wall was made of jasper, and the city of pure gold, as pure as glass. The foundations of the city walls were decorated with every kind of precious stone"* (emphasis added).

If the New Jerusalem is 1,400 miles high, its height shall exceed Earth's stratosphere. Is it not possible that Eden also did? This is speculation on my part, but I venture to say that Yah's Temple was the center of the city, and the city, the core of the cosmos. The mechanics and science of that theory are beyond my paygrade. However, what I am saying is this. Adam was created perfectly, not limited as a fallen man but clothed in righteousness and covered by light. He functioned (had accessibility) in all the dimensions, as does every other righteous son of Yah.

Moses' Tabernacle in the Wilderness, which he patterned after the one "not made with hands,"[47] contained the following:

- Brazen altar
- Place of Meeting
- Table of Showbread
- Altar of Incense
- Golden Lampstand
- Holy of Holies

The brazen altar was placed between the entrance and the Holy Place. At the far end of the tabernacle's compound was the Place of Meeting.

- Mount Moriah corresponds with the brazen altar and the tree of knowledge.
- Mount Zion with the Place of Meeting and the Tree of Life.

Genesis 2:16-17 (paraphrased): "And Yahweh, the Creator, commanded the *adam* (man), saying, "of every tree in my Temple Garden you may freely eat but not from the tree, which will cause you to be joined to the adversary, for in the day you partake of it you shall die a death from which you, by yourself, cannot return."

"Surely die" – means what? Well, in a literal sense, it did not mean Adam would die immediately, for he lived 930 years. However, if 1,000 years is the same as a "day," then yes, Adam died the day he ate the

---

46 Hebrews 10:11
47 Hebrews 9:11

forbidden fruit, for he died 70 years shy of a complete "day."

Eve ate from the forbidden tree. Did she become naked the moment she ate? Probably not, since Adam was her covering. Adam, as a Melchizedek, was required to maintain a continuous state of righteousness. And since he was her righteousness, as long as he remained righteous, then she was virtuous. Not until both had eaten were they both naked and ashamed. Yet, that has nothing to do with the meaning of "surely die."

Leviticus 26:14-17, *"But if you will not listen to me and carry out all these commands, and if you reject my decrees and abhor my laws and fail to carry out all my commands, and so violate my covenant, then I will do this to you: I will bring upon you sudden terror, wasting diseases and fever that will destroy your sight and drain away your life. You will plant seed in vain because your enemies will eat it. I will set my face against you so that you will be defeated by your enemies; those who hate you will rule over you, and you will flee even when no one is pursuing you."*

Adam was warned that if he ate of the forbidden tree, he would be disqualified and forfeit the right to the **everlasting** throne assigned to him as the Melchizedek regent. Of course, he was not warned with those words, but that was what "surely die" meant for him. In actuality, Adam fell prey to "the spirit of death." Disobedience corrupted his DNA and made him dis-eased.

The fruit of the tree of knowledge was confusion, the fruit of chaos. It was neither wholly good nor wholly evil but a mixture of both. Adam experienced a sudden terror as a wasting dis-ease pulled him from the path of righteousness and directed him toward his demise. The partaking of the forbidden fruit jolted Adam's soul and spirit into a state of confusion. Galatians 5:10, *"I am confident in the Lord that you will take no other view. The one who is throwing you into confusion will pay the penalty, whoever he may be."*

1 Corinthians 14:33, *"For God is not the author of confusion, but of peace, as in all churches of the saints."*

James 3:16, *"For where envying and strife are, there is confusion and every evil work."*

> Genesis 2:18-23, *"Yahweh Elohiym God said, 'It is not good for the man to be **alone**. I will **make a helper suitable** for him.' Now, Yahweh Elohiym formed out of the ground all the beasts of the field and all the (Aleph-Tav) birds of the air. He brought them to the man to see what he would name them, and whatever the man called each living creature, that was its name. So, the man gave names to all the livestock, the birds of the air, and all the beasts of the field. But for Adam, no suitable helper was found. So, Yahweh Elohiym caused the man to fall into a deep sleep; and while he was sleeping, he took one of the man's ribs and closed up the place with flesh. Then the Yahweh Elohiym **made a woman from the** (Aleph-Tav) **rib** he had taken out of the man, and he brought her to the man"* (emphasis added).

- Alone is bad – really! The word "alone," according to Strong's OT#905, spelled *bet-dalet*, is transliterated into *"bad"* and means solitary, separate, apart from others.
- Make – *'asah*; to appoint.
- Helpmate – *'ezer* is an aid who stands boldly as a counterpart.

After showing Adam all the other living breathing creatures, Yahweh perhaps said, "Come, you need to see what I have made for you. You need to name them since you are to dominate over them. And while you are naming them, see if any of them are your equal."

Among the creatures of *'erets*, Adam found none to be "suitable" as a mate. None were created in the same manner, and none were comparable, substantiating that Adam was *mono-genesis* – one of a kind.

As he named those brought to him, Adam received authority over them. In the naming of the animals, Adam placed a mark upon them, an imprint of reign. When no suitable mate was found, Yahweh caused a deep sleep to fall upon Adam. Strong's OT#8639 described it as *tardemah* (tar-day-maw), a sleep so deep the sleeper appears as if they were dead. While in that deep sleep, Yahweh removed one of Adam's ribs.

"Since it was the day of Preparation, and so that the bodies would not remain on the cross on the Sabbath (for that Sabbath was a high day), the Jews asked Pilate that their legs might be broken and that they might be taken away. So, the soldiers came and broke the legs of the first and of the other who had been crucified with him. But when they came to Jesus and saw that he was already dead, they did not break his legs. But one of the soldiers pierced his side with a spear, and at once there came out blood and water," John 19:31-34.

Seeing that the two crucified with Jesus were still breathing, the Roman executioners broke their legs, prohibiting them from pushing their bodies up to breathe. The breaking of their legs caused death to occur within minutes. However, in the case of Jesus, the executioner realized that since he was already unconscious, he was most likely already dead. A spear was shoved into the side of Jesus, under his ribs, to confirm their suspicion. The pericardial sack ruptured and caused blood and water to flow from the cut and down his side.

Matthew Henry's Commentary: The Creator pierced and opened Adam's side to create his wife, Eve. Likewise, Jesus Christ, the second Adam, suffered when his own side was pierced and opened for his own bride to be created.[48]

Genesis 2:22 *"And from the (Aleph-Tav) rib… made He woman."*

Made - Strong's OT#1129 *banah* (baw-naw) is a primitive root that means to build (both literally and figuratively).

Matthew 16:18-20, *"And I tell you that you are Peter, and on this rock, I will* **build my church,** *and the gates of Hades will not overcome it. I will give you the keys of the kingdom of heaven; whatever you bind on earth will be bound in heaven, and whatever you loose on earth will be loosed in heaven"* (emphasis added).

---

[48] http://www.biblicaljesus.org, retrieved October 24, 2019

> Genesis 2:23-25, *"And Adam said: '**<u>This</u> is now bone of my bones and flesh of my flesh; she shall be called Woman** because she was **taken out of Man.**' For this reason, a man will leave his (Aleph-Tav) father and (Aleph-Tav) mother and be united to his wife, and they will become one flesh. The man and his wife were both **naked, and they felt no shame**"* (emphasis added).

Zoth is the irregular feminine version of *zeh* (sheep). The *zoth* in the text is Strong's #2063 (zothe). *Zoth* is most often used as an adverb, not a noun or pronoun, as we see in this verse. Spelled ⊏◯† in pictograph form (*zayin-aleph-tav*), the weapon belongs to the strong leader; it seals the covenant. WOW! The woman (the bride) seals the covenant! She is a weapon in the hands of the Strong Leader!

Adam, the Melchizedek regent, needed a suitable mate. So, Yahweh took a rib and formed a woman, yet both he and she were literally one flesh, a single collection of DNA.

The Bride of Christ was created while he hung on the Cross. At his second advent, Yeshua and his bride shall marry. She is the reason for his return! Like Eve to Adam, the Bride of Christ is bone of his bone, essence of his essence, the strength of his strength.

Jesus left His Father in the Eternal and joined himself to the bride. Song of Songs 4:9-12, *"You have stolen my heart, my sister, my bride; you have stolen my heart with one glance of your eyes, with one jewel of your necklace. How delightful is your love, my sister, my bride! How much more pleasing is your love than wine and the fragrance of your perfume than any spice! Your lips drop sweetness as the honeycomb, my bride; milk and honey are under your tongue. The fragrance of your garments is like that of Lebanon.* **You are a garden locked up, my sister, my bride; you are a spring enclosed, a sealed fountain**" (emphasis added).

Ashamed is defined by Strong's OT#954 *buwsh* as a primitive root that means to pale; thus, by implication, to be ashamed; to be disappointed or delayed; confused. In the beginning, Adam and Eve were unaware of their nakedness – they were neither ashamed nor confused.

In the 1950s, it was discovered that living organisms emit bioluminescence, and it is now an established fact, DNA emits organic light as a means of communication. This then means light is not only emitted; it is also absorbed. That correlates with what Scripture states about angels - they come as beings of light. Should then we not think that Adam and Eve were covered by light? They were neither naked nor ashamed because they, as light-covered beings, could interact with spirit entities and not be ashamed.

James 1:17-18, *"Every good gift and every perfect gift is from above and comes down from the Father of lights."* In this verse, the term "lights" was translated from the Greek *phos*, which means to make shine. Yahweh made Adam *phos*. This correlates with when Jesus *"was transfigured before them. His face shone like the sun, and His clothes became as white as the light* (phos)" Matthew 17:2.

However, there is another reason that Adam and Eve were not ashamed. Note the Hebrew states they were both *'ărûmmîm* (the plural form) of *'ărûm*, which means cunning or wise. Ironically, *'ărûm* is also used in the following verse as a descriptive value assigned to the "serpent." Perhaps the last verse of Genesis 2 is a banter used to set the stage for Genesis 3. It is quite possible the true meaning of Genesis 2:25 is both Adam and Eve were wise in the ways of Yahweh and not confused until the "serpent" paid them a visit.

Genesis Three

> Genesis 3:1-7, *"Now the **serpent** was more **cunning** ('ărûm) than any **beast of the field** which Yahweh had made. And he said to the woman, 'Has Elohiym indeed said, "You shall not eat of every tree of the garden?"' And the woman said to the serpent, 'We may eat the fruit of the trees of the garden; but of the fruit of the tree, which is in the midst of the garden, Elohiym has said, "You shall not eat it, nor shall you touch it, lest you die."' Then the serpent said to the woman, 'You will not surely die. For Elohiym knows that in the day you eat of it, your eyes will be opened, and you will be like elohim, knowing good and evil.' So, when the woman saw that the tree was good for food, pleasant to the eyes, and a tree desirable to make one wise, she took of its fruit and ate. She also gave to her husband with her, and he ate. Then the eyes of both of them were opened, and they knew that they were naked, and they sewed fig leaves together and made themselves coverings"* (emphasis added).

Serpent, or *nachash*, is defined by Strong's OT#5175 (naw-khawsh). We shall unpack the full definition in a moment. But first, we note that as used in Genesis 3, *nachash* is a metaphor.

Since the root of *nachash* infers the making of enchantments, such as the whispering of invocations or spells, "the cunning snake, the one who was craftier than any other creature, (might have) hissed…." But that is not what was being implied. Moses did not use the word *nachash* for that reason. Moses was intentionally derogatory with his description, yet I doubt he intended for anyone to think in literal terms that this entity who spoke to Eve was a crawling critter. Moses was intentionally associating the characteristics of a "serpent" with the entity who conversed with Eve. That is to say, he was linking the perverse use of power with the entity in question. In that era, icons of serpents were commonly used as symbols of superior force, especially to conjure the image of "gods" and kings.

> "Using all the meanings of the ש in Semitic range. That is, Eve was not talking to a snake. She was speaking to a bright, shining upright being who was serpentine in appearance and who was trying to bewitch her with lies." [49]

Isaiah 27:1, *"In that day the Lord with his sore and great and strong sword shall punish leviathan the piercing serpent* (nachash), *even leviathan that crooked serpent* (nachash); *and he shall slay the dragon that is in the sea."* Yahweh punished the leviathan, yet not before the leviathan pierced his victim. "Piercing" simply means the leviathan hit his target then quickly fled. He didn't hang around and watch his victim suffer, for he feared for his own life. Since he knew one more powerful was after him, the leviathan ran quickly, hoping not to be caught, which images the actions of the Genesis 3 "serpent."

"And no wonder, for satan himself masquerades as an angel of light" 2 Corinthians 11:14. The entity that approached Eve was adversarial in nature. He was confrontational. I suspect he sought to prosecute Adam before the Divine Council so, he appeared as *elohim* to Eve. Still, I believe his real target was Adam in that he wanted to

---

[49] https://www.pidradio.com/wp-content/uploads/2007/02/nachashnotes.pdf, retrieved October 24, 2019

unseat Yahweh's representative, which meant he had to entice Adam to sin. So, he found Adam's weakness and played upon it. What was Adam's weakness? Eve!

There are at least three ways to translate *nachash*:
1. As the subject of a sentence. When used as the subject, *nachash* is usually translated as "serpent."
2. As a verb, it means divination or something similar.
3. As an adjective, it refers to the color of bronze, such as the brightness of shiny brass.

Genesis 3:1, *"Now the serpent was more cunning than any beast of the field which the Lord God had made."* The *nachash* was cunning, *'ărûm*. Adam and Eve were also *ărûmmîm*,[50] yet the *nachash* was more so. Of all the life forms the Creator made, this entity was the wisest.

Ezekiel 28:12-13, *"You were the seal of perfection, full of wisdom and perfect in beauty. You were in Eden, the garden of God"* (emphasis added). The phrase "seal of perfection, full of wisdom" conveys a document sealed by wax. The Ezekiel 28 entity was the seal marking the scroll of wisdom as a completed work. All information available was transcribed, and the scroll was sealed because nothing was left unstated. Thus, he was "full" of knowledge and marked perfected.

"Thy heart has been lifted up because of thy beauty; thy knowledge has been corrupted with thy beauty," Ezekiel 28:17 from the Greek-English Septuagint: Brenton Edition.

His knowledge, however, became corrupted because of his "brightness."[51] Hence, before his fall, this entity was all-knowing, containing all available information. No other created entity knew more regarding any subject than he. He understood the laws of government, of the cosmos. That would mean he knew quantum physics, spacetime, all the mechanics of science that make the universe work, including music, art, and so forth. So, he understood the correlation between information and DNA.

As of now, I suspect that the serpent who approached Eve was either Chaos, the "Destroyer," or his cohort, "Death." Both possess characteristics that match the descriptive terms of Ezekiel 28 and Isaiah 14. And apparently, these two work as a team. However, I suspect they are in competition with one another. And if I had to guess between these two, I choose Hades.

Nearly all ancient cultures asserted there were at least two "chief" gods of great import. One ruled over the netherworld, and the other, over the atmosphere of *'erets*. You are probably more familiar with their Greek names, Hades and Zeus. Hades controlled the underworld, Zeus the upper region, the land of the living. (Please understand this information is not given as factual data. But provided to assist in conceptualizing why Moses portrayed this being as a serpent.)

The underworld or netherworld became the "holding cell" assigned to humans when they died. But it was not formed for that reason.

---

50 *'Ărûm* means wise or full of understanding.
51 Brightness is one of the meanings of "beauty."

This nether-place belonged to the fallen gods - it was their realm. This concept was abstracted long before Israel became a nation. The Israelites simply named the underworld *shĕôl* [52] and often referred to it as *ăbaddôn*.

Abaddon, as a term, came from a root word that means to destroy. When used as a proper noun, *ăbaddôn* most often refers to the place of destruction, decay, the grave, and to hell. However, when used in the Greek New Testament, Abaddon denotes the proper name[53] of a god who was lord over *Sheol* - the lord of the dead. Yet, we find him in Eden. Ezekiel 28:13-15 from the NKJV: *"You were in **Eden, the garden of God**; every precious stone was your covering: The sardius, topaz, and diamond, beryl, onyx, and jasper, sapphire, turquoise, and emerald with gold. The workmanship of your timbrels and pipes was prepared for you on the day you were created. You were the **anointed cherub** who covers; **I established** you. You were **on the holy mountain of God**. You walked back and forth in the midst of **fiery stones**. You were perfect in your ways from the day you were created till iniquity was found in you"* (emphasis added).

These same verses from the Septuagint, Brenton Edition: *"Thou wast in the **delight of the paradise of God**; thou hast bound upon thee every precious stone, the sardius, topaz, emerald, carbuncle, sapphire, jasper, **silver, and gold**,[54] ligure, agate, amethyst, chrysolite, beryl, and onyx. Thou hast filled thy treasures and thy stores in thee **with gold**. From the day that thou wast created, thou wast with the **cherub**: I set thee on the **holy mount of God**; thou wast in the midst of **the stones of fire**. Thou wast faultless in thy days, from the day that thou wast created until iniquity was found in thee"* (emphasis added).

Please note the difference between the NKJV and the Septuagint. Primarily verse thirteen, *"you were in Eden, the garden of God,"* versus *"thou wast in the delight of the paradise of God."* The transliterated Hebrew, *b'eden gan elohim*, refers to the mountain (government) of *Elohiym*. In other words, to Yah's Throne.

How Ezekiel describes this being causes me to think he was either an anointed cherub or the overseer of the cherubim (Throne Guardians). He acted as a cover, a buffer between the court and God himself, by protecting those who approached the Divine Throne. The concept we are presented with is he guarded them against the "presence" of Yahweh. In other words, he stood between Yah and all who approached, protecting them from the striking force of God's holiness.

Isaiah 6:1-3, *"I saw also the Lord sitting upon a throne, high and lifted up, and his train filled the temple. Above it stood the seraphim, each one had six wings; with twain, he covered his face, and with twain, he covered his feet, and with twain, he did fly. And one cried unto another, and said, Holy, holy, holy, is the LORD of hosts: the whole earth is full of his glory"* (KJV emphasis added).

Seraph is an exchange term with *cherub*. *Seraph* is Egyptian, whereas *cherub*, Canaanite. Both refer to the "fiery

---

52 Barstad, H. M. (1999). *Sheol*. In K. van der Toorn, B. Becking, & P. W. van der Horst (Eds.), *Dictionary of deities and demons in the Bible* (2nd extensively rev. ed., p. 768). Leiden; Boston; Köln; Grand Rapids, MI; Cambridge: Brill; Eerdmans.
53 Hutter, M. (1999). *Abaddon*. In K. van der Toorn, B. Becking, & P. W. van der Horst (Eds.), *Dictionary of deities and demons in the Bible* (2nd extensively rev. ed., p. 1). Leiden; Boston; Köln; Grand Rapids, MI; Cambridge: Brill; Eerdmans.
54 Gold equates with royalty and perfection, silver with wisdom and purity.

beings" (fiery stones) guarding the Throne of El Elyon. Ancient literature refers to the *seraphim* as "lights" or as "fire," yet when manifesting, typically, they appear as beings with bronze-toned flesh. It is also speculated that these beings are shapeshifters (they reveal themselves more or less fearsome, whatever the situation warrants). Many believe this species of celestials to be the "Reptilians."

Their function is more in line with that of a priest. In that, they are commissioned to preserve the Holiness of Yah. The more I studied the Septuagint's rendering of Ezekiel 28, the more confident I became that this "god" was in the ancient, pre-Adamic Eden as a prince and high priest. If the *nachash* of Genesis 3 is also the Ezekiel 28 cherub, then according to the description provided of his breastplate, he was a high priest. That is until he grew proud and joined Chaos' rebellion against Yahweh.

55

So, how did he gain access to the re-created *'erets*; the *gan* of Eden if he was removed from the Throne Room? His knowledge of spacetime gave him access. This *nachash* was in the field (*'erets*), and he gained accessed to the cosmic Mountain of Yah in Adam's Eden because he had yet to be imprisoned in "outer darkness." Probably just like this: Job 1:6-7, *"Now there was a day when the sons of God came to present themselves before the Lord, and Satan also came among them. And the Lord said to Satan, 'From where do you come?' So, Satan answered the Lord and said, 'From going to and fro on the earth, and from walking back and forth on it.'"*

Eve was not frightened when the *nachash* approached. I doubt it entered her thoughts to think this *elohim* had an ulterior motive. Nor was she surprised when he spoke to her. Eve, like Adam, was accustomed to associating with divine beings. After all, she lived on the mountain of Yah. She readily engaged in conversation and, when she was asked if *Elohiym* commanded them, *"not [to] eat of every tree of the garden?"* Eve answered, *"We may eat the fruit of the **trees** of the garden except for the **tree** that is in the midst of the garden; we cannot eat of it, nor touch it lest we die."* Eve's words were insightful, although spoken innocently. For in the prophetic sense, she said, "We can't go to the brazen altar (the Cross) or even touch it – lest we die."

Nevertheless, she did not know the implication hidden in her words. More importantly, neither did the

---

55 A "winged bull" throne guardian that stood in the palace of Sargon II.

serpent. Yet, both were considered "wise."

"Touch" or *naga* is defined by Strong's # OT5060 as "touching" by laying a hand upon someone. It can also mean to lie with a woman. Those two meanings seem unrelated. Yet, there's a connection. The touching of someone or something that does not belong to you, which is not your private property, is the same as acquiring a possession illegally. This meaning of *naga* also implies anger, and therefore, *naga* can punish or destroy. Note the following usages of *naga*:

- → Genesis 12:17, *"And the Lord* **plagued** *Pharaoh and his house with great plagues because of Sarai, Abram's wife."*
- → Exodus 12:22, *"And ye shall take a bunch of hyssops, and dip it in the blood that is in the basin and* **strike** *the lintel and the two side posts with the blood that is in the basin; and none of you shall go out at the door of his house until the morning."*
- → Exodus 29:37, *"Seven days thou shalt make an atonement for the altar and sanctify it; and it shall be an altar most holy: whatsoever* **touches** *the altar shall be holy."*
- → Psalms 105:15, *"Saying,* **'Touch** *not mine anointed, and do my prophets no harm.'"*
- → Isaiah 6:7, *"And he laid it upon my mouth, and said, 'Lo, this hath* **touched** *thy lips; and thine iniquity is taken away, and thy sin purged.'"*

While researching this subject, several articles came to my attention that suggested Eve's encounter with the serpent was sexual. Primarily, these papers were based solely on the sexual implication of *naga*. There are several flaws in that notion. 1) Eve was naïve, not stupid. She was Adam's mate, formed from his rib. I'm not suggesting Eve considered herself Adam's property. The point I make, she was of Adam's "species" and not of the *elohim*. She knew she differed from the *elohim*, hence, of a differing "kind." Any sexual encounter with the *elohim* would be a sin. Eve did not sin. 2) Eve's reference was to touch the tree, not the *elohim*. Additionally, I find it hard to imagine Eve processed her reasoning through a fallen mentality. She would not have desired the *elohim*. Hence, she would not have participated in a sexual act willingly. Therefore, any sexual act would have been rape. There is no indication she was taken advantage of in that regard.

Careful examination of the text provides another perspective. In saying, "we are not to touch the tree," Eve declared that they were not to strike the tree with an intent to destroy it. She referred to the tree, not to its fruit. Fundamentally, she was saying they were not to remove it from the garden.

Eve clearly believed the tree was harmful. Yet, to remove it was an act of disobedience. Not self-aware, Eve desired to please those of her world. Yahweh, Adam, and the *elohim*.

Adam and Eve lived in the garden, at the pleasure of Yahweh. The tree was there, also at the "pleasure" of Yahweh. Though there was a warning attached to it, which read, "This tree is detrimental to life." Eve was fully aware she had access to all the trees, except that one. Until Yahweh said otherwise, Adam and Eve were to avoid the fruit of that tree. In other words, "leave the tree alone - don't try to reason out why. Don't eat of this tree; obey Yahweh, for there is a purpose for the tree even though to you it is detrimental."

No entity, spirit or otherwise, knew that tree was planted in the garden as a brazen altar. And that, in time, it would become the Cross assigned to Yeshua. It was given to the Eternal Melchizedek before the foundations of *'erets* were laid, but only Yahweh knew.

Eve was in effect saying, "We must not devour the fruit of the tree or destroy the tree even though the fruit is harmful, else we die." Quickly, the adversary turned the meaning of her words back to her by saying, *"You will not surely die. Elohiym knows when you eat of the fruit, your eyes will be opened, and* **you will be like elohim,** *knowing good and evil."*

The serpent twisted Yahweh's words, "You will not die a certain death. God is aware that the fountain of your understanding will be opened on the day you devour the fruit. You will be like the gods of the Divine Council, able to discern both good and evil and render accurate judgments."

This caused her to compare herself to the *elohim*. Made her feel inferior. The serpent told her that her "eyes would be opened." Implying they were closed. That there was a shortfall in her intellect. But since they stood before a "tree of knowledge," he was telling her that problem was easily solved. Sadly, that tactic was effective, and Eve's focus changed. She ceased thinking in terms of obedience and focused on a perceived lack that was non-existent. And that, my friend, was the deception!

Strong's OT#5869 defines eyes or *'ayin* (ah'-yin) as a primitive root denoting the eye (literally or figuratively). Symbolically, the eye is a fountain of seeing (understanding).

Yahweh had said: "in the **day** you consume (the fruit of confusion), you shall surely die *(muwth muwth)."* *Muwth* is Strong's OT#4191 (mooth). It means to die (literally or figuratively); causatively, to kill. The sentence's structure caused the first usage of *muwth* to be an adverb and the second usage a verb. Therefore, rendering it "a certain death, you shall die."

Adam and Eve were given a similar life force as the *elohim*; they too were immortal. So, note it was not lifespan that was the temptation. Eve faltered because she desired to be better. Meaning she wanted to serve Adam as his helper by understanding good and evil. The deceiver effectively caused her to feel inferior in that area, which indicates that she was sensitive toward Adam. The innate desire to please Adam was used against her blinding her to all other factors.

"So, when the woman **saw** *that the tree was* **good for food,** *that it was pleasant to the eyes, and a tree desirable to* **make one wise***, she took of its fruit and* **ate.***"*

Eve **saw** (*ra'ah*). She took a second look at the tree and didn't see evil (*'ra*); instead, she noted that the tree's fruit was edible. So, believing that it would make her wise, in her naiveté, Eve ate. Don't lose sight of the fact she ate because a member of the *elohim* told her the fruit was good, edible. His words caused her perception to change. We might say that she bought into the lie that the fruit of the tree was wisdom. Yet, it was not; it was confused knowledge. But what Eve really lost sight of is that obedience is better than sacrifice!

As indicated, the tree represented the brazen altar. In keeping with that motif, it was an altar without blood. Therefore, as an altar, it held no "eternal value." In the spiritual context of this event, the serpent took Eve (the king's bride) to the altar and asked that she partake of a bloodless sacrifice. On the other hand, Yeshua returned the bride to the altar and there, spilled his own blood, as the needed sacrifice that he might restore her to righteousness!

Tree - Strong's OT#6086 *'ets* (ates) is a primitive root that means to fasten (or make firm). Eve did not eat the tree. She ate its fruit. In other words, she ate of the tree's reward, which was knowledge, not wisdom. There was no immediate change in her appearance when she ate. 2 Corinthians 11:3-4, *"But I am afraid that just as Eve was deceived by the serpent's cunning…."*

Eve ate. Then she gave to Adam the fruit that he too might partake. *"She gave…"* or *nathan,* which according to Strong's OT#5414 (naw-than) means to give when applied with the greatest of latitude. Eve gave - Adam ate. The fruit was handed to Adam, but that did not lessen his sin. Adam was the king and high priest, thus, held to a higher standard.

Perhaps, for a moment, Adam stood and looked the fruit over as he weighed the consequence. But then, because Eve ate, Adam ate. In other words, he ate to please her. For the exact same reason she ate, he ate. Which characterizes the "cunningness" of the serpent; he understood that Adam's commitment to Eve, and hers to him, surpassed theirs to Yahweh.

The Spirit of God leads the sons of God. They do not judge by what they see or what they hear. Per Isaiah 11:3, the king is *"not (to) judge by what he sees with his eyes or decide by what he hears with his ears."* 2 Corinthians 5:7 states this same tenet, *"We live by faith, not by sight."* As I already indicated, Adam more than likely did not see a visible change in Eve. Conceivably, for that reason, he listened to her, believing the lie she repeated. More likely, Adam simply wanted to please Eve. Therefore, he took from her the offered fruit and ate.

The point is, Adam was not deceived; he disobeyed. Regarding this more profound understanding, the one pertaining to disobedience, the reality is that Adam did not trust the warning given to him. The legal meaning of trust involves property, the title to property. Adam failed to uphold Yahweh's title to the tree.

Adam was human, but he sinned as the Melchizedek Regent. He made a choice to listen to Eve's voice rather than respect Yahweh's property. The word hearken simply means he placed more weight on her words than those of Yahweh. Yahweh had said, *"in the day you eat of the tree, you will die."* Eve wasn't dead, or at least she did not appear to be dead. So, possibly Adam thought: *Hey, what is the harm if it makes her happy?*

Yet, that is no excuse. Adam was the Regent, his obligation to represent Yahweh surpassed all other responsibilities. To disobey and eat without permission was unlawful. Therefore, an act of unrighteousness.

I'm hesitant to accept the idea that it was immediately apparent Eve ate the fruit. She was not the Melchizedek. Therefore, no sin was attributed to her. Adam, on the other hand, was her Melchizedek, her righteousness. As her high priest, he was responsible for the remission of "all sin." So, when Adam failed to function as her priest, he instead joined himself to the deception. Then they became naked and exposed to the spirit of destruction.

> *"And he ate... then the eyes of both of them were opened, and they knew that they were naked, and they sewed fig leaves together and made themselves coverings."*

When both ate, they "knew" absolute shame, and their "glory" departed; their "covering of light" vanished, causing both to be aware of their nakedness. The nakedness Adam and Eve experienced was more than being without clothing. It was a downgrade of perception, a significant drop in their bandwidth.[56] The irony is that Eve and Adam ate to gain wisdom and received confusion in mind, soul, and spirit. I believe they lost the ability to access the higher dimensions of the spirit realm because their perception of them became impaired. For the first time, they saw the physical world without spiritual eyesight.

Hebrews 4:12-13, *"For the word of God is living and active. Sharper than any double-edged sword, it penetrates even to dividing soul and spirit, joints, and marrow; it judges the thoughts and attitudes of the heart. Nothing in all creation is hidden from God's sight.* **Everything is uncovered and laid bare before the eyes of him to whom we must give account."**

"So, they sewed fig leaves together…."

- Sewed – Strong's OT#8609 *taphar* (taw-far) to sew.
- Fig – Strong's OT#8384 *te'en* (teh-ane) the fig (tree or fruit). Symbolically, a fig tree represents a covenant.
- Leaves – Strong's OT#5929 *'aleh* (aw-leh) a leaf on a tree in a collective manner, as foliage, which represents life.
- Apron – Strong's OT#2290 *chagowr* (khag-ore) a belt for the waist as armor.

"The fig tree is a fit emblem of Israel. Its peculiarity is that the blossoms of the fruit appear before the leaves. Naturally, therefore, we should look for fruit on a tree in full leaf. This accounts for why Jesus cursed the fig tree that had on it nothing but leaves.[57] The presence of the leaves led Him to expect fruit, and when He found none, He cursed the tree for its fruitlessness."[58]

Adam and Eve covered themselves with fig leaves. They did not sacrifice animals. Seemingly they never thought to do so to show blood. Hence, Adam and Eve did not clothe themselves properly. Furthermore, they had broken their covenant with Yahweh. The shame of their disobedience could not be lessened without restitution. From that moment onward, humanity was without a suitable "light covering" – that is, until the Lamb was slain. Selah!

---

[56] Bandwidth is the energy or mental capacity required to deal with a situation.
[57] Matthew 21:18-20
[58] https://www.blueletterbible.org/study/larkin/dt/29.cfm, retrieved October 25, 2019

> *"Then the man and his wife **heard the** (Aleph-Tav) **sound** of Elohiym Yahweh as he was **walking** in the garden in the **cool of the day**, and they **hid** from the LORD God **among the trees** of the garden. But the LORD God called to the man, 'Where are you?' He answered, "I heard you in the garden, and I was afraid because I was naked; so, I hid.' And he said, 'who told you that you were naked? Have you eaten from the tree that I commanded you not to eat from?' The man said, 'The woman you put here with me--she gave me of the tree, and I ate it.' Then the LORD God said to the woman, 'What is this you have done?' The woman said, 'The serpent deceived me, and I ate.'"*

Heard, or *shama'* is identified by Strong's OT#8085 (shaw-mah) as to attend intelligently, often with an implication of attention, obedience, et cetera. It can also causatively mean "to tell." Adam and Eve listened to a distinct sound, the sound of Yahweh walking. According to Strong's OT#6963, "sound" or *qowl* (kole) was taken from an unused root that means to call aloud as with a loud voice or sound. So, did they hear God walking or the voice of Yahweh as it called to them?

Halak implies the movement of walking. According to Strong's OT#1980, *halak* (haw-lak) can be interpreted in several ways. Mainly as "to walk" (literally and figuratively), but the more stringent translation would signify that a relationship must exist between the one who walks and the one who hears the walking. For example, Enoch walked with Yahweh. *"Enoch halak with the Elohiym and he was not; for Elohiym took him,"* Genesis 5:24. In the process of walking, Enoch developed a relationship with *Elohiym*.

To fully understand what transpired in Genesis 3, we must add the phrase, *"cool of the day."* "Cool," is *ruach*. *Ruach* is spirit, breath, or wind, relating to the unseen realm. Thus, the cool of the day is the time of the day when "spiritual" activity is prone to occur. Adam heard Yahweh walking with spiritual ears, not with physical ones. Adam listened to the invisible Yahweh and entourage walking while he hid among the physical trees. When the Eternal King called out. Adam, ashamed, continued to hide.

Yahweh asked Adam, "Where are you?" Of course, God knew where Adam was. He wanted Adam to realize there was now a "veil" that separated them. That veil kept Adam from seeing Yahweh. So, in that regard, Yahweh's question was rhetorical. Yet, God wanted Adam to respond by asking for help, for mercy. The cosmic Supreme Judge wanted Adam to come before him and demand justice. Instead, Adam replied he was afraid and uncovered.

To stand, face to face before a Holy Righteous God is a fearful thing. "Afraid" in Hebrew is *'yare* and means to "fear Yahweh" because he is Holy! Having lost his robes of righteousness, Adam was ashamed and hid among the trees. Metaphorically, however, Adam hid among the entire human race, for he was no longer capable of being 'their' righteous king.

Yahweh asked of him, "who told you that you are naked? Have you consumed that which was not yours to consume?" Adam replied, "Yes, the woman, whom you gave me, gave me of the tree, and I ate."

Genesis 3:12: *"The **man** (not named in the text) said, 'The **woman you put here with me** (appointed to me), **she gave** (apportioned) **me some fruit** ("some fruit" is also not in the Hebrew text) **from the tree, and I ate it.'* That response was the same as if he had said, "the woman you appointed gave me the tree (the Cross), a burden I can not carry."

Hence, the spiritual implication is Eve gave Adam the assignment that belonged to the Eternal Melchizedek. These subtleties must not be overlooked, for what occurred in the Garden would take four thousand years to undo. Adam's failure to be Eve's High Priest cost him. He lost the capability to sit with the Divine Council in their assembly. However, he remained the regent king of *'erets*. But note, at that point, Adam, like Eve, required the services of a High Priest.

As the Melchizedek, Adam was created from *'erets* that he might represent Yahweh **in** the realm of *'erets*. Eve as "flesh of my flesh" represented Adam. Yet, Adam submitted to Eve. In so doing, he disobeyed Yahweh and thereby equipped the Deceiver. Meaning the Deceiver could rightly accuse Adam of rebellion.

Although it is not stated in the text, the implications suggest that a "high court" was held, and judgments were handed down. Perhaps, the Deceiver demanded the Divine Court renounce Adam by removing him as the regent king.

Some four thousand years later, in that exact location, another garden existed. And the Eternal Melchizedek would also petition Yahweh on behalf of his bride. John 17:6-19, *"I have manifested your name to the men whom you have given me out of the world. They were yours, you gave them to me, and they have kept your word. Now they have known that all things which you have given me are from you. For I have given to them the words which you have given me; and they have received them and have known surely that I came forth from you, and they have believed that you sent me. I pray for them. I do not pray for the world but for those whom you have given me, for they are yours. And all mine are yours, and yours are mine, and I am glorified in them.* **Now I am no longer in the world, but these are in the world, and I come to You. Holy Father, keep through your name those whom you have given me, that they may be one as we are.** *While I was with them in the world, I kept* (guarded) *them in your name. Those whom you gave me I have kept; and none of them is lost except the* **son of perdition** (destruction), *that the Scripture might be fulfilled. But now I come to you, and these things I speak in the world, that they may have my joy fulfilled in themselves. I have given them Your word, and the world has hated them because they are not of the world, just as I am not of the world.* **I do not pray that you should take them out of the world but that you should keep them from the evil one. They are not of the world, just as I am not of the world. Sanctify them by your truth. Your word is truth. As you sent Me into the world, I also have sent them into the world. And for their sakes, I sanctify myself, that they also may be sanctified by the truth"** (emphasis added).

Ephesians 5:23, *"For the husband is the head of the wife as Christ is the head of the church...."* Ephesians 5:25-28, *"...just as Christ loved the church and gave himself up for her to make her holy, cleansing her by the washing with water through the word, and to present her to himself as a radiant church, without stain or wrinkle or any other blemish, but holy and blameless."*

Note the challenge alluded to in Yeshua's prayer: He guarded his "bride" against the "son of perdition." In other words, Yeshua came to *'erets* to undo the events of the Garden in Eden and the work of the "evil one." And while it is true, Yeshua was referring to Judas. We note that Jesus called Judas the "son" of destruction or the son of the Destroyer. The Destroyer is *Abaddon*. Revelation 9:11, *"And they had as king over them the angel of the bottomless pit, whose name in Hebrew is Abaddon, but in Greek, he has the name **Apollyon**[59]"* (emphasis added).

Adam loved Eve; he did not blame her or Yahweh for his predicament. He blamed himself. So, Yahweh turned to Eve and asked, "Why did you do this?" She answered, "The *elohim* deceived me, and so I ate believing the tree's fruit would make me knowledgeable and acceptable as the Melchizedek's bride."

"All of us have become like one who is unclean, and all our righteous acts are like filthy rags," Isaiah 64:6. Thank God we are now clothed by Yeshua and are encouraged to *"come boldly unto the throne of grace, that we may obtain mercy, and find grace to help in time of need,"* Hebrews 4:16. *"…we know that if our earthly house of this tabernacle were dissolved, we have a building of God, a house not made with hands, eternal in the heavens. For in this we groan, earnestly desiring to be clothed upon with our house which is from heaven: If so, be that being clothed we shall not be found naked."* 2 Corinthians 5:1-3.

> **Decree one:** Genesis 3:14-15, *"So Yahweh said to the serpent, 'Because you have done this, you are cursed more than all cattle, and more than every beast of the field; on your belly you shall go, and you shall eat dust all the days of your life. And I will put enmity between you and the woman, and between your seed and her Seed; He shall bruise your head, and you shall bruise His heel.'"*

- Curse – Strong's OT#779 *'arar* (aw-rar) to execrate; to bitterly curse.
- Cattle – Strong's OT#929 *behemah* (be-hay-maw) from an unused root (meaning to be mute) a dumb beast, especially any large animal.
- Beast – Strong's OT#2416 *chay* (khah-ee) to be alive.
- Field – Strong's OT#7704 *sadeh* (saw-deh) from an unused root meaning to spread out; an area (flat).
- Belly – Strong's OT#1512 *gachown* (gaw-khone) the external abdomen; belly.
- Dust – Strong's OT#6083 *'aphar* (aw-fawr) dust (as powdered or gray) hence, clay, earth, mud, ashes, ground, mortar, powder, rubbish.
- Enmity – Strong's OT#342 *'eybah* (ay-baw) hostility, enmity, hatred.
- Seed – Strong's OT#2233 *zera'* (zeh'-rah) seed, offspring; figuratively, fruit, plant.
- Bruise – Strong's OT#7779 *shuwph* (shoof) is a primitive root that means to gape, or snap at; figuratively, to overwhelm; to break, to bruise.
- Head – Strong's OT#7218) *ro'sh* (roshe) from an unused root meaning to shake the head in literal terms; in figurative, it refers to rank.

---

[59] According to Greek mythology Apollo was the son of Zeus. It is possible to connect Apollo to *Abaddon* (Hades) and from there back to *Enlil*. If we dig deep, it is also possible to connect Zeus to *Ba'al*, and Saturn, who I believe is the god, Chaos (death). In my opinion, the "sting" of these two was removed with the first coming of Yeshua. And with his second coming, Yeshua will remove all of their power, completely forever. Then at the end of the age, Death (*Thanatos*) and Hades will be *"cast into the lake of fire."*

- Heel – Strong's OT#6119 *'aqeb* (aw-kabe) a heel; a track; figuratively, the rear troops of an army.

Genesis 3:14-15 paraphrased by the author: "You are execrable, more so than any dumb beast. You shall walk as they do, according to desire, the seat of your desires. As you are like the serpent, you shall consume the ash and the dust of perversion as you roam *'erets*. The perversion of your desires shall control you, causing hatred to rise up between you and the woman; between your seed and her Seed, there shall be hostility. Your army will snap at the rear guard of his army. But his army shall overwhelm the leaders of yours."

Note the emotion with which Yahweh spoke to the "serpent." He was angry. Yahweh viewed the deception perpetrated against Eve as high treason. When this decree was issued, I don't think the Divine Council or Court fully understood its judgment. At least not the prophetic implications.

The god, who had served previously as a guardian, prosecuted his case, yet he did not win. Instead, a judgment was rendered against him: He had deceived his victim, acted unlawfully, and was not entitled to anything except to "roam *'erets*." It was made clear to all; subsequently, he was an adversary of the Throne and cursed to be controlled by what motivated him to deceive the woman, jealousy, and hate.[60]

Ezekiel 28:14-17, *"You were the anointed cherub who covers; I established you; you were on the holy mountain of God; you walked back and forth in the midst of fiery stones. You were perfect in your ways from the day you were created till iniquity was found in you.* **By the abundance of your trading,** *you became filled with violence within, and you sinned. Therefore, I cast you as a profane thing out of the mountain of God, and I destroyed you, O covering cherub, from the midst of the fiery stones. Your heart was lifted up because of your beauty; you corrupted your wisdom for the sake of your splendor; I cast you to the ground"* (emphasis added).

Job 1:6-7, *"One day the bene elohim* (members of the Divine Court) *came to* (station themselves and report as required) *before Yahweh, and* (the adversary) *also* ("also" is **"gam"** in Hebrew – it means in like manner) *came with them. Yahweh said to* (the adversary), *"Where have you come from?"* (The adversary) *answered Yahweh, "From roaming through the earth and going back and forth in it."*

Gam implies that the adversary was no longer a member of the *'bene elohim* but came with them anyway. The Ezekiel 28 passage notes the adversary "traveled about filled with violence from within." Violence or *chamac* infers a violation of authority. Perhaps this would be better stated if we said he went beyond his sphere of influence purposefully to corrupt others. He "traded" righteousness for evil. Traded is defined by Strong's OT#7402 *rakal* (raw-kal') as a primitive root that means to travel for trading. So again, we can connect the curse spoken to the "serpent" as a decree that permitted him to be a Traveler for a "limited" season.

Travelers were allowed access to all realms and dimensions. Yet, they were not allowed to "abide" anywhere except in the netherworld. The opening verses of Job portray a traveling satan who roamed the earth. He came with the *elohim* before Yahweh. The Hebrew text states he *shuwt-halak*, which implies that this satan

---

[60] There is another judgment standing against this "satan," but that judgment is apart from this curse.

approached the throne of Yahweh after walking back and forth through all realms.

The ancients believed one's belly was the seat of their emotions; hence the expression the "serpent" was "bound" to his belly. He was tied to the motivation that caused the deception. Yet, for all intents and purposes, he was placed under the subjugation of the Melchizedek Kingdom. The reality of that subjugation waited for the advent of the Eternal Melchizedek. That's why it's crucial to understand that the adversary's powers (abilities) were not made void. He was not stripped of power; instead, of authority.

Yeshua told his disciples, *"I saw Satan fall like lightning from heaven. I have given you authority to trample on snakes and scorpions and to overcome all the power of the enemy; nothing will harm you,"* Luke 10:18-19. Yeshua was speaking of authority. He witnessed the adversary lose his.

The only other occasion *gachown* (belly) is used in Scripture is Leviticus 11:42. *"Whatsoever goes upon the* **belly**, *and whatsoever goes upon all four, or whatsoever has more feet among all creeping things that creep upon the earth, you shall not eat for they are an* **abomination**" (emphasis added). Abomination refers to an idolatrous purpose.

Yahweh then said, *"I will put enmity…."* Meaning: "I will put hatred between you and her Seed (the Eternal Melchizedek). You will bruise those who are in the rear of his army, but he will overwhelm the leadership of yours."

These terms are militaristic and equate with war. "To bruise" correlates with "shock and awe." "Heel" is an army's rear flank. The nuance of these terms offers prophetic insight, relating to the "end times" and coinciding with tribulation against the saints and ending with the battle of Armageddon.

Revelation 12:7-9: *"And there was war in heaven. Michael and his angels fought against the dragon, and the dragon and his angels fought back. But he was not strong enough, and they lost their place in heaven. The great dragon was hurled down that ancient serpent called the devil, or Satan, who leads the whole world astray. He was hurled to the earth* (literally onto the soil), *and his angels with him."*

> **Decree two:** Genesis 3:16, *"To the woman He said: 'I will greatly multiply your sorrow and your conception; in pain, you shall bring forth children; your desire shall be for your husband, and he shall rule over you.'"*

- Greatly multiply - *rabah* – Strong's OT#7235 (raw-baw), a primitive root meaning to increase (in whatever respect).
- Sorrow – *'itstabown* – Strong's OT#6093 (its-tsaw-bone) to worry with labor pain; sorrow; toil.
- Conception – *herown* - Strong's OT#2032 (hay-rone) a pregnancy; conception.
- Pain – *'etseb* – Strong's OT#6089 (eh'-tseb) is usually (painful) toil; also, a pang (whether of body or mind) that is grievous; labor, sorrow.
- Bring forth – *yalad* – Strong's OT#3205 (yaw-lad), a primitive root meaning to bear young; causatively to beget; medically, to function as a midwife; specifically, to show lineage.
- Children – *ben* (bane) Strong's OT#1121 a son (as a builder of the family name), in the broadest sense (literal and figurative) a direct relationship, including grandchild.

- Desire – *teshuwqah* Strong's OT#8669 (tesh-oo-kaw) in the original sense to stretch out after; a longing; desire.
- Rule – *mashal* – Strong's OT#4910 (maw-shal) is to rule (have or make to have) dominion; governor; reign; have power.

Yahweh would "multiply her sorrow," which indicates she was sorrowful. I have no doubt Eve regretted she listened to the *elohim*. Also, I'm sure Eve was worried about the future. She was aware life would not remain the same. That must have weighed heavily upon her mind. However, instead of an angry God, a loving Father turned from the serpent to speak to her.

To grasp the fulness of Yahweh's words, let's connect Genesis 3:16 to John 3:16. Yahweh spoke prophetically. He gave her the pattern of the solution and not a curse. We have been conditioned to think Genesis 3:16 was a curse. No, it was not; Yahweh was decreeing unto her a son. John 3:16, *"For God so loved, He gave a Son!"*

Yahweh addressed the spiritual problem by assigning to her a Savior and providing restoration. Both would be fulfilled with the coming of her Seed. You see, after declaring war, a Seed War with the serpent, Yahweh turned to Eve and began to prophesy. A Seed would be given to her. A Seed who would destroy the works of her enemy. That Seed would come "through" her feminine nature, he would overcome the adversary and reverse the devastation that arose from the deception inflicted upon her. Yahweh said: "Eve, you will toil, and your labor will be painful, but that must be for you will conceive the Melchizedek lineage. To fulfill this prophecy, I have placed a desire within you. From now on, a renewed passion shall enable you to receive Melchizedek seed from your husband."

Remember, Eve's passion was to please Adam. That passion was the "twist" used by the adversary to provoke her to eat the forbidden fruit. God took that same passion, blest it anew, and by it, she would be fruitful. Through that passion, she would receive the Melchizedek's seed. God had already placed within her the ability to receive the seed. Yet as of that moment, she had not. So, Yahweh lit her passion with new "fire."

Passion and fire are interchangeable terms in the language of the spirit. Years later, Yahweh would repeat this process with Sarah and Abraham. Even so, as Yahweh spoke to Eve, He released the future, all future Melchizedeks into *'erets*. As Yahweh's words entered Eve, they created a pathway for the Eternal Melchizedek and for those who are his inheritance. Thus, God gave a Son in Genesis 3:16 by pre-writing the genealogies recorded in Matthew 1 and Luke 3. It would be 4,000 years until the birth of the Promised Seed. Still, in the moment of Genesis 3:16, the lineage of Yeshua was established, and his birth was authorized.

By comforting Eve, Yahweh showed compassion and assured her that she would again be approved. That, again, she would be accepted as righteous. Although, her validation could return only by relationship. She had to relate to her husband by allowing him to once again be her priest, her Melchizedek. Beloved, there must be a relationship between the Melchizedek and the bride for validation to occur!

Ephesians 5:23-28, "For the husband is the head of the wife as Christ is the head of the church, his body, of which he is the Savior. Now, as the church submits to Christ, so also wives should submit to their husbands in everything. Husbands, love your wives, just as Christ loved the church and gave himself up for her to make her holy, cleansing her by the washing with water through the word, and to present her to himself as a radiant church, without stain or wrinkle or any other blemish, but holy and blameless. In this same way, husbands ought to love their wives as their own bodies. He who loves his wife loves himself."

Decree three: Verses 17-19: *"Then to Adam He said, 'Because you have heeded the voice of your wife and have eaten from the tree of which I commanded you, saying, "You shall not eat of it,"* **cursed is the ground for your sake.** *In toil, you shall eat of it all the days of your life. Both thorns and thistles will bring forth for you, and you shall eat the (Aleph-Tav) herb of the field. In the sweat of your face, you shall eat bread until you return to the ground, for out of it you were taken; for dust you are, and to dust, you shall return.'"*

Adam had listened to Eve rather than heeding the warning issued by Yahweh. As a result, due to his rank, he had to be judged. But if we examine the decree of Genesis 3:17-19 carefully, we note Adam was not cursed. The ground was cursed for Adam's sake. I need to emphasize that once more. Adam was not cursed; he was judged.

Essentially Adam was removed as the "everlasting" regent to the Melchizedek Throne. Everlasting is the keyword, the one that must be parsed. Eternal means without beginning or end. Everlasting has a start but no end in sight. So, the key to unlocking the truth is knowing that Adam represented the Eternal Melchizedek. The Eternal Melchizedek is eternal; his throne is everlasting. The Eternal Melchizedek would at some point take possession of his throne, but conditions had to be met. In other words, time was a factor. Until all contingencies were finalized, Adam sat as a regent. However, Adam was no longer "everlasting." He was weakened and consequently subjugated to "Death."

It was now up to Adam to replace himself by finding another regent, one who "imaged" him. Thankfully, Yahweh had given him seed.

The reason a curse was not placed upon Adam requires additional explaining. Think back to when the "rain" of Holy Spirit first fell on *'erets*. He watered the soil to sanctify the *adamah* as *Aleph-Tav*. That caused it to be suitable material for the *Aleph-Tav* man's body. The raining of the Holy Spirit on the *adamah* caused it to become *Aleph-Tav*.

Once Adam sinned, Yahweh was forced to decide whether to remove Adam as the Melchizedek or revoke the *Aleph-Tav* blessing from the *adamah*. If the *adamah* was *Aleph-Tav*, it would "serve" the Melchizedek, and he could "till" the soil by speaking to it. On the other hand, if Yahweh removed Adam, the covenant, sworn by oath[61] to Yeshua, would be broken. The Melchizedek Throne would be vacated, having no "sitting" king

---

61 Psalms 110

or regent.

In theory, Yahweh would be forced to start over – establishing another government system that was not Melchizedek. That option was unacceptable – also not possible. If Yahweh went that route, He would be breaking a sworn oath.

If Adam could not be redeemed, the Eternal Melchizedek would lose his inheritance. Remember, Adam was explicitly created to represent the Eternal Melchizedek. There was no other like Adam in the whole cosmos. He was one of a kind. But in that fact, was another problem. Even if Adam remained the regent, he had sinned; he owed a death penalty. So, Yahweh took two actions on Adam's behalf. 1) He placed the penalty of Adam's sin on the Eternal Melchizedek, and 2) Adam's act of disobedience upon the *adamah*, thereby cursing the *adamah*.

Keep in mind that Yahweh is eternal; He is always in the "now." So, He could look into the future of *'erets*, see the Cross, and mark Adam's penalty as paid. Additionally, He saw Yeshua's blood on the altar and flowing down from the Cross to the *adamah* so that it "showed blood," which in the moment of Genesis 3 it did not.

The Cross would pay Adam's penalty – and provide for the eventual removal of the curse from the *adamah*. But until then, access to Yah's Holy Place needed to be protected. Its portal was shut. Perception into the spirit realm was no longer readily possible. Adam and Eve lost the ability to physically access the spiritual domain of Yah.

So, Yahweh cursed the *adamah* was cursed. The serpent was cursed, but neither Eve nor Adam was cursed. But they would remain in their fallen state until they could be "born again."

Allow me to remind you that *adamah*, as defined by Strong's OT#127, is soil. The root word of *adamah* is *adam*, which means to show blood. Did the *adamah* show blood - No! And that was the point. The *adamah* could be cursed and denounced since it had failed to serve its "anointed" purpose.

Although, once it was cursed, the *adamah* was no longer subjugated to serve Adam. In rebellion, the soil would bear thorns and thistles. Essentially, the *adamah* and Adam were exchanged, one for the other. Something, though, had to mark the exchange. So, emblematically, Yahweh took the "*hei*" from the spelling of *adamah* and placed it "within" Adam.

The importance of this exchange added "breath" (*hei*) to Adam's life. Instead of dying an instant death, Adam lived for 930 years. On the flip side, the *adamah* died. It was no longer, *Aleph-Tav*, capable of producing life.

Instead of Adam being required to show blood, that requirement was placed upon the *adamah*, and when it failed to "show" blood, it was cursed. Yet, it did show blood four thousand years later. Yeshua's Cross paid the penalty Adam owed, and when his blood fell on the *adamah*, the *adamah* showed *(Aleph-Tav)* blood.

The announcement of the Promised Seed was given to the "serpent." It was announced to Eve that the

Seed given would come through sorrow. And to Adam, it was announced he would work, struggle to keep the throne occupied until the advent of the Promised Seed.

God decreed the *'erets* as good on Day Three of Creation. It was deemed righteous. Literally and figuratively, *'erets* has had its third day. Still, it waits for the fulfillment of Day Six when according to Romans 8:19-22, it shall be redeemed by the Melchizedek's seed: *"The creation waits in eager expectation for the sons of God to be revealed. For the creation was subjected to frustration, not by its own choice, but by the will of the one who subjected it, in hope that the creation itself will be liberated from its bondage to decay and brought into the glorious freedom of the children of God. We know that the whole creation has been groaning as in the pains of childbirth right up to the present time."*

Only a Melchizedek, who knew no sin, could free Adam from the clutches of Death. Only a Melchizedek with a divine nature, having the authority of the King/High Priest, could redeem Adam and reunite him with Yahweh. So, Adam's soul, his spirit, was forced to wait in the netherworld for the advent of the Eternal Melchizedek. Adam did not lose the authority of the Melchizedek Kingdom. Instead, he lost the power that accompanies that authority. He became dependent upon the Courts of Heaven to assist him with the ruling of *'erets*.

In a manner of speaking, Adam was subjugated to the *adamah*. He would toil for provision. But the actual subjugation he faced was unto Death. Death was allowed to hold him captive in *Sheol* until the advent of Yeshua. Once Yeshua came and then died innocently, Adam was freed and returned to the Father. So, basically, the serpent lost authority and Adam, power. Yet, in the "wings of time," Adam's Redeemer waited to be born!

One last point: Entropy (death and chaos) existed in the atmosphere of the cosmos. Yet it was not until Adam sinned that decay could touch his physical body or Death allowed access to his soul. Death did not reign anywhere until Adam sinned. Until Adam sinned, the spirits of death and decay had no legal means by which they could touch Adam or anything in his dominion. So, Adam did not lose possession of Earth; it was never his. He was assigned to reign, not to own. And at the risk of being extremely repetitive, allow me to say that Adam, when created, possessed all power and authority over all of the dominions of *'erets*. Only after Adam partook of what was not permitted did the spirits of death, decay, and deception have a legal case they could prosecute against Adam. Their case was primarily since Adam's body was formed from the cursed adamah - and since he had failed to show Melchizedek blood, he was doomed. Therefore, they could legally take him to the netherworld and hold him there as unredeemed. To redeem a thing is to repurchase it! To reclaim Adam, Yahweh would have to purchase Adam back from the "gods" of the Underworld.

Adam did not die immediately. Still, when he did, it was because he ate the forbidden fruit. The consumption of confusion corrupted his DNA. His disobedience gave access to the spirit of decay to work against him. So, Adam's physical body became "at dis-eased."

"Though he (Yeshua) were a Son yet learned he obedience by the things which he suffered, and being made perfect, he became the author of eternal salvation unto all of them that obey him, called of God, a high priest after the order of Melchizedek." Hebrews 5:8-10.

> Genesis 3:20-24, *"And Adam called his wife's name Eve because she was the mother of all living. For Adam and his wife also did Yahweh made tunics of skin and clothed them. Then Yahweh said, 'Behold, the man has become like one of Us, to know good and evil. And now, lest he put out his hand and also take of the tree of life, and eat, and live forever, Yahweh sent him out of the **garden** of Eden to till the (Aleph-Tav) ground from which he was taken. So, he drove out the (Aleph-Tav) man; and he placed (Aleph-Tav) cherubim at the **east** of the garden of Eden and an (Aleph-Tav) flaming sword which turned every way, to **guard the way to the tree of life**"* (emphasis added).

The first question we need to ask is what does it mean to know good and evil? "Know," used in this sense, infers an intimate relationship. To know has the effect of integrating a concept into the psyche. Adam and Eve ingested information that was both "good and evil." In that regard, they became like the *elohim*. They were capable of good thoughts and of evil ones. Meaning Adam was no longer exceptional "like" Yahweh, innately seeking good.

Previously, in describing man and DNA, we noted that information is the "third fundamental universal quantity." One of the observed principles relating to information is it cannot exist without a "mental" origin or without a transmitter. The "fruit" of the forbidden tree of knowledge transmitted information. The fruit of knowledge modified the quality of life in Adam and Eve. That fruit, whatever it was, had the effect of being epigenetic.[62] I must be clear; obviously, the tree had edible fruit since they ate. However, that fruit was not apples or any other fruit that we usually consume. So, do not overlook the importance of the "name" assigned to the tree – *da'ath* of *tôb* and *ra'* – knowing good and evil. The fruit of that tree passed to its partaker knowledge in the form of information. The information rewrote DNA. Perhaps, the fruit contained a virus. Still, whatever it was, it damaged Adam and Eve permanently as it entered their genetics, which they passed on to the next generation as a "sin nature."

Adam needed to be "fixed." At the very least, he needed a reinstatement of righteousness. So, Yahweh built an altar and slaughtered at least one animal, probably more, and from their skins made garments, coverings for both Adam and Eve. *"And the garments of skin which God made for Adam and his wife when they went out of the garden"*[63] covered their nakedness and gave them a temporary status of righteousness. Yet, those garments did not redeem them from a fallen state.

Blood was shed because animals were sacrificed. The blood of animals fell to the *adamah*, foreshadowing the work of the Cross. Yet, that blood was not Melchizedek. At best, it was representational. While the Bible is not definitive as to what kind of animals were sacrificed to make tunics of skin, most likely, Yahweh used lambs. Revelation 13:8, *"… in the book of life of the Lamb slain from the foundation of the world."*

Yahweh sent Adam out of the "garden." My translation: Adam was sent from the Mount of Assembly, meaning he was no longer permitted to sit among the Divine Council in their cosmic reality. Yet, he did not

---

62 Epigenetic literally means "above" or "on" the top of genetics.
63 Johnson, Ken. *Ancient Book of Jasher* (p. 17) Kindle Edition, Chapter 7:24

leave the territory of Eden. He left the "garden." The doors of the Temple were closed to Adam. That had the same effect as removing the temple from the physical Eden. Simply put, Adam lost physical access to the spiritual cosmic Holy Place and Mercy Seat.

Note the phrasing of Genesis 3:24, *"He drove out the man, and He placed cherubim at the east of the garden of Eden, and a flaming sword which turned every way,* **to guard the way to the tree of life.***"* Revelation 2:7, *"He who has an ear, let him hear what the Spirit says to the churches. To him who overcomes, I will give the right to eat from the tree of life,* **which is in the paradise of God***"* (emphasis added).

Revelation 22:1-3, *"Then the angel showed me the river of the water of life, as clear as crystal, flowing from the throne of God and of the Lamb down the middle of the great street of the city. On each side of the river* **stood the tree of life,** *bearing twelve crops of fruit, yielding its fruit every month. And the* **leaves of the tree are for the healing of the nations***. No longer will there be any curse. The throne of God and of the Lamb will be in the city, and his servants will serve him"* (emphasis added).

Genesis 3:24 states cherubim guard the ancient gate leading to the Tree of Life with *(Aleph-Tav)* flaming swords. "Flaming swords" refer to enriching words that enrapture the listener. Therefore, the Tree of Life is also information. It, however, speaks words of healing. The Greek word used in Revelation is *"therapeían."* The same Greek word that means "therapeutic." Since Adam and Eve were removed from the garden and could no longer physically access the *Gan of Yah*, why assign cherubim at its ancient gate? Why protect the way to the Tree of Life? From whom were they protecting it? My supposition is that the cherubim stand between the Tree of Life and fallen entities who desire restoration, either for themselves or their ill-gotten offspring.

Genesis Four

Before diving into Genesis 4, we need to familiarize ourselves with Hebrews 12:23. It calls the believer to *"the **general assembly** and **church of the firstborn**, which are written in heaven, and to God, the Judge of all, and to the spirits of just men made perfect…"* (emphasis added).

"General assembly," translated from *paneguris* (pan-ay-goo-ris), is a combination of *pas* (the whole of a thing) and *agora* (town square.) *Paneguris* means the "whole" town square. So essentially, when paraphrased, this verse states, "When we stand on Mount Zion, Yah's holy city, we are united with those who serve as heaven's host and the Church of the Firstborn."

The "general assembly" refers to the divine beings who judge the cosmos. But what about the Church of the Firstborn? It is the *Ekklēsía* of the *Protos-Tikto*. *Ekklēsía* means those who are called from a thing, such as an erroneous belief, to think differently. Yeshua is the Firstborn, the *Protos Tikto* (*protos* meaning the foremost; the original). *Tikto* means seed. So, in other words, the *Ekklēsía* of *Protos-Tikto* is the Church of the Promised Seed.

Note this same verse in the NIV with the addition of verse twenty-four. *"But you have come to Mount Zion, to the heavenly Jerusalem, the city of the living God. You have come to thousands upon thousands of angels in joyful assembly, to the church of the firstborn, whose names are written in heaven. You have come to God, the judge of all men, to the spirits of righteous men made perfect, to Jesus the mediator of a new covenant, **and to the sprinkled blood that speaks a better word than the blood of Abel.**"*

That final phrase links to, and thus, is relevant to Genesis 4.

> Genesis 4: 1-2: *"And Adam knew (Aleph-Tav) Eve, his wife; and she conceived, and bore (Aleph-Tav) Cain, and said, 'I have gotten a man from (Aleph-Tav) Yahweh.' And she again bore (Aleph-Tav) his brother (Aleph-Tav) Abel."*

Adam knew Eve. He was intimate with her, knowing her function was to assist him in pro-creating "himself." She conceived and gave birth to Qayin and said, *"I have gotten a man from* (Aleph-Tav) *Yahweh."* Conceive is *harah*, and in this context, it implies that she received her child from the "head" of the government. Indeed, Eve credited Yahweh saying, "I have gotten a man-child from Yahweh." Please understand Eve did not say she conceived "by" Yahweh, but that the life given to her child came from Yahweh.

Eve named the son born to her first, *Qayin* (Cain). His name was a play on words. Strong's OT#7014 (kah-yin) indicates this name is a derivative of the term *qanah* (kaw-naw). *Qanah* means to create or to procure by purchase. Eve considered her son to be a procurement. She likely thought he would restore the Melchizedek Kingdom to its original purpose.

Carefully noting the wording of Genesis 4:2, we find that Eve bore again. She had another son. Eve did not conceive again; conception occurred only once. Therefore, since she gave birth twice, she delivered twins. This understanding is not exclusively mine; the rabbis of the Second Temple also taught that Cain and Abel were twins.

Havel (Abel), the second son, was also Aleph-Tav. According to Strong's OT#1892, *Havel (heh'bel)* means emptiness, a vapor, or vanity. Figuratively, *havel* is something transitory and unsatisfactory. *Havel* is most often used as an adverb rather than a noun. Wow! Abel was viewed as the spare heir having no "true" value. He was perceived as having "...*no beauty or majesty to attract us to him, nothing in his appearance that we should desire him. He was despised and rejected by men, a man of sorrows, and familiar with suffering,*" Isaiah 53:2-3.

> Genesis 4:3-5a, *"And Abel was a keeper of sheep, but Cain was a tiller of the ground. And in the process of time, it came to pass that Cain brought from the fruit of the ground an offering unto Yahweh. And Abel also brought; he brought of the firstlings of his flock and of the fat thereof. And the Yahweh had respect unto Abel and to his offering: But unto Cain and to his offering he had not respect."*

Abel was a *ra'ah*, a shepherd. In the figurative sense, he represented the good shepherd. Yeshua said, *"I am the good shepherd. The good shepherd gives His life for the sheep,"* John 10:11.

Cain was a "tiller of the ground." Tiller is *'abad* and literally means "one who serves." Adam was expelled from the garden and sent forth to "till" the *adamah*. He was to till the soil (preach the gospel of the kingdom) throughout *'erets* until it was ready for harvest. Because he was the elder twin, Cain was expected to continue Adam's work.

When these two brothers became men and reached the age of maturity, they were taken to the altar of Yahweh. They were there to humble themselves so they might find acceptance. For that reason, each came with a sacrifice. However, they were aware that only one could be anointed as Firstborn. Therefore, Yahweh's approval of what they offered was crucial.

They were sent to Yahweh's altar for His determination, which He would accept as Adam's Firstborn. Obviously, Cain expected to be the Firstborn. But Adam must have been uncertain since he took both sons to the altar.

Cain went with the fruit of the *adamah*. Whether he intended it or not, his offering represented the fruit of what Yahweh had cursed. Abel brought the firstling of his flock. Strong's OT#1062 *bekowrah* (bek-o-raw) defines a "firstling" as the firstling of man or beast; the firstling represents the birthright of a firstborn.

Abel brought to the altar his birthright. In the literal sense, Abel went to the altar with an animal as a substitute. Figuratively, he went to worship Yahweh, foreshadowing the work of the Cross. No wonder Yahweh respected Abel's offering: his actions foreshadowed the Messiah!

Hebrews 11:4, *"By faith, Abel offered God a more excellent sacrifice than Cain, through which he obtained witness that he was righteous, God testifying of his gifts; and through it, he being dead still speaks."*

Cain and Abel undoubtedly had heard stories of the Garden of Eden. They were familiar with the deception perpetrated against their parents. That knowledge would include the need for a Redeemer. Inclusive of that understanding was the purpose of sacrifices; to represent the removal of sin. Thus, to invoke righteousness. At best, it was temporary righteousness, yet it would do until the Promised Seed could come and redeem them from death. However, the brothers had not come to the altar to obtain a right standing for themselves. Or for anyone else. They were not yet priests. Instead, they came as candidates for the priesthood. Even so, they knew a Redeemer would come, and all hope (faith) was to be placed in him. But until that Redeemer appeared, the animal sacrificed symbolized the future. It represented the anticipated transferrence of sin.

Galatians 5:6, *"The only thing that counts is faith expressing itself through love."*

Abel was in love with Yahweh's prophetic promises; he came to the altar expecting to enter the priesthood because he honored his birthright and sought righteousness. On the other hand, Cain went to the altar out of duty. In other words, he came because he felt an obligation to represent his father, Adam. In that manner, he came offering the fruit of his labor, not seeking righteousness.

- Abel came to the altar because he loved his birthright, so he came in faith.
- Cain came because his birthright gave him access to the altar; he came according to works.

Two motives, each vastly different. Abel trusted and respected the protocol. Therefore, aligned himself with Yahweh. On the other hand, Cain came to the altar because he was Adam's son, born first. God judges the heart. Cain's heart was not in alignment with the Melchizedek Kingdom. Consequently, Yahweh did not regard Cain's offering but acknowledged Abel's as acceptable and righteous. Thus, Abel received his desired petition; he was accepted as the Firstborn of his generation.

> Genesis 4:5b-7 *"And Cain was very wroth, and his countenance fell. And Yahweh said unto Cain, Why are you wroth? And why is your countenance fallen? If you do well, shall you not be accepted? If you do not well, sin lies at the door. And unto you shall be his desire, and thou shalt rule over him.'"*

Cain was angry. His face [*paniym*] was downcast. Yahweh asked, "Why are you so angry? Why are you downcast? If you do well, I will accept you into the Assembly of the Firstborn. However, sin will grab you if you do not do what is acceptable. It is already at the door of your heart. You can rule over sin, but if you don't, "he" will rule over you!"

The spiritual reality is Cain picked up "an offense." He was jealous. Yahweh was, in essence, saying, "Your heart must be right before me so that you are upholding the law of love. Do not pick up an offense because I chose Abel and not you – do not be ruled by a spirit of jealousy."

1 Corinthians 13:4-7, *"Love suffers long and is kind; love does not envy; love does not parade itself, is not puffed up; does*

not behave rudely, does not seek its own, is not provoked, thinks no evil; does not rejoice in iniquity, but rejoices in the truth; bears all things, believes all things, hopes all things, endures all things."

Adam failed to love Yahweh more than Eve while standing before the tree of knowledge. Cain did not love his brother as himself while standing before the altar of sacrifice. Again, we have a parallel. The tree of knowledge and the altar of sacrifice foreshadow the Cross, whose purpose was not fully honored in both instances.

> Genesis 4:8-15 *"And Cain **talked** with Abel, his brother: and it came to pass, when they were in the field, that Cain rose up against Abel his brother, and slew him. And the Lord said unto Cain, 'Where is Abel your brother?' And he said, 'I know not. Am I my brother's keeper?' And he said, 'What have you done? The voice of thy brother's blood cries unto me from the ground. And now are you cursed from the earth, which has opened (Aleph-Tav) her mouth to receive (Aleph-Tav) your brother's blood from your hand. When you till the (Aleph-Tav) ground, it shall not henceforth yield unto you, her strength; a fugitive and a vagabond shall you be in the earth.' And Cain said unto Yahweh, **'My punishment is greater than I can bear**. Behold, thou hast driven me out this day from the face of the earth; and from your face shall I be hidden, and I shall be a fugitive and a vagabond in the earth; and it shall come to pass, that everyone that finds me shall slay me.' And Yahweh said unto him, 'Therefore whosoever slays Cain, vengeance shall be taken on him sevenfold.' And Yahweh set a mark upon Cain, lest any finding him should kill him"* (emphasis added).

Genesis 4:8 from Young's Literal Translation: *"And Cain said unto Abel, his brother, (Let us go into the field') and it came to pass in their being in the field, that Cain rose up against Abel his brother, and slew him."*

"And Cain **said**..." Typically when the word "said" is used, someone says something, and a conversation follows. Not here. The words Cain said were not recorded. Or they were lost in the transcribing process. Perhaps, the original scroll detailing the conversation was mislaid. Whatever the case, the Bible gives no account concerning what Cain and Abel said to the other.

Nonetheless, the discussion is memorialized by *Jasher*, which has the two brothers quarreling over the land. On the surface, they clashed over who was to oversee the field.[64] The deeper understanding is they disagreed about the responsibilities assigned to the Firstborn. *Jasher* indicated, "Qayin was jealous… and sought a pretext to slay him (Havel)."

Cain slew his brother; subsequently, a judgment was rendered. It was a peculiar punishment, containing three distinct conditions:
1. Cain was cursed from the '*adamah*.
2. Cain would no longer receive the '*adamah's* strength.
3. Cain would be banished from his father's house, becoming a vagabond, a fugitive within '*erets*.

---

[64] This is a reasonable assumption in that '*erets* is allegorically, a field.

Since the Levitical Law did not yet exist, the judgment against Cain was not based on an "eye for an eye." Yahweh dealt with Cain based on Kingdom rules. Additionally, the decision against Cain came from Yahweh – Cain had transgressed against a Firstborn – all Firstborns belong to Yahweh. I am not saying that Cain did not sin. Instead, I present the case that the ruling against him from Yahweh related to the wrong Cain committed against Yahweh. In other words, the matter was between Yahweh and Cain.

The conversation between Yahweh and Cain when something on this order: "Where is Abel, your brother?" Cain answered, "I know not. Am I my brother's keeper?" Yahweh responded, "What have you done? The voice of your brother's blood cries unto me from the *adamah*."

Please note Abel's well-being was not being questioned. Yahweh knew where Abel was. Yahweh was providing an opportunity for Cain to confess his sin. Confession is vital. It initiates forgiveness. Instead of seizing upon that opening, Cain pushed his accountability away and looked for a scapegoat. In that he did, causes the symbolism in the story to be all the more potent. Essentially, it is a repeat of the garden.

Adam passed all blame unto his "brother," the Eternal Firstborn. Yeshua entered *'erets* as the second "Adam."

Believing that Yahweh had rejected him and not just his offering, Cain replied, "Hey, I'm not the Firstborn. My brother is now my "elder." It is his responsibility to report to you. Accountability rests upon him. Not upon me. I am not his keeper, not his shepherd. He is mine. You picked him, so it's the other way around; he is responsible for me."

Yahweh's response, "The voice of your brother's blood cries to me from the *'adamah*."

We need to pause for the full impact of that statement. Abel's blood was not appointed to remove the curse upon the *adamah*. It couldn't; he was not a Melchizedek. This is why Hebrews 12:24 says, "*...to Jesus the mediator of a new covenant, and to the sprinkled blood that speaks a better* (stronger- more powerful) *word than the blood of Abel.*"

What did Abel's blood speak? Primarily, Abel's blood cried out to God that an appointed and anointed Firstborn was denied his destiny. The irony? In denying his brother the ability to serve, Cain also denied his own destiny. As the only living candidate to be Adam's successor, he couldn't qualify for the position because of the blood on his hands.

Hebrews 11:4, "*By faith, Abel offered God a better sacrifice than Cain did. By faith, he was commended as a righteous man when God spoke well of his offerings. And by faith, he still speaks, even though he is dead.*"

Abel's voice was no longer heard in *'erets*, but it wasn't silenced in a cosmic sense. Yahweh heard him speaking from the netherworld. The sound of a Firstborn cannot be muted because of the anointing he carries; it's cosmic. Abel cried out for cosmic justice. In the strictest sense, Cain was cursed because he removed the Firstborn from *'erets*. So, he was sent from Eden. Essentially, he lost his connection with authority. Cain's descendants would never serve as Melchizedeks. In fact, they all died in the great flood.

Cain's response, "My punishment is more than I can bear… you have driven me out before the faces of the *'adamah*. Before your face, I will be absent, removed, and shaken as one who mourns. Everyone who 'finds' me shall slay me."

Avon refers to iniquity or guilt. Cain did not say that his punishment was more than he could take. Instead, he said his sin was greater than he could withstand. The phrasing of Genesis 4:13 suggests that Cain was not asking that his punishment be negated. He was stating his guilt was greater than he could bear.

Adam could not "pay the penalty" to have his sin remitted. So, Adam's sin was more than he could bear. That same concept was repeated with Cain.

Cain was convinced that the decree against him would cause everyone he met to attempt to remove him from among the living. He believed others would seek to "kill" him in an attempt to remove the curse he carried. Yahweh responded to Cain by saying, "No, if anyone attempts to take your life, my retribution will be sevenfold upon him."

I cannot promise you with absolute certainty that the mark Yahweh drew upon Cain's forehead was the *tav*. Nonetheless, I have no doubt that it was. We are told he was marked with an *'owth*, which means a sign or a token. In receiving the *tav* as a mark, Cain was sealed by covenant. The *tav* represents covenant and ownership. At that time, the "mark" would have been drawn as † - a cross.

Adam was sealed by the Cross. Cain, too, was sealed with a "cross" and personally protected by the Supreme God, Yah.

Ezekiel 9:4, *"And the Lord said unto him, 'Go through the midst of the city, through the midst of Jerusalem, and set a **mark** upon the foreheads of the men…'"* This marking, defined by Strong's OT#8420, was "the mark of *tav*."

> *Genesis 4:16, "And Cain went out from the presence of Yahweh, and dwelt in the land of Nod, on the east of Eden."*

Cain went from the "face of Yahweh," this phrasing simply means he left Eden. Remember Yah's Mountain is Eden. This also indicates Cain was no longer a member of the Melchizedek House, for he lived east of Eden, in the land called Nod (Strong's OT#5113).

> Genesis 4:17-24 *"And Cain knew his wife, and she conceived, and bare Enoch: and he built a city, and called the name of the city, after the name of his son, Enoch. And unto Enoch was born Irad: and Irad begat Mehujael: and Mehujael begat Methusael: and Methusael begat Lamech. And Lamech took unto him two wives: the name of the one was Adah and the name of the other Zillah. And Adah bore Jabal: he was the father of such as dwell in tents, and of such as have cattle. And his brother's name was Jubal: he was the father of all, such as handle the harp and organ. And Zillah, she also bore Tubal-*

> *Cain, an instructor of every artificer in brass and iron: and the sister of Tubal-Cain was Naamah. And Lamech said unto his wives, Adah and Zillah, 'Hear my voice; you wives of Lamech, hearken unto my speech for I have slain a man to my wounding, and a young man to my hurt. If Cain shall be avenged sevenfold, truly Lamech seventy and sevenfold.'"*

None of Cain's offspring served in the order of the Melchizedek. Although Cain and his children were royal, they were denied access to the throne. From the book of *Jubilees*, we learn Cain took his sister, Awan, as a wife. She gave him a son, who they named Enoch. Enoch's name means discipline ("that which comes from correction"). At some point, after the birth of Enoch, Cain obtained more children.

- Enoch (discipline) fathered Jared (fugitive).
- Jared (fugitive) fathered Mehujael (smitten by God).
- Mehujael (smitten of God) fathered Methusael (man of God).
- Methusael (man of God) fathered Lamech (the meaning of this name is uncertain but is believed, made low.)
- Lamech took two wives: *Adah* and *Zillah*.

Adah bore *Jabal* and *Jubal*. Metaphorically, Lamech fathered two streams through honor. One stream dwelled in temporal dwellings, and the other became those who learned to worship.

- *Adah* - Strong's O#5711 (aw-daw) ornament and, thus, a source of honor.
- *Jabal* - Strong's OT#2989 *Yabal* (yaw-bawl) "to flow" as a stream. Jabal was the first to dwell in tents and perhaps the first to trade in livestock.
- *Jubal* - Strong's OT#3106 *Yubal* (yoo-bawl) a stream; to flow like a stream. Jubal was the source through which musical instruments were introduced.

Zillah bore *Tubal-Cain* and *Naamah*. Figuratively, Lamech fathered a procurement of confusion through shade and shadows, bringing chaos.

- *Zillah* - Strong's OT#6741 *Tsillah* (tsil-law) a shade; a shadow whether literally or figuratively.
- *Tubal-Cain* - Strong's OT#8423 (too-bal' kah'-yin) from OT#2986 (a stream) and *Qayin* (a procurement). *Tubal-Cain* taught men how to make objects of brass and iron; he was a blacksmith. Brass and iron represent confusion and chaos.
- *Naamah* - Strong's OT#5279 (nah-am-aw) pleasantness. There was no supporting information as to why the Bible mentioned Naamah. I searched until I discovered mention of her in an obscure masonic relief. It depicted her as talented in the arts. My assumption is those were dark carnal arts.

> Genesis 4:23-24, *"And Lamech said unto his wives, Adah and Zillah, 'Hear my voice; you wives of Lamech, hearken unto my speech for I have slain a man to my wounding, and a young man to my hurt. If Cain shall be avenged sevenfold, truly Lamech seventy and sevenfold.'"*

Jasher states that Lamech accidentally killed Cain and a young shepherd boy. Afterward, Lamech said, "If

Yahweh would avenge Cain when he was guilty, since I, Lamech, am humbled and have accidentally killed these two, Yahweh will avenge me seventy times more." "Seventy times more" is an expression denoting the number 490:

- 70 x 7 = 490
- 490 symbolizes forgiveness
- 70 symbolizes God's administration of judgment
- 7 symbolizes a completed work

Matthew 18:21-22, *"Then Peter came to Jesus and asked, 'Lord, how many times shall I forgive my brother when he sins against me? Up to seven times?' Jesus answered, 'I tell you, not seven times, but seventy, seven times.'"*

The ancients held that a 490-year cycle equated to a Great Jubilee, such as the four listed here:

1. From Abraham's birth to the Exodus
2. From the Exodus to the 1st temple in Jerusalem
3. From the 1st Jerusalem Temple until a decree was given to rebuild that destroyed temple
4. From the rebuilding of the 2nd temple until the Cross

Daniel 9:24, *"Seventy 'sevens are decreed for your people and your holy city to finish transgression, to put an end to sin, to atone for wickedness, to bring in everlasting righteousness, to seal up vision and prophecy and to anoint the most holy."*

Genesis 4:25-26, *"And Adam knew (Aleph-Tav) his wife again; and she bore a son and called (Aleph-Tav) his name Seth: 'For God,' said she, 'has appointed me another seed instead of Abel, whom Cain slew.' And to Seth, to him also there was born a son; and he called (Aleph-Tav) his name Enos: then began men to call upon the name of Yahweh."*

Melchizedek Adam again knew Eve after the death of Abel. She brought forth another son who would serve as Firstborn. She named him Seth because he was a substitute for the ONE who was slain. Seth also had a Firstborn son whom he named Enos. Enos means mortal. After the birth of Enos, humanity became hostile toward Yahweh. That *"men began to call upon the name of Yahweh."* Men did not call upon Yahweh to worship. They began to use His name "as vain."

Genesis Five

> Genesis 5:1-2 *"This is the book of the generations of Adam. In the day that God created man, in the likeness of God made he him; male and female created he them; and blessed them and called their (Aleph-Tav) name Adam, in the day when they were created."*

Genesis 5 is a listing, or a roster if you prefer, of the pre-flood Firstborns. Not all reigned over *'erets* as Melchizedek. Based on how we interpret Genesis 5 and the Apocrypha, at least seven Firstborns served before the flood as Melchizedek. The Apostle Peter suggested there were eight pre-flood Firstborns. However, he adds Noah to the list.

> Genesis 5:3-5, *"And Adam lived a hundred and thirty years, and begat a son in his own likeness, after his image; and called his name (Aleph-Tav) Seth, and the days of Adam after he had begotten (Aleph-Tav) Seth were eight hundred years: and he begat sons and daughters, and all the days that Adam lived were nine hundred and thirty years: and he died."*

Previously I indicated that Adam was created, as the celestials are, gender non-specific. That understanding is implicit because he was made as one flesh, man and woman.

At the age of 130, Adam begot another *Aleph-Tav*. Certainly, Seth was not "the" first of his generation. Yet, he is listed as the Firstborn because he was the only one appointed and anointed to serve in his father's stead. And, of course, Seth was also subjugated to the spirit of death.

> Genesis 5:6-8, *"And Seth lived a hundred and five years and begat (Aleph-Tav) Enos, and Seth lived after he begat (Aleph-Tav) Enos eight hundred and seven years, and begat sons and daughters, and all the days of Seth were nine hundred and twelve years: and he died,"*

> Genesis 5:9-11, *"And Enosh lived ninety years and begat (Aleph-Tav) Cainan, and Enosh lived after he begat (Aleph-Tav) Cainan eight hundred and fifteen years and begat sons and daughters and all the days of Enos were nine hundred and five years: and he died."*

> Genesis 5:12-14, *"And Cainan lived seventy years and begat (Aleph-Tav) Mahalal'el, and Cainan lived after he begat (Aleph-Tav) Mahalal'el eight hundred and forty years, and begat sons and daughters, and all the days of Cainan were nine hundred and ten years: and he died."*

"And Cainan grew up and at forty years of age became wise; knowledgeable, and skilled with wisdom, and he reigned over all the sons of men, and he led the sons of men to wisdom and knowledge, for Cainan was a very wise man having understanding in all wisdom, and with his wisdom, he ruled over spirits and demons; and Cainan knew by his wisdom that God would destroy the sons of men for having sinned upon the earth and that the Lord would in the latter days bring upon them the waters of the flood. And in those days, Cainan wrote upon tablets of stone, what was to take place in time to come, and he put them in his treasures. And Cainan reigned over the whole earth, and he turned some of the sons of men to the service of God."[65]

> Genesis 5:15-17, *"And Mahalal'el lived sixty and five years and begat (Aleph-Tav) Jared, and Mahalal'el lived after he begat (Aleph-Tav) Jared eight hundred and thirty years and begat sons and daughters, and all the days of Mahalal'el were eight hundred ninety and five years: and he died."*
>
> Genesis 5:18-20, *"And Jared lived a hundred sixty and two years, and he begat (Aleph-Tav) Enoch, and Jared lived after he begat (Aleph-Tav) Enoch eight hundred years, and begat sons and daughters, and all the days of Jared were nine hundred sixty and two years: and he died."*
>
> Genesis 5:21-24, *"And Enoch lived sixty and five years and begat (Aleph-Tav) Methuselah, and Enoch walked with (Aleph-Tav) Elohiym after he begat (Aleph-Tav) Methuselah three hundred years, and begat sons and daughters, and all the days of Enoch were three hundred sixty and five years, and Enoch walked with (Aleph-Tav) Elohiym: and he was not; for Elohiym took him."*

Hebrew 11:5-6, *"By faith Enoch was taken from this life so that he did not experience death; he could not be found, because God had taken him away. For before he was taken, he was commended as one who pleased God. And without faith, it is impossible to please God because anyone who comes to him must believe that he exists and that he rewards those who earnestly seek him."*

"And all the days that Enoch lived upon earth were three hundred and sixty-five years. And when Enoch had ascended into heaven, all the kings of the earth rose and took Methuselah, his son, and anointed him, and they caused him to reign over them in the place of his father. And Methuselah acted uprightly in the sight of God, as his father Enoch had taught him, and he likewise, during the whole of his life, taught the sons of men wisdom, knowledge, and the fear of God, and he did not turn from the good, either to the right or to the left. But in the latter days of Methuselah, the sons of men turned from the Lord, they corrupted the earth, they robbed and plundered each other, and they rebelled against God, and they transgressed, and they corrupted their ways, and would not hearken to the voice of Methuselah, but rebelled against him."[66]

> Genesis 5:25-27, *"And Methuselah lived a hundred eighty and seven years and begat (Aleph-Tav) Lamech, and Methuselah lived after he begat (Aleph-Tav) Lamech seven hundred eighty and two years, and begat sons and daughters and all the days of Methuselah were nine hundred sixty and nine years: and he died."*
>
> Genesis 5:28-31, *"And Lamech lived a hundred eighty and two years and begat a son, and he called his (Aleph-Tav) name Noah, saying, 'This same shall comfort us concerning our work and toil of our hands, because of the ground which the Lord hath cursed.' Lamech lived after he begat (Aleph-Tav)*

---

[65] Johnson, Ken. *Ancient Book of Jasher* (p. 9) Kindle Edition. Chapter 2:11-14
[66] Ibid, Chapter 4:1-4

Noah five hundred ninety and five years, and begat sons and daughters and all the days of Lamech were seven hundred seventy and seven years: and he died."

Lamech preceded his father in death by five years. Lamech never served as Melchizedek Regent. However, he was the Firstborn of his generation. King Methuselah died five days before the great flood. The birth of Noah, the 10th Firstborn, signaled the completion of a cycle, the culmination of an era of time.

Firstborns		Kings/High Priests
Abel	1	Adam
Seth	2	Seth
Enosh	3	Enosh
Cainan	4	Cainan
Mahalal'el	5	Mahalal'el
Jared	6	Jared
Enoch	7	Methuselah
Methuselah	8	Noah
Lamech	9	
Noah	10	

Ten generations from Adam to Noah, ten Firstborns but eight Melchizedeks. By removing Enoch and Lamech from the count, there were eight who served as regents. 2 Peter 2:4-5, *"For if God spared not the angels that sinned, but cast them down to hell, and delivered them into chains of darkness, to be reserved unto judgment; and spared not the old world, but saved Noah* **the eighth person, a preacher of righteousness,** *bringing in the flood upon the world of the ungodly...."* (Emphasis added). Peter did not indicate that Noah and seven others were on the ark. In fact, the ark is not mentioned or implied in these verses. Peter declared that Noah, as the eighth messenger of righteousness, preached righteousness. Thus, he was the "eighth" Melchizedek Regent, which was the point of Peter's reasoning, why God spared Noah from judgment. The word Peter employed to describe Noah as a "preacher" is *kerux* [Greek] and is defined by Strong's NT#2783 as one who heralds a truth. A herald announces or proclaims something. What did Noah reveal? That a divine judgment was pending against earth. If the people did not return to Yahweh's system of righteousness, they would be destroyed. Noah's message was not new. All the kings who served as Melchizedek before Noah knew an impending judgment was against *'erets*. They all proclaimed as much. Even Adam. In fact, they had a duty to do so.

§7 [1.7] of Josephus: "They also were the inventors of that peculiar sort of wisdom which is concerned with the heavenly bodies, and their order. And that their inventions might not be lost before they were sufficiently known, upon Adam's prediction that the world was to be destroyed at one time by the force of fire and at another time by the violence and quantity of water, they made two pillars, the one of brick, the other of stone: they inscribed their discoveries on them both, that in case the pillar of brick should be destroyed by the flood, the pillar of stone might remain, and exhibit those discoveries to mankind, and also inform them that there was another pillar of brick erected by them. This remains in the land of Siriad (Egypt) to this day. [67]

King-Father	Firstborn-Son	Age at Son's Birth	Years Lived	A.M Date of Birth	A.M. Date of Death
Adam	Seth	130	930	0	930
Seth	Enosh	105	912	130	1042
Enosh	Cainan	90	905	235	1140
Cainan	Mahalal'el	70	910	325	1235
Mahalal'el	Jared	65	805	395	1290
Jared	Enoch	162	962	460	1422
Enoch	Methuselah	65	-	622	987
Methuselah	Lamech	180	969	687	1656
Lamech	Noah	182	777	874	1651
Noah	Shem	500	950	1056	2006

- Adam means – man
- Seth means – substitute
- Enosh means – mortal
- Cainan means – possession
- Mahalal'el means – praised of God
- Jared means – to descend
- Methuselah means – to extend the attack
- Noah means – rest and comfort

Genesis 5:32, *"And Noah was five hundred years old: and Noah begat (Aleph-Tav) Shem, (Aleph-Tav) Ham, and (Aleph-Tav) Japheth."*

---

[67] Josephus: *Antiquities of the Jews*, PC Study Bible formatted electronic database Copyright © 2006 Biblesoft, Inc. All rights reserved.

DAY TWO

Genesis Six

> Genesis 6:1-2, *"Now **it came to pass when men began to multiply** on the face of the earth, and **daughters were born to them**, that the **sons of God saw the daughters of men**, that they were **beautiful**, and they **took** wives for themselves of **all whom they chose**"* (emphasis added).

"What came to pass?" is the question I asked when I first read verse one. My eyes kept going back to that little word, "it." Curious, I reached for my Interlinear Bible and immediately noted that *"Now it came to pass"* was one word, not five. The first word of Genesis 6:1 is *hayah*. *Hayah* is defined by Strong's OT #1961 as something existing because time had passed. The question then became, was Moses saying that "time passed" or that something or another occurred as time passed? If the latter was his intent, what was the "it"?

Looking closer, I further realized the spelling of *hayah* began with a *vav*, not a *hei*. If you recall, this was also the case with Genesis 1:1; the *vav* in that verse connected heaven and earth. So, knowing that a *vav* may function much like an "and," combining two things into one, I realized Moses joined the ending thought of Chapter 5 with the first sentence of 6.

Grabbing a pencil, I rewrote the verses. The result: Noah was five hundred years old when he became the father of Shem, Ham, and Japheth AND, when men began to increase in number on the earth, and daughters were born to them, (when) the sons of God saw that the daughters of men were (good), and they took any of them they chose.

Two things sprang to mind. 1) Moses provided a timeline, and 2) Luke 17:26, *"As it was in the days of Noah, so it will also be in the days of the Son of Man."*

> Genesis 6:3, *"And Yahweh said, 'My Spirit shall not **strive with man** forever, for **he is indeed flesh**; yet **his days shall be one hundred and twenty years.'** There were **giants on the earth in those days, and afterward, when the sons of God came into the daughters of men**, and they **bore children** to them. Those were the **mighty men who were of old, men of renown**. Then Yahweh saw that **the wickedness of man was great in the earth** and that every **intent of the thoughts of his heart was only evil continually**. And Yahweh was **sorry that He had made man on the earth**, and He was grieved in His heart. So, Yahweh said, 'I will destroy man whom I have created from the face of the earth, both man and beast, creeping thing and birds of the air, for I am sorry that I have made them.' But **Noah found grace** in the eyes of Yahweh"* (emphasis added).

Understanding Genesis 6 is crucial. One must comprehend this chapter to grasp the remaining Scripture, not just Genesis, but the entire Bible. Therefore, to unpack this chapter, we shall do so bit by bit and even reiterate things previously presented to layer our understanding.

Moses did not provide his readers with the minutia concerning the "sons of God." That is to say, he did not explicitly state who they were. Neither did he outline what these "sons" did, but clearly, Yahweh was not pleased. From extra-canonical writings, we discover Yahweh did not spontaneously declare He was weary with "man" and then bring a flood. He, in fact, had informed Adam hundreds of years before that there would be a "judgment" that would come by water.

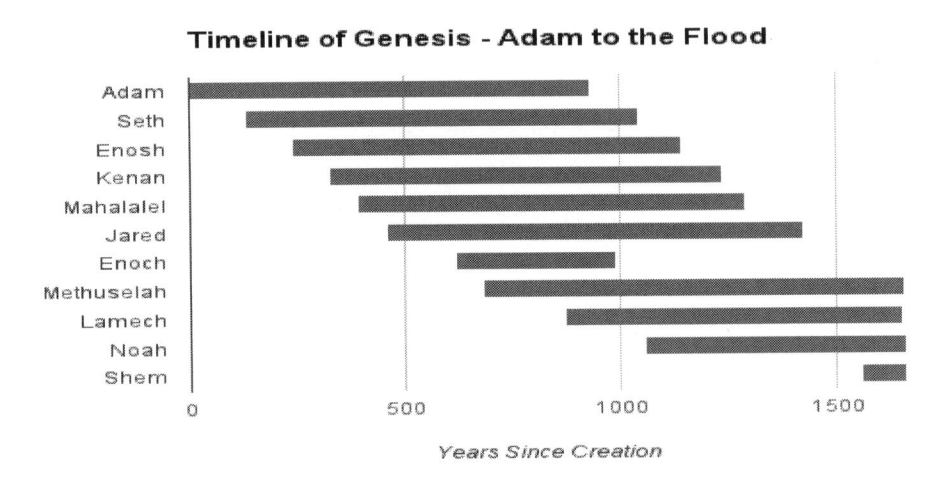

Timeline of Genesis - Adam to the Flood

Years Since Creation

As Moses transitioned from Adam to the flood, Noah became his focus. Noah is introduced in Genesis 5:29. But Moses ignores him until he is five hundred years old, and his sons are born to him. Still, he connects Noah's day with the "sons of God" who took women as wives.

So, let's go back to Genesis 5. "***This is the book of the genealogy of Adam.*** *In the day that God created man,* ***He made him in the likeness of God. He created them male and female and blessed them, and*** *called them Mankind in the day they were created. And Adam lived one hundred and thirty years, and* ***begot a son in his own likeness, after his image…,***" Genesis 5:1-3 (emphasis added).

Adam was created in the likeness of God. However, his descendants: Seth, Enosh, Cainan, Mahalalel, Jared, Enoch, Methuselah, Lamech, and Noah, were not. They were like Adam in many ways, but Adam was unique. There has never been another as he; he was one of a kind.[68] So, his sons were "pro-created" as "his" kind, but they were different in that they did not represent Yahweh; they characterized Adam.

Genesis 5 does not list every child of Adam. It lists only those considered "Adam's" sons, who served as the Firstborns; the pre-flood *ekklēsía*.[69] There were nine Firstborns. That is if we do not count Adam as a Firstborn. There was one for each generation. And I remind you that a Firstborn was selected because he met specific requirements. To choose a Firstborn, the Melchizedek (usually the son's father, but certainly a direct progenitor) started with the son born first. However, a second son became eligible for consideration if

---

68 *Mono* = only + *genes* = race
69 Hebrews 12:23, "…*to the general assembly and church of the firstborn who are registered in heaven, to God the Judge of all…*,"

the first son had blood on his hands or failed to attend to his father's business in an exemplary and cautious manner. If the second son did not please his father, the appointment fell to the third son. And so on and so forth. Until, at last, a son was found who was right by being righteous. The selected son was appointed and taken to the altar, where he was placed before Yahweh. Once Yahweh accepted the appointed son, he was anointed. In a public forum, the appointee was then ceremonially presented as the next anointed priest of the Melchizedek Priesthood, the Firstborn of his generation.

All Firstborns could prove their lineage, that they held a direct descent from Adam. This proof was vital for it attested that the Firstborn had a "birthright" to the succession of the Melchizedek's[70] scepter as a regent. That he qualified to rule *'erets* and establish righteousness.

Let's be clear: There are only two superior non-appointed thrones in the cosmos – Yahweh's and Yeshua's. That is it! All other thrones are appointed as secondary thrones, or they are illegal pretenders. The connection to Adam was crucial because Adam was a son of God. So, records were kept of origin to provide a direct link to Adam. While every human born can claim they descended from Adam, not every human can lay claim to the line of succession to the throne on which Adam sat. Firstborn sons were tested, and their "righteousness" was determined.

We must remember that Adam was appointed as the regent for the Eternal Melchizedek. Only he or one who came from him could legally continue the regency. Therefore, all who followed him to sit on the throne in *'erets* were placeholders in his image. So, Genesis 5 is the line of succession from Adam to Noah for that position.

Moses ended the roster of Genesis 5 with Noah **and** his three sons. The Firstborn of Noah's sons had yet to be established. That Firstborn would not be confirmed until after the flood. Moses, of course, knew which of the three would ultimately be chosen. He deliberately withheld that information until later. Moses instead transitioned from Genesis 5 to 6 with – *"and it came to pass."*

As we studied previously, Adam did not leave Eden; he lost access to the Garden. From Adam to Lamech (Noah's father), each generation anticipated the coming of the Promised One. However, they knew his arrival was not imminent. Yet, they hoped since it was expected of him to restore mankind to the Garden of Yah. And during that same time, Day One, *'erets* grew divided. Another kingdom entered the field and began spreading seeds of darkness. This rival kingdom sought out the living souls of mankind, drawing them away from Yahweh.

Evil intensified. The "gods" who perverted the purpose of humanity seemingly had free reign. So much so, they thought of this era as "Golden," for they were convinced they had gained control of *'erets*. But that wasn't the case.

---

[70] The people of the pre-flood era did not call their king Melchizedek, or their kingdom, the Melchizedek Kingdom. This terminology is used here in to delineate the righteous.

*Yahweh saw that **the wickedness of man was great in the earth** and that every **intent of the thoughts of his heart was only evil continually**. So, Yahweh said, "**I will destroy** man whom I have created from the face of the earth, both man and beast, creeping thing and birds of the air, **for I am sorry that I have made them**."*

Yahweh's decree of judgment was not against the righteous but directed toward the evil. To grasp my meaning, think back to Genesis 1, when the Creator implemented His plan. Six days – six steps, each day representing an era of 1,000 years. It was planned from the beginning of time, 6,000 years, then the Eternal Melchizedek shall be seated on his throne forever.

- א – *Aleph* - Day One - light; the kingdom is revealed
- ב – *Bet* - Day Two - Holy Spirit begins His work
- ג – *Gimel* - Day Three - the soil receives the King's seed
- ד – *Dalet* - Day Four - the doorway into the kingdom opened, and the bride announced
- ה – *Hei* - Day Five - the hosts of heaven are assembled and made ready for war
- ו – *Vav* - Day Six – the Melchizedek Kingdom is positioned

During Day One, God began revealing the plan, yet not everything was exposed - not entirely. Adam functioned in his position with partial revelation. He knew a Divine natured Promised Seed would restore the glory of the Melchizedek Kingdom, but I doubt he knew when. Yet the Regent knew there would be a Day Two, and that "day" would begin a new work. He, however, did not witness the new day nor the workings of the Holy Spirit in a new way.

Chapter 4, Jubilees 4:29 – 30, "[930 A.M.] thereof, Adam died, and all his sons buried him in the land of his creation, and he was the first to be buried in the earth. And he lacked seventy years of one thousand years; for one thousand years are as one day in the testimony of the heavens…."[71]

Adam was not the first person to be buried but the first Melchizedek Regent to die. Additionally, he was not the only regent during those first one thousand years. Seth also served in that position. After Seth, his son, Enosh. Genesis 4:26, "*And as for Seth, to him also a son was born; and he named him Enosh.* **Then men began to call on the name of the Lord**" (emphasis added).

Once again, the key to unlocking understanding is in the Hebrew spelling and phrasing. The spelling of "to call" places a *lamed* at the beginning of the word "*qara,*" which nuances an understanding that men began to "goad" Yahweh. They provoked Him with the misuse of His name.

"In that time, the sons of men began to multiply and to afflict their souls and hearts by transgressing and rebelling against God. And it was in the days of Enosh that the sons of men continued to rebel and transgress against God, to increase the anger of the Lord against the sons of men. And the sons of men went, and they served other gods, and they forgot the Lord who had created them in the earth, and in those days, the sons of men made images of brass and iron, wood, and stone, and they bowed down and served them. And every man made his god, and they bowed down

---

[71] *Old Testament Pseudepigrapha: Book of Jubilees*, PC Study Bible formatted electronic database © 2007 by Biblesoft, Inc. All rights reserved

to them, and the sons of men forsook the Lord all the days of Enosh and his children, and the anger of the Lord was kindled on account of their works and abominations which they did in the earth."[72]

Enosh was born 235 A.M. (*Anno Mundi*, which means "in the year of the world). So, these gods who began appearing in Enosh's day were not the Watchers of Genesis 6:4. If they were, they had yet to make their unholy pact on Mount Hermon. So, who were they, and where did they come from? Obviously, they came from the unseen realms. And that they encouraged or even allowed men to replicate their image means they were blasphemous.

Genesis 1 portrays destruction (chaos) and death as extant before Adam sinned. That means there are at least two "chief" spirits (gods) that qualify as a candidate for the Isaiah 14 and Ezekiel 28 "god." I hold these two are Chaos (Zeus) and Death (Thanatos).[73] So, perhaps they set up their own cosmic mountain north of Eden. And from their own high place, they proclaimed they were the Creator's replacement. Of course, they also claimed to be the benefactors of mankind. And because they believed, men forgot Yahweh, who created them. The notion that Yahweh ceased to exist was the great lie (deception) of Day One, which was told then and continues today.

It was taught that created humans can become gods. They can do so by tapping into the residue of the Creator's "spirit." Additionally, the gods proclaimed Yahweh was weakened by the process of creating. They reasoned it was because He put too much of Himself into Adam.[74] And if we dig deep into Greek mythology, we find this same notion is repeated repetitiously. But not only did the Greeks believe this so did the Romans. In other words, the pagan world accepted the idea that gods and humans were of the same "kind."

All ancient cultures had their creation stories. And in those stories is an element of truth. Created gods transgressed into Yahweh's *'erets* and attempted to prevent His rule. That is chaos!

Accordingly, to these pagan teachings, it all began with chaos. In the beginning, Chaos existed, and he gave birth to (created) Nyx (the goddess of night). Her siblings were Gaia (Mother Earth), Tartarus (the god of the netherworld), and Erebus (the god of darkness). By Erebus, she brought forth Hypnos (sleep), Thanatos (death), Aether (goddess of the upper sky), and Hemera (the god of the day). Gaia became the mother of Pontus (god of the sea) without a consort.

Following Enosh, the next global king was Cainan. "And Cainan grew up, and he was forty years old, and he became wise and had knowledge and skill in all wisdom, and he reigned over all the sons of men, and he led the sons of men to wisdom and knowledge; for Cainan was a very wise man and had understanding in all wisdom, … And Cainan reigned over the whole earth, and he turned some of the sons of men to the service of God."[75]

The righteousness of that generation was short-lived. Mankind began transgressing again during the time of

---

[72] Johnson, Ken. *Ancient Book of Jasher* (pp. 8-9), Kindle Edition (Author's emphasis added).
[73] I have presented their Greek names because these monikers are the most familiar.
[74] This is known as the Doctrine of Emanations.
[75] Johnson, Ken. *Ancient Book of Jasher* 2:11-14

Mahalalel (the son of Cainan), "men caused their wives to drink a draught that would render them barren, so that they might retain their figures and whereby their beautiful appearance might not fade."[76]

However, that was not all they began to do. People began to venerate the dead. Idols were made of ancestors who had passed. It was believed that worshipping ancestors 1) made them "happy." Happy ancestors made life effortless in the here and now. And 2) happy ancestors made the progression into immortality easier. One example of ancestor veneration from the post-flood era is the reverence they falsely placed upon Eve.

"Various scholars have concluded from these that **a goddess lies behind Eve**. Thus, the **Sumerian divine name nin. ti, 'Lady of Life,'** which is structurally similar to the etiology for Eve and is itself ambiguous in meaning, also having the sense '**Lady of the Rib**,' is cited by Gaster. Kikawada draws attention to the **Akkadian formula bēlet kala ili, 'Mistress of all the gods,'** applied to the goddess Mami, suggesting that Mami underlies Eve. She is, however, supposedly demythologized. We may also add, from a nearer cultural milieu, the epithets of Ugaritic Athirat (→Asherah), *qnyt ilm* ('Progenitrix of the gods'), and *um il[m]*, ('mother of the gods.' A goddess named *Ḥwt* appears in a votive stela from the Carthaginian necropolis, beginning with the invocation *rbt ḥwt 'lt mlkt...*: 'Great Lady, Havvat, Goddess, Queen(?)!' Hrozny proposed that *ḥwt* is related to the Hurrian divine name →Hebat. She was the consort of Teshub, the Hurrian storm god.[77]

Essentially, the gods began to take on the persona of the dead to deceive the living and gain control of *'erets*.

Mahalalel fathered a son, [461 A.M.] "and he called his name Jared, **for in his days the angels of the Lord descended on the earth, those who are named the Watchers, that they should instruct the children of men,** and that they should do judgment and uprightness on the earth."[78]

"And it came to pass when the children of men had multiplied that in those days, born unto them were beautiful and comely daughters. And the angels, the children of the heaven, saw and lusted after them, and said to one another: 'Come, let us choose us wives from among the children of men and beget us, children.'"[79]

> Genesis 6:2, "... *the sons of God saw the daughters of men, that they were beautiful; and they took wives for themselves of all whom they chose.... There were giants in the earth* **in those days; and, after** *that,* **when the sons of God** *came in unto the daughters of men, and they bore children to them, the same became mighty men which were of old, men of renown,*" Genesis 6:4 (emphasis added).

Jude wrote that *"the* **angels who did not keep their proper domain** *but* **left their own abode,** *He has reserved in everlasting chains under darkness for the judgment of the great day...."* (emphasis added).

---

[76] Ibid, Chapter 2:20
[77] Wyatt, N. (1999). Eve. In K. van der Toorn, B. Becking, & P. W. van der Horst (Eds.), *Dictionary of deities and demons in the Bible* (2nd extensively rev. ed., pp. 316–317). Leiden; Boston; Köln; Grand Rapids, MI; Cambridge: Brill; Eerdmans.
[78] Charles, R.H. *The Book of Jubilees* (Kindle Locations 499-500) Kindle Edition (Author's emphasis added).
[79] Enoch. *The Book of Enoch* (p. 4). Kindle Edition.

The Watchers descended on Mount Hermon approximately five hundred years after Adam left the Garden of Eden. So, let's dig deeper by looking back at Genesis 3:5-6 – *"For God knew that in whatever day you eat of it your eyes would be opened, and **you will be as gods, knowing good and evil**"* (emphasis added).[80]

Evil was translated from *"ra."* Strong's OT#7451 defines *"ra"* as evil, adversity, wickedness, et cetera. It comes from a root that means to spoil by making a thing harmful. If information is corrupted, it is harmful. Adam and Eve became like the *elohim*, able to harm themselves and one another. Of course, that "knowledge" was passed to the next generation. So, the knowledge that came "with" the eating of the forbidden fruit confused the purpose of mankind. After Adam ate, mankind's relationship with Yahweh was damaged.

Even so, Yahweh is without rival, no matter the domain. However, he has adversaries, predominantly those who seek to keep Yeshua from being installed as the Eternal Melchizedek. So, the tactic taken by the fallen gods in their "war" against righteousness was to deceive mankind, so humans would transgress of their own volition. Proverbs 29:18, *"Where there is no **prophetic vision** (the ability to see or discern), **the people cast off restraint** (the people run wild); but happy is he who keeps the law."* Basically, where there is no revelation, there is chaos.

Those who brought evil were gods. They worked against Yahweh by working against mankind. Essentially, we could rightfully say it was the *elohim* who brought evil. Genesis 3:4-5, *"And the serpent said to the woman, Ye shall not surely die. For God knew that in whatever day ye should eat of it your eyes would be opened, **and ye would be as gods, knowing good and evil**"* (emphasis added Greek-English Septuagint: Brenton Edition).

We could go further and say that the evil of the adversarial *elohim* was based on two elemental desires. 1) They wanted an abode other than the one assigned to them. 2) They must keep the Eternal Melchizedek from taking possession of his throne. When he does, it is all over!

They knew then, as they do now, that their time was limited and that their six days run concurrently with the timing of the Eternal Melchizedek's inheritance.

Corresponding with Adam leaving the Garden, the gods abandoned their habitation in the netherworld and began building cosmic mountains. But not just the fallen realm, we also note that the Watchers of Mount Hermon also wanted to leave their habitation. Those 200 Watchers were from the upper region (heaven). So, the *"elohim"* of heaven and those of *Sheol* went from their abodes to construct cosmic mountains.

Why? Simply put, they wanted *'erets*. In other words, they wanted access to the domain assigned to mankind for their self-aggrandizing purposes. Their cosmic mountains provided doors or portals that accessed the physical "dimensions." But what if their real goal was to take control of the physical *'erets*? To do so, wouldn't they need to modify humanity for that purpose? Keep that thought in mind.

---

80 Greek-English Septuagint: Brenton Edition. Biblesoft Formatted Electronic Database. Copyright © 2020 by Biblesoft, Inc. All rights reserved.

While Adam preached righteousness in Eden, proclaiming that Yahweh would send a Promised Seed, Cain, and his sons, built cities on the other side of the river. "And at that time, Cain went out from the presence of the Lord, from the place where he was, and he went moving and wandering in the land toward the east of Eden."[81] The meaningful phrase is "Cain went out from the presence of Yahweh." *"And he built a city, and he named the city after the name of his son, Enoch"* Genesis 4:17.[82]

It is speculated that this city of Genesis 4:17 was not named after Cain's son but his grandson, Irad. If that is the case, the city was Eridu. Eridu was an antediluvian city and is considered by some to be the first city in the world.[83] It presumably was built by the great Sumerian god Enki before the flood.[84] And supposedly, the Tower of Babel, post-flood, was constructed in Eridu.

Humanity, at that time, was not plowing fields to barely make a living, cooking in gourds over open fires, or sleeping in mud huts. They were building a civilization, a sophisticated culture. In fact, that "age" was the Golden Age of interaction between humans and the gods. If Atlantis was real, then this was the era it existed.

Adam was created without flaws. The range of his knowledge must have been incredible. He knew how to access the spirit realm while he lived in the physical. Adam conversed with the Creator. I feel sure he understood the laws of physics, mathematics, aerodynamics, and much more. Probably, Adam was telepathic and could levitate large objects. These things he would have passed on to Cain, Abel, and Seth. That gave them the needed capabilities to build cities with edifices that are, to this day, a mystery.

Among the Dead Sea Scrolls are fragments that refer to the capital of the whole earth, a pre-flood city named Salem. Salem's leading citizen was the King of kings (Melchizedek).

"Fragment 1, Column 2, seems to teach that the capital pre-flood city would be rebuilt afterward and be the center for God's glory again. It was first called Salem, but then was later renamed Jerusalem."[85]

"Fragment 2 (of the Dead Sea Scrolls) seems to be stating there were angels … that fought for control. God judges each situation, punishing some and forgiving others. Fragments 3-5 are too small to really understand the complete context. They seem to indicate that God is in control and has decreed certain ages where certain powers rule, but ultimately God is always in control, and evil will be judged on the Day of Judgment. There is also a mention of the *Moedim*, the appointed times."[86]

Much of what I am presenting to you is known by academia. But it is not taught. To do so would be equivalent to saying evolution is bunk.

---

[81] Johnson, Ken. *Ancient Book of Jasher* (p. 8) Kindle Edition.
[82] Greek-English Septuagint: Brenton Edition. Biblesoft Formatted Electronic Database. Copyright © 2020 by Biblesoft, Inc. All rights reserved.
[83] I hold that Salem was the first city built but since I want to build support for my case, I withhold any explanation.
[84] https://www.worldhistory.org/eridu retrieved October 5, 2021
[85] Johnson, Ken. *Ancient Testaments of the Patriarchs: Autobiographies from the Dead Sea Scrolls* (pp. 12-13). Kindle Edition.
[86] Ibid (p. 13). Kindle Edition.

Adam and Eve would have told their children about the *elohim* and their experiences with them. So, when the *elohim* manifested, none thought it strange. But then, *"it came to pass...the sons of God saw the daughters of men...and they took ...for themselves of all whom they chose."*

Initially, the Watchers came to give mankind "instructions" but, at some point, said, "Come, let us choose wives from among the children of men and beget children." And their leader, Semyaza, said to them, "I am afraid that you will not truly agree to do this deed, and I alone will have to pay the penalty of this great sin." They all answered him, saying, "We should all swear to bind ourselves by a mutual oath not to abandon this plan but to do this thing." So, altogether, they bound themselves by an oath. There were two hundred, total, that descended in the days of Jared upon Ardis, the summit of Mount Hermon. They called it Mount Hermon because they had sworn and bound themselves by oath upon it.... These leaders led the rest of the two hundred angels.[87]

Louis Ginzberg, *Legend of the Jews*: "The depravity of mankind, which began to show itself in the time of Enosh, had increased monstrously in the time of his grandson Jared, by reason of the fallen angels. When the angels saw the beautiful, attractive daughters of men, they lusted after them and spoke: 'We will choose wives for ourselves only from among the daughters of men and beget children with them.' Their chief Semjaza said, 'I fear me, ye will not put this plan of yours into execution, and I alone shall have to suffer the consequences of a great sin.' Then they answered him and said: 'We will all swear an oath, and we will bind ourselves, separately and together, not to abandon the plan, but to carry it through to the end.' Two hundred angels descended to the summit of Mount Hermon, which owes its name to this very occurrence because they bound themselves there to fulfill their purpose...."[88]

Jasher 1422 AM – Jared died. "And Jared the son of Mahalalel died in those days, in the three hundred and thirty-sixth [336] year of the life of Noah; and all the days of Jared were nine hundred and sixty-two years, and he died. And **all who followed the Lord died in those days before they saw the evil which God declared** to do upon earth."[89]

The Septuagint: Brenton Edition, translation of Genesis 6:4 is *"Now the giants were upon the earth in those days; and after that when the sons of God were wont to go in to the daughters of men, they bore children to them, those were the giants of old, the men of renown."*

The sons of God, the *bene elohim,* produced the *gibboriym*. Strong's OT#1368 *gibbowr* [ghib-bore'] or (the shortened version) *gibbor*, which means the powerful and, by implication, warriors, tyrants. Yet, there was more going on than what seemingly is inferred. Perhaps because the ancients of human society did not know DNA existed, they could not fully express what was happening. Yet, the *elohim* did, make no mistake about that. They were not waiting for the twentieth century A.D. and for Watson and Crick.

Genesis 3:15, *"I will put enmity between you and the woman, and between your seed and her Seed."* Seed is *zera*, which means posterity. Yahweh was obviously saying that the *nachash* would have offspring. The progeny of the *nachash* is anti-Messiah. At this time, I shall not develop that concept further except to say the full extent of these words were understood by the serpent; he realized that he would produce a "son."

---

[87] Johnson, Ken. *Ancient Book of Enoch* (pp. 18-19. Kindle Edition
[88] Ginzberg, Louis. *The Legends of the Jews — Volume 1* (Kindle Locations 1443-1449) Kindle Edition.
[89] Johnson, Ken. *Ancient Book of Jasher* (p. 13). Kindle Edition (emphasis added by author).

So, when the Watchers descended on Mount Hermon, were they looking to produce "sons" by procreation? Or something more, and procreation was merely a means to an end? Genesis 6:4 in the KJV, *"and they bare children to them, the **same** became mighty men...."* The offspring were the "same" (*hem*). *Hem* is often translated as "like."

The *bene elohim* desired for beings "like" themselves, in their "own" image, and sought out the daughters of men for that purpose. They believed human women could provide them with offspring "like" themselves. This is what Genesis 6:2 means when it states the daughters of men were "beautiful." The daughters of men were "*towb*." *Towb* means good, or to make good. Whether *towb* is used as a noun or an adjective depends on context. In my opinion, Genesis 6:2 should read: The daughters of *adam* made good the purpose of the *bene elohim*.

We should not place "human" emotion or innate desire onto those of the *elohim*. Insisting that these "sons of God" committed these sins because their primary desire was sexual or that they loved the women is misleading. The Watchers strategized. They knew what they planned was a sin. They considered the cost and even debated it. Yet, I think their desire to have their own dominion was more potent than their need to remain faithful to the Creator.

Each of the two hundred chose a wife for himself, and they began to go in unto them and to mate with them, and they taught them sorcery and enchantments, and the cutting of roots, and made them acquainted with plants. These women became pregnant and gave birth to great giants, whose height reached up to three thousand ells. These giants consumed all the food, and when men could no longer sustain them, the giants turned against them and devoured mankind. They also began to sin against birds, beasts, reptiles, and fish, and devour one another's flesh, and drink the blood. Then the earth laid accusations against the lawless ones.[90]

Bottom-line, the Watchers were experimenting with human, animal, and even plant DNA. They '*bow*' (came and went), taking or *laqach* (carrying away what they seized), those who they *bachar* (found acceptable for their chosen purpose). The women, who were taken, bore giants. The giants were (*'isyh*) – male hybrids. *'Isyh* denotes masculinity. Those whom the women bore were not *adam* (human) males. They were *gibbor* males, like their fathers. They were hybrids with supernatural strength. Therefore, their names (*ha'shem*) were well known and kept alive even after the flood.

Recently, I watched a program where Dr. Thomas Horn suggested, "the Watchers wanted to leave their proper sphere of existence. To enter earth's three-dimensional reality, they viewed women's genetic material as proper or fit for their cause." When I heard this notion, I found it intriguing. Especially since I had realized an extended meaning in Jude's comment, "they left their 'own' abode." I have come to believe the Watchers and their seed modification program exacerbated the activities of the adversarial kingdom to a whole new level.

In that same documentary, Dr. Horn wondered if what the Watchers were doing was searching for the right

---

[90] Johnson, Ken. *Ancient Book of Enoch* (p. 19) Kindle Edition

combination of genetic matter to bring forth "soulless" bodies for themselves to inhabit. Instead, they kept creating beings with souls without regard or respect for life forms. In other words, the Watchers created monsters, flesh-eating gargoyles, and the like. Of course, they also produced the Titans and the Olympian demi-gods.

> Genesis 6:5, *"Then the Lord saw that the wickedness of man was great in the earth and that every intent of the thoughts of his heart was only evil continually."*

Loyalty is best described as a strong feeling of allegiance. Allegiance is a commitment. Loyalty and allegiance in spiritual terms are faithfulness and obedience. *"My Spirit shall not strive* **with man** (*ba'adam* – the species of adam)." Yahweh did not look among the *elohim* for loyalty but among the terrestrials. None among them was righteous, only Noah. The fallen gods had succeeded in turning mankind from righteous thought.

> Genesis 6:6-8, *"And the Lord was sorry that He had made man on the earth, and He was grieved in His heart. So, the Lord said, 'I will destroy man whom I have created from the face of the earth, both man and beast, creeping thing and birds of the air, for I am sorry that I have made them.' But Noah found grace in the eyes of the Lord."*

Luke 20:9-16, *"Then He began to tell the people this parable: 'A certain man planted a vineyard, leased it to* **vinedressers,** *and went into a far country for a long time. Now at vintage-time, he sent a servant to the vinedressers so that they might give him some of the fruit of the vineyard. But the vinedressers beat him and sent him away empty-handed. Again, he sent another servant, and they beat him, treated him shamefully, and sent him away empty-handed. And again, he sent a third, and they wounded him also and cast him out.*

"Then the owner of the vineyard said, 'What shall I do? I will send my beloved son. Probably they will respect him when they see him.' But when the vinedressers saw him, they reasoned among themselves, saying, 'This is the heir. **Come, let us kill him, that the inheritance may be ours.'** *So, they cast him out of the vineyard and killed him. Therefore, what will the owner of the vineyard do to them? He will come and destroy those vinedressers and give the vineyard to others."*

Consider the vinedressers of this parable as *"elohim"* and the servants as the regents appointed to represent the Son. Do you see the parallel? And the motivation of the fallen "vinedressers"? They know they shall be destroyed, yet they continue to deny the owner and kill his son, hoping to change their appointment for destruction.

Upon hearing the decree that all life on the "face of the earth" would be destroyed, the Watchers knew their punishment was imminent. They had anticipated a harsh sentence but not the eradication of their offspring. The Watchers begged their case before Enoch, "Please seek a reprieve for our doomed children."

"The Watchers asked Enoch to petition Yahweh on their behalf because from this point on, they could not speak with Yahweh or lift up their eyes toward heaven, ashamed on account of the shame of their sins for which they were condemned."[91]

Enoch, residing with the *elohim,* granted the Watchers a hearing. He listened to their plea. Then "went off and sat down" to think about what the Watchers had asked of him. Falling asleep, he dreamed. When he woke, he returned to the Watchers. He recounted the dream, saying, "This is the record of the words of righteousness, and the reprimand of the eternal Watchers I was commanded to give by the Holy Great One in that vision. I will now relate what I saw in my dream with my tongue of flesh and the breath of my mouth that you may understand with your whole heart. Just as He created man with the power of understanding the word of wisdom, He has created me and given me the power to reprimand the Watchers, the children of heaven. I wrote out your petition, but in my vision, I saw that your petition will not be granted unto you throughout all the days of eternity. Your judgment is final. The decree is from this point on, you will be bound on earth throughout all the days of the world. You will not be able to reenter heaven. But before you are bound, you will see all your loved ones destroyed. You will not be able to possess them; you will only be able to watch them fall by the sword. Your petition on their behalf, or for yourselves, will not be granted, even though you weep and pray. This I have written."[92]

Enoch continued, "You are immortals, of the spirit world, you had no cause to take wives; to pro-create… you defiled yourselves and the women you lay with. While I dreamed, I heard… giants born from flesh become evil spirits and remain on the earth. Because they were created from above, from the holy Watchers, at death, their spirits will come forth from their bodies and dwell on the earth. They will be called evil spirits. The heavenly spirits will dwell in heaven, but the terrestrial spirits who were born on earth will dwell on earth. The evil spirits of the giants will be like clouds. They will afflict, corrupt, tempt, battle, work destruction on the earth, and do evil; they will not eat nor drink but be invisible. They will rise up against the children of men and against the women because they have proceeded from them. When the giants die, and their spirits leave their bodies, their flesh will decay without judgment. In this way, the race will cease to exist until the great judgment in which the age will be wholly consummated over the Watchers and the godless."[93]

Enoch saw the future and understood that the disembodied Nephilim would become demonic spirits. They would roam "to and fro" over the face of *'erets* seeking to do evil.

"And God looked upon the earth, and behold, it was corrupt; for all flesh had corrupted his way upon the earth," Genesis 6:12.

Why flood the entire earth? "All flesh (*basar* – 'preaches') deception." The purpose of DNA was corrupted. It preached or spoke profanely. Chiefly, no man walked "the way" of Yahweh except Noah. So, let's spend a few moments discussing the importance of walking with Yahweh. In Hebrew, there's a word, *ōběrîm* – a plural form of a verb that means "to pass from one side to the other." This term is often translated as "travel" or "traveler," primarily noting a passing from one existence to another, much like how the ancient

---

[91] Ibid (p. 26) Kindle Edition
[92] Ibid (pp. 27-28) Kindle Edition
[93] Johnson, Ken. *Ancient Book of Enoch* (p. 31) Kindle Edition

Greeks viewed the dead traveling across the River Styx to reach or return from the underworld.[94]

In a broad sense, Enoch was a Traveler. He walked with the *elohim* from one plane of existence into another. "Enoch walked with God after having begotten Methuselah, and he served the Lord and despised the evil ways of men. And the soul of Enoch was wrapped up in the instruction of the Lord, knowledge, and understanding; and he wisely retired from the sons of men and secreted himself."[95]

"And he (Enoch) was taken from amongst the children of men... into the Garden of Eden[96] in majesty and honor, and behold there he wrote down the condemnation and judgment of the world and all the wickedness of the children of men."[97]

Genesis 5:18, *"Jared lived a hundred sixty and two years, and begat Enoch..."* and Enoch *"walked with God."* This was not said of any other Firstborn. So, why Enoch? If we look at the Hebrew text, we find Moses used two different words, both translated into English as "walked." Although the first empowered the second. *Yalak* (verse 22) infers a process of "to come, to go." *Halak* (verse 24) is analogous *to yalak* but is expanded in meaning suggesting that walking brings advancement toward a chosen goal. In other words, *halak* is achieved when one repeats the behavior of *yalak* – of coming and going. Enoch walked with the *elohim* – he came and went with them. Doing so repeatedly.

Enoch was not a time traveler. He was not returned in time to the Garden of Eden when Adam lived there. Instead, he was taken into heaven, to the Garden of Eden and the temple there. Genesis 5:24 *"Enoch walked with God: and he was not for God took him,"* because *"Enoch pleased the Lord, and was translated,* **being an example of repentance to all generations.***"*[98]

Whoa! Enoch was "an example of repentance!" What? Example means "an illustration of." Enoch "illustrated" repentance. He was translated to exemplify repentance for "all generations."

'*Erets* had to be kept safe since it is the designated field for Yah's harvest. That harvest is the Son of God's inheritance. If you recall, one of the primary functions of a Melchizedek was to officiate at Yahweh's altar as the high priest. Enoch was translated (made interdimensional) to function as a high priest, to seek Yahweh's approval for *'erets*, in the cosmic mountain of the Garden, for all generations. That is until the Eternal Melchizedek is seated and receives his inheritance.

Annually, Yahweh declared *'erets* righteous, to keep it sacred, and from being claimed by the adversary as abandon. That meant the serving regent, in *'erets*, witnessed (assured) the necessary protocols were obeyed. But his word alone was not sufficient. As the high priest, officiating as the Adonizedek of *'erets,* he placed blood (the blood of an animal) upon an altar dedicated to Yahweh. The blood was applied first for himself

---

[94] Gilbert, Sharon K. *Veneration: Unveiling the Ancient Realms of Demonic Kings and Satan's Battle Plan for Armageddon* (p. 87). Defender. Kindle Edition.
[95] Johnson, Ken. *Ancient Book of Jasher* (p. 10 Kindle Edition.
[96] Enoch was not taken to Adam's day but to the Garden in heaven.
[97] Charles, R.H. *The Book of Jubilees* (Kindle Locations 513-517) Kindle Edition.
[98] Ecclesiasticus 44:16 – also called Sirach.

and then for the people. Yahweh, seated as Judge, saw the blood and immediately reminded the Divine Court that Adam's penalties were paid (in the future) and therefore, *'erets* was righteous.

Eternal Yahweh saw the blood of the Eternal Lamb slain before the foundations of *'erets* were formed. He did not look at the altar and see the blood of animals. Then God would nod and say, "Yes, I see the blood, and Adam redeemed. So, righteousness exists in the Kingdom of Righteousness. Go your way, sin no more!"

And every year, a shout would come from the adversary, "Where is your witness?" Enoch would rise from his seat, the one assigned to him in the Garden temple, and say, "I'm here as a witness for the Melchizedek Kingdom! I proclaim it is righteous also. As a Melchizedek Prophet, I, too, see that atonement has been made." *"And they overcame him by the blood of the Lamb, and by the word of their testimony,"* Revelation 12:11.

Hebrew 11:5, *"By faith Enoch was translated that he should not see death; and was not found, because God had translated him:* **for before his translation he had this testimony, that he pleased God."**

"Pleased" or *euaresteo* [Greek] means to be entirely gratified. In other words, Enoch satisfied all the requirements that deemed him a holy Adonizedek, allowing him to give testimony. Testimony (*martureo* – also Greek) means to bear witness. Enoch gave testimony before the courts of the Divine Council and directly to the throne of Yahweh every year from his translation to the day Yeshua went to the Cross. From that point onward, all of heaven has given witness. There is blood on the altar!

Enoch was taken and remained there, then "all the kings of the earth rose and took Methuselah, his son and anointed him, and they caused him to reign over them in the place of his father. And Methuselah acted uprightly in the sight of God, as his father Enoch had taught him, and he likewise, during the whole of his life, taught the sons of men wisdom, knowledge, and the fear of God, and he did not turn from the good way either to the right or to the left. But in the latter days of Methuselah, the sons of men turned from the Lord, they corrupted the earth, they robbed and plundered each other, and they rebelled against God, and they transgressed, and they corrupted their ways, and would not hearken to the voice of Methuselah, but rebelled against him."[99]

Genesis 6:9 also states that Noah walked with God: *"These are the generations of Noah: Noah was a just man and perfect in his generations, and Noah walked with God."* Noah's walk credited him with righteousness. Meaning that because he walked with the Supreme God, he was without defilement. However, Noah did not *yalak* and *halak*. He did not come and go into the unseen realm - he remained bound to *'erets*.

- Enoch's walk translated him, seating him in the Courts of Heaven.
- Enoch's walk protected him from death.
- Noah's walk deemed him righteous.
- Noah's walk protected him from global judgment.
- Enoch (the dedicated) was translated - Noah (the peaceful) was saved.

Jasher: 1536 AM – God warns of a coming flood. "And after the lapse of many years, in the four hundred and

---

[99] Johnson, Ken. *Ancient Book of Jasher* (p. 12) Kindle Edition.

eightieth year of the life of Noah, when all those men, who followed the Lord had died away from amongst the sons of men, and only Methuselah was then left, God said unto Noah and Methuselah, saying, "Speak ye, and proclaim to the sons of men, saying, 'Thus says the Lord, return from your evil ways and forsake your works, and the Lord will repent of the evil that he declared to do to you so that it shall not come to pass.' For thus says the Lord, 'Behold I give you a period of one hundred and twenty years; if you will turn to me and forsake your evil ways, then will I also turn away from the evil which I told you, and it shall not exist,' says the Lord."[100]

Even after God had resolved upon the destruction of the sinners, He still permitted His mercy to prevail, in that He sent Noah unto them, who exhorted them for one hundred and twenty years to amend their ways…,[101]

Jasher: 1651 AM – Lamech died. "And Lamech, the father of Noah, died in those days… And Noah rose up, and he made the ark, in the place where God had commanded him, and Noah did as God had ordered him."[102]

Enoch Chapter 9: Then Michael, Gabriel, Raphael, and Uriel looked down from heaven and saw all the bloodshed on earth by the extreme lawlessness. They said one to another, "the earth is laid waste, and the voice of all the dead cries up to the gate of heaven. The souls of men cry out to the holy ones of heaven, saying, 'bring our cause before the Most High.'" They said to the Lord, the King, "Lord of lords, God of gods, and King of kings, the throne of Your glory endures throughout all the ages, and Your name is holy, glorious, and blessed unto all the ages! You have made all things and have power over all things, and You see all things; nothing is hidden from You. You see what Azazel has done, teaching unrighteousness on earth, and revealing the eternal secrets concealed in heaven. Semjaza and those he has authority over have taught sorcery. And they have defiled themselves by sleeping with the daughters of men and revealed to those women these kinds of sins. These women have begotten giants, and by their children, the whole earth has been filled with blood and unrighteousness. Now the souls of the dead are crying out to the gates of heaven because of the lawlessness which has taken place on the earth. You know all things before they come to pass. You allow this but have not told us what we should do to the giants who are destroying your creation.[103]

Enoch, Chapter 10: … The Lord said to Gabriel, "Proceed against the bastards, the reprobates, against the children of fornication.[104] Destroy the children of fornication and the children of the Watchers from amongst men. Cause them to go forth against one another that they may destroy each other in battle, for they will not have long life. Grant no request that their fathers may make to you on behalf of their children, for they hope to live an eternal life, but none of them will live past five hundred years.[105]" The Lord said to Michael, "Go, tell Semjaza and his associates who have defiled themselves by marrying women that they and all those they contaminated will be destroyed. When they have seen their sons slay one another and all their loved ones destroyed, bind them for seventy generations[106] under the valleys of the earth, until the day of their judgment and of their end, till their last judgment be passed for all eternity.

---

100 Ibid (p. 13). Kindle Edition.
101 Ginzberg, Louis. *The Legends of the Jews — Volume 1* (Kindle Locations 1737-1738) Kindle Edition.
102 Ibid.
103 Johnson, Ken. *Ancient Book of Enoch* (pp. 20-21) Kindle Edition.
104 There were at least two clans of pre-flood giants - They begat sons, the *Nâphîdîm,* and they were all unlike, and they devoured one another: and the Giants slew the *Nâphîl,* and the *Nâphîl* slew the *Eliô [Elioud],* and the *Eliô,* mankind, and one man another. *Jubilees* 7: 22
105 Within five hundred years of this prophecy, the giants fought their civil war, which annihilated their race.
106 According to Luke 3: 23-38, there were seventy generations from Enoch to Jesus Christ. The miracles associated with the Azazel ritual preformed on Yom Kippur each year stopped when the Messiah died on the cross. See *Ancient Messianic Festivals* pp. 99, 119. Jesus made atonement and ascended to heaven. The fallen angels remained bound until the seventy generations passed, and Christ completed His work. Now they await their last judgment, to be cast into the lake of fire.

In those days, they will be led off to the fiery abyss, to the torment and the prison in which they will be confined forever. And whosoever was condemned and destroyed will from thenceforth be bound together with them to the end of all generations.[107]

2 Peter 2:4-11, *"For if God did not spare the angels who sinned, but cast them down to hell and delivered them into chains of darkness, to be reserved for judgment; and did not spare the ancient world, but saved Noah, one of eight people, a preacher of righteousness, bringing in the flood on the world of the ungodly; and turning the cities of Sodom and Gomorrah into ashes, condemned them to destruction, making them an example to those who afterward would live ungodly; and delivered righteous Lot, who was oppressed by the filthy conduct of the wicked (for that righteous man, dwelling among them, tormented his righteous soul from day to day by seeing and hearing their lawless deeds) — then the Lord knows how to deliver the godly out of temptations and to reserve the unjust under punishment for the day of judgment, and especially those who walk according to the flesh in the lust of uncleanness and despise authority. They are presumptuous, self-willed. They are not afraid to speak evil of dignitaries, whereas angels, who are greater in power and might, do not bring a reviling accusation against them before the Lord."*

Jude 5-11, *"But I want to remind you, though you once knew this, that the Lord, having saved the people out of the land of Egypt, afterward destroyed those who did not believe. And the angels who did not keep their proper domain, but left their own abode, He has reserved in everlasting chains under darkness for the judgment of the great day; as Sodom and Gomorrah, and the cities around them in a similar manner to these, having given themselves over to sexual immorality and gone after strange flesh, are set forth as an example, suffering the vengeance of eternal fire. Likewise, also these dreamers defile the flesh, reject authority, and speak evil of dignitaries. Yet Michael the archangel, in contending with the devil, when he disputed about the body of Moses, dared not bring against him a reviling accusation but said, "The Lord rebuke you!" But these speak evil of whatever they do not know, and whatever they know naturally, like brute beasts, in these things they corrupt themselves. Woe to them! For they have gone in the way of Cain, have run greedily in the error of Balaam for profit, and perished in the rebellion of Korah."*

Matthew 24:37-40: *"**But as the days of Noah were, so also will the coming of the Son of Man be**. For as in the days **before the flood**, they were eating and drinking, marrying, and giving in marriage, until the day that Noah entered the ark, and did not know until the flood came and took them all away, **so also will the coming of the Son of Man be.**"*

> Genesis 6: 8-21, *"But Noah found grace in the eyes of the Lord. This is the genealogy of Noah. Noah was a just man, **perfect in his generations**. Noah walked with God. And Noah begot three sons: Shem, Ham, and Japheth. The earth also was corrupt before God, and the earth was filled with violence. So, God looked upon the earth, and indeed it was corrupt, for all flesh had corrupted their way on the earth. And God said to Noah, 'The end of all flesh has come before Me, for the earth is filled with violence through them; and behold, I will destroy them with the earth. Make yourself an (Aleph-Tav) ark of gopherwood; make rooms in the ark and cover it inside and outside with pitch. And this is how*

---

[107] Johnson, Ken. *Ancient Book of Enoch*. Kindle Edition

> *you shall make it: The length of the ark shall be three hundred cubits, its width fifty cubits, and its height thirty cubits. You shall make a window for the ark, and you shall finish it to a cubit from above; and set the door of the ark in its side. You shall make it with lower, second, and third decks. And behold, I Myself am bringing (Aleph-Tav) floodwaters on the earth, to destroy from under heaven all flesh in which is the breath of life; everything that is on the earth shall die. But I will establish My (Aleph-Tav) covenant with you, and you shall go into the ark — you, your sons, your wife, and your sons' wives with you. And of every living thing of all flesh, you shall bring two of every sort into the ark, to keep them alive with you; they shall be male and female. Of the birds after their kind, of animals after their kind, and of every creeping thing of the earth after its kind, two of every kind will come to you to keep them alive. And you shall take for yourself of all food that is eaten, and you shall gather it to yourself, and it shall be food for you and for them.'"*

At last, we have come to my favorite portion of this chapter - the ARK.

Noah and his grandfather, Methuselah, traveled 'erets preaching righteousness, but alas to no avail. Then suddenly, after living 777 years, Lamech died, leaving the Melchizedek Priesthood with only two priests – Methuselah and Noah. Shortly after that, Noah was given the command to build the ark. It took him five years to complete the mission. But when finished, almost immediately, Methuselah died at the age of 969.

Hebrews 11:7, *"By faith Noah, being divinely warned of things not yet seen, moved with godly fear, prepared an ark for the saving of his household, by which he condemned the world and became the heir of righteousness, which is according to faith."*

"Perfect" or *tamiym* means without blemish, without spot, pure in heart. Sacrificial animals were required to be *tamiym*. They were to be without blemish. Psalms 119:1, *"Blessed are the undefiled* (tamiym) *in the way, who walk in the law of the Lord."* 1 Peter 1:18, Jesus is the ultimate *"lamb without blemish and without spot."*

Noah walked according to the law of the Kingdom of Righteousness and kept his bloodline untainted; his heart filled with truth, so grace was extended to Noah. Grace (*chen*) is defined by Strong's OT# 2580 as subjective kindness, favor, and objective beauty.

Noah was told, *"go and build yourself a **box** to represent my house."* The ark was not a boat; it was a box. Ark or *tebah* infers a box. *Tebah* (*tav-bet-hei*) in pictographic lettering is ✝ ⊔ ⍦ "the sign of the house – behold."

What sign? What house? God's house. Its emblem has always been the "cross." The ark was noted by Scripture as being *Aleph-Tav*, belonging to Melchizedek. It foreshadowed the work of the Cross.

Approximately 510 feet in length, the ark was over fifty feet in height, giving it the cargo capacity of 450 semi-trailers!

It was built from "one" tree, not many trees. The wood was gopherwood. The pictograph of *gopher- ets* translates as - "the lifting up – of the word - of the Leader." That lifting was above the dark floodwaters of deception, foreshadowing the lifting of the "Word of God" on the Cross.

The ark had many rooms. John 13:36, *"In my Father's house are many* (rooms) *if it were not so, I would have told you.*

I go to prepare a place for you."

Noah was instructed to cover the ark with pitch (*koper*), inside and out, to prevent the ark from taking on water. *Koper* is spelled *kaf-pey-resh* and equates with atonement, cleansing, and forgiveness. As a result, the coating of "pitch" represented righteousness – inwardly and outwardly.

The length of the ark was three hundred cubits. In Hebrew, three hundred is represented by *shin*. The width of it was fifty cubits. Fifty is expressed by the *nun*. The height was thirty cubits or the *lamed*. *Shin* means to consume. *Nun* represents seed. *Lamed* equates with authority, particularly that associated with a shepherd since it is drawn as a shepherd's staff.

Even the ark's dimensions foreshadowed the Messiah. He is the Seed, the Good Shepherd, who consumes the works of the adversary.

Like the Ark of the Covenant, Noah's ark was a rectangle-shaped box. Both arks were proportional in shape and size, their ratio equaling *pi*. Meaning both were perfectly stable since *pi* is geometric perfection (wisdom).

Noah was to '*asah* (make or appoint) a window. *Tsahor* (window) loosely translates as "the sun's radiance at midday." The root of *tsahor* means to glisten as oil or to press out the oil. Even the window was representational, signifying the anointing placed upon the Eternal Melchizedek as the Messiah, the one anointed to be the Light of the World.

Note that the window was overhead, on top of the ark. That window (much like Holy Spirit) hovered above and allowed light to flow within.

The ark was assigned one door – literally and figuratively – one access point. That door was placed in "its side." John 19:34, *"But one of the soldiers with a spear pierced his side...."*

John 10:7,9: *"Then said Jesus unto them again, 'Verily, verily, I say unto you, I am the door..., I am the door: by me, if any man enters, he shall be saved."*

Next, we note that there were three levels to the ark: Lower, Mid, and Upper. These levels represented the realms of existence (heaven, earth, and hell). Yeshua has access to all dominions. He came to the realm of *'erets* as the Promised Seed in submission to the Eternal Father, empowered by the Holy Spirit. Descending from the upper level to the lower level, he took the keys of Hades.

Yeshua, on the Cross, reached out and up and down. He brought the two states of human existence (the righteous dead and the righteous living) together as one family so they might forever "be his kingdom."

Sheniy, the mid-level, symbolized a "doubling" in that it represented the middle realm, *'erets*. Yeshua came to *'erets* as the "second" Adam and established his kingdom. He then returned to the upper level (the unseen realm of "eternal government") as the Adonizedek (High Priest). When he doubles back again (his second advent), he will do so by returning to *'erets* as the Eternal Melchizedek – the King!

Yeshua died in the middle realm, descended into the netherworld, and doubled back to *'erets* before ascending to the Father, where he currently governs from the spiritual realm. For that reason, the *tachity*, the lower level of the ark, also represents the Pit. *Tachity* means the nether part.

The third level, the upper level, also portrayed the coming of the *shaliysh* - the third day – the resurrection. Yahweh seeded *'erets* on the third day of creation; Yeshua rose from the grave on the third day.

1656 A.M. – And it was at that time Methuselah the son of Enoch died, nine hundred and sixty-nine years old was he, at his death. At that time, after the death of Methuselah, the Lord said to Noah, "Go with your household into the ark; behold, I will gather to you all the animals of the earth, the beasts of the field, and the fowls of the air, and they shall all come and surround the ark." [108]

Methuselah's death caused Noah to be the only Melchizedek priest in the field. The literal translation of Genesis 7:1, *"For you, I have seen **as** the righteous, before me in this age."* The old had passed, and it was appointed for the new to commence, so Noah entered the ark. He went in seven days before the rain began to fall. Seven should be perceived as sacred, primarily because it represents covenant, perfection, and completion. *Sheba* (seven), as presented in Genesis 7:4, *"For seven days yet…,"* possesses a feminine tense. Noah represented the future Melchizedek Bride.

Noah, representing mankind, was perfected "in" the ark with the passing of seven days. Whether we refer to seven days or seven thousand years, seven represents a time of perfection; perfecting the Melchizedek Kingdom requires seven thousand years.

The name Methuselah translates as: "straightforward attack." The death of Methuselah ended Yahweh's direct attack against the adversary. Noah personified rest, and the "rest" he brought, brought peace. Peace was a new weapon. Hebrews 13:20-21, *"May the God of peace, who through the blood of the eternal covenant brought back from the dead our Lord Jesus, that great Shepherd of the sheep, equip you with everything good for doing his will, and may he work in us what is pleasing to him, through Jesus Christ, to whom be glory forever and ever."*

1 Thessalonians 5:23-24, *"May God himself, the God of peace, sanctify you through and through. May your whole spirit, soul, and body be kept blameless at the coming of our Lord Jesus Christ. The one who calls you is faithful, and he will do it."*

Romans 16:20, *"The God of peace will soon crush Satan under your feet."*

Chaos "rained" outside the ark, but the Prince of Peace was "within." Genesis 6:18 should read: *"I will confirm my (Aleph-Tav) covenant BY abiding with you in the ark…."*

---

[108] Johnson, Ken. *Ancient Book of Jasher* (p. 14). Kindle Edition

Genesis Seven

> Genesis 7:1-5, *"And Yahweh said unto Noah, 'Come, you and all of your house into the ark for you have I approved as righteous before me in this generation. Of every clean beast, you shall take unto you by sevens, the male, and his female: and of beasts that are not clean by two, the male and his female. Of fowls also of the air by sevens, the male, and the female; to keep seed alive upon the face of all the earth. For yet seven days, and I will cause it to rain upon the earth forty days and forty nights, and every living substance that I have made will I destroy from off the face of the earth.' And Noah did according unto all that the Lord commanded him."*

The opening verses of Genesis 7 seemingly repeat those that ended Genesis 6. Both warn of the impending judgment. However, the tenor is different. Notice the subtlety:

→ Genesis 6: Elohiym spoke to Noah authoritatively as the Supreme Judge of the Divine Council.

→ Genesis 7: Yahweh spoke as Father, signifying relationship.

In a metaphoric sense, Yahweh said, "I shall bring floodwaters, representing a healing flow of words. These words will destroy the corruption and deception upon *'erets,* my field, and make it clean again. It is not just the lies told by the gods that have distorted my purpose. They have also corrupted the DNA of my field, polluting my expected harvest. Hence, no flesh is as it was ordained. Noah, you, and your family, I deem as righteous. You have obeyed my law and kept your seed pure. You and your family must go into the ark, for I must cleanse *'erets* of this perversion while it is still your era, so the soil is ready to be sown with my Seed in Day Three."

To grasp the extent of damage perpetrated by the fallen realm, we should think of "flesh" as DNA. DNA unites one generation to the next by retaining traits. You have probably heard the term "familiar spirits." Family traits and familiar spirits are technically the same. It is possible to pass corruption through epigenetic means by continuing a lie.

The gods had corrupted the information stored in the genetics of mankind. Which in turn brought forth characteristics not intended by Yahweh. To make matters worse, the Watchers mixed "kinds." Sowing their non-terrestrial seed (DNA) into not just humanoids, they also perverted the animal and plant kingdoms with their DNA. Even beyond that, they cross-bred the genes of the different species by placing animal DNA into humans, plant DNA into animals, and so forth.

Though Noah was the Melchizedek Regent, and he built the ark, the ark was Yahweh's. Which marked it *Aleph-Tav.*

Too often, we misread the intent in the actions of the ancients. They lived according to a different set of rules. At no time in the ancient past was any society predicated upon democratic conventions. They built their civilizations as theocracies.

Noah understood that the ark belonged to Yahweh. He needed permission for his family to board it. Genesis 6:18 gave permission, and Genesis 7:1 issued the sanctioned command.

Genesis 6:19-20, *"You are to bring into the ark two of all living creatures, male and female, to keep them alive with you. Two of every kind of bird, of every kind of animal, and of every kind of creature that moves along the ground will come to you to be kept alive."* Genesis 7:2-3, *"Take with you seven* (sheba' sheba') *of every kind of clean animal, a male, and its mate, and two of every kind of unclean animal, a male and its mate, and also seven of every kind of bird, male and female, to keep their various kinds alive throughout the earth."*

The instructions of Chapter 6 involved two of all living creatures, yet in Chapter 7, Noah was told to take seven pairs of clean animals. So, the numbers seven and two are essential data points.

- Two doubles a thing (7 x 2 = 14)
- One male plus one female (of the same species) equals two of the same kind.
- The *"bet,"* the number two, represents family, a house.
- Noah was commanded to take *sh'nayim* of every sort into the ark, a male and a female. *Sh'nayim* is the feminine tense of *sheniy* and translates as "the doubling or the duplicating of a thing."
- The duplicating of a "kind" results in a new life. (Male + Female = new life).
- Psalms 12:6, *"The words of the Lord are pure words, like silver tried in a furnace of earth, purified seven times."* Yahweh's words are pure and are represented by the number seven.
- In Genesis 7:2, *sibah'* was written twice; thus, *sibah'* should be doubled.
- God created in six days yet did not deem creation complete until the seventh day when he rested.
- The ancients considered seven a sacred number representing the completion of a thing; they reckoned seven as the expression of divine perfection.
- There are seven notes in the music scale; seven primary colors in the light spectrum; seven continents; seven large bodies of water; seven eclipses a year; seven yearly feasts.
- Seven priests, each blowing a shofar, marched about the walls of Jericho for seven days. On the seventh day, those seven priests went around the walls seven times. On the seventh go-around, the people gave up loud shouts, and the walls of Jericho fell.
- Seven, or the seventh letter of Hebrew, is the *zayin* – it represents a weapon, a harvest, and the perfecting of a thing.

Since seven and two appeared together in this manner, the perfecting process is duplicated. The simple subliminal message is that there shall be another harvest, one that shall be perfected. In other words, the numbers hint at another "age" that correlates to the "Days of Noah. That second harvest will be perfected – clean, made pure by the perfected Ark, who we shall soon discover is Yeshua.

Noah would be on the ark for approximately a year. During that time, it would be required of him to offer sacrifices. Additionally, Noah and his family would need to eat. And so, while the instructions Noah received implied the expectation of clean animal sacrifices,[109] it was also necessary that he take clean animals

---

[109] Genesis 4 (the story of Cain and Abel) refers to sacrifices so we can know the rules of acceptable offerings were already established.

for the consumption of meat. Wait! How did he know the clean from the unclean, the Levitical law had yet to be written?

Tahowr, clean, is defined by Strong's OT#2889 as pure physically or chemically; ceremonially made pure; pure in a moral sense. *Tahowr* is the opposite of unclean.

Genesis 6:21, *"You are to take every kind of food that is to be eaten and store it away as food for you and for them."* Yahweh did not say take only grains, vegetables, or fruit. He said "every kind of food" - *ma 'akal*, that which is edible. *Ma'akal* is inclusive of all food types, that includes meat.

Genesis 7:4, *"Seven days from now I will send rain on the earth for forty days and forty nights, and I will wipe from the face of the earth every living creature I have made."* Young's Literal Translation: *"…for after another seven days, I am sending rain on the earth, forty days and forty nights, (wiping) away all the substance that I have made from off the face of the ground"* (this verse was slightly modified by the author for the sake of clarity).

"And Noah was six hundred years old when the flood of waters was upon the earth" Genesis 7: 6.

Antiquities of the Jews: §14 [1.14] God afforded them a longer time of life on account of their virtue and the good use they made of it in astronomical and geometrical discoveries, which would not have afforded the time of foretelling [the periods of the stars] unless they had lived six hundred years; for the great year is completed in that interval. Now I have for witnesses to what I have said, all those that have written Antiquities, both among the Greeks and barbarians; for even Manetho, who wrote the Egyptian History, and Berosus, who collected the Chaldean Monuments, and Mochus, and Hestieus, and, besides these, Hieronymus the Egyptian, and those who composed the Phoenician History, agree to what I here say: Hesiod also, and Hecatseus, Hellanicus, and Acusilaus; and, besides these, Ephorus and Nicolaus relate that the ancients lived a thousand years. But as to these matters, let everyone look upon them as he thinks fit.[110]

Josephus wrote that living six hundred years indicated an individual, upon obtaining that age, achieved "a great year." That meant they had witnessed all the vital astronomical signs and geometric designs; therefore, they were deemed wise and full of knowledge. While this might seem trivial or less significant, the ancients were much more attuned to the "celestial" sky than we. They looked for and regarded the placement of luminary bodies as revelatory or spiritual information. The reason for studying the alignment of constellations wasn't to diagram horoscopes but instead to know Yahweh's timing for the events prophesied, especially the arrival of the Promised Seed.

---

[110] Josephus: *Antiquities of the Jews*, PC Study Bible Copyright © 2003, 2006 by Biblesoft, Inc. All rights reserved

> Genesis 7:7-10, *"And Noah went in, and his sons, and his wife, and his sons' wives with him, into the ark, because of the waters of the flood. Of clean beasts, and of beasts that are not clean, and of fowls, and of everything that creeps upon the earth, two by two they came to Noah, into the ark; the male and the female, as God had commanded Noah. And it came to pass after seven days, that the waters of the deluge were upon the earth,"* Young's Literal Translation.

Noah didn't look for the critters of *'erets* – they came to him, to their king, the Melchizedek. This demonstrates Yahweh's reasoning for Adam naming all the creatures. Did they go to Noah because some innate sense warned a disaster loomed upon the horizon? Or were they driven to the ark by the *elohim*? Or did Noah call out - commanding them "to come?" Whatever the answer, they came because he was their king.

Romans 8:20-22, *"For the creation was subjected to futility, not willingly, but because of Him who subjected it in hope, because the creation itself also will be delivered from the bondage of corruption into the glorious liberty of the children of God. For we know that the whole creation groans and labors with birth pangs together until now."* **Creation longs to be delivered from destruction – from the adversary – and it seeks for the righteous"** (emphasis added.)

Josephus §7 [1.7] And that their inventions might not be lost before they were sufficiently known, upon Adam's prediction that the world was to be destroyed at one time by the force of fire and at another time by the violence and quantity of water....[111]

Adam predicted two global judgments, one of water and the other of fire. Apostle Peter made a few observations concerning the fire judgment, which are rather interesting: *"But the day of the Lord will come as a thief in the night; in which the heavens shall pass away* (go away) *with a **great noise**, and **the elements** (the orderly arrangement) **shall melt** (dissolve and break up) with fervent heat* (be set on fire), *the earth also and the works that are therein shall be burned up* (consumed). *Seeing then that all these things shall be dissolved, what manner of persons ought you to be in all holy conversation and godliness, looking for and hasting unto the coming of the day of God, wherein the heavens being on fire shall be dissolved, and the elements shall melt with fervent heat?"* 2 Peter 3:10-12 (emphasis added).

Peter stated the fire judgment would come "with a great noise" and dissolve the disorder in *'erets*. I would venture to say that the flood occurred comparably – with a great noise. I suspect that the planet was hit by a comet, or at the very least by several meteors, which caused the earth's crust to rupture, resulting in volcanoes and such. Probably, shaking the planet so hard it shifted on its axis.

> Genesis 7:11, *"In the six hundredth year of Noah's life, in the second month, the seventeenth day of the month* (chodesh), *the same day were all the fountains of the great deep broken up, and the windows of heaven were opened."*

---

[111] Ibid.

Upon reading verse eleven, I paused and wondered why Noah's age and the date were provided. The date was the 17th day of the 2nd month. Noah was six hundred, which meant the year was 1656 A.M. The date was Iyar 17, 1656 A.M. or 17/2/1656. After summing the numbers (1+7+2+1+6+5+6 = 28), I wrote the sum as *bet-chet*. The *bet* symbolizes a house, and the *chet* signifies a "separation for a new beginning." Ah-ha! Yahweh was sending a message. His House was being separated from the "unrighteous," and a new beginning was on the horizon. This notion is confirmed by the term *chodesh*.

Verse 11 is phrased as to use *chodesh* twice. In most cases, *chodesh* is translated as "month." However, *chodesh* also refers to the new moon. Consequently, *chodesh* symbolizes a period of rebuilding. A new moon is a time of "rebuilding" the fullness of the moon's light. A new moon is dark; essentially, it is hidden because the earth blocks the sun's rays from reflecting upon the moon's surface. Yet as the moon continues its cycle, it rebuilds its light, and its brilliance intensifies.

Yahweh commanded "all the fountains of the great deep" to break. The inference: The deep (*Sheol*) broke apart, but the windows of heaven were opened. God sent His army, and they *baqa* - rooted out those who were corrupting '*erets*. Principally, the rebellious *elohim* were removed from their places of esteem, their temples.

Yahweh sent his loyal spiritual forces to '*erets*, and they cast the Watchers out of their cosmic mountains and into the abyss. The adversary's army was removed, temporarily "kicked" out, and "bound" to the netherworld.

Forty equates to judgment, and as a judgment, it can also mean massive water.

Yahweh commanded Raphael to "bind Azazel hand and foot and cast him into the darkness. Make an opening in the desert, which is in Dudael, and bind him there. And place upon him rough and jagged rocks, and cover him with darkness, and let him abide there forever, and cover his face that he may not see light. And on the day of the great judgment, he will be cast into the fire."[112] And to Gabriel, Yahweh said, "Proceed against the bastards, the reprobates, against the children of fornication. Destroy the children of fornication and the children of the Watchers from amongst men."[113]

2 Peter 2:4-5, *"For if God did not spare the angels who sinned, but cast them down to hell and delivered them into chains of darkness, to be reserved for judgment; and did not spare the ancient world, but saved Noah…,"*

> Genesis 7:13-17, **"On the very same day Noah** and Noah's sons, Shem, Ham, and Japheth, and Noah's wife and the three wives of his sons with them, **entered** the ark — they and every beast after its kind, all cattle after their kind, every creeping thing that creeps on the earth after its kind, and every bird after its kind, every bird of every sort. And they went into the ark to Noah, two by two, of all flesh in which is the breath of life. So those that entered, male and female of all flesh, went in as

---

[112] Johnson, Ken. *Ancient Book of Enoch* (pp. 21-22) Kindle Edition.
[113] Ibid

*Elohiym had commanded him; and Yahweh shut him in. Now the flood was on the earth forty days. The **waters increased and lifted up the ark, and it rose high above the earth**"* (emphasis added).

- "On the same day" (*'estem*) equates to substance, strength, and bone.
- Noah entered, *'bow*. He went in to abide.
- Elohiym commanded – *tsavah* - appointed.
- Noah was shut-in – *cagar* -enclosed.
- Waters increased – *rabah* means produced an abundance.
- Lifted up – *nasa'* means to accept; to lift.
- Rose above – *ruwm 'al* means to exalt above.
- Earth – *'erets* the land - the surface of the earth.

To paraphrase Genesis 7:13-17: When the full measure of all who were righteous was within the ark as appointed, *Elohiym* commanded them to be enclosed. The waters grew to abundance, and the judgment against the celestials was executed. Yet, those within the ark were safe because Yahweh's authority exceeded all other authority. So, as the waters rose, the ark rose above the judgment and the devastation, which covered *'erets*.

Genesis 7:18-24, *"The waters prevailed and greatly increased on the earth, and the ark moved about on the surface of the waters. And the waters prevailed exceedingly on the earth, and all the high hills under the whole heaven were covered. The waters prevailed fifteen cubits upward, and the mountains were covered. And all flesh died that moved on the earth: birds and cattle and beasts and every creeping thing that creeps on the earth, and every man. All in whose nostrils was the breath of the spirit of life, all that was on the dry land, died. So, He destroyed all living things which were on the face of the ground: both man and cattle, creeping thing, and bird of the air. They were destroyed from the earth. Only Noah and those who were with him in the ark remained alive. And the waters prevailed on the earth one hundred and fifty days."*

The "waters" prevailed exceedingly. The waters pushed beyond their established boundaries and flowed together as one body of water. Rivers, oceans, and seas overflowed as the flood increased until even the hills and mountains were covered with water.

Genesis Eight

> Genesis 8:1 *"Then God remembered Noah, and every living thing, and all the animals that were with him in the ark. And God made a wind to pass over the earth, and the waters subsided...."*

Determining that it was time for Noah to rebuild, Yahweh sent a spirit to force the waters to recede. Yahweh had not forgotten Noah; the more accurate rendering would be: "Yahweh was mindful of Noah." *Zakar* is translated as remembered, but in my opinion, in this instance, the better translation would be "make mention." God sent wind (a spirit, probably an angel) to pass over the earth.

Interestingly, the waters of the text are "pissing waters." This idiom denoted conflict, a contest. You got the implication, I'm sure.

> So, *"the fountains of the deep surrendered and the windows of heaven were also stopped* (commanded to cease). *Thus, the rain from heaven restrained,"* Genesis 8:2.

Wow! Such picturesque language indicates that a battle in the spirit realm affected the physical world, and the flood resulted. So, suppose we view the scene figuratively rather than on a strict literal basis. The spiritual message then is that the battle that raged in the domain of the spirit world was finished after forty days and nights.

The phrase *"the windows of heaven"* directs our attention toward the holy ones. Whereas *"the fountains of the deep"* points toward the netherworld. These expressions position the spiritual forces of good and evil in opposition. Suggesting that the armies of the spirit world battled for supremacy and that "heaven's hosts" won.

During the forty days and nights, underground springs and rivers burst through to the surface, where they combine with rainwater. Even after the rain ceased, the waters rose for another 110 days. Hence the waters prevailed for 150 days. Then after the wind began blowing, the waters receded continually and returned to their established boundaries.
- → 50 = *nun*, which symbolizes a seed.
- → 100 = *qof* and pictures an end to a cycle.

The 150 days annihilated the Watchers' progeny; the Nephilim's reign of terror was over.

> Genesis 8:3, *"And the waters receded continually from the earth. At the end of the hundred and fifty days, the waters decreased."*

Genesis 7 speaks to the prevailing waters, whereas Genesis 8 speaks of diminishing waters.

> Genesis 8:4, *"Then the ark rested in the seventh month, the seventeenth day of the month, on the mountains of Ararat."*

The floodwaters had prevailed for five months. But note, while the waters were still at their peak, the ark rested. The ark rested (*nuwach*) upon the (*hars*) of Ararat. (Ararat is also spelled A-r-a-t-t-a.)

Ararat is a mountain range in the far north,[114] and in this instance, it rested in the region currently known as Turkey. However, the phrase "far north" implies "up" (as over the head), not a direction on a compass. Figuratively, "far north" means heavenly places within the cosmic sphere. Pictographically, Ararat means - "strong leader of the highest rank rules supreme over clay containers." Which actually pictures the ark as resting on the God of clay vessels. In other words, Yeshua (Ark) rests on Yahweh (God of mankind). This also pictures Yeshua sitting on his throne next to Yahweh before his enemies are thoroughly defeated. Yeshua took his seat as High Priest when the war in the spirit realm was still at its zenith.[115] He is at rest because he trusts his Father. The ark rested upon the mountain's crest, not at its base to signal that point.

We also note that the flood began in the 2nd month. Though the matter, the judgment, was not perfected until the seventh. The symbolism indicates that the judgment against the fallen realm, which began in Noah's era, shall not be perfected until the millennial reign. Meantime, Yeshua-Yahweh is at rest.

The waters crested on day seventeen of the 7th month. From that date to the first day of the 10th month is 73 days. Noah did not see the top of any mountain other than Ararat for a total of 73 days. 7 + 3 = 10, and 10 represents Divine Order.

> Genesis 8:5-6, *"And the waters decreased continually until the tenth month. In the tenth month, on the first day of the month, the tops of the mountains were seen. So it came to pass, at the end of forty days, that Noah opened the window of the ark he had made."*

Noah opened the Melchizedek window into the heavens and saw '*erets* as cleansed, prophetically. With spiritual eyes, he noted that the thrones of the fallen gods were gone. Seeking verification that order was restored, Noah released two birds: a raven and a dove.

> Genesis 8:7-9, *"Then he sent out a raven, which kept going to and fro until the waters had dried up from the earth. He also sent out from himself a dove to see if the waters had receded from the face of the*

---

[114] "North" in relation to Jerusalem. Biblical direction places Jerusalem as the center of all activity.
[115] Daniel 7 also describes this scene.

ground. But the dove found no resting place for the sole of her foot, and she returned into the ark to him, for the waters were on the face of the whole earth. So, he put out his hand and took her and drew her into the ark to himself."

Ravens are large, black-feathered birds that primarily feed by scavenging on carrion.[116] Doves are emblems of peace and love (Holy Spirit descended on Yeshua "like a dove." In Song of Songs, the Bridegroom called his bride "my dove," saying her eyes were like those of a dove.[117]

After Noah released the birds, they flew off. The raven going "to and fro" - did not return. It remained outside the ark. However, the dove returned to Noah, and she was received when he brought her back to himself and then into the ark. Initially, upon her release, the dove found no resting place for the sole of her foot. That phrasing indicates the dove attained no rest for the hollow of her hand. There was nothing to grab and hang on to. Symbolically, Noah received his "peace" or rest once again. Since *'erets* was not ready, there was no work other than to wait upon Yahweh!

Genesis 8:10 -11, "And he waited yet another seven days, and again he sent the dove out from the ark. Then the dove came to him in the evening, and behold, a freshly plucked olive leaf was in her mouth, and Noah knew that the waters had receded from the earth."

Noah waited another seven days before releasing the dove once again. She did not immediately return because Divine Order had been restored to the mountain tops. Consequently, she found a branch, which she brought Noah. Isaiah 11:1-4, *"And a Branch shall grow out of his roots, and the spirit of the Lord shall rest upon him, the spirit of wisdom and understanding, the spirit of counsel and might, the spirit of knowledge and of the fear of the Lord; and shall make him of quick understanding in the fear of the Lord: and he shall not judge after the sight of his eyes, neither reprove after the hearing of his ears. But with righteousness shall he judge the poor and reprove with equity for the meek of the earth: and he shall smite the earth with the rod of his mouth, and with the breath of his lips shall he slay the wicked."*

Genesis 8:12, "So he waited yet another seven days and sent out the dove, which did not return to him anymore."

Noah waited another seven days after the dove returned with the olive branch. Then he sent her out again. There are three sets of seven days. Each represents a segment, more specifically, a two-thousand-year period. The Essenes called that first 2,000-year period the Age of Chaos. The second they referred to as the Age of the Torah, and the third as the Age of Grace. The Age of Chaos started with Creation and ended with the calling of Abraham. From Abraham to the coming of the Messiah was the Age of Torah. The Age

---

[116] https://www.conservapedia.com/Raven - retrieved April 22, 2020
[117] http://www.weseejesus.com/bibledictionary/dove.html - retrieved April 22, 2020

of Grace commenced with Yeshua's first coming and shall extend to the second.

The dove returned the first time empty-handed. She returned the second time with a Branch. Once the Kingdom is in place, she shall not return. Eternal peace shall be restored.

> Genesis 8:13-14, *"And it came to pass in the six hundred and first year, in the first month, the first day of the month, that the waters were dried up from the earth; and Noah removed the covering of the ark and looked, and indeed the surface of the ground was dry. And in the second month, on the twenty-seventh day of the month, the earth was dried."*

Noah removed the ark's covering on the anniversary of his great year.

Nisan is the first month, so the waters dried on November 1st, 1657 A.M. The earth was not dried until Iyar 27th. Nisan means to "pull out" or embark on a journey. Iyar means to glow, to blossom. The journey was over; it was time to blossom. So, Yahweh commissioned Noah to subdue *'erets* – as he had with Adam, saying, "Go forth and be fruitful!"

> *"God spoke to Noah, saying, 'Go out of the ark, you and your wife, and your sons and your sons' wives with you. Bring out with you every living thing of all flesh that is with you: birds and cattle and every creeping thing that creeps on the earth, so that they may abound on the earth, and be fruitful and multiply on the earth.' So, Noah went out, and his sons and his wife and his sons' wives with him. Every animal, every creeping thing, every bird, and whatever creeps on the earth, according to their families, went out of the ark. Then Noah built an altar to the Lord and took of every clean animal and of every clean bird and offered burnt offerings on the altar. And the Lord smelled a soothing aroma. Then the Lord said in His heart, 'I will never again curse the ground for man's sake, although the imagination of man's heart is evil from his youth; nor will I again destroy every living thing as I have done. While the earth remains, seedtime and harvest, cold and heat, winter and summer, and day and night shall not cease,'"* Genesis 8:15-22.

Noah proclaimed *'erets* was again a sanctified realm, cleansed, holy, submitted to the purposes of Yahweh. Yahweh responded, "I will never again devastate the *adamah* for man's sake although the *adamah* is cursed; I will never again destroy the living. Seedtime and harvest will continue like cold and heat, winter, and summer; day and night."

Genesis Nine

Genesis 9:1-7, "So God blessed Noah and his sons, and said to them: 'Be fruitful and multiply and fill the earth. And the fear of you and the dread of you shall be on every beast of the earth, on every bird of the air, on all that move on the earth, and on all the fish of the sea. They are given into your hand. Every moving thing that lives shall be food for you. I have given you all things, even the green herbs. But you shall not eat flesh with its life, that is, its blood. Surely for your lifeblood I will demand a reckoning; from the hand of every beast, I will require it, and from the hand of man. From the hand of every man's brother, I will require the life of man. **Whoever sheds man's blood, by man his blood shall be shed; for in the image of Elohiym was the man appointed.** *And as for you, be fruitful and multiply, bring forth abundantly in the earth and multiply in it"* (emphasis added).

Let's imagine that we secretly observe the Divine Council as they assembled to watch Noah set up an altar. They gathered around a massive plasma screen T.V. Then, suddenly, Yahweh interrupted, "We need to bless Noah and his sons." He motioned for an angel and, with great satisfaction filtering through His voice, said, "Go tell Noah and his sons to be fruitful and multiply." Then, catching a scribe's eye, the Almighty shook a forefinger in the air and continued, "You need to put this in the record. As it was with Adam, so it will be with Noah." Murmurs of agreement filled the hall as Yah added, "remind Noah that Adam was given every tree of the garden, from which he could freely eat. Adam, as the king, named all living creatures, so they are still under the dominion of the regent. However, it will be different now; the animals shall fear mankind, even the birds of the air. It is permissible for humans to consume the meat of clean animals. Yet, they must not do so if the flesh still has life." Yah paused and then lowered His voice, "life is in the blood. I will demand a reckoning of all lifeblood, even from the beasts that think they are gods; I will require it."

Gasps of surprise filled the air, and someone standing in the back, asked, "Is this to be a law?" Narrowing his brow, Yahweh nodded, "Yes! Whoever sheds the blood of Adam's offspring, his life shall be put out, for Adam was made in the image of God." Unexpectedly, fear filled the great hall, and all grew silent. Slowly and deliberately, annunciating each word with keen deliberation, Yahweh explained, "Adam represented me. I will not tolerate the corruption of my word. I gave my name and word to my Son that his inheritance would come through Adam. Anyone who seeks to remove the life of Adam's progeny seeks to remove my name and my word. Whether it be man or beast, he will be judged. All of you and Noah must judge *'erets* with that in mind."

We witnessed the "fear of the Lord," called *mora*. That type of fear is akin to dread. To anger Yah is a fearful thing, so Yah sent a message to the fallen realm: "Leave my kids alone!"

In the preceding scene, this type of fear (respect) was present in the Divine Council because they knew firsthand the vastness of power and authority within Yahweh. However, fear of this nature was new in the animal kingdom. It was placed within them post-flood to "type or typify" – respect. Pre-flood, the animals came willingly to Noah. Post-flood, the creatures would flee from all of mankind. An innate sense of dread (fear) would exist between animals and mankind. Yahweh did this to safeguard the animal kingdom but also to make an example of them. Noah typed the Melchizedek, and the animals (beasts) represented the fallen realm. Henceforth, there would be a new "fear" in the fallen realm. As we shall see, this fear made the fallen gods more cautious, but they did not stop being beasts though their tactics changed.

From the beginning, the Melchizedek Regent was to protect the animals from abuse. Yet, the Nephilim consumed animals while they still lived. This was not to be, ever again. Noah was to safeguard against such practices. Eating meat was allowed, but not if the creature lived. The thought of that is appalling, yet some records suggest the Nephilim did precisely that. Yahweh was offended. Therefore, Noah was told, *"you shall not eat flesh with its life."* This also explains why Yah stated all human blood needed to be accounted for. Genesis 9:5, *"And surely your blood of your lives will I require; at the hand of every beast will I require it."*

There is no court for animals, nor do animals have hands, so this phrasing was figurative. Yahweh was voicing His view of the adversaries, that they are beasts. He was addressing the spirit beings who murder, telling them that they shall account for the lives they take. And additionally, the regent king was commanded to judge them. Or anyone who murders. Noah and those who would come after him were instructed to charge the adversarial kingdom with the unlawful removal of Yahweh's "image" from *'erets*.

Henceforth it would be required of the Melchizedek to require blood in exchange for human blood. In other words, an atonement was required. Yahweh was moving mankind toward the concept of personal accountability. Accordingly, all men would be held responsible for knowing the "truth" and being loyal to God and the king.

And in that regard, Noah and his sons were to "go forth – be fruitful (increase) – multiply (excel)– bring an abundance (abound) – multiply (extend the authority of the priesthood)." Genesis 9:2-7 is a four-part plan of restoration: 1) Maintain, 2) Provide, 3) Extend accountability, 4) Establish honor.

Genesis 9:8-11, "Then God spoke to Noah and to his sons with him, saying, 'And as for Me, behold, I establish My (Aleph-Tav) covenant with you and with your (Aleph-Tav) descendants after you, and with every living creature that is with you: the birds, the cattle, and every beast of the earth with you, of all that go out of the ark, every beast of the earth. Thus, **I establish My covenant with you***: Never again shall all flesh be cut off by the waters of the flood; never again shall there be a flood to destroy the earth"*
(emphasis added).

The Hebrew text of Genesis 9:8 reads: "Elohiym spoke to (*Aleph-Tav*) Noah and to his (*Aleph-Tav*) seed with him." As the Supreme Judge of the Cosmos, Yahweh spoke to the "three" with Noah at the altar. They were there as the (*Aleph-Tav*) seed of the Melchizedek Regent, not as "sons" of Noah. One of the three would become the next Firstborn of his generation. Still, apparently, at that moment, the Firstborn had yet to be chosen.

Past teaching has inferred that the three with Noah were there because they were sons of Noah. That is misleading. It leads to the assumption Yahweh included them in His directive. *Elohiym* spoke with the regent king and the one who would inherit the regency. The order was authoritative and formal; kingdom business was being conducted.

So yes, the sons of Noah heard the words, but they did so collectively. These three were not being brought into the covenant Yahweh held with the Melchizedek Kingdom. They were there because Yahweh wished to address the next Firstborn while He addressed Noah. In other words, Yahweh desired for the next regent to hear His instructions.

Noah, like Adam, was a regent for the Eternal Melchizedek. Yahweh was affirming the regent was to maintain righteousness. In return, Yahweh would protect him. Genesis 9 is viewed by many as the giving of a new covenant. Perhaps it would be best to consider these verses as Yahweh reaffirming His covenant with Adam.

Yahweh said, "I will establish." Establish is *quwm*. However, *quwm* connotes a "lifting up again" - arising for the second time. In other words, Yahweh was saying, "I place before you and your (*Aleph-Tav*) seed, my Melchizedek Covenant. Therefore, never again shall *'erets* be consumed by floodwaters."

Biblical covenants are classified as:
1. Blood Covenant - a blood covenant required the "cutting" of sacrificial animals, thus the shedding of blood (this type of covenant is described in Genesis 15).
2. Salt Covenant - a salt covenant bound one party to another as a seal of loyalty and friendship.
3. Sandal Covenant - also known as the "marriage covenant." The stipulations of this covenant included those of the blood and salt covenants. In other words, it was a "cutting" that required loyalty and friendship. It almost always transferred the ownership of property or provided for an inheritance.

The making or cutting of a covenant required adherence to established ritualistic protocols. Genesis 9 does not indicate that any such protocols were implemented on that specific occasion. The covenant that formed the Melchizedek Kingdom was not between Adam and Yahweh but between Yahweh and Yeshua. Adam was a substitute for the Eternal Melchizedek. Logistically, Adam was included in the covenant, but not as a covenant partner. In that same vein, Noah (Adam's son) inherited his covenant rights from Adam. So, Yahweh re-established to Noah that he had the protection of the Melchizedek Covenant. In that respect, the covenant between Yahweh and Yeshua was passed from generation to generation until the Messiah's first advent.

Adam's death did not abolish the Melchizedek Covenant. In fact, the death of a covenant partner does not cancel a covenant, not as it does with contractual law. Covenants were made to understand that future generations were also bound to all stipulations. Such was the case with the Melchizedek Covenant. It bound Adam as the placeholder until the advent of the Eternal Melchizedek for as many generations as it would be required.

Post-flood, Noah was a restart – a reaffirmation – a renewing of original intent. That was why Yahweh addressed Noah's Firstborn. He, too, would be a Melchizedek Regent.

"See, I have set before you today life and good, death and evil," Deuteronomy 30:15. With Moses, this scene in Deuteronomy was much the same as what we witness with Noah in Genesis 9. *"I call heaven and earth as witnesses today against you, that I have set before you, life and death, blessing and cursing; therefore, choose life, that both you and your descendants may live,"* Deuteronomy 30:19.

The words were not expressed explicitly in Genesis 9 as in Deuteronomy. Still, that *chay* (life) was spoken six times is significant. Twice the word *'chay* was translated as "beast;" and four times as "living."

John 6:63, *"It is the spirit who gives life; the flesh profits nothing. The words that I speak to you are spirit, and they are life."*

"Furthermore, we have had fathers of our flesh which corrected us, and we gave them reverence: shall we not much rather be in subjection unto the Father of spirits, and live?" Hebrews 12:9.

The life force of an individual and his spirit are intertwined – woven together – wonderfully made. Romans 8:11, *"But if the Spirit of him that raised up Jesus from the dead dwell in you, he that raised up Christ from the dead shall also quicken your mortal bodies by his Spirit that dwells in you."*

Quicken is an old English term referring to the process known as "trimming the wick." Cutting the wick became necessary so that a lantern or candle would burn without smoke, without producing smut. God gave man His Spirit to quicken mankind so that man's light would burn efficiently. Basically, that was the purpose of this message in Genesis 9. We could paraphrase it this way: "See, I am putting before you life. Choose life. Be filled by the anointing, which rests upon you, serve me, and burn efficiently. I have removed the waters of deception, and while it is true that Death still exists – I give you the rainbow to show you that my Melchizedek Covenant still stands."

Genesis 9:9, *"As for me, behold, I establish* (lift again) *MY* (Aleph-Tav) *covenant with you and with your* (Aleph-Tav) *descendants."* The covenant is Psalms 110:4, *"Yahweh has sworn and will not relent, 'You are a priest forever according to the order of Melchizedek.'"* As a sign of that covenant, Yahweh placed a rainbow in the clouds.

"And God said, 'This is the sign of the covenant which I make between Me and you, and every living creature that is with you, for perpetual generations. I set My rainbow in the cloud, and it shall be for the sign of the covenant between Me and the earth. It shall be when I bring a cloud over the earth that the rainbow shall be seen in the cloud, and I will remember My covenant which is between Me and you and every living creature of all flesh. The waters shall never again become a flood to destroy all flesh. The rainbow shall be in the cloud, and I will look on it to remember the everlasting covenant between God and every living creature of all flesh that is on the earth.' And God said to Noah, 'This is the sign of the covenant which I have established between Me and all flesh that is on the earth.'" Genesis 9:12-17

Yahweh placed within the atmosphere of *'erets* the symbol of His throne – a rainbow. *"I do set my bow in the cloud as a token."*

- → Cloud - *'anan*[118] suggests the practice of dark magic.
- → Bow - *qashah*[119] refers to the act of laying a snare.
- → Token - *'owth* [120] a flag as a sign.

The darkness alluded to is the secret place (hiding place) of the fallen realm. But Yahweh openly put the sign of His government in the sky, so all could see. That was the snare; the adversaries are entrapped by their actions, which they do in the dark.

Every word that Yahweh speaks is weighty. Therefore, His words are commitments. Which causes the repeated use of the word "covenant" in Genesis 9 to be the correct word. Yahweh is committed to His Son and His Son's inheritance.

Revelation 4:3-5, *"And the one who sat there had the appearance of jasper and carnelian.* **A rainbow resembling an emerald encircled the throne.** *Surrounding the throne were twenty-four other thrones, and seated on them were twenty-four elders. They were dressed in white and had crowns of gold on their heads. From the throne came flashes of lightning, rumblings, and peals of thunder. Before the throne, seven lamps were blazing. These are the seven spirits of God."* Revelation 10:1-3, *"He was robed in a cloud, with* **a rainbow above his head**; *his face was like the sun, and his legs were like fiery pillars. He was holding a little scroll, which lay open in his hand. He planted his right foot on the sea and his left foot on the land, and he gave a loud shout like the roar of a lion. When he shouted, the voices of the seven thunders spoke"* (emphasis added).

Note, at no time, did Yahweh ask anything of Noah other than faithfulness and obedience.

Genesis 9:18-24, "Now the sons of Noah who went out of the ark were Shem, Ham, and Japheth. And Ham was the father of Canaan. These three were the sons of Noah, and from these, the whole earth was populated. And Noah began to be a farmer, and he planted a vineyard. Then he drank of the wine and was drunk and became uncovered in his tent. And Ham, the father of Canaan, saw the nakedness of his father and told his two brothers outside. But Shem and Japheth took a garment, laid it on both their shoulders and went backward and covered the nakedness of their father. Their faces were turned away, and they did not see their father's nakedness. So, Noah awoke from his wine and knew what his younger son had done to him. Then he said, 'Cursed be Canaan, a servant of servants, he shall be to his brethren.'"

The pertinent details of this story are:
- Noah's sons went out of the ark.
- Their names were Shem, Ham, and Japheth.

---

[118] Strong's OT# 6051
[119] Strong's OT#7198
[120] Strong's OT#226

- Ham was the father of Canaan.
- Noah's sons repopulated the whole earth.
- Noah became a farmer - he planted a vineyard.
- He drank the wine and became drunk.
- Noah became uncovered in his tent.
- Ham, the father of Canaan, saw the nakedness of Noah.
- Ham told his brothers that their father was naked.
- Shem and Japheth took a garment; laid it across their shoulders.
- Walking backward into the tent, Shem and Japheth covered Noah's nakedness.
- Neither Shem nor Japheth saw their father's nakedness.
- Noah woke; he knew what his "young son" had done.
- Noah cursed Canaan.

These details aren't the whole story so let's unpack verses 18-24, bit by bit.

"The sons of Noah went (*yatsa'*) from the ark." *Yatsa* means "to go after."[121] After leaving the ark, the sons of Noah populated *'erets*.

Shem, Ham, and Japheth left the ark, and then almost as an afterthought, Moses wrote: "Ham was the father of Canaan." Let's explore why that was the case.

- Shem = the name
- Ham = enclosed chaotic water
- Japheth = enlarge
- Canaan (Kena'an) = brought low

First, note the way the names of Noah's sons were listed in verse 18. They were listed according to rank, not how they exited the ark or their birth order. Shem became the Firstborn of their generation.

Next, while his sons scattered, Noah planted a vineyard. In other words, he put down roots, no pun intended.

While drinking wine, Noah became drunk, then uncovered himself. He didn't do so in public but in his tent. However, in spiritual terms, Noah drank the wine of his making, not the wine of Holy Spirit. He lost his (*Aleph-Tav*) mantle – his royal covering. Ham saw Noah's (*Aleph-Tav*) nakedness.

Returning to the literal sense, Ham entered Noah's tent and saw his father's nakedness. After leaving the tent, Ham found his two brothers and told them of their father's condition. Upon hearing that their father was naked, Shem and Japheth found a covering; walking backward, they entered the tent and laid a mantle over Noah. They did so without looking upon their father's nakedness. Noah woke, knowing what had happened.

---

121 Strong's OT#3318

Ezekiel 17:1-2, "The word of the LORD came to me: 'Son of man, set forth an allegory and tell the house of Israel a parable."

Okay, we know the literal. Now let's examine the allegory. Which is that Yah had three sons with whom he made a covenant. The three went straightway from his throne into the cosmos. They scattered throughout all the realms of existence.

Meanwhile, Yah planted a garden and appointed a husbandman to administer his garden, whom he named Adam. Intoxicated with joy, overcome with delight in his garden and its husbandman, Yah visited the garden daily. He was so pleased Yah was seemingly unaware of everything else in the cosmos. After noting his Father's joy, one of the sons entered the garden to find out what filled his Father with so much pleasure. Immediately, that son was jealous when he witnessed his Father's great love for Adam. Surreptitiously, that son, who was chaotic in behavior, uncovered and exposed Adam, which dishonored his Father's purpose for Adam.

Nonetheless, that son was pleased with what he had done. He dashed, found his brothers, and reported that their Father was vulnerable because Adam was stripped and lay naked in the garden. The son who bore the father's name, Yah-Yeshua, along with the one whose responsibility was to enlarge the King's territory, Yah-Spirit, sought and found an acceptable raiment. Then walking back through time, the two carried the shame of Adam upon their own shoulders. They covered Adam and concealed his nakedness, restoring honor to their Father's garden and its husbandman. Seeing what was done to Adam, Yah acknowledged that "a" lesser son had transgressed. To that son, Yah said, "Cursed be my son who has humiliated himself. He shall labor in bondage; he shall fall before his brothers."

The purpose of this allegory is to expose the emotion of betrayal. Yahweh was betrayed by a rebellious son. Yeshua loves his Father so much that he gave everything to reverse the damage caused by the rebellious sons.

> Genesis 9:25-27, *"Then he said, 'Cursed be Canaan; a servant of servants he shall be to his brethren.' And he said,* **'Blessed be Yahweh, the God of Shem**, *and may Canaan be his servant. May Elohiym enlarge Japheth, and may he dwell in the tents of Shem, and may Canaan be his servant."*

Noah blessed Yahweh, referring to him as the *Elohiym* of Shem. These two verses are the first to indicate that Shem was the Firstborn. It is also meaningful that Ham was not mentioned. Only Shem, Japheth, and Canaan.

Ham was on the ark, which meant he was accepted as righteous while there. Yet, at some point, post-flood, he faltered.

Still, I believe Ham belonged to Yahweh because Yahweh had received him on the ark. That suggests Noah could not curse Ham without first seeking Yahweh's permission. Ham's sons were not on the ark, Noah, as Melchizedek could legally curse them, for they were not "acknowledged" as Yahweh's.

Allow me to restate: Firstborns belong to Yahweh. Ham was not chosen by Yahweh as the Firstborn, but that he was on the ark, he had been received as belonging to the Ark (it symbolized covenant – and symbolized Yeshua). This principle harkens back to Cain and the protection given him.

Next, note Moses places Canaan in the middle of the story. Genesis 9:22, *"Ham, the father of Canaan, saw the* (Aleph-Tav) *nakedness of his father."* So perhaps we should surmise that Canaan was somehow involved. Maybe he saw Noah first. However, it was Ham who openly spoke about Noah's nakedness.

Nakedness is *'ervah* and means disgraced; naked; uncovered. In other words, Ham saw the king uncovered and immediately went forth and spoke about it to his brothers. "Told" is *nagad,* meaning to announce, expose, stand out boldly and declare a thing. Did he laugh? Did he jest? Maybe.

Psalms 105:15, *"Saying, Touch not mine anointed, and do my prophets no harm."*
- → Touch – *naga'* – to bring down; to cast down; to strike out as to punish
- → Anointed – *mashiyach* – one who has been consecrated, such as a king or priest
- → Prophet – *nabiy'* – an inspired man
- → Harm – *ra'a* – to afflict; to make mischief; to physically, socially, or morally spoil.

Ham left the Melchizedek uncovered and then exploited the situation. Why didn't he find a covering for his father? The only reason I can imagine is that the intent of his heart was not pure, and thus he had no desire to "cover" his father – the king! The fact that Ham was willing to leave Noah uncovered is telling. It explains why the sin in this story must be placed upon Ham. This incident did not somehow make Noah unrighteous. Noah was still the Melchizedek Regent and was still decreed "righteous." And because Noah was the anointed Melchizedek, he knew what had been done to him when he awoke.

Noah cursed Canaan and then immediately blessed the God of Shem. The phrasing of these verses strongly suggests that Shem was appointed and anointed as Firstborn before this incident. If that be true, neither Ham nor his seed was a part of the Melchizedek Priesthood.

"Younger" is *qatan* and means the lesser, literally in size or figuratively, in age or importance. And do not be thrown by the term "son." In Hebrew, it's *"ben"* and is often associated with grandsons.

Now for my thoughts as to what happened in Noah's tent. This mystery was solved for me by the following excerpt from *Jasher:* And God made the garments of skin for Adam and his wife when they went out of the garden were given to Cush. After the death of Adam and his wife, the garments were given to Enoch, the son of Jared. When Enoch was taken, they were given to Methuselah, his son. And at the death of Methuselah, Noah took them and brought them to the ark, and they were with him until he went out of the ark. And while going out, Ham stole those garments from Noah, his father, and he took them and hid them from his brothers.[122]

Noah woke, and upon noting that he was covered by a garment that was not his, he questioned where the garment came from. Or perhaps, he recognized the garment and knew its origins and thereby knew what

---

[122] Johnson, Ken. *Ancient Book of Jasher* (p. 17). Kindle Edition.

had happened. Yet we must not lose sight of the fact that Noah was anointed; thus, as high priest of the Melchizedek Priesthood, he knew by Holy Spirit what had happened. Upon hearing what Ham had said to his brothers, Noah was dismayed. You see, I suspect Noah knew Ham had taken Adam's garments. Perhaps that was the reason Shem was appointed Firstborn over Ham and Japheth. The stealing of the Melchizedek garments would have immediately disqualified Ham from consideration for the appointment of Firstborn. (In the following chapter, we shall discuss why Japheth was not chosen.)

By now, you have realized that everything affects or is affected by the Melchizedek and his kingdom. Thus, the hidden message in this story concerns the loss of the Melchizedek covering (mantle).

Genesis 3:21, *"... for Adam and his wife the Lord God made tunics of skin and clothed them."* Genesis 9:21, *"(Noah) drank of the wine and was drunk and became uncovered in his tent."*

Adam got it wrong – Noah got it wrong – everybody got it wrong – Yeshua got it right!

These two points are undeniable: 1) Adam became naked and 2) Noah became uncovered. And both men were kings and high priests; both devoted to Yahweh. Yet both were uncovered! Adam lost his Divine covering when his sin left him naked and ashamed. Noah lost his mantle when it was stolen from him, which left him uncovered and humiliated.

Yahweh arrayed (literally and figuratively) Adam with tunics of skin, foreshadowing the work of the future Eternal Melchizedek. The tunics were temporary mantles, covering a temporary Melchizedek. Still, they represented a spiritual concept of immense importance that equated with stealing the Melchizedek's anointing. Ham "stole" and then made fun of it. He left the regency vulnerable to the adversary.

One more vital point about these matters, they exposed Noah's passivity. He failed to properly exercise his God-given authority over his house (family tent). We shall see in the next chapter that he also was unable to exercise his Melchizedek authority over Yahweh's house. The taking of the Melchizedek garments foreshadowed Noah and Nimrod, who became Noah's humiliation.

Noah came to his senses and immediately knew what his son had done. He took no action against Ham and laid the matter's blame at Canaan's feet. Why Canaan? Perhaps because Noah was prophetic and could see the future. However, there is another possibility. Louis Ginzberg suggested that Canaan told Ham of Noah's drunkenness. Yet some of the punishment was inflicted upon him on his own account, for Canaan had drawn Ham's attention to Noah's revolting condition.[123]

Genesis 9:26, *"And may Canaan be his* (Shem's) *servant."*

Noah also prayed that Elohiym (the God of Shem) would increase Japheth and that he would abide in the "house" of Shem. Noah desired for Japheth to be protected by Shem. If Japheth chose correctly and remained with Shem at the altars of Yahweh, Japheth and his offspring would be prosperous.
Noah blessed Shem and Japheth, but not Ham. Ham's nature became chaotic, and his offspring became a

---

[123] Ginzberg, Louis. *The Legends of the Jews — Volume 1* (Kindle Locations 1914-1915) Kindle Edition.

humiliation.

> Genesis 9:28-29, *"And Noah lived after the flood three hundred and fifty years. So, all the days of Noah were nine hundred and fifty years; and he died."*

Genesis Ten

Chapter 10: *"Now this is the genealogy of the sons of Noah:* **Shem, Ham, and Japheth.** *And sons were born to them after the flood.*

"The sons of **Japheth** *were Gomer, Magog, Madai, Javan, Tubal, Meshech, and Tiras. The sons of Gomer were Ashkenaz, Riphath, and Togarmah. The sons of Javan were Elishah, Tarshish, Kittim, and Dodanim. From these,* **the coastland peoples of the Gentiles** *were separated into their lands, every one according to his language, according to their families, into their nations.*

"The sons of **Ham** *were Cush, Mizraim, Phut, and Canaan. The sons of Cush were Seba, Havilah, Sabtah, Raamah, and Sabtechah; and the sons of Raamah were Sheba and Dedan.* **Cush begot Nimrod: he began to be a mighty one on the earth. He was a mighty hunter before the Lord; therefore, it is said, "Like Nimrod, the mighty hunter before the Lord." And the beginning of his kingdom was Babel, Erech, Accad, and Calneh, in the land of Shinar. From that land, he went to Assyria and built Nineveh, Rehoboth Ir, Calah, and Resen between Nineveh and Calah (that is the principal city). Mizraim begot** *Ludim, Anamim, Lehabim, Naphtuhim, Pathrusim, and Casluhim* **(from whom came the Philistines** *and Caphtorim).* **Canaan begot Sidon, his firstborn, and Heth; the Jebusite, the Amorite, and the Girgashite; the Hivite, the Arkite, and the Sinite; the Arvadite, the Zemarite, and the Hamathite. Afterward, the families of the Canaanites were dispersed. And the border of the Canaanites was from Sidon as you go toward Gerar, as far as Gaza; then as you go toward Sodom, Gomorrah, Admah, and Zeboiim, as far as Lasha. These were the sons of Ham,** *according to their families, according to their languages, in their lands, and in their nations.*

"And children were born also to **Shem, the father of all the children of Eber,** *the brother of* **Japheth, the elder.** *The sons of Shem were Elam, Asshur, Arphaxad, Lud, and Aram. The sons of Aram were Uz, Hul, Gether, and Mash. Arphaxad begot Salah, and Salah begot Eber. To Eber were born two sons: the name of one was Peleg, for in his days the earth was divided; and his brother's name was Joktan. Joktan begot Almodad, Sheleph, Hazarmaveth, Jerah, Hadoram, Uzal, Diklah, Obal, Abimael, Sheba, Ophir, Havilah, and Jobab. All these were the sons of Joktan. And their dwelling place was from Mesha as you go toward Sephar, the mountain of the east. "These were the sons of Shem, according to their families, according to their languages, in their lands, according to their nations.*

"These were the families of the sons of Noah, according to their generations, *in their nations; and* **from these, the nations were divided on the earth after the flood"**
(emphasis added).

Genesis 10 is known as the 'Table of Nations.' It provides the record of the sons of Noah… *"in their nations… divided… after the flood."* Primarily it is a roster listing the tribes of *'erets* that will later be known as the Gentile nations. Note that Israel is not listed. It did not become a nation until hundreds of years later. And when it did form, it came through Abraham, who was also not included in this list.

Post-flood, the three sons of Noah divided the realm of *'erets* after "tribal governments" began forming. However, the complexity of what occurred was a bit more involved. It was more than just a few men sitting around a campfire deciding to go their separate ways, as Hollywood might have you believe.

Tribes were families that became nations. They were autonomous, territorial, and sophisticatedly structured. To grasp the significance of the message in this chapter, we need this basic understanding:

- → Pre-flood, all of *'erets* was under the authority of the Melchizedek Kingdom.
- → Post-flood *'erets* was divided into territories with many kings and kingdoms.

It is uncertain who insisted *'erets* be divided among Shem, Ham, and Japheth. This division, however, should be viewed as "the uncovering of Noah." And possibly, for that reason, we can lay the blame on Ham.

Ancient records tell of Japheth and his sons going north[124], Ham and his sons going south, while Shem and his descendants spread across the Middle East, even venturing as far east as the Orient. Shem, however, remained in Eden, residing in Salem (modern-day Jerusalem).

We also note that Genesis 10:21 names Japheth as the elder son. That meant he should have been the Firstborn. Yet, he was not. Why? The truth is, I am uncertain. However, based upon the account given concerning Shem, we find that he was the only one of Noah's three sons who remained righteous. Which would indicate that Japheth and Ham had committed an offense.

We are aware of Ham's offense but are unclear about Japheth's. My assumption is that Japheth "abandoned his father's business."

All postulates to the Melchizedek Priesthood were to concern themselves solely with the kingdom. Apparently, Japheth sought to go his own way. When we carefully consider the words concerning Japheth in Genesis 10:5, it is possible to conclude Japheth walked away from Noah., *"From these, the coastland peoples of the* **Gentiles** *were* **separated** *into their lands, every one* **according to his** *language,* **according to their** *families, into their nations."* This was the first use of the word "gentile." So, the association of Japheth with the word "gentile" is a hint. The root of the Hebrew term used in this verse is *goy*, which connotes "a turning of the back," primarily against Judaism. Gentile is Latin, meaning not Jewish. However, at that time, there were no Jews. So in this instance, we adhere to the extended meaning of *goy*.

Japheth and his sons went north, first to the isles, then into the mountains of Turkey and Greece. By doing so, Japheth placed a considerable distance between himself and his father – he turned his back. Note the following concerning the House of Japheth:

---

[124] Remember Jerusalem is the center point of biblical geography.

- **Japheth's sons**: Gomer, Magog, Madai, Javan, Tubal, Meshech, and Tiras.
- The sons of Gomer (Celtics): Ashkenaz, Riphath, and Togarmah.
- The sons of Javan (Greece and Rome): Elishah, Tarshish, Kittaim, and Rodanim.

Although Japheth had seven sons, the text expands upon only Gomer and Javan. I wondered about that, and as I considered possible reasons, the thought came that there was a message in their names. So, I grabbed my Hitchcock's Bible Names Dictionary.

- <u>Gomer</u> – to finish; complete
- Ashkenza- a fire that spreads
- Riphath- release; pardon
- Togarmah- all bone
- <u>Javan</u> – mire
- Elishah – it is God; the lamb of God, that saves
- Tarshish – his excellency; dove
- Kittim (Chittim)- breaking; invade
- Rodanim (Dodanim)- to move slowly

Next, I placed those meanings in sentence form: The elder brother's sons produced a bloodline, which will finish what began in Eden, the **completion** of the kingdom. The Elder was promised **a fire spreading** across *'erets*, burning the **restraints** placed upon mankind by **Death**. The **miry** clay of human flesh will look upon the **Lamb of God that saves** and align with His **Excellency** and together **invade darkness** as the message of the Kingdom spreads **slowly** throughout *'erets*.

Well, that was fun. So, I did the same with Ham's descendants:

- **Ham's sons:** Cush, Mizraim, Phut, and Canaan.
- The sons of Cush: Seba, Havilah, Sabtah, Raamah, and Sabteca.
- The sons of Raamah: Sheba and Dedan.
- Ham (chaos)
- Cush (darkness)
- Mizraim (tribulation)
- Phut (words that bind)
- Canaan (humiliation)
- Seba (intoxication)
- Havilah (surrounds)
- Sabtah (thunder)
- Raamah (depressing)
- Sabtechah (unsure of the correct meaning of this name)
- Raamah - the covenant
- Sheba (slowly)
- Dedan (probably – to judge)

Chaos (Ham) fathered **darkness** (Cush), **tribulation** (Mizraim), **deception** (Phut), and **humiliation** (Canaan). **Darkness, intoxicated** by pride, **surrounded** *'erets* with **thunderous** threats; **depressing** truth; distorting the **covenants** of Yahweh, slowly bringing **judgment** to *'erets*.

As you can see, names carry messages. Yet, I am not saying that the preceding exercise was Holy Spirit-inspired. The intent was to demonstrate that names are meaningful and in the Holy Writ for a reason.

Ham fathered Mizraim, who was the progenitor of Egypt and Philistia. Ham also fathered Phut. Phut was the progenitor of the people that became Persia (modern-day Iran). And, of course, Ham fathered Canaan.

Note that the principal enemies of Israel were fathered by Ham. Which were Egypt (including the Philistines), Persia (Babylon), and the Canaanites tribes of the Amorites.

Canaan and his sons moved into Eden and most of the Middle East, overthrowing Shem's offspring. Ham's descendants' past, present, and future have waged war, in one manner or another, against the Melchizedek Kingdom since the time of Genesis 10.[125]

Genesis 10:8, *"Cush begot Nimrod; he began to be a mighty one on the earth."*

The name Cush means dark. Darkness begot Nimrod. If there was ever an individual conceived by the personification of Darkness, it was Nimrod. It is essential to say this upfront, Nimrod was the first "Anti-Messiah." I suspect he, or at least the spirit of who he became, is the Anti-Christ yet to be revealed. But let's develop this line of thought a bit more slowly.

Genesis 10:8 does not read that Nimrod was born a giant but that he became one. If you recall the word *gibbowr* from our study of Genesis 6:4, you remember that the *Nephilim* were *gibbowr*. So, did Nimrod become a Nephilim, a hybrid? 1 Chronicles 1:10 also states, "Cush begot Nimrod; he began to be a mighty one (*gibbowr*) on *'erets*." Scripturally, we have two separate witnesses that state Nimrod began to be *gibbowr*. To fully grasp what Nimrod became, we first must determine what is implied by the term *gibbowr*. Does this term mean that Nimrod became a giant or powerful? Or both?

In that, Nimrod "began to be *gibbowr* on *'erets*," hints that whatever he became was intentional and different from the normal. Yet, both Genesis 10:8 and the I Chronicles 1:10 texts assert that Cush begot Nimrod. This would mean that Nimrod received twenty-three of his forty-six chromosomes from Cush. And since there is no record of *gibborim* in Cush's ancestry, we are left with three possibilities as to how Nimrod became *gibbowr*:
1. Nimrod's mother was a giant, or someone up lineage from her was a giant.
2. In this instance, *gibbowr* doesn't mean giant.
3. Nimrod transformed through some supernatural means and became a giant.

---

[125] This subject will be developed with greater detail in Day Three.

I think the most likely possibility is either 2 or 3. So, let's explore these by turning to Genesis 10:8 in the Septuagint: *"And Cush begot Nebrod: he **began** to be a **giant** upon the earth."* Well, that eliminates the number two possibility. Nimrod was a giant but wasn't born one. So, he transformed.

- Strong's OT#3205 *yalad* (yaw-lad) a primitive root; to bear young; causatively, to **beget**; medically, to function as a midwife; specifically, to show lineage.
- Strong's OT#2490 *chalal* (khaw-lal) a primitive root properly, to bore, by implication to wound, to dissolve; figuratively, **to profane a person**, place, or thing, to break (one's word), to begin.
- Strong's OT#1961 *hayah* (haw-ya) a primitive root; to exist, to be or **become**, "come to pass" (always emphatic, and not a mere copula or auxiliary).
- Strong's OT#1368 *gibbowr* (ghib-bore or gibbor) **powerful;** by implication, **warrior, tyrant,** champion, chief, **giant,** man, mighty (man, one), strong (man), valiant man.

Nimrod began as "normal" and became something more, which is what is inferred. Nimrod existed (*hayah*) as something profane (*chalal*). In other words, in some manner, he was transformed into something, and whatever that was, was powerful and blasphemous, going beyond the ordinary into the supernatural.

A warlord is profane. So is a giant. Both blasphemes the purpose of mankind. Profane is usually defined as disrespectful of religious or sacred practices. Given that perspective, we consider that God did not create giants nor teach men to war. War and giants disrespect the sacred intent of humans as a species.

1908 AM – And Cush the son of Ham, the son of Noah, took a wife in those days in his old age, and she bare a son, and they called his name Nimrod, saying, At that time the sons of men again began to rebel and transgress against God, and the child grew up, and his father loved him exceedingly, for he was the son of his old age. And the garments of skin which God made for Adam and his wife when they went out of the garden were given to Cush…. And Nimrod became strong when he put on the garments.[126]

Louis Ginzberg wrote nearly the same: The first among the leaders of the corrupt men was Nimrod. His father Cush had married his mother at an advanced age, and Nimrod, the offspring of this belated union, was particularly dear to him as the son of his old age. He gave him the clothes made of skins that God had furnished Adam and Eve when they left Paradise. Cush himself had gained possession of them through Ham.[127]

To avoid conjectures that have little basis, let's rethink what *Jasher* and Ginzberg wrote concerning this matter. *Jasher* attributed Nimrod's rise to power to the garments that belonged to Noah. Interesting theory! Rest assured, we shall discuss this notion. However, allow me to state with absolute certainty: The garments did not possess magic. Yet, how these garments came into Nimrod's possession is insightful. It affirms the appetite for power and greed in Ham, Cush, and Nimrod. All were driven to be "great" – to outdo others and, more significantly, to profane the name of Yahweh.

Nimrod's determination drove him to possess his own global kingdom. So, rather than think the garments

---

[126] *The Book of Jasher,* unknown author, Global Grey eBooks, (Kindle Locations 467-470).
[127] Ginzberg, Louis. *The Legends of the Jews — Volume 1* (Kindle Locations 1999-2002) Kindle Edition.

mystically empowered him, we should conclude Nimrod bargained for power. And possibly for his kingdom. In doing so, he surrendered his soul to "the evil one." That he, perhaps sold his soul for his own kingdom, would not have made him a physical giant but instead a man of great power and prestige. Again, there is something else hidden that we need to understand.

According to *Jasher,* Nimrod was born in the year 1908 A.M., which was 252 years after the flood. Using the dates provided in *Jasher*'s account Cush was approximately 250 years of age, and Noah (Nimrod's great-grandfather) 852. Ham (Nimrod's grandfather) was close to three hundred. By that time, post-flood, the population of Earth neared one million.

Another fact to consider is that Noah's three sons ventured off in different directions to build separate kingdoms. That detail is vital because they competed, in the physical and spiritual realms, for control of *'erets*. Fundamentally, the consequence of that opposition pitted Nimrod against the Melchizedek Kingdom.

At the time of Nimrod's birth, Cush was the king of Nubia. Nubia was located along the Nile (southern Egypt - northern Sudan). Nubia pre-dated Egypt.

The ancients called Nubia, *Ta-Seti* (land of the bow - as in bow and arrow). Later, the Egyptians would call that same area Kush. *Cushi* is the Greek rendering of the Egyptian term. It is also a derivative that references the ancient Kingdom of Kush.[128] Artifacts from the region of the Nile suggest that *Ta-Seti* also was the birthplace of the pharaonic civilization. *Ta-Seti* was a powerful self-governing kingdom; more importantly, it was an intricate civilization.

Cush had other sons: *"The sons of Cush were Seba, Havilah, Sabtah, Raamah, and Sabtechah; and the sons of Raamah were Sheba and Dedan,"* Genesis 10:7. These five older sons, born while Cush was still a young man, meaning they, not Nimrod, were heirs to his kingdom. His brothers were senior to Nimrod by at least a hundred years, indicating that the five had likely already inherited Cush's kingdom by the time Nimrod was born. Born too late, Nimrod was out of luck.

Although Jasher stated that Nimrod's mother was a wife, the implication is that she was not "legal" according to the laws of royal alliances. If that were the case, it explains Nimrod's warrior tenancies. He was driven to have his own kingdom, apart from his half-brothers, superior to theirs.

Cush kept the garments that Ham gave to him in secret. He, too, concealed them from his brothers and his older sons. This perhaps indicates the relationship between Cush and his older sons was strained.

Now, these garments were supposedly those Yahweh gave to Adam. That being the case, they were Melchizedek garments and represented the mantle or covering, foreshadowing the righteousness of Yeshua. Adam wore them as a mantle, meaning he wore them when officiating as the King of kings, the Lord of lords, and the Melchizedek high priest. So, they belonged to whoever served as the high priest of *'erets,* and as the global king - they represented global authority.

---

128 https://en.wikipedia.org/wiki/Cushitic_peoples#History retrieved May 1, 2020

Ham likely gave the garments to Cush in an equivalent manner to how they were given to Nimrod, secretly. Ham might have hoped that Cush would overthrow the Melchizedek Kingdom and become the king of a new order. A new global kingdom based upon the Golden Age, the era when the gods interacted freely with men. In other words, the new order would resurrect the pre-flood Doctrine of Emanation.

Did Cush hold on to the garments hoping he would become the king of the new order one day? Then, as an old man realized that would never be. So, he gave the garments to Nimrod, and Nimrod put them on, thereby taking on the dream of being the king of the new world order. Though we cannot be absolutely sure, it appears that was the case. And if so, Nimrod would have been told of the promise attached to the garments. Of course, that promise was that the final ruler of *erets* would be a Divine.

"He (Nimrod) *was a mighty hunter before the Lord; therefore, it is said, 'Like Nimrod, the mighty hunter before the Lord.' And the beginning of his kingdom was Babel, Erech* (Uruk), *Accad* (Akkad), *and Calneh* (Nippur), *in the land of Shinar* (Sumer). *From that land, he went to Assyria and built Nineveh, Rehoboth-Ir, Calah, and Resen between Nineveh and Calah (that is the principal city),"* Genesis 10:8-12. In referencing these cities, a connection is created between Nimrod to ancient Sumer.

Enmerkar and the Lord of Aratta, an epic story, interestingly provided another link. The poem, written about 2000 B.C., mentions the confusion of the languages. Among other tidbits, it points to the Temple of Babel.

Ararat (a Hebrew term) is pronounced Aratta in Aramaic. As I'm sure you recall, Ararat is the mountain upon which the ark came to rest. The poem tells of the Lord of Aratta (Ararat) and his adversary, Enmerkar. It hints metaphorically that the Lord of Aratta is Noah and Enmerkar is Nimrod. In the poem, Enmerkar is notably referred to as "the son of Utu" (the Sumerian sun god), saying that Enmerkar was the founder of Uruk and the builder of a temple built at Eridu[129]. He was even credited with writing upon clay tablets to threaten the Lord of Aratta into submission. Enmerkar sought to restore the disrupted linguistic unity of the inhabited regions around Uruk, listed as Shubur, Hamazi, Sumer, Uri-ki (the area around Akkad), and the Martu (Amorite) land.[130]. There is also a Sumerian Kings List, a listing of the first House of Uruk, also known as the First Dynasty of Uruk. Legend has the House of Uruk descended from the sun god, Utu. Ancients Sumerians viewed their kings as superhuman, capable of mighty deeds in that they were deities. They memorialized these kings as powerful men: Enmerkar, Lugalbanda, Dumuzi, and Gilgamesh are not only on that list but also have monuments dedicated to them that date back to the Uruk Period (c. 3800-2850 BC).

The House of Uruk (Enmerkar) yielded one of the most remarkable and outstanding eras in all ancient Mesopotamian history.[131] Erech or Uruk (pronunciation depends on whether the translation is Hebrew or Greek) was founded by Enmerkar. Therefore, many have concluded that Nimrod was Enmerkar, a king of great significance. By the way, Nimrod was not a name but a descriptive term. Hitchcock's Dictionary

---

[129] Refer to the chapter on Genesis 6 for the understanding, Eridu was the city named for Cain's grandson.
[130] https://en.wikipedia.org/wiki/Enmerkar retrieved May 1, 2020
[131] https://www.ancient-origins.net/history/sumerian-heroes-0012916 retrieved May 1, 2020

defines it as Assyrian and translates "nimrod" as rebellion.[132]

It is beyond the scope of this study to search for conclusive evidence proving Nimrod was Enmerkar, so instead, I offer indirect proof and logic. Enmerkar was viewed as a god, as a demi-god. So, it is reasonable to assume that Nimrod, as Enmerkar transformed from humble beginnings, rose above his station and sat on the world's stage as the king of kings of a new order. Did he become immortal? Well, that is debatable, for what I have failed to discuss with you, up to now, is the matter of the *Rephaim*.

There is a legend that the House of Uruk descended from the sun god, Utu. That connection is another vital component. Note the progenitor "descended" from Utu.

Utu was worshipped in Babylonia (Sumer) as the sun god. His twin, Inanna, was revered as the Queen of Heaven. They both were the offspring of Enlil (Hêlēl). Ah-ha! Hopefully, you just made the connection to Ezekiel 28. This progression of revealing clues described an entity who Paul stated in 2 Thessalonians 2:3-4 was *"the son of perdition, who opposes and exalts himself above all that is called God or that is worshiped, so that he sits as God in the temple of God, showing himself that he is God."*

Later, in the era associated with the Greeks, Utu was called Apollo, and his twin, Artemis. Their father was Zeus. So, the same gods of the pre-flood returned post-flood, using different names but having the same personas. And these gods also brought forth offspring. Genesis 6:4. *"There were giants on the earth in those days, and also afterward...,"*

Sumerian artifacts suggest Enmerkar was much taller than the average human male. How was a physical transformation possible? Take note of the following: And he found a writing which former (generations) had carved on the rock, and he read what was thereon, and he transcribed it and sinned owing to it; for it contained the teaching of the Watchers in accordance with which they used to observe the omens of the sun and moon and stars in all the signs of heaven. And he wrote it down and said nothing regarding it, for he was afraid to speak to Noah about it lest he should be angry with him on account of it.[133]

Evidently, the Watchers left "teachings" – the mysteries of the celestial world. Which I suggest was DNA manipulation. Clearly, the Watchers knew how since they created chimeras. But did they also leave spells that could transform a man into a demi-god? Or did they teach incantations that would awake the dead, and the *Rephaim* returned to instruct the living? The answer is yes to both. Don't forget information is a core element. DNA is structured information.

Did Nimrod invoke the spiritual netherworld and, through that invocation, open a portal to release evil when he put on the garments of Adam? The answer likely is yes.

He was a global king, the first, not a Melchizedek Regent. In my opinion, Nimrod was the first anti-Messiah (Christ). He was *anti*-the-Anointed Melchizedek. *Anti* means "in the place of." He was the adversary of Noah and Shem and, for all intents and purposes, the one who uncovered Noah.

---

[132] *Hitchcock's Bible Names Dictionary*, PC Study Bible Copyright © 2003, 2006 Biblesoft, Inc. All rights reserved.
[133] Charles, R.H. *The Book of Jubilees* (Kindle Locations 691-694). Kindle Edition.

Nimrod built the "Babylonian" system, although it was not called Babylon in Nimrod's time. Nimrod was the post-flood father of the false system by any name or title.

Genesis 10:13-14, *"Mizraim begot Ludim, Anamim, Lehabim, Naphtuhim, Pathrusim, and Casluhim - from whom came the Philistines and Caphtorim."* Mizraim means to be captured by trouble, to be besieged.

Genesis 10:15, *"Canaan begot Sidon his firstborn…,*

- → Like Nimrod, Sidon opposed the Melchizedek Kingdom.
- → Like Nimrod, he too built a counter-system to the Melchizedek Kingdom
- → Sidon (Tsiydon – also spelled Zidon) opposed the lordship of Noah and Shem.

"Beloved, do not believe every spirit but test the spirits, whether they are of God because many false prophets have gone out into the world. By this, you know the Spirit of God: Every spirit that confesses that Jesus Christ has come in the flesh is of God, and every spirit that does not confess that Jesus Christ has come in the flesh is not God. And this is the **spirit of the Antichrist**, *which you have heard was coming and is now* **already in the world** (cosmos)," 1 John 4:1-3 (emphasis added.)

At first, as families grew in number, they formed tribes. As the tribes increased, cities were built.

"These were the sons (the seed) *of Ham* (chaos), *according to their families* (tribes), *according to their languages* (babbling speech), *in their lands and in their nations,"* Genesis 10:20.

"And children were born also to Shem (the Name), *the father of all the children of Eber* (those who cross over), *the brother of Japheth* (the one who Yahweh enlarges), *the elder,"* Genesis 10:21. *"The sons of Shem were Elam* (concealed), *Asshur* (blessed), *Arphaxad* (a healer and releaser), *Lud* [?], *and Aram* (elevated)," Genesis 10:22.

"Arphaxad (a healer and releaser), *begot Salah* (the sent one), *and Salah begot Eber* (those who cross over)," Genesis 10:24. *"To Eber were born two sons: the name of one was Peleg* (an earthquake), *for in his days the earth was divided; and his brother's name was Joktan* (made little)," Genesis 10:25.

Note that the progeny of Elam, the son born first to Shem, was not included in this listing. Instead, Moses focused on Arphaxad [v. 24] and Eber [v.25] and Peleg. The omission of Elam's offspring meant Elam was not selected to serve as Firstborn. Apparently, that honor became Arphaxad's. However, Arphaxad died before Shem. As of this writing, I have yet to find any account of Arphaxad serving as a Firstborn. On the other hand, Eber did, leading me to believe he was the Melchizedek immediately following Shem's death.

Genesis 10
The 'Table of Nations'

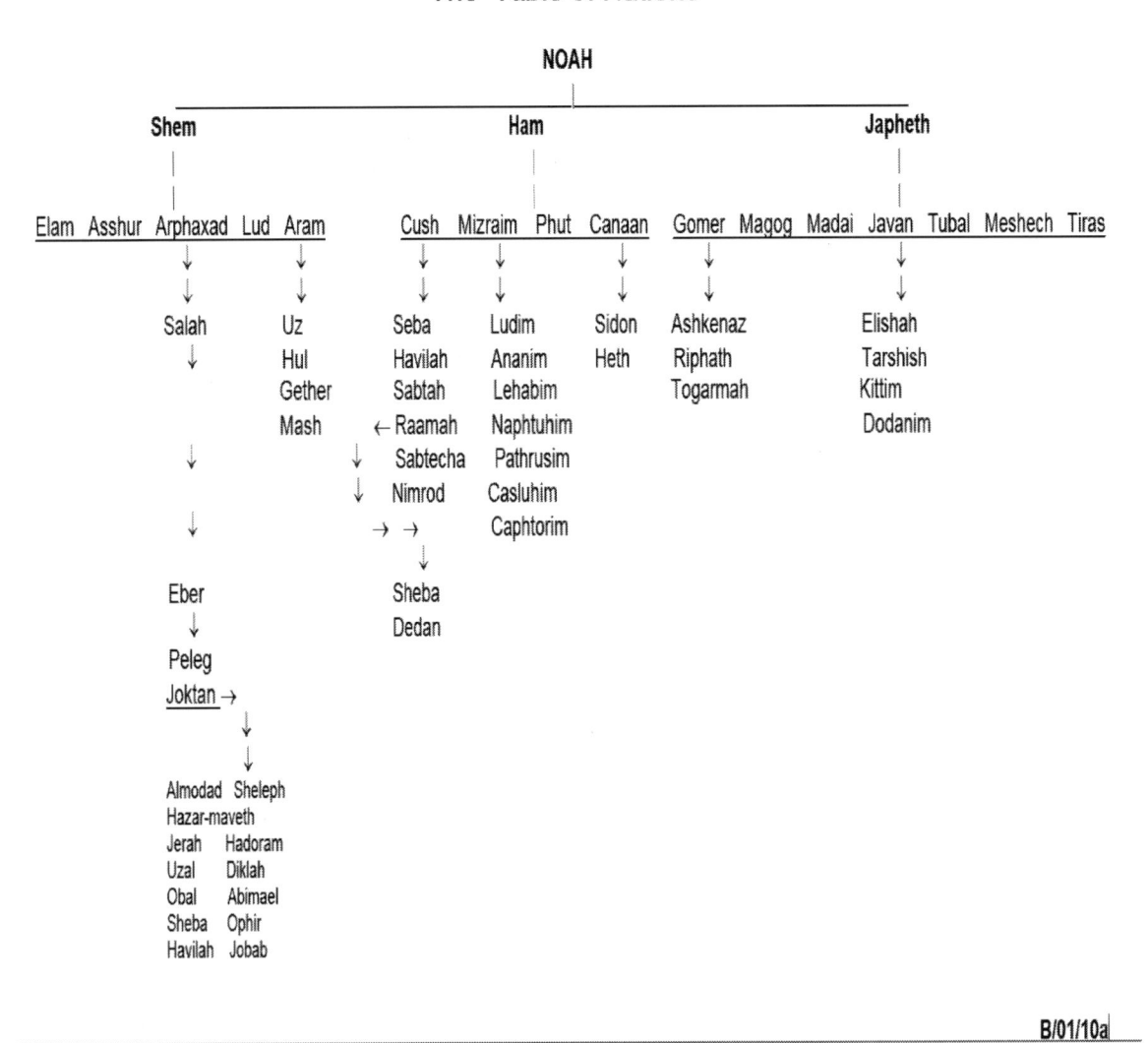

```
                                    NOAH
                                      |
        Shem                          Ham                           Japheth
          |                            |                               |
 Elam Asshur Arphaxad Lud Aram    Cush Mizraim Phut Canaan    Gomer Magog Madai Javan Tubal Meshech Tiras
              ↓       ↓            ↓     ↓          ↓           ↓                   ↓
            Salah    Uz          Seba   Ludim      Sidon      Ashkenaz           Elishah
              ↓      Hul         Havilah Ananim    Heth       Riphath            Tarshish
                     Gether      Sabtah Lehabim               Togarmah           Kittim
                     Mash     ←Raamah   Naphtuhim                                Dodanim
                              ↓ Sabtecha Pathrusim
                              ↓ Nimrod   Casluhim
                                → →      Caphtorim
              ↓                   ↓
                               Sheba
            Eber               Dedan
              ↓
            Peleg
            Joktan →
                    ↓
                    ↓
          Almodad  Sheleph
          Hazar-maveth
          Jerah   Hadoram
          Uzal    Diklah
          Obal    Abimael
          Sheba   Ophir
          Havilah Jobab
```

Genesis Eleven

Genesis 11:1-9, *"**Now the whole earth had one language and one speech**. And it came to pass, as they journeyed from the east, that they found a plain in the land of Shinar, and they dwelt there. Then they said to one another, 'Come, let us make bricks and bake them thoroughly.' They had brick for stone and they had asphalt for mortar. And they said, 'Come, let us build ourselves a city and a tower whose top is in the heavens; let us make a name for ourselves, lest we be scattered abroad over the face of the whole earth.' But the Lord came down to see the city and the tower which the sons of men had built. And the Lord said, 'Indeed the people are one, and they all have one language, and this is what they begin to do; now nothing that they propose to do will be withheld from them. Come, let us go down and confuse their language, that they may not understand one another's speech.' So, the Lord scattered them abroad from there over the face of all the earth, and they ceased building the city. Therefore, its name is called Babel, because there the Lord confused the language of all the earth; from there the Lord scattered them abroad over the face of all the earth."*

Genesis 11:10-26, *"**This is the genealogy of Shem:** Shem was one hundred years old, and begot Arphaxad two years after the flood. After he begot Arphaxad, Shem lived five hundred years and begot sons and daughters. Arphaxad lived thirty-five years and begot Salah. After he begot Salah, Arphaxad lived four hundred and three years and begot sons and daughters. Salah lived thirty years and begot Eber. After he begot Eber, Salah lived four hundred and three years and begot sons and daughters. Eber lived thirty-four years and begot Peleg. After he begot Peleg, Eber lived four hundred and thirty years and begot sons and daughters. Peleg lived thirty years and begot Reu. After he begot Reu, Peleg lived two hundred and nine years and begot sons and daughters. Reu lived thirty-two years and begot Serug. After he begot Serug, Reu lived two hundred and seven years and begot sons and daughters. Serug lived thirty years and begot Nahor. After he begot Nahor, Serug lived two hundred years and begot sons and daughters. Nahor lived twenty-nine years and begot Terah. After he begot Terah, Nahor lived one hundred and nineteen years and begot sons and daughters. Now Terah lived seventy years and begot Abram, Nahor, and Haran."*

Genesis 11: 27-32, *"**This is the genealogy of Terah:** Terah begot Abram, Nahor, and Haran. Haran begot Lot. And Haran died before his father Terah in his native land, in Ur of the Chaldeans. Then Abram and Nahor took wives: the name of Abram's wife was Sarai, and the name of Nahor's wife, Milcah, the daughter of Haran, the father of Milcah and the father of Iscah. But Sarai was barren; she had no child. And Terah took his son Abram and his grandson Lot, the son of Haran, and his daughter-in-law Sarai, his son Abram's wife, and they went out with them from Ur of the Chaldeans to go to the land of Canaan; and they came to Haran and dwelt there. So, the days of Terah were two hundred and five years, and Terah died in Haran."*

Almost as if it were a parenthetical thought, the story surrounding the Tower of Babel is sandwiched between the genealogies of Genesis 10 and those of Genesis 11. When I first noted this, I asked why. Immediately I thought about Exodus 34:10-17, *"Then Yahweh said, 'I am making a covenant with you. Before all your people, I will do wonders never before done in any nation in all the world. The people you live among will see how awesome is the work that I, Yahweh, will do for you. Obey what I command you today. I will drive out before you the Amorites, Canaanites, Hittites, Perizzites, Hivites, and Jebusites.* **Be careful not to make a treaty with those who live in the land where you are going, or they will be a snare among you.** *Break down their altars, smash their sacred stones, and cut down their Asherah poles. Do not worship any other god, for Yahweh, whose name is Jealous, is a jealous God. Be careful not to make a treaty with those who live in the land, for when they prostitute themselves to their gods and sacrifice to them, they will invite you, and you will eat their sacrifices. And when you choose some of their daughters as wives for your sons, and those daughters prostitute themselves to their gods, they will lead your sons to do the same. Do not make cast idols.'"*

Deuteronomy 7: 1-11, *"When Yahweh, your God, brings you into the land, which you go to possess, and has cast out many nations before you, the Hittites and the Girgashites and the Amorites and the Canaanites and the Perizzites and the Hivites and the Jebusites, seven nations greater and mightier than you, and when Yahweh, your God, delivers them over to you, you shall conquer them and utterly destroy them. You shall make no covenant with them nor show mercy to them. Nor shall you make marriages with them. You shall not give your daughter to their son nor take their daughter for your son. For they will turn your sons away from following Me, to serve other gods; so, the anger of the Lord will be aroused against you and destroy you suddenly. But thus, you shall deal with them: you shall destroy their altars, and break down their sacred pillars, and cut down their wooden images, and burn their carved images with fire.* **For you are a holy people to Yahweh, your God; Yahweh, your God, has chosen you to be a people for Himself, a special treasure above all the peoples on the face of the earth. Yahweh did not set His love on you nor choose you because you were more in number than any other people, for you were the least of all peoples; but because Yahweh loves you, and because He would keep the oath which He swore to your fathers, Yahweh has brought you out with a mighty hand,** *and redeemed you from the house of bondage, from the hand of Pharaoh king of Egypt. Therefore, know that Yahweh, your God, He is God, the faithful God who keeps covenant and mercy for a thousand generations with those who love Him and keep His commandments; and He repays those who hate Him to their face, to destroy them. He will not be slack with him who hates Him; He will repay him to his face. Therefore, you shall keep the commandment, the statutes, and the judgments which I command you today, to observe them."*

It appears that Moses' intent regarding the presentation of history between these two chapters was to direct the attention of the offspring of Abraham toward Shem, the last globally recognized Melchizedek. I suspect his purpose was to repair their self-esteem. To transform them from a slave mentality to one of Hebrew exceptionalism.

Although Isaac took possession of the regency, it was void of power and authority – Isaac was Melchizedek in name only. That was also true for Jacob; he too was king/high priest in name only. The fallen realm had seemingly won and rendered the Melchizedek system null and void. Yet, Yahweh was not defeated. That was Moses's message, the purpose of why he wrote the history of their beginnings as he did. Yahweh was returning Israel, as a nation, to Eden, in preparation for the advent of the Eternal Melchizedek.

The amount of detail that I'm skipping over is vast – but this is the point: The descendants of Abraham, Isaac, and Jacob held the scepter to the Melchizedek Kingdom, for it was hidden in Judah. However,

Yahweh desired that the entire nation of Israel be Melchizedek, not merely the one tribe of Judah. Yet, Israel failed to understand. So, while they waited for Moses at Mount Horeb, in their ignorance, they sinned.

Still, Yahweh was not defeated – He still had a plan! His promise to the Eternal Melchizedek would still be fulfilled through Abraham's offspring. To that end, Yahweh instructed the Israelites to facilitate the cause. They needed to become Hebrew by crossing over from the world's system.

Adam had weakened the Melchizedek Kingdom, and Noah lost its covering. Then, Terah made himself subservient to Nimrod and Babylon. So, Moses separated the genealogies of Shem and Terah. Yet, through Abraham, the system of the Melchizedek would again reign.

What is most notable about the genealogy of Shem as presented in Genesis 10 is how it differs from the one of Genesis 11. Genesis 10 lists the offspring of Shem – the tribes from Shem to Joktan.

The Genesis 10 genealogy would best be described as listing Shem's children. By the way, Arabic legend holds that Joktan was the progenitor of the Arabic tribes. So, this list isn't about Firstborns.

But Genesis 11 is, and that is the difference. The sons deemed firstborn, from Shem to Terah, is how the descendants are recorded. However, note that listing is not exclusive to generational Firstborns – it switches. From Peleg down to Terah, the list becomes "legal" firstborns. Legal firstborns administrated their father's estate. You see, in the days of Peleg, *'erets* was divided.

Genesis 11:1-2, *"Now the whole earth had one language and one speech. And it came to pass, as they journeyed from the east, that they found a plain in the land of Shinar, and they dwelt there."* *'Erets* had one language (*saphah*) - one speech (*dabar*). Figuratively and literally, no borders existed at that time, *'erets* was a global community - with one manner of speech.

Men journeyed to the east and sought to rebuild that elusive Golden Age of the pre-flood world. People traveled east to the plain (*biq'ah* – the breach between mountains) in Shinar (Babylonia), and there they dwelt (*yashab* – remained). The phrasing of "the breach between mountains" alludes to their desire to find a portal. An opening that they believed existed "between" the cosmic mountains of the gods. In other words, they sought to find the breach between the netherworld and the upper regions of the cosmic planes.

Shinar is most likely a corruption of the Hebrew term *shene neharot* (two rivers). Shinar refers to the Mesopotamian Valley stretching between Euphrates and Tigris. It is also possible that Shinar is a derivate of *shene arim* (two cities). In addition, there is the thought that Shinar was derived from the Hebrew pronunciation of the Akkadian word, Šumeru.[134]

Shinar is Hebrew, whereas Babylonia is Greek. They both refer to the same place –the birthplace of post-flood counter-systems. While the word, Babylon, is Greek, it is an adaptation of the Akkadian term *Babilli*. *Babilli* means "Gate of God" or, more precisely, the "gateway to the gods." Hebrew spells *Babilli* as *Bavel*. *Bavel* is often translated as confusion due to its close resemblance to the Hebrew verb *bilbél*, which means

---

134 https://en.wikipedia.org/wiki/Shinar retrieved May 6, 2020

"to confuse."

And he (Nimrod) placed Terah the son of Nahor the prince of his host, and he dignified him and elevated him above all his princes. And whilst he was reigning according to his heart's desire, after having conquered all his enemies around, he advised with his counselors to build a city for his palace, and they did so. And they found a large valley opposite to the east, and they built him a large and extensive city...[135] And all nations and tongues heard of his fame, and they gathered themselves to him, and they bowed down to the earth, and they brought him offerings, and he became their lord and king, and they all dwelt with him in the city at Shinar, and Nimrod reigned in the earth over all the sons of Noah, and they were all under his power and counsel. And all the earth was of one tongue and words of union, but Nimrod did not go in the ways of the Lord, and he was more wicked than all the men that were before him, from the days of the flood until those days.[136]

And king Nimrod reigned securely, **and all the earth was under his control**, and all the earth was of one tongue and words of union. And all the princes of Nimrod and his great men took counsel together; Phut, Mitzraim, Cush, and Canaan with their families, and they said to each other, Come let us build ourselves a city and in it a strong tower, and its top reaching heaven, and we will make ourselves famed, so **that we may reign upon the whole world, in order that the evil of our enemies may cease from us, that we may reign mightily over them, and that we may not become scattered over the earth on account of their wars.** And they all went before the king, and they told the king these words, and the king agreed with them in this affair, and he did so. And all the families assembled consisting of about six hundred thousand men, and they went to seek an extensive piece of ground to build the city and the tower, and they sought in the whole earth, and they found none like one valley at the east of the land of Shinar, about two days' walk, and they journeyed there, and they dwelt there. And they began to make bricks and burn fires to build the city and the tower that they had imagined to complete. And the building of the tower was unto them a transgression and a sin, and they began to build it, and whilst they were building against **the Lord God of heaven, they imagined in their hearts to war against him and to ascend into heaven.**[137]

Genesis 11:3 *"Then they said to one another, 'Come, let us make bricks and bake them thoroughly.' They had brick for stone, and they had asphalt for mortar."*

The *Book of Jasher* is not Bible canon, but it does afford a historical perspective. The people, led by Nimrod, sought to overthrow their enemies. Who were their enemies? If Nimrod ruled over all the earth, his only viable enemy would be Noah, later Shem. Both opposed what Nimrod attempted.

Noah represented Yahweh. Nimrod knew that. That's why it is believed he sought to ascend into "heaven" - to war with Yahweh. Incredibly that had to be possible. Nimrod was not stupid, nor were his "great men."

Genesis 11:4, *"And they said, 'Come, let us build ourselves a city, and a tower whose top is in the heavens; let us make a name for ourselves, lest we be scattered abroad over the face of the whole earth.'"*

Now it was Nimrod who excited them to such an affront and contempt of God. He was the grandson of Ham, the son of Noah, a bold man of great strength of hand. He persuaded them not to ascribe it to God, **as if it was through**

---

[135] Unknown Author. *The Book of Jasher* (Kindle Locations 485-488). Global Grey eBooks. Kindle Edition.
[136] Ibid. (Kindle Locations 490-494).
[137] Ibid (Kindle Locations 596-606).

his means they were happy, but to believe that it was their own courage that procured that happiness. He also gradually changed the government into tyranny, seeing no other way of turning men from the fear of God but to bring them into a constant dependence on his power. He also said he would be revenged on God if he should have a mind to drown the world again; for that, he would build a tower too high for the waters to be able to reach and that he would avenge himself on God for destroying their forefathers! Now the multitude were very ready to follow the determination of Nimrod, and to esteem it a piece of cowardice to submit to God, and they built a tower, neither sparing any pains, nor being in any degree negligent about the work: and, by reason of the multitude of hands employed in it, it grew very high, sooner than anyone could expect; but the thickness of it was so great, and it was so strongly built, that thereby its great height seemed, upon the view, to be less than it really was. It was built of burnt brick, cemented together with mortar, made of bitumen that it might not be liable to admit water. [138]

Jasher and Josephus both recorded that it was Nimrod who incited the building of the Tower of Babel, a ziggurat with a height that reached toward the heavens.

Genesis 11:5-6, *"But Yahweh came down to see the city and the tower which the sons of men had built. And Yahweh said, 'Indeed the people are one, and they all have one language,* **and this is what they begin to do; now nothing that they propose to do will be withheld from them."**

If Yahweh thought they could achieve their goal, shouldn't we? Therefore, I am going to propose to you that Nimrod had indeed learned how to be interdimensional. Somehow, his DNA had been manipulated, bringing about a transformation. That transformation added perception to his natural human senses. This increased bandwidth allowed him to access the underworld and the higher cosmic dimensions. In other words, his data bank of "language information" had become one with the netherworld, and he could communicate with them at will. Which means he could also perceive all cosmic dimensions. Nimrod was unified, soul and purpose, with the fallen gods.

Let us build:
- A city - Strong's OT#5892 *iyr* (pronounced - eer) a city, a place guarded by a watch (military term); in the broadest sense, an encampment; a military post; a court. It is also plausible that this term refers to the Watchers and thus, implies the people built the "tower" for the Watchers.
- A tower - Strong's OT#4026 *migdal* – a derivate of *gadal*, which means to twist. A *migdal* is a tower due to its size and height, by analogy, a rostrum. Figuratively, it was a pyramidal bed of flowers constructed for worship.
- A name for ourselves - Strong's OT#8034 *shem* is a mark or memorial of individuality; by implication, honor; authority; character; name; renown.

Genesis 11:4, "…let us build us, for the Watchers, a **tower** whose **top** will **transport us unto their cosmic mountains,** so we may **make us a name**, or else we will be scattered abroad as nothing upon the face of the whole earth" (paraphrased by the author).

Nimrod and his followers made a pact like the one made by the Watchers on Mount Hermon. They agreed

---

[138] Josephus, *Antiquities of the Jews*, PC Study Bible Copyright © 2003, 2006 by Biblesoft, Inc. All rights reserved.

to: "obtain children (the meaning of build) and through them erect a place from which we shall rule and have our own divine court. Our tower will have a platform from which we shall unite with our gods. Our gods will rule as the *elohim* of heaven's court. The leader of our gods will keep us together – keep us from being scattered (dashed into pieces)."

Wow! Another coup d'état. Again the fallen realm sought to destroy Yahweh and His Melchizedek. They did not win then, nor shall they in the future. Revelation 18:21, *"Then a mighty angel took up a stone like a great millstone and threw it into the sea, saying, 'Thus with violence the great city Babylon shall be thrown down, and shall not be found anymore.'"*

This conflict we think of as the Tower of Babel was between Noah and Nimrod. It's the story of a counter-king who seeks to destroy the true king. Precisely, it parallels the conflict between Yeshua and the Anti-Christ. Hidden in the figurative language of these stories is deep-rooted jealousy harbored against the rightful king. Remember that Noah represented the Eternal Melchizedek, whereas Nimrod, the "son of Destruction."

This same type of struggle existed between Ham and Shem. Ham desired to be the Firstborn of his generation, like Cain. And like Cain, Ham was not chosen. Instead, he became ranked as the "lesser" son.

To the *Jasher* account of Ham stealing Adam's garments, we add the following facts:
- → Noah's first-born son was Japheth – the birth year 1556 A.M.
- → Noah's second sons were twins – Shem and Ham – birth year 1558 A.M.

Jasher 5 states the following: Noah went and took a wife, and he chose Naamah, the daughter of Enoch, and she was five hundred and eighty years old. And Noah was four hundred and ninety-eight years old when he took Naamah for a wife. And Naamah conceived and bare a son, and he called his name Japheth, saying, God has enlarged me in the earth; and she conceived again and bare a son, and he called his name Shem, saying, God has made me a remnant, to raise up seed in the midst of the earth. And Noah was five hundred and two years old when Naamah bare Shem, and the boys grew up and went in the ways of the Lord… [139]

Jasher made no mention of a third conception. So, either Ham was Japheth's twin, or he was Shem's. The logical choice is that he was Shem's twin. In this regard, we note *Jasher's* first mention of Ham: "And these are the names of the sons of Noah: Japheth, Ham, and Shem…."[140] To connect the dots, we add the following:

- → Genesis 6:10, *"And Noah begot three sons:* **Shem, Ham, and Japheth.**"
- → Genesis 7:1, *"Come into the ark, you and all your household, because I have seen that you are righteous before Me in this generation."*
- → Genesis 9:18-19, *"Now the sons of Noah who* **went out of the ark were Shem, Ham, and Japheth.** *And Ham was the father of Canaan."*
- → Genesis 9:22-24, *"And Ham, the father of Canaan, saw the nakedness of his father and told his two brothers outside. But Shem and Japheth took a garment, laid it on both their shoulders and went backward and covered the*

---

[139] Johnson, Ken. *Ancient Book of Jasher* (pp. 13-14). Kindle Edition.
[140] Ibid (p. 16). Kindle Edition.

*nakedness of their father. Their faces were turned away, and they did not see their father's nakedness. So, Noah awoke from his wine and knew what his **younger** son had done to him."*

If Japheth was the eldest and Shem the second son, why not list them in that order? Why list them as Shem, Ham, and Japheth? The only logical reason is that Shem was the chosen Firstborn, and Moses gave Shem his proper rank. Yet if that is the case, why place Ham before Japheth? The answer lies in knowing "Japheth the elder" was disqualified from being the Firstborn before Shem was chosen. If that were the case, then Shem and Ham were contenders as twins. That is until he dishonored Noah.

The Bible ranks them according to royal status. For example, Noah was the king. Therefore, all his sons were princes. Yet Shem was more than a prince. He was the Firstborn of his generation, a priest in the Melchizedek Priesthood. So, he outranked his brothers regardless of age.

Once Shem was chosen as the Firstborn, his position was superior to his brothers, which I believe made Ham bitter with jealousy. The king of the darkness, recognizing the bitterness in Ham, used it to his advantage by inciting Ham with reckless rage. In turn, Ham became the Melchizedek Kingdom's number one enemy.

Jealousy is perverse and persistent, even spreading its tentacles into the third and fourth generations. Numbers 14:18, *"The Lord is longsuffering and abundant in mercy, forgiving iniquity and transgression; but He by no means clears the guilty, visiting the iniquity of the fathers on the children to the third and fourth generation."*

Josephus: Nimrod excited them to such an affront and contempt of God. He was the grandson of Ham, the son of Noah, a bold man of great strength of hand. He persuaded them not to ascribe it to God (Yahweh), as if it was through his means they were happy, but to believe that it was their own courage which procured that happiness. He also gradually changed the government into tyranny, seeing no other way of turning men from the fear of God but to bring them into a constant dependence on his power. He also said he would be revenged on God if he should have a mind to drown the world again; for that, he would build a tower too high for the waters to be able to reach and that he would avenge himself on God for destroying their forefathers! [141]

Essentially, Nimrod positioned himself as the supreme ruler over a "new world order." That meant he had to dismantle the Melchizedekian order.

Genesis 11:3-4 is a list of weapons:

- Bricks – Strong's OT#3843 *lebenah* (leb-ay-naw') a brick (from the whiteness of the clay); can also refer to an altar of bricks.
- Burn – Strong's OT#8313 *saraph* (saw-raf') is a primitive root that means to be (causatively) set on fire.
- Bitumen – Strong's OT#2564 *chemar* (khay-mawr') is a slime that boils underground.
- Thoroughly – Strong's OT#8316 *serephah* (ser-ay-faw') is derived from the Hebrew word that equates to cremation.

---

141 Josephus, *Antiquities of the Jews*, PC Study Bible Copyright © 2003, 2006 by Biblesoft, Inc.

- Mortar – Strong's OT#2563 *chomer* (kho'mer) is a bubbling up of the earth.
- Stone – Strong's OT#68 *'eben* (eh'-ben) means to build; the root of *'eben* is *ben* (son).

Let's develop sentences around these definitions: No tribal or national borders separated the people at that time. They spoke one language as a unified body. As time passed, the people began looking to the past, to the time before the great flood when the *bene 'elohim* set up their sovereignties and opposed Yahweh's Melchizedek. In that same manner, the people proposed to do the same again. They journeyed, like Cain, into the east and found a vast space between the two rivers of the east, where before the flood, Cain had built a vast city. They "camped" between the rivers. In between "heaven" and "hell." Then, one said to the others, "Come, let us make an altar and burn a sacrifice so that it is cremated. We will then cover **him** with slime, which boils up from the underworld – **he** will be our offering to gain entrance into the *elohim*." They agreed, as with one voice, and with like mind, they built a place for their common cause that they might worship as divine beings.

For additional insight, note the following from *Veneration: Unveiling the Ancient Realms of Demonic Kings and Satan's Battle Plan for Armageddon*: Traditions and sources outside the Bible identify the builder of the tower as the shadowy figure named Nimrod. Our best guess is that he lived sometime between 3500 and 3100 BC, a period of history called the Uruk Expansion. This tracks with what little is told in the Bible about Nimrod. Genesis 10:10, we read, "the beginning of his kingdom was Babel, Erech, Accad, and Calneh, in the land of Shinar."[142] Scholars have learned that the name "Babylon" was interchangeable with other city names, including Eridu. So "Babylon" didn't always refer to the city of Babylon in ancient texts.[143] Now, this is where we tell you that *abzu* (*ab* = water + *zu* = deep) is where we get our English word "abyss." And the name *"Enki"* is a compound word. *En* is Sumerian for "lord," and *ki* is the word for "earth." Thus, *Enki*, god of the *abzu*, was "lord of the earth." Do you remember Jesus calling someone "the ruler of this world"? Or is Paul referring to "the god of this world"? Who were they talking about? Satan. The lord of the dead.[144]

Isaiah 14:12, *"How you have fallen from heaven, O morning star, son of the dawn! You have been cast down to the earth, you who once laid low the nations!"*

Ezekiel 28:16, *"By the abundance of your trading you became filled with violence within, and you sinned; therefore, I cast you as a profane thing out of the mountain of God; and I destroyed you, O covering cherub, from the midst of the fiery stones."*

"Now, we will tell the interpretation of it before the king. You, O king, are a king of kings. For the God of heaven has given you a kingdom, power, strength, and glory; and wherever the children of men dwell, or the beasts of the field and the birds of the heaven, He has given them into your hand, and has made you ruler over them all **— you are this head of gold**.*"* Daniel 2:36-38. Nebuchadnezzar, however, was not the founder of the Babylonian Kingdom but the ruler of it when Daniel wrote. The founder was Nimrod. Nebuchadnezzar ruled about 1,000 years later and over the Neo-Babylonian Empire. The point being the timeline allotted to the idolatrous gentile counter-systems

---

142 Gilbert, Veneration: Unveiling the Ancient Realms of Demonic Kings and Satan's Battle Plan for Armageddon (p. 244). Defender. Kindle Edition.
143 Ibid.
144 Ibid.

began with Nimrod.

As Noah and the Melchizedek system diminished, the gentile system increased. Yet, the gentile kingdoms shall decrease. "*... the iron, the clay, the bronze, the silver, and the gold were crushed together and became like chaff from the summer threshing floors; the wind carried them away so that no trace of them was found...*"[145] for they were broken to pieces and scattered to the wind.

Luke 21:24, "*... and Jerusalem shall be trodden down of the Gentiles until the times of the Gentiles be fulfilled.*"

- → Times [*kairos* – Greek for a set time]
- → Gentiles [*ethnos* – Greek for pagan]
- → Fulfilled [*pleroo* – Greek meaning to satisfy; complete; accomplish]

Genesis 11:8-9, "*So,* **the Lord scattered them abroad** *from there over the face of all the earth, and* **they ceased building** *the city. Therefore, its name is called Babel, because there the Lord confused the language of all the earth; from there the Lord scattered them abroad over the face of all the earth.*"

...and God knew all their works and all their evil thoughts, and he saw the city and the tower which they were building. And when they were building, they built themselves a great city and a very high and strong tower... And the Lord knew their thoughts... And they built the tower and the city, and they did this thing daily until many days and years elapsed. And **God said to the seventy angels** who stood foremost before him, to those who were near him, saying, Come let us descend and confuse their tongues, that one man shall not understand the language of his neighbor, and they did so unto them. And from that day following, they forgot each man his neighbor's tongue, and they could not understand to speak in one tongue... And those who were left amongst them, when they knew and understood the evil which was coming upon them, they forsook the building, and they also became scattered upon the face of the whole earth. And they ceased building the city and the tower; therefore, he called that place Babel, for the Lord confounded the Language of the whole earth; behold, it was at the east of the land of Shinar. And as to the tower which the sons of men built, the earth opened its mouth and swallowed up one-third part thereof, and a fire also descended from heaven and burned another third, and the other third is left to this day, and it is of that part, which was aloft, and its circumference is three days' walk. And many of the sons of men died in that tower, a people without number.[146]

Louis Ginzberg also referred to the seventy angels. Who were these seventy angels? How do they fit into the story? The answer is found in Deuteronomy 32 and Psalms 82. But first, let's back up to Genesis 10:25. "*To Eber were born two sons: the name of one was Peleg, for in his days the earth was divided*" (*palag* means to literally split or figuratively divide). *Peleg* and *palag* are spelled identically. The difference is not the Hebrew letters but how the "points" are placed. Points, or diacritic marks, indicate vowels. The proper name, Peleg, means earthquake. Yet as a verb, it refers to channeled water.

Deuteronomy 32:7-9, "*Remember the days of old; consider the generations long past. Ask your father, and he will tell you, your elders, and they will explain to you.* **When the Most High gave the nations their inheritance when he**

---

145 Daniel 2:45
146 Johnson, Ken. *Ancient Book of Jasher* (pp. 21-22) Kindle Edition.

divided all mankind, he set up boundaries for the peoples according to the number of the sons of El for Yahweh's portion is his people, Jacob his allotted inheritance."

Yahweh *"nachal"* the nations. He "divided" the nations as allotments of "inheritance" to seventy *elohim* "princes." The "people" who were gifted as an inheritance to the seventy were *goy*. The seventy princes were assigned territories (principalities) and commanded to "spread out;" and go into their appointed regions. Yet, that is not what happened. Instead, the people and their judges unified and purposed to build a tower.

My translation of Deuteronomy 32: 7-8 and Genesis 11:6-8. "Your father will show you, and your elders will tell you. When divided according to their inheritance, El Elyon dispersed the *goyim* of Adam's sons. He appointed the boundaries of their tribes by the number of the sons of El." Then notice, "Yahweh said, 'Indeed the people are one, having one language.'" The people came together; they did not stay in their assigned territories. "And this is what they begin to do," which was to erect a tower, a means by which they could access Yah's sacred mountain. "Now, nothing that they propose to do will be withheld from them." Why? Because they were unified, but not just with each other, the people were united to the fallen realm.

So, Yahweh said to His righteous ones, "Come, **let us go down** and **there confuse their language**, that they may not understand one another's speech." Yahweh descended to the lower regions of the enemy. He "mixed" up His enemies. He *"balal"* them. Essentially, Yahweh terminated their ability to pass "knowledge" (celestial information) between their ranks, especially to the *goyim*. That action translates as a reduction of bandwidth within the *goyim*. And, in my opinion, a confusion of purpose in the fallen realm; after that, they became territorial. Daniel speaks of the "prince of Persia," the "prince of Greece," and so on.[147] This action also weakened the fallen realm's ability to communicate with mankind on a global basis. *"So, the Lord scattered them abroad from there over the face of all the earth, and they ceased building the city."*

Psalms 82: *"God stands in the congregation of the mighty; He judges among the gods.* **How long will you judge unjustly and show partiality to the wicked?** *Defend the poor and fatherless; do justice to the afflicted and needy. Deliver the poor and needy; free them from the hand of the wicked.* **They do not know, nor do they understand; they walk about in darkness; all the foundations of the earth are unstable.** *I said, 'You are gods, and all of you are children of the Most High. But you shall die like men and fall like one of the princes.' Arise, O God, judge the earth; for You shall inherit all nations."* What foundations were unstable? Righteousness and justice!

The Table of Nations of Genesis 10 presents seventy tribes or nations formed from the offspring of Noah's three sons. When the sons of Noah divided *'erets,* the seventy were removed from Melchizedek's control. A Divine Council judge was assigned to serve as an overseer of each. Those seventy judges were to "protect and care" for their assigned nation.

Note that all seventy nations were considered "gentile" and that Israel was not included. The word "gentile" simply means not "Hebrew," a foreign people, believers in the false system.

---

147 See Daniel 10:20

Noah and Shem had no "nation of people" aligned with them. As already stated, Israel was omitted from the text because it was not yet a nation. That is why the Melchizedek Priesthood was temporarily suspended with Noah, Shem, and Eber. Abram was on the horizon, and the Third Day was around the corner.

The word "divided" was translated from a Hebrew root that is usually used as a descriptive value to note the "separation" of humans by race as "gentile." The root, *parad,* is also used to substantiate a long-held rabbinical observation that Genesis 10-11 was the reasoning supporting the following verse. Deuteronomy 32:8, *"he divided all mankind according to the number of the sons of El."*

Israel was never assigned to any deity – she was Yahweh's portion. So, the reference to seventy "sons of Israel" in the Masoretic text of Deuteronomy 32 is misleading. Perhaps, understandable in that Genesis 46:27 and Exodus 1:5 stated that seventy members of Jacob's family went to Egypt in the days of Joseph.[148]

However, the number seventy of Deuteronomy 32 was a correlation – a parallel not inclusive of Israel herself. "Literary and conceptual parallels discovered in the literature of Ugarit, however, have provided a more coherent explanation for the number seventy in Deuteronomy 32:8 and have furnished support for textual scholars who argue against the 'sons of Israel' reading. Ugaritic mythology plainly states that the head of its pantheon, *El* (who, like the God of the Bible, is also referred to as *El Elyon*, (the 'Most High') fathered seventy *sons*, thereby specifying the number of the "*sons* of *El*" (Ugaritic, *bn il*)."[149]

"The *dt'ilm* (assembly of *El* / the gods) of Ugaritic texts represents the most precise parallel to the data of the Hebrew Bible. Psalm 82:1 also uses the same expression for the council (*dt'ilm*), along with an indisputably plural use of the word '*elohim* (God or gods): God ('*elohim*) stands in the council of *El*/the divine council (*ba'adat 'el*); among the gods ('*elohim*) he passes judgment. The second occurrence of '*elohim* must be plural due to the preposition 'in the midst of.' The Trinity cannot be the explanation for this divine plurality since the psalm goes on to detail how Israel's God charges the other '*elohim* with corruption and sentences them to die 'like humankind.' Psalm 89:5-7 [6-8] places the God of Israel 'in the assembly of the holy ones' (*biqhal qedosim*) and then asks who in the clouds can be compared to Yahweh. Who is like Yahweh among the sons of God (*bene 'elim*), a god greatly feared in the council of the holy ones (*besod qedosim*)? Psalm 29:1 commands the same sons of God (*bene 'elim*) to praise Yahweh and give him due obeisance. These heavenly sons of God (*bene 'elim*), or the (*bene 'elohim*) appear in other biblical texts (Gen 6:2.4; Job 1:6; 2:1; 38:7; and Deuteronomy 32:8-9, 43 [LXX, Qumran]) … At Ugarit, the divine council and its gods met on a cosmic mountain, the place where heaven and earth intersected and where divine decrees were issued. This place was at the 'source of the two rivers' (*mbk nhrm*) in the 'midst of the fountains of the double-deep' (*qrb apq thmtm*). This well-watered mountain was the place of the 'assembled congregation' (*phr m 'd*). *El* dwelt on this mountain and, with his council, issued divine decrees from the 'tents of *El*' (*dd 'il*) and his 'tent shrine.'"[150]

Before Yahweh confused their language, there were no national boundaries. *'Erets* functioned as a global community. Afterward, language became the boundary that distinguished one tribe or nation from another. *Saphah,* translated into English as "language," also means a border.

---

148 https://digitalcommons.liberty.edu Bibliotheca Sacra158 (January-March 2001) 52-74 DEUTERONOMY 32:8 AND THE SONS OF GOD Michael Heiser

149 https://digitalcommons.liberty.edu Bibliotheca Sacra158 (January-March 2001) 52-74 DEUTERONOMY 32:8 AND THE SONS OF GOD, Michael Heiser

150 http://www.thedivinecouncil.com/HeiserIVPDC.pdf

The *Book of Jasher* suggests that the earth swallowed one-third of the tower. Possibly. However, the following is my interpretation of Genesis 11:5-10: "But Yahweh descended that he might see the court and the platform, which the sons of men had set up. And Yahweh said, 'Behold, this collective group of people have one language: one manner. What they profanely appoint they will complete, for nothing will be inaccessible should they proceed with what they determine. They shall do what they are united with the fallen realm to do. So go and confuse their language that they may not discern one another's speech.' So, Yahweh scattered them abroad from there, across the face of the earth, and they ceased building the city. Accordingly, the name of that place became Babel because there, Yahweh appointed a confused language for each tribe on the earth. Broken apart, they were scattered across the face of all the earth."

Speculations abound as to the cause of the tower's toppling – but the exact cause is unknown. A meteorite could have hit it, or a tornado of great force weakened the structure, causing it to collapse under its weight.

The Genesis 10 genealogy listing of Shem differs from the one in Genesis 11 mainly due to the addition of the Bible's first mention of Abram, Genesis 11:26.

The Genealogy of Shem

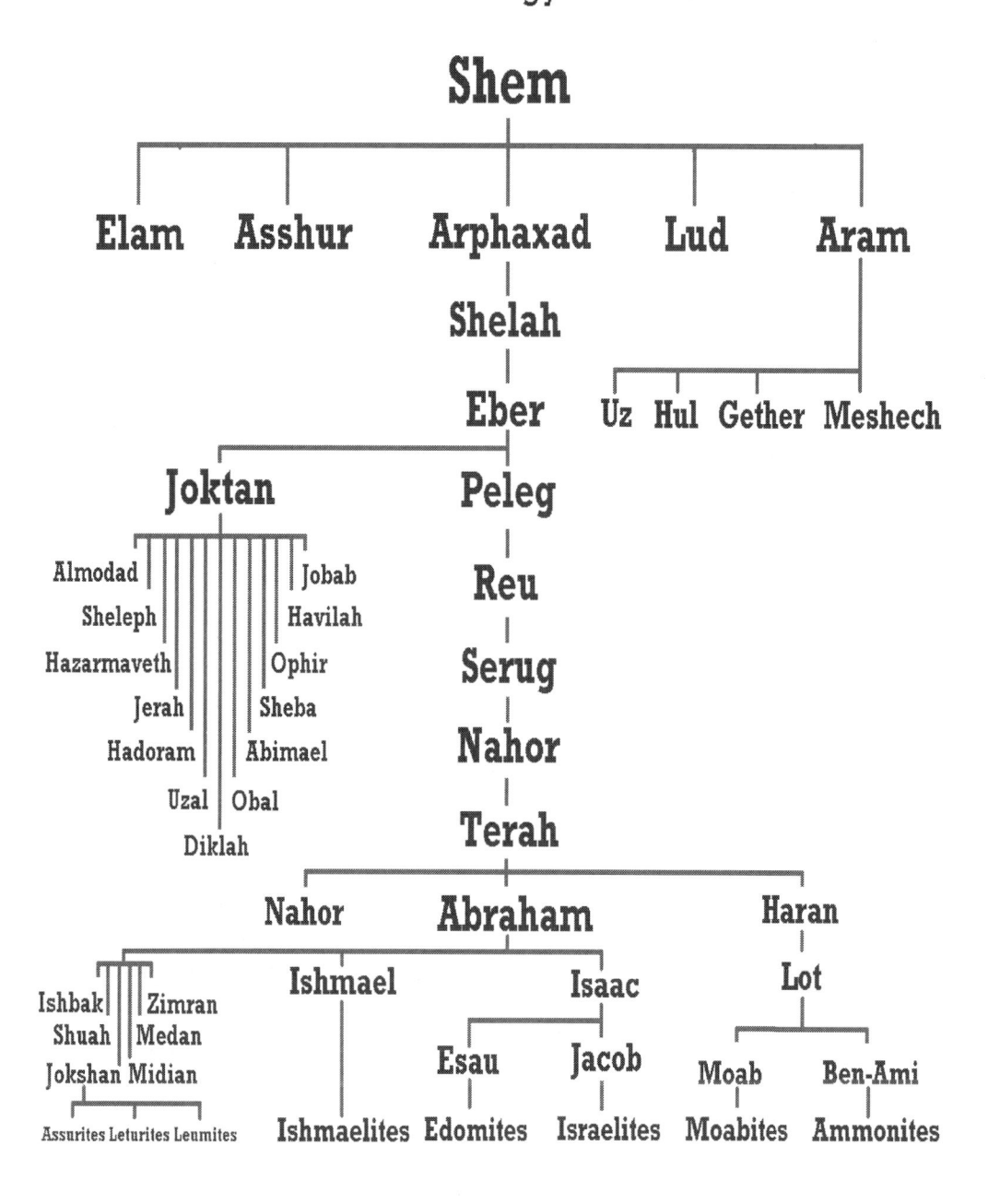

Shem
- Elam
- Asshur
- Arphaxad
  - Shelah
    - Eber
      - Joktan
        - Almodad
        - Sheleph
        - Hazarmaveth
        - Jerah
        - Hadoram
        - Uzal
        - Diklah
        - Obal
        - Abimael
        - Sheba
        - Ophir
        - Havilah
        - Jobab
      - Peleg
        - Reu
          - Serug
            - Nahor
              - Terah
                - Nahor
                  - Ishbak
                  - Shuah
                  - Jokshan
                    - Assurites
                    - Leturites
                    - Leumites
                  - Zimran
                  - Medan
                  - Midian
                - Abraham
                  - Ishmael → Ishmaelites
                  - Isaac
                    - Esau → Edomites
                    - Jacob → Israelites
                - Haran
                  - Lot
                    - Moab → Moabites
                    - Ben-Ami → Ammonites
- Lud
- Aram
  - Uz
  - Hul
  - Gether
  - Meshech

DAY THREE

Genesis Twelve

"Now the Lord had said to Abram: 'Get out of your country, from your family and from your father's house to a land that I will show you. I will make you a great nation; I will bless you and make your name great, and you shall be a blessing. I will bless those who bless you, and I will curse him who curses you, and in you, all the families of the earth shall be blessed." Genesis 12:1-3

'Amar, said, challenges; commands; appoints. In the context of Genesis 12:1, it was an imperative command. Yahweh commanded Abram to leave the country of his birth, his kindred, and his father's house. Yahweh appointed Abram to *"the land I will show you."*

Acts 7:2-3, *Brethren and fathers, listen: The God of glory appeared to our father Abraham when he was in Mesopotamia, before he dwelt in Haran, and said to him, "Get out of your country and from your relatives and come to a land that I will show you."*

And Abram remained in the land three years, and at the expiration of three years, the Lord appeared to Abram and said to him; I am the Lord who brought thee forth from Ur Casdim and delivered thee from the hands of all thine enemies. And now, therefore, if thou wilt hearken to my voice and keep my commandments… and go to the land of Canaan and remain there, and I will there be unto thee for a God, and I will bless thee.[151]

The serpent entered the garden on Adam's watch. On Noah's, the Tower of Babel was built. And in between, the Watchers descended and brought unspeakable chaos. It's not plausible to evaluate which of these was the most horrific. Each attributed to evil. Even so, it is imperative to understand each, considering Abram's calling. These three evils were the reason Abram was commanded to leave Ur. However, as usual, we cannot go the direct route; vital details would be overlooked. So, we are going around the proverbial mountain to find the truth.

"The earth also was corrupt before God, and the earth was filled with violence. So, God looked upon the earth, and indeed it was corrupt…."[152] Yahweh permitted the flood to *"destroy from the face of the earth all living things"* [153] because *"there were giants on the earth in those days, and afterward when the sons of God came into the daughters of men, and they bore children to them. Those were the mighty men who were of old, men of renown."*[154] Then Yahweh *"came down to see the city and the tower which the sons of men had built. He said, 'Indeed the people are one, and they all have one language, and this is what they begin to do; now nothing that they propose to do will be withheld from them. Come, let Us go down and there confuse their language, that they may not understand one another's speech.' So, Yahweh scattered them abroad from there over the face of all the earth, and they ceased building the city."*[155]

---

151 Johnson, Ken. *Ancient Book of Jasher* (p. 30). Kindle Edition
152 Genesis 6:11-12
153 Genesis 7:4.
154 Genesis 6:4
155 Genesis 11:5-9

Using the NJKV, we can determine that Abram was born 1,948 years after Adam was created or "In the year of the world, 1948 Anno Mundi." Interestingly, Israel as a nation was born in 1948, Anno Domini, in the year of our Lord.

As we discovered in the previous section, Day Two was anything but peaceful. So, Yahweh had specific reasons for commanding Abram to leave Ur and exacting ones that directed him to Canaan. This means we need to know more about Canaan. And why we need to go around the mountain to get there.

It is widely accepted that the *Book of Job* is the oldest of the Old Testament scrolls. Due to recent archeological findings, the question of when the scroll was penned has resurfaced. However, since *Job* contains no references to the Law of Moses, the assumption remains that it was written before the Exodus. If that is the case, then Job most likely lived in the same era as Abraham.

Job 1:1-2, *"There was a man in the land of Uz* (Uts), *whose name was Job* (Iyovb), *and that man was blameless and upright, and one who feared* (revered) *God* **(Elohiym)** *and shunned* (turned from) *evil."* Genesis 10:21-23, *"And children were also born to Shem, the father of all the children of Eber, the brother of Japheth, the elder. The sons of Shem were Elam, Asshur, Arphaxad, Lud, and Aram. The sons of Aram were* **Uz**, *Hul, Gether, and Mash"* (emphasis added).

Bible scholars believe that the "land" of Uz was named for Shem's grandson. This also infers Job and Abram were likely generational contemporaries. Yet, it is doubtful they were acquainted. Nonetheless, we should view their respective spheres of influence and the environments they lived in to be similar. So, like Abram, Job was an influential chieftain, a man of great wealth possessing much. Also, like Abram, he revered Yahweh as his *Elohiym*.

Job shunned evil. That phrase suggests that Job served only Yahweh. It also aligns him with the Melchizedek of his day, who I believe was Noah. Furthermore, by turning from evil, Job turned away from the false system of government that demanded that he worship the fallen gods. Acting as a priest, probably since he did not live near Noah or Shem, Job offered burnt offerings on behalf of his family. That indicates he was familiar with the duties of a priest and the Melchizedek system. And when we read passages like the following, we can be assured that Job was familiar with Adam's and Noah's teachings.

Job 19:25-27, *"For I know that my* **Redeemer lives**, *He shall stand at last on the earth; after my skin is destroyed, this I know, that in my flesh I shall see* **Eloah**, *whom I shall see for myself, and my eyes shall behold, and not another. How my heart yearns within me!"* (Emphasis added).

Job expected a Divine Messiah. This means he was familiar with the decrees given to Adam and Eve. Thus, he knew the Messiah would be born of a virgin. That distinct understanding of an expected Messiah was common, even at that time. By stating that his Redeemer existed, Job was, in fact, proclaiming his personal faith in a Divine person who would come and act upon his behalf as his kin. Another way to express Job's words: "My Redeemer shall avenge me and deliver me from the abyss, as my next of kin."

The virgin birth of the expected eternal king was written in the stars. Adam had that revelation, and so did Noah, Job, and Abram. It's vital to understand that Abram knew the "gospel" message of the Mazzaroth.

"The heavens declare the glory of God, and the firmament shows His handiwork. Day unto day utters speech, and night unto night reveals knowledge. There is no speech nor language where their voice is not heard. Their line has gone out through all the earth, and their words to the end of the world. In them, He has set a tabernacle for the sun, which is like a bridegroom coming out of his chamber and rejoices like a strong man to run its race. Its rising is from one end of heaven and its circuit to the other end, and there is nothing hidden from its heat." Psalms 19:1-6

Job 1:6-13, *"Now there was a day when the **sons of God** came to present themselves before* (Yahweh), *and* (haSaataan) *also came among them. And* (Yahweh) *said to* (haSaataan), *'From where do you come?' So* (haSaataan) *answered* (Yahweh) *and said, 'From **going to and fro on the earth, and from walking back and forth on** it.' Then* (Yahweh) *said to* (haSaataan), *'Have you considered My servant Job, that there is none like him on the earth, a blameless and upright man, one who fears* (Elohiym) *and shuns evil?'* (haSaataan) *answered* (Yahweh) *and said, 'Does Job fear* (Elohiym) *for nothing? Have You not **made a hedge around him, around his household, and around all that he has on every side**? You have blessed the work of his hands, and his possessions have increased in the land. But now, stretch out Your hand and touch all that he has, and he will surely curse You to Your face!' And* (Yahweh) *said to* (haSaataan), *'Behold, all that he has **is in your power**; only do not lay a hand on his person.' So* (haSaataan) *went out from the presence of the Lord"* (emphasis added).

In the previous sections, we noted that the accuser was a Traveler. The Hebrew word rendered "traveler" is *ōbĕrîm*, a plural form of the verb *'br*, which means "to pass from one side to the other." In this context, then, a Traveler is a spirit that passes from one plane of existence to another, in the same sense that the ancient Greeks believed the dead had to travel across the River Styx to reach or return from the underworld.[156]

Yahweh gave the traveling accuser access to Job, allowing the prosecutor to go beyond the protection perimeter placed around Job. But then, in Job 41:9-11, Yahweh declared, *"Indeed, any hope of overcoming him* (the leviathan) *is false; shall one not be overwhelmed at the sight of him? No one is so fierce that he would dare stir him up. Who then can stand against Me? Who has preceded Me that I should pay him? Everything under* (below) *heaven is Mine."*

Yahweh stated that He possesses the ultimate say. He is in control, and "everything below" heaven belongs to Him, as heaven is His. *'Erets,* or earth, is below heaven. Hell is below heaven. Hence, Yahweh possesses absolute authority over all realms. Yet, He allows "His" adversaries to continue to exist.

Removing the serpent from the garden, the Watchers from Mount Hermon, or crashing the Tower of Babel didn't stop the rebellion. I suggest the reason is that Yahweh is committed to ridding the entire cosmos of evil. But shall do so legally, so none can accuse Him of an unjust act.

No one knows for sure how many gods initially rebelled. Nevertheless, over time their number increased. Genesis 3:4 portrays only one, but by Genesis 6:4, there are at least two hundred more. Then the seventy judges we discussed in the previous chapter joined the rebellion.

Revelation 12:4 suggests one-third of all celestials chose to align with the god of chaos. (*"His tail drew a third*

---

[156] Gilbert, Sharon K.; Gilbert, Derek P. *Veneration: Unveiling the Ancient Realms of Demonic Kings and Satan's Battle Plan for Armageddon* (p. 87). Defender. Kindle Edition.

of the stars of heaven and threw them to the earth.")[157]

Revelation 12:7-9, *"And war broke out in heaven, Michael and his angels fought with the dragon, and the dragon and his angels fought, but they did not prevail. Nor was a place found for them in heaven any longer. So, the great dragon was cast out, that serpent of old called the Devil and Satan, who deceives the whole world; he was cast to the earth, and his angels were cast out with him."*

Approximately three hundred years post-flood, all of *'erets* was under the false system. Eden also, except Salem. (However, Yahweh had a remnant. Job belonged to that group.)

Abram was aware of these details. He knew an ongoing war existed between Yahweh and the fallen realm. He was also aware that Noah lost his authority over *'erets,* as its global king, to Nimrod.

"Terah was seventy years old when he begat him, and Terah called the name of his son that was born to him Abram (exalted father) because the king (Nimrod) had raised him (Terah) in those days and dignified him above all the princes that were with him."[158]

"He (Abram) went to Noah and his son, Shem, and remained with them to learn the instruction of the Lord and his ways, and no man knew where Abram was, and Abram served Noah and Shem for a long time.[159]

1988 A.M., when "Abram was in Noah's house thirty-nine years… Abram knew the Lord (Yahweh) from three years old, and he went in the ways of the Lord (Yahweh) until the day of his death, as Noah and his son Shem had taught him."[160] The *Book of Jasher* continues with how Abram grew and excelled under the tutelage of Noah and Shem. Yet, at the same time, Terah served other gods by erecting idols and practicing necromancy. He venerated the fallen gods and his dead ancestors.

By the time Abram was forty, Nimrod was reigning securely over *'erets* and was building the Tower Babel. Then Yahweh took down the tower in 1993 A.M. Later, "in the fiftieth year of the life of Abram,[161] son of Terah, Abram came forth from the house of Noah and went to his father's house. And Abram knew Yahweh, and he went in his ways and instructions, and Yahweh, his God, was with him. And Terah, his father was in those days, still captain of the host of king Nimrod, and he still followed strange gods."[162]

After Abram spoke openly against Nimrod's "many gods," Nimrod sought to put Abram to death. But instead, Abram's older brother (Sarai's father) was slain while Abram supernaturally escaped harm. Sometime later, Nimrod allowed Abram to return to his father's house in Ur. It was at that time that Abram married Sarai.

In 2000 A.M. Nimrod sought once again to kill Abram. "Abram hastened and ran for safety to the house of Noah and his son Shem, and he concealed himself there and found a place of safety, and the king's servants came to

---

[157] "Stars" is figurative and used frequently in Scripture an epithet regarding the *elohim*.
[158] Johnson, Ken. *Ancient Book of Jasher* (p. 18). Kindle Edition.
[159] Ibid
[160] Ibid
[161] 1998 A.M.
[162] Johnson, Ken. *Ancient Book of Jasher* (p. 24). Kindle Edition.

Abram's house to seek him, but they could not find him, and they searched throughout the country, and he was not to be found, and they went and searched in every direction, and he was not to be met with. And when the king's servants could not find Abram, they returned to the king, but the king's anger against Abram was stilled, as they did not find him, and the king drove from his mind this matter concerning Abram. And Abram was concealed in Noah's house for one month until the king had forgotten this matter, but Abram was still afraid of the king, and Terah came to see Abram, his son, secretly in the house of Noah, and Terah was very great in the eyes of the king."[163]

Abram urged his father, Terah, to leave Nimrod and live with him in Canaan, out of the reaches of Nimrod in Mesopotamia (Ur)... And Abram ceased to speak when Noah and his Son Shem answered Terah, saying, True is the word Abram hath said unto thee. And Terah hearkened to the voice of his son Abram, and Terah did all that Abram said, for this was from the Lord, that the king should not cause Abram's death."[164]

"And Terah took his son Abram and his grandson Lot, the son of Haran, and Sarai his daughter-in-law, the wife of his son Abram, and all the souls of his household and went with them from Ur Casdim to go to the land of Canaan. And when they came as far as the land of Haran, they remained there, for it was exceedingly good land for pasture."[165]

While they started for Canaan, Terah stopped at Haran (current-day Turkey). "And Abram remained in the land (Haran) three years...."[166] Then Abram returned to Canaan, to Noah," 2003 A.M. "At that time, at the end of three years of Abram's dwelling in the land of Canaan, in that year (2006 AM), Noah died."

Abram was fifty-eight when Noah passed, and Shem took over as Melchizedek. Although Jasher states Abram continued to live in Canaan, the reality is that Abram was dwelling with Shem in Salem. Jasher continues Abram's story, stating that Yahweh said in the fifteenth year of his dwelling with Shem, "I brought you out of Ur to give you this land for an inheritance." Yet, Abram moved back to Haran, to Terah's house. "At that time Abram returned and went to Haran to see his father and mother, and his father's household, and Abram and his wife and all belonging to him returned to Haran, and Abram dwelt in Haran five years."[167]

Once again, Yahweh appeared, this time to Abram in Haran. And according to the *Book of Jasher*, "Behold, I spoke unto thee these twenty years back saying, go forth from thy land, from thy birth-place, and from thy father's house to the land which I have shown thee." [168]

At the age of seventy-five, Abram, with his wife and all they owned, returned to the land of Canaan. Lot, Sarai's brother, also went with them. This "return" to Canaan is the Genesis 12 account.

Abram descended from Shem. Which, of course, meant Abram was Noah's offspring. According to the chronologies given in the Masoretic Texts, Noah was nearly nine hundred years old when Abram was born. If that timetable is accurate, Noah was alive and still the Melchizedek.

---

163 Ibid.
164 Ibid.
165 Ibid
166 Ibid
167 Ibid
168 Ibid.

So, in that aspect, that he was descended from Noah and Shem, Abram possessed the proper lineage. But Abram's father, Terah, never served as a Firstborn. Truthfully, Terah would have never passed the test of righteousness, which meant Abram could not be appointed a Firstborn because his father was not one. Without first being a Firstborn, Abram could not be a Melchizedek Regent. Still, Yahweh was placing Abram in "Canaan" to give him the land of the Melchizedek as an inheritance. How and why – is the story of Abram (Genesis 12-24).

> Genesis 12:4-8, *"So Abram departed as the Lord had spoken to him, and Lot went with him. And Abram was seventy-five years old when he departed from Haran. Then Abram took Sarai, his wife, and Lot, his brother's son, and all their possessions that they had gathered and the people whom they had acquired in Haran, and they departed to go to the land of Canaan. So, they came to the land of Canaan.* **Abram passed through the land to the place of Shechem,** *as far as the terebinth tree of* **Moreh.** *And the Canaanites were then in the land. Then the Lord appeared to Abram and said,* **'To your descendants, I will give this land.'** *And there* **he built an altar** *to the Lord, who had appeared to him"* (emphasis added).

Genesis 12:7 "Unto your **Seed** I will give land **this** …." Galatians 3:16-18, *"Now to* **Abraham and his Seed** *were the promises made. He does not say, 'And to seeds,' as of many, but as of one,* **'And to your Seed,'** *who is Christ* (the Anointed One). *And this I say that the law, which was four hundred and thirty years later,* **cannot annul the covenant that was confirmed before by God in Christ,** *that it should make the promise of no effect. For if the* **inheritance** *is of the law, it is no longer of promise; but* **God gave it to Abraham by promise"** (emphasis added).

Romans 4:13-25, **"For the promise that he would be the heir of the world** *was* **not to Abraham or to his seed through the law, but through the righteousness of faith.** *For if those who are of the law are heirs, faith is made void and the promise made of no effect because the law brings about wrath; for where there is no law, there is no transgression. Therefore, it is of faith that it might be according to grace so that the promise might be sure to all the seed, not only to those who are of the law but also to those who are of the faith of Abraham, who is the father of us all (as it is written, 'I have made you a father of many nations) in the presence of Him whom he believed — God, who gives life to the dead and calls those things which do not exist as though they did; who, contrary to hope, in hope believed, so that he became the father of many nations, according to what was spoken, 'So shall your descendants be…,' he did not waver at the promise of God through unbelief, but was strengthened in faith, giving glory to God, and being fully convinced that what He had promised He was also able to perform. And therefore, 'it was accounted to him for righteousness.' Now it was not written for his sake alone that it was imputed to him, but also for us. It shall be imputed to us who believe in Him who raised up Jesus our Lord from the dead, who was delivered up because of our offenses and was raised because of our justification"* (emphasis added).

Seed or *zera* can mean child, children, or fruit, posterity. Apostle Paul wrote to the Galatians that Abraham's Seed is the Christ. The *zera* of Genesis 12:7 was singular in form, not plural. That's an important distinction. The "land" - (*ha'erets*) belongs to the Promised Seed. However, there is an associated meaning hidden in the nuance of Hebrew, which infers "feminine sheep." Within the Hebrew, Holy Spirit hid a promise to the future Messiah and his bride. *"To your Seed, I give (Aleph-Tav) land, this (sheep) ...."* When we break down the meaning, we find that the *aleph-tav* acts as a preposition to modify two nouns: land and sheep. The land belonged to the *(Aleph-Tav)* Melchizedek and his "sheep." No wonder Yeshua is the Good Shepherd!

Yet, another view to consider is that God was speaking to Abram's DNA. The Creator was marking him as a chosen pathway for the future Eternal Melchizedek to come to "the land." We might phrase that concept this way: Yahweh was correcting (purifying) the patriarchal lineage from which the Seed would come; God was refining the royal system. Adam, Noah, and their sons had tarnished the kingdom, but God would bring a refreshing to the eternal kingdom through Abram's DNA. How? By faith, not by works.

"Come, I will show you the bride, the Lamb's wife.' And he carried me away in the Spirit to a great and high mountain (the cosmic mountain of Yah). *He showed me the great city* (the *gan* of Eden populated by the righteous Bride), *the holy Jerusalem, descending out of heaven from God, having the glory of God,"* Revelation 21:9-11.

So, Yahweh adopted Abram in a sense, making him divine royalty. The collaboration between Yahweh and Abram was structured much like the bond between the Melchizedek Regent and the Firstborn. If we view their relationship that way – this was the linking of the Eternal Melchizedek to the "Firstborn" of Faith.

Genesis 12:2-3, *"I will make you a great nation; I will bless you and make your name great; you shall be a blessing. I will bless those who bless you, and I will curse him who curses you; and in you, all the families of the earth shall be blessed."*

- *"I will make"* – will appoint.
- *"a nation"* – a people.
- *"I will bless you"* – cause men to kneel before you.
- *"Make your name great"* – that which is said about you shall be excellent.
- *"You shall be a blessing"* - those who know you and align with your purpose shall prosper.
- *"I will bless those who bless you"* – those who kneel before your purpose shall be blessed.
- *"I will curse him who curses you"* – those who bring contempt or abate your purpose shall be execrated.
- *"In you, all the families of the earth shall be blessed."* – Through you, because of the purpose you serve, all of those born of Adam shall be blessed.

Romans 8:14-17, *"For as many as are led by the Spirit of God, these are sons of God. For you did not receive the spirit of bondage again to fear, but you received the Spirit of adoption by whom we cry out, Abba, Father. The Spirit Himself bears witness with our spirit that we are children of God, and if children, then heirs — heirs of God and joint-heirs with Christ."*

Ephesians 1:3-6, *"Blessed be the God and Father of our Lord Jesus Christ, who has blessed us with every spiritual blessing in the heavenly places in Christ. Just as He chose us in Him before the foundation of the world, that we should be holy and without blame before Him in love, having predestined us to adoption as sons by Jesus Christ to Himself, according to the good pleasure of His will, to the praise of the glory of His grace, by which He made us accepted in the Beloved."*

Expanding Genesis 12:4-5, we discover that the first father (Abram) departed (Haran) as Yahweh had commanded. His natural covering (Lot) went with him. Abram was judged and received grace when he exited the place of dryness (Haran) because he went forth in obedience. Abram took his wife (his helpmate) and the mantle given to him by his elder brother (Adam's spiritual mantle; the knowledge of Yahweh). Taking all he possessed, including his servants acquired in anger and dryness, Abram went to the place of humiliation (Canaan) that was trafficked in the adversary's commerce.

As an author, I appreciate Holy Spirit's expertise in "wordplay." Holy Spirit intentionally named the land to which Abram went, saying it was Canaan. Yet, in Abram's day, that region was not known as Canaan. Not until several hundred years later. But Holy Spirit wanted the reader to understand Abram went to the land that was "humiliated." It was inhabited by those who worshipped pagan gods.

When Abram "crossed over" from Sumer (Ur), the eastern region of Mesopotamia, and entered the Levant, he moved into a spiritual war zone. But note, he passed through. Meaning Abram did not stop to abide. That is until he came to Shechem. He *"passed through (Canaan) to the place of Shechem, as far as the terebinth tree of Moreh."*

Ham, not Shem, was Canaan's father. Canaan was subjugated to serve his brothers. So, how was it Canaan and his sons dwelt in the territory of Shem? All of Mesopotamia was assigned to Shem. However, within a few hundred years, after the earth was divided by the three sons of Noah, all Shem possessed was Salem (Jerusalem).

Consider the following:

→ Genesis 9:18, *"And the sons of Noah that went forth of the ark, were Shem, and Ham, and Japheth: and **Ham is the father of Canaan**"* (emphasis added).

→ Genesis 9:25-26, *"And he said, '**Cursed be Canaan; a servant of servants** shall he be unto his brethren.' And he said, 'Blessed be the Lord God of Shem, and **Canaan shall be his servant**'"* (emphasis added).

→ Ezekiel 28:12-16, *"Son of man, take up a lamentation for the king of Tyre, and say to him, 'Thus says the Lord God: You were the seal of perfection, full of wisdom and perfect in beauty. You were **in Eden, the garden of God** (Yahweh)…, I established you. You were on **the holy mountain of God** (Yahweh). You walked back and forth in the midst of fiery stones. You were perfect in your ways from the day you were created until iniquity was found in you. By the abundance of your trading, you became filled with violence within, and you sinned. Therefore, I cast you as a profane thing **out of the mountain of God**, and I destroyed you, O covering cherub, from the midst of the fiery stones"* (emphasis added).

→ Genesis 2:8, *"The Lord God planted a garden eastward in Eden, and there He put the man whom He had formed."*

→ Revelation 21:10, *"And he carried me away in the Spirit to a great and high mountain and showed me the great city, the **holy Jerusalem….**"* (Emphasis added).

→ Micah 4:1-3, *"Now it shall come to pass in the latter days that the mountain of the Lord's house shall be established on the top of the mountains and shall be exalted above the hills and peoples shall flow to it. Many nations shall come and say, "Come, and let us go up to the mountain of the Lord, to the house of the God of Jacob. He will teach us His ways, and we shall walk in His paths." For out of Zion, the law shall go forth, and the word of the Lord from Jerusalem. He shall judge between many peoples and rebuke strong nations afar off. They shall beat their swords into plowshares and their spears into pruning hooks. Nation shall not lift up sword against nation, neither shall they learn war anymore."*

Jerusalem – *Hierousalem* is the Greek, whereas *Yerushalayim* is Hebrew. *Yerushalayim* is a combination of two words that mean – "to teach" and "peace." Yahweh intended for Jerusalem to be the capital of *'erets*, the place where "peace is taught." It was also the place where *'erets* and *shamayim* came together to connect as one. Jerusalem was meant to be the center of all cosmic government activity. And it will, during the millennial reign of Yeshua.

To understand the significance of Jerusalem, we need to recall this same area was where the Garden **in** Eden was fastened to *'erets*. Suppose we think of Jerusalem as the "Mount of Yahweh," which means it is a Holy Place. Thus, the geographical Eden was essentially the physical outer court of Yahweh's cosmic temple. The terrestrial Jerusalem was the "door" into Yahweh's interdimensional Throne Room.

As previously mentioned, the garden was the location of the Mount of Assembly and the Throne of Yah. The Assembly Hall is the court of the cosmic judges. The Throne Room is the court where the principalities (princes – sons of God) meet to rule the cosmos. Thus, we are not discussing a physical mountain drawn on a topography map.

However, physically Eden was the land between the Euphrates and the Nile. And Jerusalem is midway on that map, or thereabout, between the Nile and the Euphrates.

When Adam sinned, he was removed from the garden, not from Eden. However, the garden was removed, or better stated, "hidden from view." Allow me to restate that premise. The garden is where it was fastened. It is still connected to *'erets*. Only we can't see it. Yet, when God rolls back the heavens, there it shall be. It shall be seen again, for it is the city John wrote about in Revelation 21.

This next point is vital. Yahweh intended for the Melchizedek Regent to protect Eden and, simultaneously, have dominion over *'erets*. However, Adam failed to do so, and so did Noah. Hence, Yahweh had to assign judges over the field (the gentile nations) and turn His attention to Eden. It was overrun by power-hungry gods, particularly in the high places (the mountains north and south of Jerusalem).

Eve's Deceiver, among other fallen gods, still roamed *'erets*. As anthropomorphic entities, they interfered with mankind, with Yahweh's purpose for humankind. A principal objective they sought to execute was to destroy the seed of mankind, thereby destroying the inheritance of the Eternal Melchizedek. Abiding with these gods were the *Rephaim,* the spirits of the dead Nephilim.

In the era of the Old Testament, the demonic realm was viewed slightly differently than in the New Testament era. The *Rephaim* were called demons in Jesus' day. The *Rephaim* were consigned to Hades but roamed *'erets* looking for bodies to possess.

Unable to remove Noah as the Melchizedek or Shem as the anointed Firstborn, the fallen realm used Ham, Canaan's father, by exposing Noah's vulnerabilities. Simply put: They uncovered Noah. That is the meaning of Genesis 9. The curse that Noah issued against Ham's offspring, Canaan, was straightforward: *"Cursed be Canaan; a servant of servants he shall be to his brethren - Blessed be Yahweh, the Elohim of Shem, and may Canaan be his servant – may Elohim enlarge Japheth, and may he dwell in the tents of Shem, and may Canaan be his servant."*

Canaan was to be a "servant" to the "servants" of Shem and Japheth. More significantly, he was to serve Yahweh. The meaning of servant, as used in the text, is bondman, a slave. The definitions of these terms were different in the ancient world. A slave could earn freedom and release if he met certain conditions.

Canaan never served Shem nor Japheth; more significantly, he never served Yahweh. Hence, Canaan and his offspring were never released from their bondage to Yahweh. However, instead of serving Yahweh, they allied with the underworld as worshippers of fallen gods, particularly the *Rephaim* demi-gods.

Canaan set his face against the Melchizedek Kingdom, hating Noah in the same way Nimrod hated. He also constructed a counter-system of worship as he aligned with Nimrod. And for their mutual benefit, Canaan and his sons inhabited Eden illegally.

Briefly, let's define the term "Hebrew." Since Abram "passed through" Canaan – he crossed over. *'Abar* and *'Eber* are both spelled *resh-bet-ayin*. The masculine possessive tense is added by adding a *yod* to *'abar* or *'eber*. Genesis 14:13 describes Abram as *"the Hebrew,"* suggesting Abram earned the title *"Ivrie* (or Hebrew)*"* because he crossed over the Jordan River and entered Canaan, whereas his father had not. Even so, it is true that Eber was an ancestor to Abram. Yet, Abram was not a Hebrew because of Eber. After all, Terah was also related to Eber but was not called a Hebrew. Joshua 24:3, *"I took your father Abraham from the other side of the river, led him throughout all the land of Canaan."*

Yah is more than a single word can describe, meaning He is without limit. He alone is eternal. Eternal means without end or beginning. Again, that does not define God. Instead, merely refers to His existence. The reality is that the vastness of His power, His authority, and His wisdom knows no boundaries. But then, that is also true concerning His love. That is why words such as righteousness, justice, truth, and peace describe Him but do not define Him. They only annunciate aspects that are implicit and explicit. Yahweh **is** Love; **Faithful; Truth; Just; Righteous** - all the time, simultaneously. All these factors set Yahweh apart from the *elohim* – He, alone, is *qodesh*. His Presence, His glory is *qodesh*. You have my meaning – Yahweh is immeasurable – beyond description.

Yahweh is the Supreme Power of the entire cosmos. He is God the Father, thus the Creator. However, Yah is, was, and always shall be the Eternal One, the source of all life, including the life of the *elohim*. That some have rebelled does not negate the truth. They must obey Him.

So, here is the chief thing, the Bible is a love story. It tells of the love the Father has for the Son and the Son has for the Father. Then that they love their Creation. Jesus, when quoting Deuteronomy, added, **"The first of all the commandments** *is: 'Hear, O Israel, the Lord our God, the Lord is* **one**. *And you shall love the Lord your God with all your heart, with all your soul, with all your mind, and with all your strength.'* **This is the first commandment. And the second, like it, is this: 'You shall love your neighbor as yourself.' There is** *no other commandment greater than these.*"[169]

Love unlocks the Kingdom of Yahweh, the Melchizedek Kingdom. Faith and love work in tandem as one. Abram needed to prove his love by walking in faith. Yahweh appeared to him and offered to bring Abram into the Father's love. Abram had to cross over and permanently leave behind all other associations. He was required to commit fully to Yahweh through love and faith. That also necessitated Abram to pick up the burden of the message of Yah's Kingdom.

"Appeared," *ra'ah*, means to see, literally or figuratively. In other instances, *ra'ah* was translated as approved, discern, experience, gaze, and so forth. It is uncertain if Yahweh manifested physically or merely spoke to Abram from the spirit realm. But that Yahweh spoke meant Yahweh was "present." So, Abram was assured he had arrived at his destination; he was in the right place because he physically sensed Yahweh's presence. Accordingly, Abram received assurance that the site where he stood would pass to his Descendant!

Abram *"passed through"* Canaan (humiliation to the kingdom) and stopped when he reached the *"terebinth tree of Moreh."* Genesis 12:6, *"the place of Shechem, unto the oak* (plain) *of Moreh."* Abram stopped at Shechem to seek the next set of instructions.

Shechem, located approximately forty miles north of Salem, was considered a "high place," a place of worship. Whether Shem worshipped there is unclear, but probably not. After all, Abram had to build an altar.

During my research on Shechem, I discovered that the Canaanites venerated the Rephaim at Shechem. However, there is no mention of a confrontation in Genesis 12 between Abram and the Canaanites that dwelt there. So, it must have been insignificant if he ran into opposition at Shechem.

Shechem means a ridge or shoulder. The etymology of the word refers to burdens, whether physical or metaphoric. When used as a verb rather than a noun, the term implies – "to rise early, to make an early start." So, Shechem was the place where the burden of the kingdom passed to Abram. It was where the torch was passed from Shem to Abram, in a spiritual sense.

Moreh means teacher or teaching, also early rain. As a verb, it means to cast or to shoot. Symbolically the *"terebinth of Moreh"* designates it as a holy hill. However, it had fallen to the fallen realm. Yet, Yahweh chose that location to cast the burden of the Melchizedek Kingdom upon Abram's shoulders.

Years later, Joshua *"gathered all the tribes of Israel to Shechem and called for the elders of Israel, for their heads, for their judges, and for their officers; and they presented themselves before God. And Joshua said to all the people, 'Thus says the Lord God of Israel: Your fathers, including Terah, the father of Abraham and the father of Nahor, dwelt on the other side of the river in old times; and they served other gods. Then I took your father Abraham from the other side of the river, led him throughout all the land of Canaan, and multiplied his descendants…,"* Joshua 24:1-3.

To solidify his commitment, Abram built an altar as a monument. And the altar, since it was erected to

---

[169] Mark 12:29-31 (emphasis added).

Yahweh, belonged to Yahweh. The building of that altar sent a signal to the underworld Yahweh was now the God of Shechem. Therefore, the area no longer belonged to any god but Yahweh.

Ancient altars were raised structures that people placed sacrifices on. In the ancient world, the altar was almost exclusively built as a monument to remember or commemorate a divine occurrence that took place at a certain location. In ancient Israel, altars were very significant; they symbolized communion with the LORD. They were a place of worship and a place to remember His covenant. The "altar" was a place of "approach," a place to call upon the name of the LORD and remember His glorious promises.[170]

Abram departed from Shechem. He moved to the south and pitched his tent with Bethel on the west and Ai on the east. Again, building an altar, Abram called upon the name Yahweh. But note - *"There were Canaanites in the land,"* and they revered not Yahweh but the fallen *elohim*.

That second altar Abram built at Bethel was also a prophetic act. It sealed the words spoken at Shechem. That is why Abram addressed (*qara'*) Yahweh by His name (*shem*) at Bethel. Abram was invoking Yahweh to come as "salvation" to the land. In other words, Abram was seeking redemption for the land of Eden.

Bethel or *Beyth 'El* translates as the "house of God." Ai or *'Ay* translates as the place of ruins. Ai was east of his tent. The place of ruins was in the "past."

Bethel was west, meaning it was *yam*. *'Yam* means to roar as a sea. Prophetically, by positioning his tent in that manner, Abram was proclaiming: "The altars of the past are ruins, but God's house will roar as a 'great sea' filled with a multitude."

"Abram journeyed, going on still toward the south," Genesis 12:9.

Abram left the area north of Salem and traveled south toward the Negev. "And he removed from thence and went towards the south, and he came to Hebron and Hebron was built at that time, and he dwelt there two years, and he went (thence) into the land of the south, to Bealoth…,"[171]

That Abram chose Hebron is interesting on several levels. Primarily because Hebron was a "high place" devoted to pagan worship. But also, accessing its heights was challenging for a company as large as Abram's. The region around Hebron is mountainous and over 3,000 feet above sea level.

Artifacts recovered from the area suggest that in the beginning, Hebron was a Canaanite city serving the region as a "seat of government." Consequently, if royalty resided in Hebron, there were palaces, gardens, altars, and temples.

The term, Hebron, means friendship or alliance. It's believed the name was derived from the Hebrew word *haber* (friend). If that be the case, then in Abram's day, that community was probably not called Hebron.

---

170 https://www.bible-history.com/biblestudy/altars.html
171 Charles, R.H. *The Book of Jubilees* (Kindle Locations 900-902). Kindle Edition.

The city was the focal point of two major trading routes, serving as the last major economic center before the Negev Desert. Merchants bound for Egypt went south from Hebron into a long stretch of rugged terrain. Or they turned west toward the coastal plains of the Great Sea, which was the territory of the Philistines who, as a rule, were less amenable than the Canaanites.

While the city we know as Hebron was not as ancient as Salem, it grew to be an important city in Abram's day. Both cities were located on the same merchant trade routes.

> Genesis 12:10-20, *Now, there was a famine in the land, and Abram went down to Egypt to dwell there, for the famine was severe in the land. And it came to pass, when he was close to entering Egypt, that he said to Sarai, his wife, "Indeed I know that you are a woman of beautiful countenance. Therefore, it will happen, when the Egyptians see you, that they will say, 'This is his wife,' and they will kill me, but they will let you live. Please say you are my sister, that it may be well with me for your sake, and that I may live because of you." So it was, when Abram came into Egypt, the Egyptians saw the woman, that she was very beautiful. The princes of Pharaoh also saw her and commended her to Pharaoh. And the woman was taken to Pharaoh's house. He treated Abram well for her sake. He had sheep, oxen, male donkeys, male and female servants, female donkeys, and camels. But the Lord plagued Pharaoh and his house with great plagues because of Sarai, Abram's wife. And Pharaoh called Abram and said, "What is this you have done to me? Why did you not tell me that she was your wife? Why did you say, 'She is my sister'? I might have taken her as my wife. Now, therefore, here is your wife; take her and go your way." So, Pharaoh commanded his men concerning him, and they sent him away with his wife and all that he had.*

Abram's trek into Egypt separated him and his "house" from Eden. He became "disconnected." Big mistake, even for a short while. The repercussions of this decision would cost Abram dearly in the years to come. Spiritually, Abram "joined" himself with the Canaanites by entering Egypt.

However, in his defense, I don't think Abram, at that juncture, fully comprehended the reason he was called to the land of Canaan. If he had realized, I doubt he would have gone to Egypt.

Let's begin by defining *ra'ab* – as famine. Strong's OT #7458 indicates *ra'ab* is hunger (more or less) caused by an **extensive** famine.

Due to the famine, Abram went "down" into Egypt. He went south in a literal sense, also figuratively. The symbolism of sojourning south connotates descending into the lower dimensions. The word translated as "down" in Genesis 12:10 is the same word used in Genesis 11:5, *"And Yahweh came down to see the city…,"* – *yarad*, suggesting movement from a higher realm to that of a lower one.

Egypt, in Bible iconology, represents the "world," the kingdom of darkness, the place from where the fallen gods reign. Therefore, we should view the act of Abram leaving Hebron as his leaving Yahweh and entering the world's system to find relief from "starvation." Oh, the irony!

"And in that year, there was a heavy famine throughout the land of Canaan, and the inhabitants of the land could not remain on account of the famine, for it was very grievous. And Abram and all belonging to him rose and went down to Egypt on account of the famine, and when they were at the brook Mitzraim, they remained there some time to rest from the fatigue of the road."[172]

Abram left behind the two altars he had built for Yahweh in Shechem and Bethel. Maybe, however, the real problem was Abram had yet to build an altar in Hebron. He had been there two years, so he had plenty of time.

However, perhaps the more significant problem was that Abram had integrated with the Canaanite society in Hebron. Which might be why Hebron is called Hebron. Which would explain why he went with the Canaanites to Egypt. Abram lost sight of his mission and allied with the fallen gods by forming alliances with the Canaanites, who worshipped profanely. This message is simple: Yahweh calls believers to love their neighbors but not to make alliances with "Canaanites."

Again, the irony is incredible because the gods, who the Canaanites revered, were the same ones Abram was in the land to remove. He was there to restore the land to Yahweh by occupying it for Yahweh. But what happened? When those gods grew angry, Abram turned tail and ran down to Egypt to escape the famine caused by the gods who desired to drive Abram out of the land.

Seriously, I don't mean to be harsh, but I can't help but ask, why didn't Abram "call" on Yahweh? Yahweh did not cause the famine, but it was a divine ploy, nonetheless.

As Abram and his "house" neared the Nile, he said to Sarai, "You are beautiful. The rulers of Egypt will desire you. They will kill me to gain you. Say you are my sister, so they will allow me to live."

Over the years, Bible students have misinterpreted Abram's words. So, let's add some clarity by noting that it was a frequent practice in the house of royalty to adopt a daughter-in-law. Sarai was Terah's granddaughter, as well as his daughter-in-law. To secure her inheritance, it is highly likely Terah adopted her as his daughter when her father died. There are references made to her as Terah's daughter in the Apocrypha.

Sarai spelled '*Saray* came from the noun, '*sar,* which means sovereign or prince; the feminine version has the addition of the *yod*, making it '*sari*. This name, which the Bible assigns to Abram's wife, is a key. Sarai was revered as a princess, the daughter of a king. Abram and Sarai would have been received as royalty no matter where they traveled. They would have been afforded excellent accommodations and recognized because of their relationship with Terah and his association with Nimrod's court.

Terah had served Nimrod as a mighty king. His reputation was widespread, and though Nimrod was exiting the world's stage, he had not left it altogether. Hence, Sarai, as a princess, was a valuable prize. Her extraordinary beauty only increased the probability that a king would notice her and desire her as a bargaining tool. Kings, wanting to remain in Nimrod's good graces, were bound by protocol to pay homage to Terah's son and daughter. Mainly his daughter.

---

172 Johnson, Ken. *Ancient Book of Jasher* (p. 33). Kindle Edition.

Daughters of kings were valuable "tools" to cut a pathway through complex legalities and form alliances. Primarily, marriages were treaties. Marrying the daughter of an ally was wise – marrying the daughter of an enemy was a clever strategy.

Another reason Abram was concerned for his well-being was the prevalent belief that the pharaohs were the offspring of the gods; therefore, they were deities. Hence, it would not be murder if the pharaoh, desiring Sarai, had Abram killed to exempt her from all legal entanglement involving prior husbands. Abram knew that any aggression against him would have been viewed as an act of "the gods."

According to the *Book of Jubilees*, Abram successfully hid Sarai for five years before she was taken by Pharaoh's guards. When she was discovered, Sarai was accepted as Abram's sister and placed in Pharaoh's harem. Pharaoh's court awarded Abram sheep, cattle, donkeys, camels, horses, male and female servants, and precious metals in exchange for his sister.

And the king approached to speak to Sarai, and he reached out his hand to touch her when the angel smote him heavily; and he was terrified, and he refrained from reaching to her. When the king came near Sarai, the angel smote him to the ground and did so the whole night. The king was terrified…, and his entire household, on account of Sarai, and there was a great lamentation that night amongst the people of Pharaoh's house. Seeing the evil that befell him, Pharaoh said, "Surely on account of this woman has this thing happened to me." He removed himself at some distance from her and spoke comforting words to her. Then the king said to Sarai, "Tell me, I pray, the man with whom you came here, who is he?" Sarai answered, "He is my husband. I said to you that he was my brother, for I was afraid that you would put him to death." As long as the king kept away from Sarai, the plagues ceased from him and his household. Pharaoh knew that he was smitten on account of Sarai. He was astonished. In the morning, Pharaoh called for Abram and asked, "What have you done? Why did you say she was your sister? Because you have, I took her for a wife. Now, this heavy plague has come upon me and my household. Here is your wife, take her and go from our land or we shall all die on her account." Pharaoh took more cattle, menservants and maidservants, silver, and gold and gave to Abram. Pharaoh took a maiden[173] whom he begat by his concubines and gave her to Sarai for a handmaid. He said to his daughter, "It is better for you, my daughter, to be a handmaid in this man's house than be mistress in mine…"[174]

---

[173] It's commonly accepted that Hagar was the "maiden" given to Sarai.
[174] Johnson, Ken. *Ancient Book of Jasher* (p. 34). Kindle Edition.

AM Date	Event	BC Date
1656	The great flood	2269
1878	Terah born	2047
1908	Nimrod born	2017
1948	Nimrod usurps Noah	1977
1948	Abram born	1977
1958	Sari was born of Nahor	1967
1993	Tower of Babel fell	1932
1996	Chedorlaomer conquered Sodom and Gomorrah	1929
1997	Abram returned to Ur from Noah	1928
1998	Abram married Sari	1927
2000	Abram fled from Nimrod (returned to Noah)	1925
2006	Noah died	1919
2008	Sodom and Gomorrah rebelled against Chedorlaomer	1917
2013	Nimrod warred against Chedorlaomer	1912
2018	Abram went to Terah	1907
2023	Abram and Lot went to Canaan	1902
2034	Ishmael born	1891
2047	Circumcision commanded	1878
2048	Sodom and Gomorrah destroyed	1877
2048	Isaac born	1877
2083	Terah died	1842
2085	Isaac offered on Mount Moriah	1840
2085	Sarah died	1840
2088	Abraham married Keturah	1837
2123	Abraham died at 175	1802

Genesis Thirteen

> Genesis 13:1-4, *Then Abram went up from Egypt, he, and his wife and all that he had, and Lot with him, to the South. Abram was very rich in livestock, silver, and gold. And he went on his journey from the South as far as Bethel, to the place where his tent had been at the beginning, between Bethel and Ai, to the site of the altar which he had made there at first. And there Abram called on the name of the Lord.*

Abram left Egypt and ascended, *'alah*. The implication is he lifted himself up by going up and away from Egypt. Fundamentally, Abram reversed the act of descending. Perhaps, this should be viewed as "he repented." Abram returned to the last place he heard from Yahweh, the altar at Bethel.

Abram went north from Egypt. However, he did not return to Hebron via a direct route. Instead, he bypassed Hebron and went to Bethel. Why go to Bethel?

Abram "went up" from Egypt through the Negev Desert and made his way to Bethel, approximately forty miles out of his way, to *"the place where his tent had been at the beginning."*

Arriving at Bethel, the house of God, Abram cried out to Yahweh. I would imagine he apologized and sought forgiveness.

But consider the following Genesis 13:5-18 account from the NKJV:

> *"Lot also, who went with Abram, had flocks, herds, and tents. Now the land could not support them, that they might dwell together, for their possessions were so great that they could not dwell together. And there was strife between the herdsmen of Abram's livestock and the herdsmen of Lot's livestock. The Canaanites and the Perizzites then dwelt in the land. So, Abram said to Lot, 'Please let there be no strife between you and me, and between my herdsmen and your herdsmen; for we are brethren. Is not the whole land before you? Please separate from me. If you go left, then I will go to the right; or, if you go to the right, then I will go to the left.' And Lot lifted his eyes and saw all the plain of Jordan, that it was well watered everywhere (before the Lord destroyed Sodom and Gomorrah) like the garden of the Lord, like the land of Egypt as you go toward Zoar. Then Lot chose for himself all the plain of Jordan, and Lot journeyed east. And they separated from each other. Abram dwelt in the land of Canaan, and Lot dwelt in the cities of the plain and pitched his tent even as far as Sodom. But the men of Sodom were exceedingly wicked and sinful against the Lord. And the Lord said to Abram, after Lot had separated from him: 'Lift your eyes now and look from the place where you are — northward, southward, eastward, and westward; for all the land which you see I give to you and your descendants forever. And I will make your descendants as the dust of the earth; so that if a man could number the dust of the earth, then your descendants also could be numbered. Arise, walk in the land through its length and its width, for I give it to you.' Then Abram moved his tent and went and dwelt by the terebinth trees of Mamre, which are in Hebron, and built an altar there to the Lord.*

Now, let's read the story provided by *The Book of Jasher:* Lot the son of Haran, Abram's brother, had a heavy stock of cattle, flocks, and herds and tents, for the Lord was bountiful to them on account of Abram. And when Abram was dwelling in the land, the herdsmen of Lot quarreled with the herdsmen of Abram, for their property was too great for them to remain together in the land. The land could not bear them on account of their cattle. And when Abram's herdsmen went to feed their flock, they would not go into the fields of the people of the land, but the cattle of Lot's herdsmen did otherwise, for they were suffered to feed in the fields of the people of the land. And the people of the land saw this occurrence daily, and they came to Abram and quarreled with him on account of Lot's herdsmen. And Abram said to Lot, "What is this thou art doing to me, to make me despicable to the inhabitants of the land, that thou orderest thy herdsman to feed thy cattle in the fields of other people? Dost thou not know that I am a stranger in this land amongst the children of Canaan, and why wilt thou do this unto me? And Abram quarreled daily with Lot on account of this. Still, Lot would not listen to Abram, and he continued to do the same, and the inhabitants of the land came and told Abram. And Abram said unto Lot, "how long wilt thou be to me for a stumbling block with the inhabitants of the land? Now I beseech thee let there be no more quarreling between us, for we are kinsmen. But I pray thee separate from me, go, and choose a place where thou mayest dwell with thy cattle and all belonging to thee, but keep thyself at a distance from me, thou, and thy household. And be not afraid in going from me, for if anyone does an injury to thee, let me know and I will avenge thy cause from him, only remove from me." And when Abram had spoken all these words to Lot, then Lot arose and lifted up his eyes toward the plain of Jordan. And he saw that the whole of this place was well watered and good for man as well as affording pasture for the cattle. And Lot went from Abram to that place, and he there pitched his tent, and he dwelt in Sodom, and they were separated from each other. And Abram dwelt in the plain of Mamre, which is in Hebron, and he pitched his tent there, and Abram remained in that place many years.[175]

- Lot also gained wealth in Egypt because he was Sarai's brother.
- Abram and Lot could not adequately provide for their herds if they pastured them together.
- Lot and his men bickered with the Canaanites over grazing rights.
- Lot chose according to "sight."
- Only after Abram separated himself from Lot did Yahweh expand upon the promise made to Abram.
- After Lot's departure, Abram built his third altar at Hebron.

According to the *Book of Jasher*, Lot and Abram were close to the same age since Lot was Sarai's elder brother by a few years. Due to that brother-sister relationship, while in Egypt, Lot became a wealthy man.

There is no record of strife between Lot and Abram until after their return from Egypt. So, it's plausible that Lot was not wealthy before entering Egypt. At the very least, his wealth was not equivalent to Abram's until after Egypt. This presents a plausible reason as to why Lot left Haran with Abram. He hoped to inherit Abram's wealth, given that Abram and Sarai were childless.

Lot lacked spiritual discernment; he attached himself to unjust gods and aligned with the wrong kings. The name "Lot" is spelled (*lamed, vav, tet*). In pictograph form, it translates as "the authority of the joining is

---

[175] Unknown Author. *The Book of Jasher* (Kindle Locations 1075-1087). Global Grey eBooks. Kindle Edition

twisted." Strong's OT#3875 defines Lot as - a veil, a covering.

Abram had over three hundred men trained in weaponry, which does not account for the additional that served him as shepherds, herdsmen, and the like. It is more than plausible that the company that traveled with Abram exceeded 1,000. So, if Lot had even half as much, these two men were a "town" unto themselves. Given the size of their combined herds and flocks, any local pastures would have been quickly devastated.

Yet, Abram had not entered Canaan to war with the Canaanites. Well, not a literal war using swords and arrows. Abram was positioned in the land to "war" spiritually with the region's false gods, which he neglected to do when he went to Hebron the first time and dwelt there.

Abram had returned to Canaan to "seek" Yahweh. And he certainly would not have done so at a Canaanite altar. Even though the land of Canaan had many altars. They were erected to the fallen deities and were portals to the underworld. So, understandably, Abram went to the altar he had constructed for Yahweh at Bethel, where he last accessed Yahweh.

2 Kings 21: 2-6 provides additional insight into the rituals of the Canaanites. The following account took place hundreds of years later. Nevertheless, the patterns of worship as described in this passage were practiced by the Canaanites of Abram's time. "(Manasseh) *did evil in the sight of the Lord, according to the abominations of the nations whom the Lord had cast out before the children of Israel. For* **he rebuilt the high places** *which Hezekiah his father had destroyed; he raised up altars for Baal and made a wooden image, as Ahab king of Israel had done; and* **he worshiped all the host of heaven** (rebellious not holy "hosts") **and served them**. *He also built altars* (to his fallen realm gods) *in the house of the Lord, of which the Lord had said, 'In Jerusalem, I will put My name.' And* **he built altars for all the host of heaven** *in the two courts of the house of the Lord. Also,* **he made his son pass through the fire, practiced soothsaying, used witchcraft, and consulted spiritists and mediums***. He did much evil in the sight of the Lord, to provoke Him to anger*" (emphasis added).

Abram opened the heavens above by calling out to Yahweh. Invoking Yahweh's name in high places empowered heaven's holy warriors. It enabled them to war against the evil of the gods. Note that the word "altar" comes from *altaruim*, a Latin word that means "high." Ancient altars were built on mountain tops or high hills. Although they were constructed for offerings and sacrifices, they were perceived as portals, pathways giving access to the inhabitants of the spirit realm to travel between *'erets* and *shamayim*—earth and heaven.

Eden belonged to the Melchizedek Kingdom. Sorry, I will say that repetitively because we must lose sight of the spiritual implications of all that the patriarchs endured. Yahweh had called Abram and was preparing him for the test of Genesis 22. At Shechem, Yahweh, by Oath, began proposing to Abram's descendants. The land of Eden would be "their inheritance" when they married His Son.

To prepare the land for the Eternal Melchizedek and His Bride, Abram needed to rid it of the false system.

Hosea 6:2, *"After two days will he revive us: in the third day, he will raise us up, and we shall live in His sight."*

Abram represented the "third day." Genesis 22:4, *"Then, on the third day, Abraham lifted his eyes and saw the place afar off."* However, Abram initially did not see his mission clearly. Not until Lot's influence was removed. Compare the following two passages: Genesis 13:1, *"And Lot lifted his eyes and saw all the plain of Jordan...."* Genesis 13:14, *"And the Lord said to Abram,* **after Lot had separated from him***: 'Lift your eyes* **now** *and look from the place where you are...'"*

There are no coincidences in the spirit realm. The holy ones understood separation between Abram and Lot needed to occur. Lot was not called; Abram was. Lot was not loyal; Abram was. The two could no longer co-exist. So, when Abram returned to Bethel, where the heavens were opened, the holy warriors brought healing to Abram by provoking the one person who clouded his vision.

So, Lot "lifted his eyes" and chose the "plain of Jordan." "Lifted" or "*nasa*" means to lift in various applications, literal and figurative. Such as accept, arise, carry, contain, desire, and hold up. Lot desired the "plain of Jordan."

- Plain or *kikkar* means a circle or a loaf.
- Jordan, or *yarad*, means to descend, to literally go downward.

Genesis 13:10 explains. Lot looked and saw a *"well-watered"* valley, *"even as the garden of Yahweh."* But *"like the land of Egypt"* – *"the men of Sodom were exceedingly wicked and sinful against the Lord."*

It seems evident that Lot gave no thought to Yahweh yet wanted to dwell in the *"garden of Yahweh."* So, perhaps the correct understanding is that he was not particular about which god's garden (cosmic mountain) he associated with. He was out for himself to get whatever he could. Furthermore, I suggest that the Jordan River Valley had become a cosmic mountain of *Ba'al (El)*, primarily to resurrect those who traversed *'erets* as the Rephaim.

Note the following: "We will dig deeper into this concept as we unpack the importance of the dead in the ancient world. Gardens held a special place in the culture of the ancient Near East, and it was part of a very different way of looking at the world. This wasn't just because they lacked modern conveniences, our understanding of the sciences, and access to the Internet, but because they understood that the spirit realm was part of daily life—something we've lost in the modern world, especially in the West. Part and parcel of their reality was interacting with the dead."[176]

Deuteronomy 30:19-20, *"I call heaven and earth as witnesses today against you, that I have set before you, life and death, blessing and cursing; therefore choose life, that both you and your descendants may live; that you may love the Lord your God, that you may obey His voice, and that you may cling to Him, for He is your life and the length of your days; and that you may dwell in the land which the Lord swore to your fathers, to Abraham, Isaac, and Jacob, to give them."*

Yahweh is "life." To dwell apart from Him is to co-exist with death. Lot chose death.

Gardens or *gans* were viewed as private temples; their physical size did not determine their importance. Since

---

[176] Gilbert, Sharon K.; Gilbert, Derek P. *Veneration: Unveiling the Ancient Realms of Demonic Kings and Satan's Battle Plan for Armageddon* (pp. 10-11). Defender. Kindle Edition.

they were influential and had the means, the wealthy, especially kings, built gardens within their palatial estates. The lesser affluent built dolmens. These served several purposes.

The altars they built, dedicated to their chosen gods, were constructed alongside elaborate edifices containing their dead ancestors. Primarily this was to accommodate the lifestyle of the rich. Monthly they would venerate their ancestors, often with feasts and libation sacrifices, and celebrate their gods and good fortune. Remember that a person of wealth or royal status was believed to be blessed by the gods. So blessed, they mingled with the gods as demi-gods and held saturnalia in these stylish, even ostentatious gardens to honor their gods and ancestors.

"In the Amorite world of the ancient Near East, gardens were not simply for growing pretty flowers; it was where the cult of the royal ancestors performed the rites to summon and feed the divinized kings of old."[177]

Isaiah 66:17, *"'Those who sanctify themselves and purify themselves, to go to the gardens after an idol in the midst, eating swine's flesh and the abomination and the mouse, shall be consumed together,' says the Lord."*

Abram's Canaanite neighbors were pagans, spiritually whoring after the enemies of Yahweh - in gardens. The Jordan Valley, which Lot lifted his eyes and saw, was filled with perversion. Yet, Lot chose it over Bethel. Need further proof? Note verse eleven, *"Lot journeyed east."* Lot went into the past. As previously mentioned, *miqqedem* in the original Hebrew denotes time, not space. Lot returned to the ways of his ancestors and entered a place where the dead were worshipped in Sodom.

Sodom means "the scorch." And by the way, the place where Lot "pitched his tent" was not called Sodom until after it was destroyed. When Lot parted ways with Abram, the Jordan River Valley was not a desert but a lush vale, a prosperous community with many citizens.

After Abram separated himself from Lot - Yahweh began to speak once again. He expanded upon the promises He had previously made. Yahweh instructed Abram to *"lift your eyes and look to the north, the south, east, and west. For all the land you see, I will give it to your Seed forever."* Seed is intentionally capitalized. The Seed of this verse is the Eternal Melchizedek Seed, Yeshua the Anointed One.

Forever is *'ad olam*. *'Ad* is a preposition meaning: against, before, for, etc. *Olam* suggests from vanishing point to vanishing point. In other words, eternally.

Galatians 3:16, *"Now to Abraham and his Seed were the promises made. He does not say, 'to seeds,' as many, but as of one, 'to your Seed,' who is Christ."*

Yahweh declared, *"I will make your seed as the dust of the earth so that if a man could number the granular of dust, then he could number your seed."* The second use of *'zera'* infers the many as a multitude of people.

So, let's clarify what was said. The land belonged to Yahweh. Yet, He was assigning it to Abram to occupy for his descendants. The ultimate goal was to gift the land to the Eternal Melchizedek and the descendants

---

[177] Ibid (p. 119). Kindle Edition.

of Abram, who "married" the King. That would include anyone Hebrew or not. Hence, Yahweh was preparing for the end "harvest." But first, Abram had to be seeded – so that he by faith could reap the Seed's "harvest."

Galatians 3:7, *"Therefore know that only those who are of faith are sons of Abraham."* So, to be clear, Abraham's Seed inherited Abraham's seed. To become Abraham's seed, all one had to do was cross over from the false system and become Hebrew, aligned with the Truth.

Abram was told to look beyond the natural and see Yahweh's plan with spiritual insight. Looking to the north (*tasphon* - the unknown); the south (*negeb* – to the dry places); the east (*qedem* – what came before); and to the west (*yam* – the sea) …, *"All that you see, I 'appoint' to your Seed."* In other words, unto your Seed, I give all who come to the Kingdom, by faith, your faith.

Combine that thought with Daniel 7:13-14. *"And behold, One like the Son of Man, coming with the clouds of heaven! He came to the Ancient of Days, and they brought Him near before Him. Then to Him was given dominion and glory and a kingdom that all peoples, nations, and languages should serve Him. His dominion is an everlasting dominion, which shall not pass away, and His kingdom the one which shall not be destroyed."*

God chose Abram to begin the third day, a day of restoration, by planting "Seed/seed." Complete restoration would not occur during Abram's lifetime. Still, it began with the command: *"Arise, walk in the land through its length and width, for I give it to you."* That command was, in essence, the passing of inheritance, making it a Sandal covenant.

- Arise – abide and accomplish
- Walk – behave continually
- The land – be firm
- Length – tarry forever
- Breath – the room (space)
- Give – appoint

Abram was to abide continually in the firm knowledge that his Seed would forever occupy the space Yahweh had appointed. So, Abram moved his tent to the strong tree of Mamre in Hebron.

Judging by the wording of verse eighteen, Abram moved "next door" to royalty and then *"built an altar there to Yahweh."* Abram acted out what Yahweh communicated. His act of building this third altar shouted to the fallen realm and their cohorts, the Canaanites, "Take notice; a worshipper of Yahweh is now living among you."

Genesis Fourteen

And it came to pass in the days of Amraphel king of Shinar, Arioch king of Ellasar, Chedorlaomer king of Elam, and Tidal king of nations, that they made war with Bera king of Sodom, Birsha king of Gomorrah, Shinab king of Admah, Shemeber king of Zeboiim, and the king of Bela (that is, Zoar). All these joined together in the Valley of Siddim (that is, the Salt Sea). Twelve years, they served Chedorlaomer, and in the thirteenth year, they rebelled. In the fourteenth year, Chedorlaomer and the kings with him came and attacked the Rephaim in Ashteroth Karnaim, the Zuzim in Ham, the Emim in Shaveh Kiriathaim, and the Horites in their mountain of Seir, as far as El Paran, which is by the wilderness. Then they turned back and came to En Mishpat (that is, Kadesh) and attacked all the country of the Amalekites and the Amorites who dwelt in Hazezon Tamar. And the king of Sodom, the king of Gomorrah, the king of Admah, the king of Zeboiim, and the king of Bela (that is, Zoar) went out and joined together in battle in the Valley of Siddim against Chedorlaomer, king of Elam, Tidal king of nations, Amraphel king of Shinar, and Arioch king of Ellasar — four kings against five. Now the Valley of Siddim was full of asphalt pits, and the kings of Sodom and Gomorrah fled; some fell there, and the remainder fled to the mountains. Then they took all the goods of Sodom and Gomorrah and all their provisions and went their way. They also took Lot, Abram's brother's son who dwelt in Sodom, and his goods and departed. Then one who had escaped came and told Abram the Hebrew, for he dwelt by the terebinth trees of Mamre the Amorite, brother of Eshcol and brother of Aner, and they were allies with Abram. Now, when Abram heard that his brother was taken captive, he armed his three hundred and eighteen trained servants who were born in his own house and went in pursuit as far as Dan. He divided his forces against them by night, and he and his servants attacked them and pursued them as far as Hobah, which is north of Damascus. Genesis 14:1-15

Genesis 14:1-15 positioned Abram for Genesis 14:16-24. In turn, readied him for the supernatural encounter of Genesis 15. Moses began the story with a history lesson by naming all the players, as did Jasher: At that time, Chedorlaomer, king of Elam, sent to all the neighboring kings, to Nimrod, king of Shinar who was then under his power, and to Tidal, king of Goyim, and to Arioch, king of Elasar, with whom he made a covenant, saying, Come up to me and assist me, that we may smite all the towns of Sodom and its inhabitants, for they have rebelled against me these thirteen years. And these four kings went up with all their camps, about eight hundred thousand men, and they went as they were, and smote every man they found in their road. And the five kings of Sodom and Gomorrah, Shinab king of Admah, Shemeber king of Zeboyim, Bera king of Sodom, Bersha king of Gomorrah, and Bela king of Zoar, went out to meet them, and they all joined together in the valley of Siddim. And these nine kings made war in the valley of Siddim, and the kings of Sodom and Gomorrah were smitten before the kings of Elam.[178]

This same story, according to the Jewish historian Josephus: At this time, when the Assyrians had dominion over Asia, the people of Sodom were in a flourishing condition, both as to riches and the number of their youth. There were five kings that managed the affairs of this county: Ballas, Barsas, Senabar, and Sumobor, with the king of Bela;

---

178 Unknown Author. *The Book of Jasher* (Kindle Locations 1089-1096). Global Grey eBooks. Kindle Edition

and each king led on his own troops: and the Assyrians made war upon them; and, dividing their army into four parts, fought against them. Now every aspect of the army had its own commander; and when the battle was joined, the Assyrians were conquerors and imposed a tribute on the kings of the Sodomites, who submitted to this slavery twelve years; and so long, they continued to pay their tribute: but on the thirteenth year they rebelled, and then the army of the Assyrians came upon them, under their commanders Amraphel, Arioch, Chedorlaomer, and Tidal. These kings had laid waste all Syria and overthrown the offspring of the giants. And when they came over against Sodom, they pitched their camp at the vale called the Slime Pits, for at that time there were pits in that place; but now, upon the destruction of the city of Sodom, that vale became the Lake Asphaltites, as it is called. However, concerning this lake, we shall speak more presently. Now when the Sodomites joined battle with the Assyrians, and the fight was very obstinate, many of them were killed, and the rest were carried captive; among which captives was Lot, who had come to assist the Sodomites.[179]

The events of Genesis, Chapters 12 through 14, were not chronologically sequenced. However, the minutia of history wasn't Moses' objective. Instead, he set forth the progression of Abram's commitment to Yahweh. And Yahweh's to the children of Abraham. Mainly, Moses built his narrative around the encounters with Yahweh that presented the progression of promises that initiated the writing of a Ketubah (the Book of Covenant).

Still, it is beneficial that you have a bit of history. The great flood had occurred less than five hundred years previously. Although the Mesopotamian Crescent (Sumer) dominated the world, Egypt and Assyria were on the ascent. And Chedorlaomer had booted Nimrod out as the global king. So, basically, the entire known world, at that time, was in flux.

It is not my purpose to reconcile the Bible's timeline with a current archaeological standard. Nor shall I repeat what we have already covered concerning Nimrod. Other than to remind you, he had usurped Noah. No doubt, Nimrod was a mighty warrior. However, he did not have a corner market on that perverse attribute. After the fall of the Tower of Babel, the Elamites, led by Chedorlaomer, took Ur (Babylonia), forcing Nimrod's vassal kings into submission. Chedorlaomer began invading the outposts of Nimrod's kingdom by going to each region. After conquering whatever territory, he was in, he demanded their taxes be paid to him.

Meanwhile, Nimrod moved his headquarters to Assyria and began to muster the descendants of Ham (the Canaanites) to resist Chedorlaomer and retake his throne. Nimrod would fail. Even so, he established cities and built several fortresses in the process.

The first few verses of Genesis 14 explain why Chedorlaomer had come to the area of the Jordan River Valley. He came to gain control over the city of Sodom and its neighbors. In that respect, we must not forget Chedorlaomer, as an Elamite, was descended from Shem. Neither should we forget Nimrod was a descendant of Ham.

Events in the physical realm mirror (reflect) the actions of the spiritual. Therefore, it would be safe to

---

[179] Josephus: *Antiquities of the Jews*, PC Study Bible formatted electronic database Copyright © 2003, 2006 by Biblesoft, Inc. All rights reserved.

assume that a revolt occurred among the gods. They, too, were fighting among themselves for territorial control. And I suspect the gods were worried. Abram was building altars, and then there was Noah's proclamation: *"Blessed be Yahweh, the God of Shem, and may Canaan be his servant."*[180] These two seeming independent details must have been troubling to the Canaanite gods. Especially since Abram was more aggressive than Shem, and he was receiving instructions personally from Yahweh. That detail was not lost on any in the fallen realm.

The gods of the Canaanites were resisting those of the Elamites. Neither side was battling for Yahweh.

A Melchizedek lived in Salem, and he continued to serve Yahweh as *"the priest of God Most High."*[181] But seemingly, he was isolated from the "world." So the events of Genesis 14 were, up to a point, confined to the kings of the false system,

Moses named the four Amorite kings, so let's explore what their names represent.

- **Amraphel of Shinar** - Rabbinic sources often identify Amraphel as Nimrod; however, I hesitate to believe Nimrod would have aligned with Chedorlaomer. Nevertheless, the name Amraphel means "one that speaks of secrets." Additionally, Shinar is Hebrew and refers to Sumer, so this king was deeply involved in the occult, probably linked to Enlil or Enki.
- **Arioch of Ellasar** - This king has recently been identified as Eri-Aku of Larsa. Arioch means "servant of the moon-god." Ellasar was north of Ur, and it means rebellion.
- **Chedorlaomer of Elam** – His name means "servant of the deities." Elam, located east of the Tigris, was in the high country. Although Elam was a son of Shem, he was not considered a Semite. The Elamites became the ethnic group later known as Persians.
- **Tidal of Goyim** – Tidal was a Hittite king from Turkey. *Goyim* in Hebrew means "nations" and all who are not Hebrew.

Lot had chosen to live in the lush valley of the Jordan River and had left the more arid region of the hill country. He dwelt in Sodom, near Gomorrah, and aligned himself with their kings and gods. Sodom, or Cedom, as previously mentioned, means to scorch, whereas Gomorrah or *'Amorah* means a ruined heap. It is doubtful that Sodom nor Gomorrah was called Sodom and Gomorrah before their destruction. For they were anything but scorched or a heap of ruins. Both city-states were highly populated with thriving cultures.

The four Amorite kings of the east traveled hundreds of miles west into the Jordan River Valley to engage the five Canaanite kings of the west.

- **Bera of Sodom** - Abarim Publications presents this term as representing "evil or son of evil."[182]
- **Birsha of Gomorrah** - Son of wickedness.[183]

---

[180] Genesis 9:26
[181] Genesis 14:18
[182] https://www.abarim-publications.com/Meaning/Bera.html, retrieved June 11, 2021
[183] https://www.abarim-publications.com/Meaning/Birsha.html, retrieved June 11, 2021

- **Shinab of Adamah** - Hitchcock's Bible Names Dictionary defines Shinab as the "father of changing."
- **Shemeber of Zeboiim** - Jones' Dictionary of Old Testament Proper Names indicates that Zeboiim means "gathering of troops." Shemeber means protector or renown for strength.[184]
- **Bela (Zoar)** - the king of Bela is unnamed, although Bela means to destroy, to devour by swallowing.

The four kings (gods) spoke secrets, served the moon god, and aligned with the fallen deities that ruled those who were not Hebrew. They entered the territory of Canaan (darkness) and fought with the five kings (gods) who ruled Canaan. Those five were also evil sons of wickedness. They fathered the changes that brought devastation, destroying the deeds of the true king, the Melchizedek.

Nine kings, representing the gods, battled *"in the vale of Siddim, which is the salt sea." Siddim*, the plural form of *'sadeh,* means to spread out as a field or flat land. Bible iconology depicts *'erets* (earth) as a field, which we note was for the living. The sea is the chaotic chamber of the dead. Therefore, these verses describe, in symbolic terms, the ongoing battle amidst heaven's outcasts.

The Hebrew text of Genesis 14:4 shows twelve as ten and two. *'Esar* is ten. *Shenayim* is two or twofold. Ten represents the completion of a thing and "two," a doubling. Hence, "the Canaanite cities that served Chedorlaomer were double-minded and thus, rebelled in the thirteenth year.

"Thirteen" is three and ten. Interestingly, there is a double meaning to the root of three, *shaliysh,* for it also means captain or great lord. So, it is conceivable that the "king of Sodom" incited the others to rebel in year thirteen. Indeed, Scripture implies he was the most powerful of the five Canaanite kings.

Chedorlaomer smote the *"Rephaim, Zuzim, Emim, and the Horites."* The Gilberts unpacked the significance of this passage in *Veneration: Unveiling the Ancient Realms of Demonic Kings and Satan's Battle Plan for Armageddon:* On their way to fight the kings of Sodom, Gomorrah, and their allies, probably for control of the King's Highway, a vital trade route connecting Egypt to Mesopotamia, the kings of the east had to defeat *Rephaim* tribes along the road, which ran east of the Jordan River, parallel to the Jordan Rift Valley… This mission was apparently directed against troublemaking city-states, *Rephaim* tribes, and their allies from Mount Hermon to the Gulf of Aqaba. This was no quick police action. Marching from western Persia to the area around the Dead Sea was a three or four-month journey…, the kings of the east apparently traveled south along the King's Highway, doubled back to Kadesh (Petra), and then marched north along the west side of the Dead Sea, defeating the Amorites at Ein Gedi, and then fought the Sodom alliance somewhere north of the sea, not south, as is traditionally believed. That route makes sense, and it fits the theory that Tall el-Hammam was Sodom. It would also explain how Abraham, who was pasturing his flocks west of the Jordan, was able to get out after the eastern alliance so quickly.[185]

- ***Rephaim* in Ashteroth Karnaim**: The *Rephaim* are best described as "shades of the dead," in other words, the spirits of the dead. Strong's OT#6255 *Ashteroth Qarnayim* comes from *Ashtaroth,* which

---

[184] https://www.abarim-publications.com/Meaning/Shemeber.html, retrieved June 11, 2021
[185] Gilbert, Sharon K.; Gilbert, Derek P. *Veneration: Unveiling the Ancient Realms of Demonic Kings and Satan's Battle Plan for Armageddon* (pp. 333-334). Defender. Kindle Edition.

means double horns (a symbol associated with deity). Thus, *Ashteroth-Karnaim* was a place East of the Jordan where the *Rephaim* were giants in a physical sense and the offspring of gods or demi-gods from the underworld.
- ***Zuzim* in Ham** – "*Zuzim*" were also giants.
- ***Emim*** - giants.
- **Horites** – It is believed this ancient tribe dwelt in the caves of Seir. Later in Genesis, a connection will be made between this tribe and Esau. Like the previous three groups, the Horites descended from Ham.
- **Amorites** (*'Emoriy*) inhabited the northeastern regions of Transjordan.
- **Amalekites** (*'Amaleqiy*) dwelt south of Beersheba.

> Genesis 14:11-15, *"Then they took all the goods of Sodom and Gomorrah, and all their provisions, and went their way. They also took Lot, Abram's brother's son who dwelt in Sodom, and his goods and departed. Then one who had escaped came and told Abram the Hebrew, for he dwelt by the terebinth trees of Mamre the Amorite, brother of Eshcol and brother of Aner, and they were allies with Abram. Now when Abram heard that his brother was taken captive, he armed his three hundred and eighteen trained servants born in his own house and went in pursuit as far as Dan. Abram divided his forces against them by night. He and his servants attacked them and pursued them as far as Hobah, north of Damascus."*

Likely, the one who escaped was a servant in Lot's house since he fled to Abram. He informed Abram of Lot's capture. Abram immediately rallied his men and his neighbors, asking for help.

Interestingly, Mamre the Amorite (*Mamre' ha- 'Emoriy*) means "from seeing adversity, he rebelled." Eschol, or *'ach 'Eshkol*, means many grapes or fruit and *'Aner* – a lad; a young man; servant. These three Amorite brothers befriended Abram; the Hebrew text (*b'riyt ba'al*) indicates they formed a covenant partnership. That being the case, they were Abram's equal in standing, concerning strength and might, probably having much the same material wealth as Abram.

Chedorlaomer had attacked the Amorites *"who dwelt in Hazeaon Tamar"* before raiding Sodom. Survivors of that battle were taken captive. Whether Mamre was partially motivated by that news is uncertain. Still, their forces were combined because he and his brothers were Abram's covenant partners.

Abram armed his servants, 318 men skilled in weaponry, which indicates his men were trained warriors. Probably in what we would call guerilla tactics. We aren't told how many men were in the combined forces of Mamre and Abram. However, I seriously doubt their number exceeded that of Chedorlaomer's troops. Additionally, it is reasonable to assume Chedorlaomer's men were better equipped than were those who followed Abram. Yet, Abram pushed ahead in pursuit without stopping until reaching the outskirts of what would later be called Dan.[186]

---

[186] Dan means judgment.

Dan is north of the Sea of Galilee, in the foothills of Mount Hermon. After locating the armies of Chedorlaomer, Abram divided his forces and attacked at night. Surprised and dazed, the enemy fled north to Damascus. Damascus is an ancient city, one of earth's oldest, and its name means "dwelling place."

Abram and his troops chased their adversary to a place north of Damascus, Hobah, which means a place of hiding. All these details are significant. These events occurred - literally. Yet, given how Moses recounted them, it would be amiss not to examine the symbolism.

Because it is Yahweh's, Eden is ground zero. It's where major spiritual battles are fought. Note the following:

- *"And (Yahweh) planted a garden eastward in Eden."* [187]
- *"You were in Eden, the garden of Elohiym."* [188]
- *"I made the nations shake at the sound of its fall when I cast it down to hell together with those who descend into the Pit and **all the trees of Eden**...."* [189]

Referring to a powerful entity as a tree is an iconic image that extends beyond the Bible. In fact, many cultures believed that a tree united the underworld, earth, and sky. That ancient image was often portrayed as the center of all cosmic realms.

Trees, especially cedars and oaks, were viewed as divine entities. It is not coincidental that Jesus was crucified on a tree. Or that Adam ate from a "forbidden" tree.

Abram dwelt by the "terebinth trees of Mamre." The Hebrew word "terebinth" is *'elown*, and means oak; primarily, any strong tree.

Spirits are not ghosts floating about in the ether; they are entities. They are sentient beings that do not exist in a terrestrial body yet have bodies. Well, most do.

Dead humans are spirits. Still, disembodied human spirits are prohibited from traveling into earth's four-dimensional space. Therefore, where a spirit originates is crucial since not all are the same. I could say some are angels, but we should really avoid the word "angel." It is misleading.

So, what was going on? Spirits were battling for the control of the Jordan River Valley. That is why the following is vital to grasp– it explains why the locale of the Jordan River was so important.

First, we need to make a distinction of terms. Amorites are often lumped together with the Canaanites. To some extent, they are of the same ethnicity. However, my research has led me to realize that they were different factions of the larger group that is academically known as the Sumerians. Nomadic Amorites often clashed with the "city-dwelling" Canaanites in Sumer.[190] And Sumer, like Eden, housed cosmic mountains.

---

[187] Genesis 2:8
[188] Ezekiel 28:13
[189] Ezekiel 31:16
[190] We shall dig deeper into the Amorite culture as we progressive study Abram.

In fact, Sumer was, for all intents, the adversaries' counter of Eden. This region of the Jordan River Valley, running north and south, was the "spiritual" border between Eden and Sumer.

Genesis 13:18, *"Abram moved his tent, and went and dwelt by the terebinth trees of Mamre, which are in Hebron, and built an altar there to Yahweh."* This verse and that of Genesis 14:13 hint Abram built his altar to Yahweh, near or next to Mamre's altar, since both state Abram dwelt *"**by** the terebinth trees of Mamre."*

"The trees" of Mamre indicate a garden. In that garden would have been an altar, which most assuredly was not dedicated to Yahweh but to whatever god Mamre served. Yet, it is apparent that Abram and Mamre didn't argue. Instead, they allied. And what is thought-provoking is *that "Yahweh appeared to him (Abraham) by the terebinth trees of Mamre, as he was sitting in the tent door in the heat of the day,"* Genesis 18:1-2. What then are we to make of this association between Mamre and Abram? It's just an assumption, but I think Mamre submitted to Abram. Thus, his god fell to Yahweh.

Now, I've gone around the mountain to show you the metaphorical implications of this story: Abram and Mamre, respectively, represent the Melchizedek regency and its covenant partners. No, I'm not saying Abram was the Melchizedek Regent. I'm saying he "types" him. And I'm saying that Mamre "types" those who disassociate themselves from the fallen realm. So, when Melchizedek (Abram) heard his brother (by-law), who could not see adequately, had been taken captive, he raised an army and went in pursuit of the adversary. And in this allegory, the military of Melchizedek was comprised of those "from" his own house; (spirit warriors) and covenant partners (followers). Hopefully, you are picking up what I am putting down. The Eternal Melchizedek came to redeem his brother - Adam. As the Promised Seed – he came as the Seed of Abraham. And like Abram, Yeshua chased his adversaries to "their judgment" – their "hiding place." Then Yeshua entered Hades and took the keys to death, hell, and the grave before returning to the Ancient of Days as a victorious King! That, however, is only part of the story. So, let's return to verse one and look at those four kings as deities.

Now I watched when the Lamb opened one of the seven seals, and I heard one of the four living creatures say with a voice like thunder, "Come!" And I looked, and behold, a white horse! And its rider had **a bow, and a crown was given to him, and he came out conquering, and to conquer.** *When he opened the second seal, I heard the second living creature say, "Come!" And out came another horse, bright red. Its rider was* **permitted to take peace from the earth so that people should slay one another, and he was given a great sword.** *When he opened the third seal, I heard the third living creature say, "Come!" And I looked, and behold, a black horse!* **And its rider had a pair of scales in his hand.** *And I heard what seemed to be a voice amid the four living creatures, saying, "A quart of wheat for a denarius, and three quarts of barley for a denarius, and do not harm the oil and wine!" When he opened the fourth seal, I heard the voice of the fourth living creature say, "Come!" And I looked, and behold, a pale horse!* **And its rider's name was Death, and Hades followed him***. And they were given authority over a fourth of the earth, to kill with sword, famine, and pestilence and by wild beasts of the earth,* Revelation 6:1-8, (ESV emphasis added).

- → Rider 1) A storm god that is a warring archer.
- → Rider 2) A god of war that deceives and brings chaos.

- → Rider 3) A god of commerce, the keeper of accounts.
- → Rider 4) A god who causes death and his brother, the god of the underworld.

Note that there are two riders on the fourth horse. Four gods plus one equals five gods. Perhaps that is why we read in Genesis 14 that 4 kings pursued five kings. Whatever the case, these four are not the only gods who sinned against Yahweh. But these riders are lords of darkness; they rule over other spirits. Naming these gods is less important than knowing what they represent. They are the "satans" controlling the present world. Yet, while they are mighty, they are not all-powerful. However, they traverse interdimensional space and simultaneously manifest in numerous ways, having multiple personas.

As I studied Genesis 14, I became convinced Holy Spirit wants us to realize that the four horsemen of Revelation have been on the loose for a long time. Now, I am not claiming that the Revelation 6 gods came from the Euphrates to Canaan (Eden) to bring their offspring to heel in Abram's day. The case I am attempting to make is simply that the gods traverse outside the confines of time and space. They existed before John the Revelator was taken to the Isle of Patmos. Despite that, they were defeated by the coming of Yeshua when he went to the Cross.

Yeshua, as the Eternal Melchizedek, wins because "God Most High (El Elyon)" is his shield (*magen*). So, once again, I put this before you, Yahweh is the God of the Melchizedek. Yahweh is God Supreme, but Yeshua is King – of everything!

> Genesis 14:18-24, *"Then Melchizedek, king of Salem, brought out bread and wine; he was the priest of God Most High. And he blessed him and said: 'Blessed be Abram of God Most High, Possessor of heaven and earth; and blessed be God Most High, who has delivered* (magen) *your enemies into your hand.' And he gave him a tithe of all. Now, the king of Sodom said to Abram, 'Give me the persons, and take the goods for yourself.' But Abram said to the king of Sodom, 'I have raised my hand to the Lord, God Most High, the Possessor of heaven and earth, that I will take nothing, from a thread to a sandal strap, and that I will not take anything that is yours, lest you should say, 'I have made Abram rich'* — *except only what the young men have eaten, and the portion of the men who went with me: Aner, Eshcol, and Mamre; let them take their portion.'"*

And when he returned from smiting these kings, he and his men passed the valley of Siddim where the kings had made war together. And Bera, king of Sodom, and the rest of his men with him went out from the slime pits into which they had fallen to meet Abram and his men.[191]

And Adonizedek, king of Jerusalem, the same was Shem, went out with his men to meet Abram and his people with bread and wine. They remained together in the valley of Melech. And Adonizedek blessed Abram, and Abram gave him a tenth from all that he had brought from the spoil of his enemies, for Adonizedek was a priest before God.[192]

---

[191] Johnson, Ken. *Ancient Book of Jasher* (p. 35), Kindle Edition.
[192] Ibid

Making his way back to Hebron from winning the battle, Abram entered the Valley of the Kings from the north. At the opposite end of the valley, coming from the slime pits of the south, where he hid, the king of Sodom encountered Abram. The place where their paths crossed was northeast of Salem.

Since Adam, Salem had served as the "capital" of the Melchizedek Kingdom. So, traveling east, Melchizedek Shem entered the same valley. He came with bread and wine so that they might celebrate Abram's victory, which means he came as the High Priest[193] of the Melchizedek Kingdom with the sole purpose of blessing Abram.

Greeting Abram, Shem declared Yahweh, possessor of heaven and earth, was Abram's shield of protection and, as El Elyon, had delivered the adversary into Abram's hands. (Note these words figuratively speaks of the relationship shared by Yahweh and Yeshua. However, they also extend to Abram the protection of Yahweh. Thus, they are the offering of a Salt Covenant.)

Now note that Melchizedek was there as the High Priest, not as the Melchizedek Regent. He was blessing Abram while prophesying that the Eternal Melchizedek's enemies were defeated. Yeshua, the Lion of Judah, is counted as Abram's Seed. Therefore, Yeshua was present at this meeting. He, too, received Shem's blessing.

Responding to the offering of friendship to the Eternal King, Abram tithed to Melchizedek; in so doing, he sealed the Melchizedek blessing upon himself and his offspring. Abram gave his tithe as he partook of the elements that would later represent the Eternal Melchizedek's covenant with mankind – bread and wine.

The giving of his tithe was the same as swearing an oath: *"I have raised my hand to Yahweh, El Elyon, the Possessor of heaven and earth, that I will take nothing, from a thread to a sandal strap, and that I will not take anything that is yours, lest you should say, 'I have made Abram rich,'"* Genesis 14:22-23.

---

[193] When officiating as the High Priest the Melchizedek was called Adonizedek (my Lord is righteous).

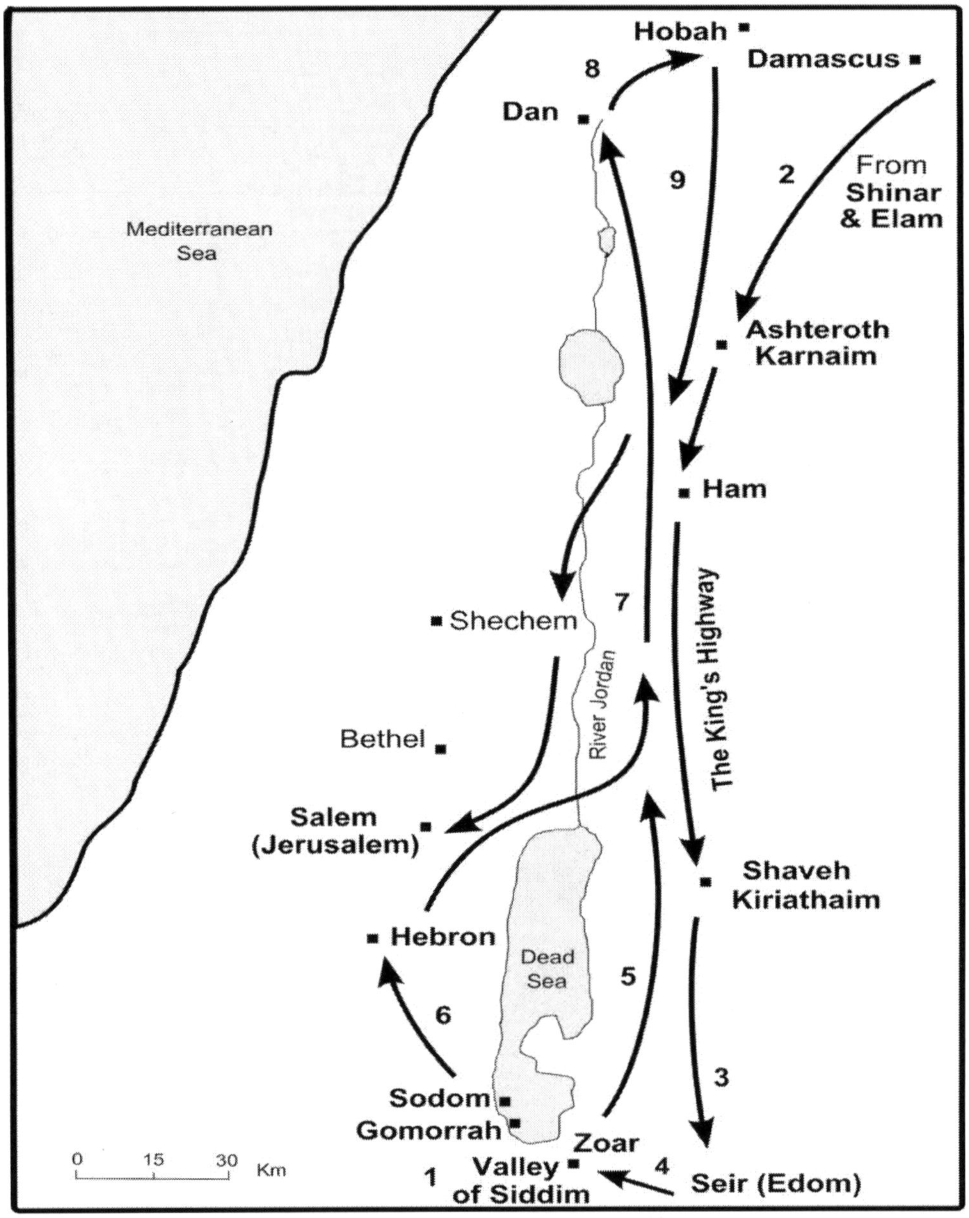
Hobah
Damascus
8
Dan
9
2
From
Shinar
& Elam
Mediterranean
Sea
Ashteroth
Karnaim
Ham
The King's Highway
7
Shechem
River Jordan
Bethel
Salem
(Jerusalem)
Shaveh
Kiriathaim
Hebron
Dead
Sea
5
6
3
Sodom
Gomorrah
Zoar
0
15
30
Km
1
Valley
of Siddim
4
Seir (Edom)

Genesis Fifteen

> Genesis 15: *After these things, the word* **(dabar)** *of the Lord* **(Yahweh)** *came to Abram in a vision, saying, "Do not be afraid, Abram. I am your shield* **(magen)**, *your exceedingly great* **(rabah)** *reward* **(sakar)." But Abram said, "Lord* **(Adonai Yahweh)** *God, what will You give me, seeing I go childless, and the heir of my house is Eliezer of Damascus?" Abram said, "Look, you have given me no offspring; indeed, one born in my house is my heir* **(yarash)!"** *Then behold, the word of the Lord came to him, saying, "That one shall not be your heir, but one who will come from your own body shall be your heir." Then He brought him outside and said, "Look now toward heaven, and count the stars if you can number them." And He said to him, "So shall your descendants be." And he believed in the Lord, and He accounted it to him for righteousness. Then He said to him, "I am the Lord, who brought you out of Ur of the Chaldeans, to give you this land to inherit it." And he said, "Lord God, how shall I know that I will inherit it?" So, He said to him, "Bring Me a three-year-old heifer, a three-year-old female goat, a three-year-old ram, a turtledove, and a young pigeon." Then he brought all these to Him and cut them in two, down the middle, and placed each piece opposite the other. Still, he did not cut the birds in two. And when the vultures came down on the carcasses, Abram drove them away. When the sun was going down, a deep sleep fell upon Abram. Behold, horror and great darkness fell upon him. He said to Abram, "Know of a certain that your descendants will be strangers in a land that is not theirs and will serve them, and they will afflict them four hundred years. And the nation whom they serve I will judge; afterward, they shall come out with great possessions. Now, as for you, you shall go to your fathers in peace; you shall be buried at a good old age. But in the fourth generation, they shall return here, for the iniquity of the Amorites is not yet complete." And it came to pass when the sun went down, and it was dark, that behold, there appeared* **a smoking oven** *and* **a burning torch** *that passed between those pieces. On the same day,* **(Yahweh)** <u>made a covenant</u> *with Abram, saying: "To your descendants, I have given this land, from the river of Egypt to the great river, the River Euphrates — the Kenites, the Kenezzites, the Kadmonites, the Hittites, the Perizzites, the Rephaim, the Amorites, the Canaanites, the Girgashites, and the Jebusites"* (emphasis added).

Abram swore an oath pledging his allegiance to the Melchizedek Kingdom, and after that, upon his return to Hebron, the "Word *(dabar)* of Yahweh" came to him.

Compare the "Word" who came to Abram to John 1:1-5. ***"In the beginning was the Word, and the Word was with God, and the Word was God.*** *He was in the beginning with God. All things were made through Him, and without Him, nothing was made that was made. In Him was life, and the life was the light of men"* (emphasis added).

Psalms 110:4, *"The Lord has sworn and will not relent, 'You are a priest forever according to the order* (dibrah) *of Melchizedek.'"* There is a special connection between Genesis 15, Psalms 110, and John 1. They all concern the "Word."

Strong's OT#1697 defines *dabar* as a "word" by implication, a matter (as spoken of) or thing; adverbially, a cause. *Dibrah* (Strong's OT#700) is the feminine version of OT#1697. The only difference between *dabar* and *dibrah* is the '*hei*.' When added to *dabar*, the *hei* causes the masculine tense of *dabar* to become feminine. "Newness" or refreshing pours forth when an additional breath is added to the pronunciation of *da-bar*, changing the term to *di-bra-ah*, so "she" may create. Ancient rabbis taught this added *hei* represented the "breath of God." His breath anointed the word and produced the effect of saying, "Behold, look at what comes from." Therefore, adding the *hei* to '*dabar*,' as in Psalms 110:4, caused the word spoken by Yahweh to become the Word described by John 1, Jesus Incarnate. We summarize by noting Jesus is our High Priest, forever, due to the breath Yahweh released upon Abram in Genesis 15. Essentially, isn't that precisely what John stated in John 1:1?

Even more amazing is how these golden nuggets are hidden throughout the Bible. And they are divinely connected even though the Bible was written by forty different people and throughout thousands of years. No one could have achieved this except the Holy Spirit.

The Word that appeared to Abram was the Word of Yahweh. I would suggest a compelling case might be made that it was the pre-incarnate Yeshua who manifested as the Divine One that Abram saw and spoke with. I would further argue that Abram had an open vision, not an inner vision or a dream.

So, if the one who came to Abram was the pre-incarnate Yeshua, why did Moses report that Yahweh conversed with Abram? The answer is complex. Nonetheless, the one I will give is short: It was taught, before the first century A.D., that Yahweh manifested as "two" powers.

"The startling reality is that long before Jesus and the New Testament, careful readers of the Old Testament would not have been troubled by the notion of, essentially, two Yahwehs— one invisible and in heaven, the other manifest on earth in a variety of visible forms, including that of a man. In some instances, the two Yahweh figures are found together in the same scene."[194]

Some take issue with the previous quote, but we need to note Abram witnessed "two" images of Yahweh later when he saw the "smoking oven" and "burning torch." Those images represented God the Father and the Son, yet both were Yahweh.

Yahweh began by saying, *"Do not be afraid, Abram. I am your shield* (magen), *your exceedingly great* (rabah) *reward* (sakar)."

- → *Magen* is defined by Strong's OT#4043 as in the plural and feminine, *meginnah* and derived from OT#1598 (to hedge) by being a shield (i.e., the small one or buckler); figuratively, a protector.
- → *Rabah* is defined by Strong's OT#7235 as a primitive root; to increase (in whatever respect).
- → *Sakar* is defined by Strong's OT#7939 as coming from OT#7936 (to hire), as a payment of a contract; concretely, salary, fare, maintenance; by implication, compensation, benefit.

In the previous chapter, Melchizedek proclaimed Yahweh as Abram's deliverer (*magen*). In this chapter,

---

[194] Heiser, Michael S. *The Unseen Realm: Recovering the Supernatural Worldview of the Bible* (Kindle Locations 2479-2482). Lexham Press. Kindle Edition.

Yahweh begins by affirming the same to Abram. Then further declares that he is Abram's "increase."

"I am your shield, your reward (the payment or benefit), *of your great* (abundant) *exceeding* (strong) *passion."* In essence, Yahweh said to Abram that He, Yahweh, was his strength and covering and the reward of his passion. Passion, in this instance, refers to the "passion" Abram shared with Sarai.

That declaration appeared to confuse Abram. So, being a practical man, he asked, *"Adonai Yahweh,* what (who and how) will You give me this reward, seeing I am childless *('ariyriy* – destitute of children). The heir *(yarash)* of my house, as of now, is Eliezer of Damascus. You have given me no offspring *(zera).* None born within my house is my heir *(yarash)!"*

Since he recognized the subject was "seed," Abram went straight to the heart of what was promised - "seed." We should examine why Abram was concerned that he had no heir from his body.

Abram was a very wealthy man; his holdings were vast. He was also a man of immense importance and responsible for many. Previously, we surmised Abram was a company of many people, probably upward of a thousand or more. While researching this matter, I found several articles claiming that Eliezer was Abram's son by a handmaiden named Masek. That could not be. A man cannot be "seedless" and, simultaneously, father a son, regardless of who the mother might be. So, since Abram in Genesis 15 was seedless, he had yet to seed (hopefully, you follow my meaning). I have no doubt Abram was faithful to Sarai. However, she was not capable of conceiving, in my opinion. I would further speculate that Yahweh had purposefully kept her womb closed.

Anyway, had Lot remained with Abram, he, rather than Eliezer, would have inherited Abram's wealth? Lot was not only Abram's brother-in-law but also his nephew. Yahweh answered Abram, *"That one shall not be your heir, but one who will come from your own body shall be your heir,"* proving my point that Abram, up to that moment in time, had no offspring.

Apparently, Eliezer of Damascus was the master steward of Abram's household. In the culture of that day, his position likened him to an adopted son. To conduct business and manage affairs of Abram, Eliezer would have presented himself as "coming in" Abram's name. In other words, Eliezer stood before whoever he was dealing with in the stead of Abram.

Eliezer means "God is my help." Still, we note he was "of Damascus." That suggests that he and Abram were not of the same bloodline, probably not the same ethnicity. Additionally, the "El" of his name more likely did not refer to Yahweh but to the Canaanite god, *"El."*

Yet, whatever the case, in that Abram mentioned Eliezer as a potential heir means he was highly trusted and well-loved by Abram. Still, Abram had yet to look and behold "who" would come from him!

Therefore, Eliezer was not Abram's reward because he was not of Abram's *me'ah* (body). So, Yahweh instructed Abram, *"Go outside. Look now toward heaven, and count the stars; if you can number them, then you can number your descendants."*

Keep in mind that Abram was in an open vision. That he was told to go outside meant he was inside. So, Yahweh sent Abram out to look at the stars. Did Yahweh show Abram the princes of heaven or the physical stars in the night sky? Or both? I leave that to your imagination. However, once Abram saw the stars, he believed Yahweh, and his faith was "counted" (*chashab* - imputed) unto him as righteousness. At that moment, Abram was officially established as a royal prophet of the Melchizedek Kingdom! The first to be joined to the Melchizedek Order according to faith.

To affirm my assertion, note that Yahweh declared, *"I am Yahweh. I brought you from Ur to give (nathan –* appoint) you **this (zo'th)** *(Aleph-Tav) land, to inherit it."* Let's rephrase so we might see the implication of what was said. "I, Yahweh, brought you out of Ur (the past) and appointed you this (the female sheep) of the Melchizedek land. Drive out, my enemies!" Abram was appointed to be a shepherd (a priest and prophet) to prepare the land for the Good Shepherd.

Abram again asked, "how?" (The NKJV presents his question as, "How shall I know that I will inherit it?") Inherit is *yarash* and means more than to occupy. By implication, the land was to be dispossessed of its current occupants. Abram was then to fill it with "sheep," followers. Appropriately, Abram was first to remove the Canaanite tenants (the wolves and vultures of the fallen gods) and then make disciples to Yahweh from his offspring.

Who shall ultimately inherit Eden? The answer is Yeshua. Yahweh gave the land to Yeshua; Eden is <u>his</u> portion! Abram was not being assigned the land to possess it for himself. He was there to reclaim it. Abram and his descendants were chosen as stewards. The mission of Abram and his offspring was to drive out the "false gods" from the land and occupy it until the time that God shall execute the final judgment on the adversaries of the Melchizedek.

I must clarify my point: The land is the inheritance of the Groom. It shall be the home of the Bride when the two are married. They shall marry when their enemies are destroyed. That is the end goal. It's spiritual in nature but must occur first in the physical. The land must be restored as Eden so it may become the home of Melchizedek and his Bride - the House of Israel. These things are cyclical. Genesis reveals Revelation, and Revelation fulfills Genesis.

Yahweh answered, *"Bring me a three-year-old heifer, a three-year-old female goat, a three-year-old ram, a turtledove, and a young pigeon."*

- → Three-year-old heifer
- → Three-year-old female goat
- → Three-year-old ram
- → Turtledove
- → Young Pigeon

Why ask for these animals? Of all the explanations I came across, the following, in my opinion, is the most accurate. "This form of making a covenant was probably the usual one used in Babylonia (Ur). Thus, Abram received the assurance of his inheritance by employing a ceremonial that he was familiar with. In most ancient languages, men cut or struck a covenant because of the solemn penalty involved if broken... The severing of the bodies was not, as some supposed to represent the two parties. But, as explained in Jeremiah 34:18-20, it set forth the penalty of perjury. Usually, with the making of the covenant, an imprecation was given. It was stated that if the covenant was broken, the same destruction applied to the slaughtered animals would be applied to the one who broke it. There is no mention of this occurrence being a sacrifice. However, the same animals are subsequently set apart for sacrifice by the Levitical law. The heifer, she-goat, and ram at three years old would each have attained their full maturity. Still, there may be a further symbolic meaning in there being three animals each three years old."[195]

Abram brought the requested animals and birds. He (Abram) divided the three animals in half and laid the pieces against one another. However, he did not divide the birds. Then birds of prey, either hawks or vultures, came down. Abram drove them away. *"Now when the sun was going down, a deep sleep fell upon Abram; and behold, horror and great darkness fell upon him,"* Genesis 15:12.

But then, Yahweh said to Abram: "It is certain, your descendants will be strangers in a land that is not theirs and will serve those among whom they shall live. They will be afflicted for four hundred years. However, I will judge the nation they are subjected to, and afterward, your offspring shall return with many possessions. Now, as for you, you shall go to your fathers in peace. You shall be buried at a good old age. But in the fourth generation that your offspring are away from here, they shall return. They shall return when the Amorites' cup of iniquity is considered full." Then, when the sun went down and darkness fell, a smoking firepot and a burning torch appeared. The pot and the torch passed between the animal pieces and the birds. At that time, Yahweh completed the covenant by saying, "To your descendants, I assign this land. Its boundaries of it are from the river of Egypt to the great river, the Euphrates. Even though it is currently inhabited by the Kenites, Kenezzites, Kadmonites, Hittites, Perizzites, Rephaim, Amorites, Canaanites, Girgashites, and the Jebusites."[196]

Let's consider how much of what was said was perceived. I believe Abram fully understood that Yahweh decreed that he, a man who had yet to father any children, would be the father of many. Additionally, he grasped that Yahweh promised him that he would be the father of a "Divine" Son, the Promised Seed; the same Seed promised to Eve. This concept might be foreign to believers today, even blasphemous. But given the culture and environment of Abram's upbringing, he understood what he "saw" and comprehended what he heard. He recognized these promises as the same ones made to Adam and Eve. Abram's concern was not who or what but how and when.

Once again, allow me to repeat that Abram was not "a" Melchizedek. He was not a Firstborn. Yet, Yahweh had instructed him to "live" in the Melchizedek's territory like a king and priest. That meant he was to build altars, which at that time, he had made three. Yahweh was preparing Abram for the fourth altar.

Altar, *"mizbeach,"* marked a divine encounter. I also remind you that the average person could not afford to

---

[195] https://biblehub.com/commentaries/genesis/15-9.htm retrieved June 21, 2021
[196] Genesis 15:13-21 paraphrased by the author.

build an altar. Only the very rich, the royalty of that day, built altars. Most altars were called "high places" or "gardens." They were constructed as unique places of worship and sacrifice. Once the altar was dedicated, it served as a portal into the cosmic dimensions that opened with prayers of supplications.

Abram was okay with building altars as an act of obedience. But to believe he would father a Melchizedek took a massive amount of faith. I imagine Abram asked himself, "How can that anointed birthright skip from Shem to me, or to a son I don't have?"

Yahweh sent him outside to look at the stars to assist Abram with understanding. That bit of information infers a) it was nighttime, b) the sky was clear, and c) Abram perceived the meaning of Yahweh's words immediately upon seeing the sky for – *"he believed." "By faith, Abraham obeyed when he was called to go out to the place which he would receive as an inheritance… By faith, he dwelt in the land of promise as in a foreign country…, for he waited for the city which has foundations, whose builder and maker is God,"* Hebrews 11:8-10.

From the get-go, Abram had walked guided by Spirit, not sight. He was connected, to Yahweh, spiritually. Abram spiritually knew the voice of Yahweh, recognizing who was speaking. Additionally, Abram was familiar with the story of the *Mazzaroth*. So, he immediately understood what the Voice of Yahweh was saying. And, at that moment, saw the cosmic purpose of the promise, that through him, the Promised Melchizedek would come, and Eden and its garden would be restored to *'erets*. That is why the writer of *Hebrews* stated Abram waited for the city whose builder and maker is God.

Romans 1:20, *"For since the creation of the world His invisible attributes are clearly seen, being understood by the things that are made, even His eternal power and Godhead…."* Psalms 19:1-6, *"The heavens declare the glory of God; and the firmament shows His handiwork. Day unto day utters speech, and night unto night reveals knowledge. There is no speech nor language where their voice is not heard. Their line has gone out through all the earth, and their words to the end of the world. In them, (Yahweh) has set a tabernacle for the sun* (Son), *which is like a bridegroom coming out of his chamber and rejoices like a strong man to run its race. Its rising is from one end of heaven, and its circuit to the other end, and there is nothing hidden from its heat."*

§7 [1.7] "They also were the inventors of that peculiar sort of wisdom concerned with the heavenly bodies and their order…" [197] Yahweh gave understanding to Adam. The revelation given to Adam was written in the stars. You may be asking, "What revelation?" The revelation of redemption. Adam was taught about a forthcoming Messiah, and Adam passed that understanding to Seth. Seth taught Enosh, and Enosh taught Cainan. Cainan taught Mahalalel, and Mahalalel taught Jared. Jared taught Enoch, and Enoch taught Methuselah. Methuselah taught Lamech, and Lamech instructed Noah. Noah instructed Abram.

Genesis 15:5, *"Then (Yahweh) brought him (Abram) outside and said, 'Look now toward heaven, and* **count (caphar)** *the stars if you can number* **(caphar)** *them'"* (emphasis added). *Caphar* – Strong's OT#5608 states *caphar* is a primitive root that correctly suggests scoring with a mark as a tally or record. Also, by implication, to inscribe and enumerate; intensively, to recount, to celebrate. Also, the KJV translates it as 'to

---

[197] Josephus: *Antiquities of the Jews*, PC Study Bible formatted electronic database Copyright © 2003, 2006 by Biblesoft, Inc. All rights reserved

commune,' (ac-) count; declare, number, penknife, reckon, scribe, shew forth, speak, talk, tell (out), writer. Psalms 19:1, "To declare" is *caphar*. I suggest Yahweh was telling Abram to commune with the stars.

"Have you not known? Have you not heard? Has it not been told to you from the beginning? Have you not understood from the foundations of the earth? It is He who sits above the circle of the earth, and its inhabitants are like grasshoppers, who stretches out the heavens like a curtain and spreads them out like a tent to dwell in. He brings the princes to nothing; He makes the judges of the earth useless. Scarcely shall they be planted, scarcely shall they be sown, scarcely shall their stock take root in the earth when He also blows on them, and they will wither, and the whirlwind will take them away as stubble. 'To whom then will you liken Me, or to whom shall I be equal?' says the Holy One. Lift up your eyes on high, and see who has created these things, who brings out their host by number. He calls them all by name, by the greatness of His might and the strength of His power. Not one is missing," Isaiah 40:21-26.

The ancients were familiar with the stars and their constellations. Their cycle, which they traverse, is the Mazzaroth, which the Greeks called the Zodiac. Whatever name we use, it is the panorama of the night. "These pictures were designed to **preserve, expound, and perpetuate the one first great promise and prophecy of Genesis 3:15** that all hope for man, all hope for Creation, was bound up in a coming Redeemer; One who should be born of a woman; who should first suffer, and afterward gloriously triumph; One who should first be wounded by that great enemy who was the cause of all sin and sorrow and death, but who should finally crush the head of 'that Old Serpent the Devil.' These ancient star pictures reveal this Coming One. They set forth 'the sufferings of Christ and the glory that should follow.' Altogether there are forty-eight of them, made up of twelve SIGNS, each sign containing three CONSTELLATIONS. These may be divided into three great books, each book containing four chapters (or Signs); and each chapter containing three sections (or Constellations)."[198]

"Adam, who first heard that wondrous promise, repeated it and gave it to his posterity as a most precious heritage, the ground of all their faith, the substance of all their hope, the object of all their desire. Seth and Enoch took it up. Enoch, we know, prophesied of the Lord's coming, saying, '*Behold the Lord cometh with ten thousand of His saints to execute judgment upon all* (Jude 14). How could these 'holy prophets, since the world began,' have recorded their prophecies better, more effectually, or more truthfully and powerfully than in these star pictures and their interpretation?"[199]

Luke 1:68-75, *"Blessed is the Lord God of Israel, for He has visited and redeemed His people, and has raised up a horn of salvation for us in the house of His servant David, as He spoke by the mouth of His holy prophets, who have been since the world began, that we should be saved from our enemies and from the hand of all who hate us, to perform the mercy promised to our fathers and to remember His holy covenant, the oath which He swore to our father Abraham: To grant us that we, being delivered from the hand of our enemies, might serve Him without fear, in holiness and righteousness before Him all the days of our life."*

Which constellations were visible in the sky the night of Genesis 15? I don't know for sure. Perhaps it was Virgo, the picture of the Virgin and her Seed. *"For unto us a child is born, unto us, a son is given, and the government shall be upon His shoulder,"* Isaiah 9:6. The constellation of Virgo, the first book of the Mazzaroth, depicts the promise made to Eve, the coming one, the Promised Seed. Nevertheless, whatever constellation or group of

---

[198] Bullinger, Ethelbert W. *The Witness of the Stars* - Illustrated Kindle Version. Kindle Edition.
[199] Ibid

stars Abram viewed, he knew in that instant that he was being chosen as a pathway for the Divine to be released to the earth. *"Therefore, the Lord Himself will give you a sign: Behold, the virgin shall conceive and bear a Son, and shall call His name Immanuel" (which means God is with us),* Isaiah 7:14-15.

There are 110 stars in Virgo. The brightest star in Virgo is *Tsemech* [Hebrew]. In Arabic, that same star is known as *Al Zimach*, the Branch. Jeremiah 33:15-16, *"In those days and at that time I will cause to grow up to David a Branch (Tsemach) of righteousness; He shall execute judgment and righteousness in the earth. In those days, Judah will be saved, and Jerusalem will dwell safely."*

We can be assured that Abram listened to the stars that night and believed. And because he did, it was credited to him as righteousness (*tsadaq*). Romans 4:9-12, *"Does this blessedness then come upon the circumcised only, or upon the uncircumcised also? For we say that* **faith was accounted to Abraham for righteousness**. *How then was it accounted for? While he was circumcised or uncircumcised? Not while circumcised,* **but while uncircumcised**. *And he received the sign of circumcision,* **a seal of the righteousness of the faith which he had while still uncircumcised, that he might be the father of all those who believe, though they are uncircumcised, that righteousness might be imputed to them also**, *and the father of circumcision to those who not only are of the circumcision but who also walk in the steps of the faith which our father Abraham had while still uncircumcised"* (emphasis added). Abram became, in that moment, the father of all who would believe. Believe in what? Who? Believe in Yahweh and in the Eternal Melchizedek. That they would redeem mankind from the curse of sin, of death.

John 3:16-17, *"For God (Yahweh) so loved the world that He gave His only begotten Son, that whoever believes in Him should not perish but have everlasting life. For God (Yahweh) did not send His Son (Yeshua) into the world to condemn the world, but that the world through Him might be saved."*

These verses and extra-canonical quotes are presented to substantiate that Abram stood under the stars that night and, in his heart, believed in the prophesied Melchizedek. And at that moment, the Kingdom was established on his faith. Before that moment, it had been built upon works of the reigning Melchizedek. The physical Melchizedek throne did not pass to Abram, but the righteousness associated with that throne did. Also, Abram did not instantly become a Firstborn priest of the Melchizedek Order. Even so, he became the first Melchizedek prophet who would preach the message of faith.

Most importantly, he became the spiritual father of **all** who came after him, who would also believe in Yahweh's Divine Redeemer, the Eternal Melchizedek. Abram set aside the when and simply accepted that his Seed was the Eternal Melchizedek. He grabbed ahold of the concept – Yahweh would send a Redeemer, and the Promised Seed would be counted as Abram's Seed. So, he asked, "how am I to be assured, legally, that I should occupy this land?"

Remember, legally, based upon Yahweh's own provisos, the Melchizedek Regent had dominion over the land. At that time, Shem was the reigning Regent. Shem and his father Noah, owing to their "blinded eyes," allowed the Amorites and Canaanites to build altars to gods other than Yahweh in that region. As a result, Eden was overrun by foreign gods. Abram was appreciative of the fact that Yahweh's Kingdom needed restructuring. That the land of Eden needed to be cleared of unrighteousness. He was asking for instructions. He was not of the mind to "step" on the authority of Shem and Eber. Yet, he needed to know how to advance his appointment. So, Yahweh answered Abram by asking for the animals and birds. But don't lose sight of this truth – God fights the battles; mankind reaps the rewards!

Being the masterful tactician that He is, Yahweh renewed the Psalms 110 covenant. We could view this move as He disconnected the past regents (Adam to Eber) and bound the future to that eternal covenant by making Abram, a witness to the renewal. Since the regency, as it existed, had to continue, Abram would be grafted into the renewal as Prophet, not king. Shem and Eber were not replaced. Their roles as negotiators were diminished. Of course, that was already obvious. Yet, it would not be until Isaac that the office of king/high priest/prophet came together again in one individual. Even then, the power of the regent king was undermined, and the authority of the priesthood diminished. Consequently, it was not until Yeshua's first advent that the Melchizedek Kingdom fully recovered.

As a result, Shem, and later Eber, continued, in name only, as Melchizedek. And Abram became the Prophet. The cutting of that covenant made the transaction legal because Abram was grafted into the covenant as Prophet. Which afforded him the right to approach the Divine Council or any spiritual entity and legally demand they submit to his authority as the "Voice" of the future. In that instant, Abram was handed full responsibility for the land. Therefore, he would represent Yahweh. That is until his death. Upon his death, another, who had to be his seed, would carry forth until, at last, the Divine Redeemer appeared.

Abram went to his herds and retrieved the requested animals and birds. He then dug a ditch, and after cutting the animals per the custom of "cutting a covenant," he placed them in the ditch and watched over their pieces until the sun went down. From the moment the trench was dug and the animals placed within, Abram protected his portion of the covenant by driving *"the fowls,"* which *"came down on the carcasses, away."* The terms used in verse eleven invoke a picture of Abram fighting off birds of prey, which biblically represent demons. He fought with them until he could "work" no more because the sun had ceased to provide light.

More than a few hours had passed since the Word of the Lord came to Abram in an open vision. I assume it was dark when the open vision began since it was dark when Abram went outside to look at the stars. So, daylight had come and gone. Therefore Genesis 15:12 says, *"And it came to pass, that, when the sun went down, and it was dark, behold a smoking furnace, and a burning lamp that passed between those pieces."*

John 9:4, "I must work the works of Him that sent me, while it is day; the night is coming, when no one can work." And as it grew dark, Abram fell into a trance because a "Spirit of Darkness" overshadowed him. Just as darkness seemed to render him immobile, Abram heard the Voice of Yahweh saying, *"Know certainly that your descendants will be strangers in a land that is not theirs and will serve them, and they will afflict them four hundred years. And the nation whom they serve I will judge; afterward, they shall come out with great possessions. Now, as for you, you shall go to your fathers in peace; you shall be buried at a good old age. But in the fourth generation, they shall return here, for the iniquity of the Amorites is not yet complete,"* Genesis 15:13-16.

- → Deep sleep - *Tardemah* (deep sleep) describes a lethargy much like a trance, implying Abram was silenced, unable to speak, but aware of his surroundings. The root word, *radam*, means to stun or stupefy.
- → Horror of great darkness - Something or someone frightened him. The word *'eymah* conveys the idea of an idol that invokes terror.

I think it would be safe to assume a satan appeared with the purpose of accusing Abram of overstepping his authority. As the sleep befalling Abram grabbed him, he heard Yahweh rendering a judgment against his accuser.

Let's explore that concept by looking for the meaning of *"a smoking furnace and a burning lamp."* Genesis 15:1, Abram is told – *"Do not be afraid, Abram. I am your shield, your exceedingly great reward."* In other words, Yahweh positioned Abram. Yahweh placed Abram before Him and then surrounded him. That's a God thing that only God can do. Abram became the beneficiary of God's Presence. I would go as far as to say that was the moment that Yahweh put the future Exodus into play. But then, I would be jumping too far ahead into the future. Yet, Yahweh is so far ahead of His enemies that there is no way they can win!

When the Spirit of Darkness immobilized Abram and his "seed" within him, his Reward and Shield stepped into the trench and dispelled the darkness. The Shield, Yahweh, and Abram's Reward, Yeshua, stepped into the ditch and walked between the pieces as Judgment and Light. The Ancient of Days, seated on the Throne of Justice, and the Son of Man, the Light of the World, might be a better rendering. For God walked together – and dispelled the works of the adversaries.

After witnessing the covenant made and hearing the prophecy, "to your descendants I have given this land," Abram knew he was to occupy the land for Yahweh. He knew a Divine judgment stood against the dark kingdom and was guaranteed of, thus comforted by this revelation when he saw Yahweh and Yeshua walking between the animal pieces. Yahweh said, *"Know of a certainty your descendants SHALL come out of bondage with great possessions. They SHALL return when the iniquity of the Amorites is complete."* And Abram saw as he heard the prophecy, *"a smoking furnace and a burning lamp passing between the pieces."*

Abram witnessed this "prophecy" unfolding before him. Subsequently, he realized he was a Prophet of Yahweh; otherwise, the Divine revelation would not have been given to him. Nor would he have been allowed to witness the Yahweh-Yeshua covenant.

Awe-struck Abram watched and heard, *"Unto your seed have I given this land, from the river of Egypt unto the great river, the river Euphrates: The Kenites, and the Kenezzites, and the Kadmonites, and the Hittites, and the Perizzites, and the Rephaim, and the Amorites, and the Canaanites, and the Girgashites, and the Jebusites."*

- → Smoking furnace – a light such as a candle or a firepot
- → Burning torch - a torch that is flaming hot

The smoking firepot is a symbol of judgment. Thus, it represented God as the Ancient of Days. The torch or lamp depicted Yeshua as the "light of the world." When the smoking firepot and the burning torch passed between the animal parts, the covenant regarding the land of Eden was ratified. Once again, we have a witness of the Great Supreme Judge of the cosmos passing to His Son his inheritance.

Abram only observed. He did not participate. Why? Abram was not capable of restoring Eden. But his Reward is – that is why his Reward walked with Yahweh through the pieces.

There you have it - two Divine powers. The God and the King of the Melchizedek Kingdom made a covenant. However, the Creator and Supreme God, Yahweh, assigned Abram and his descendants the land from the Nile to the Euphrates to occupy. That is the exact territory Adam was given oversight of in Genesis 2.

All the "ites" living at the time of this covenant within that territory were trespassers. Eventually, they would be driven out of the land. But only after the iniquity of the Amorites had reached its full measure. Iniquity means sin, a perverse and immoral evil. Yahweh stated that He was allowing the sin of the Amorites to continue for a season. Amorite kings ruled from the east of the Euphrates to the Nile, north into the area that is Turkey, and south toward Sinai and the Red Sea. The union of their tribal kings was a powerful force. However, more significant is that the Amorite culture influenced the Egyptians, Assyrians, Greeks, and Romans.

The Amorite[200] culture was "mystery Babylon." Which makes the words of Yahweh, *"They* (the children of Abraham) *shall return when the iniquity of the Amorites is complete,"* doubly potent. Abraham's spiritual seed shall return when the "fullness of the Gentiles" is determined.

(Amorites lived in eastern Mesopotamia, the area which became "Babylonia." Canaanites lived in the west, closer to the Great Sea, the Mediterranean. In using the term Amorites, Yahweh essentially referred to all the sons of Ham. They were all Amorite, including all the tribes of Canaan.)

Psalms 110: *"The affirmation of Yahweh to my Lord: 'Sit at My right hand, Till I make thine enemies your footstool.' The rod of your strength Yahweh sends from Zion. Rule amid your enemies. Your people* (are a) *free-will gift* (the descendants of Abram) *in the day of your strength, in the beauty of holiness. From the womb, from the morning, you have the dew of youth. Yahweh has sworn, and will not repent,* **'You are a priest forever according to the order of Melchizedek.'** *Adonai* (Yeshua), *on your right hand, smote kings in the day of His anger. He judges the nations and gathers the carcasses; he shall smite the head* (satan) *over the earth. From a brook by the wayside, he shall drink. Therefore, He shall lift up the head!* (emphasis added).

There is more, much more, to this chapter. The "burning torch" was the proxy for Abram's future descendants. Yahweh specified who He wanted to be His Bride. She was to be the fourth generation that "shall return." Since that point is explored extensively in *Survey Two*, we shall not do so here. Other than to note that the ratification of the covenant described in Genesis 15 marked the proposal of marriage between Yahweh and the House of Israel as perfected. To say that another way, what Yahweh began with Abram in

---

[200] The Amorite civilization and the Sumerians were the same.

Genesis 12 was completed with Genesis 15. Yet, Abram had to be tested and proved. And an exchange needed to be made between the Melchizedek and the Bride to mark them as belonging to each other.

Genesis Sixteen

Now Sarai, Abram's wife, had borne him no children. And she had an Egyptian maidservant whose name was Hagar. So, Sarai said to Abram, 'See now, the Lord has restrained me from bearing children. Please, go into my maid; perhaps I shall obtain children by her.' And Abram heeded the voice of Sarai. Then Sarai, Abram's wife, took Hagar, her maid, the Egyptian, and gave her to her husband Abram to be his wife after Abram had dwelt ten years in the land of Canaan. So, he went to Hagar, and she conceived. And when she saw that she had conceived, her mistress became despised in her eyes. Then Sarai said to Abram, 'My wrong be upon you! I gave my maid into your embrace, and when she saw that she had conceived, I became despised in her eyes. The Lord judge between you and me. So, Abram said to Sarai, 'Indeed your maid is in your hand; do to her as you please.' And when Sarai dealt harshly with her, she fled from her presence. Now the Angel of the Lord found her by a spring of water in the wilderness, by the spring on the way to Shur. And He said, "Hagar, Sarai's maid, where have you come from, and where are you going?" She said, "I am fleeing from the presence of my mistress Sarai." The Angel of the Lord said to her, "Return to your mistress, and submit yourself under her hand." Then the Angel of the Lord said to her, "I will multiply your descendants exceedingly so that they shall not be counted for multitude." And the Angel of the Lord said to her: "Behold, you are with child, and you shall bear a son. You shall call his name Ishmael because the Lord has heard your affliction. He shall be a wild man; his hand shall be against every man, and every man's hand against him. And he shall dwell in the presence of all his brethren." Then she called the name of the Lord who spoke to her, You-Are-the-God-Who-Sees; for she said, "Have I also here seen Him who sees me?" Therefore, the well was called Beer Lahai Roi; observe, it is between Kadesh and Bered. So, Hagar bore Abram, a son, and Abram named his son, whom Hagar bore, Ishmael. Abram was eighty-six years old when Hagar bore Ishmael.
Genesis 16

"At the end of ten years of Abram's dwelling in the land of Canaan, which was the eighty-fifth year of Abram's life, Sarai gave Hagar unto him."[201]

Sarai and Hagar were both princesses. The difference between them had to do with wealth and authority. Sarai was Terah's granddaughter. According to the record supplied by the book of *Jubilees*, Terah had adopted Sarai, making her a legal daughter and one of his heirs. Thus, within Terah's house (court), Sarai held a position of preeminence.

On the other hand, according to the *Book of Jasher*, Hagar was Pharoah's daughter by one of his concubines. That would have made her a daughter without legal standing. Implying that she would have been cared for but not recognized as an heir though she belonged to the Royal House of Egypt. But in no case would she have been lower caste.

Sarai gave Abram Hagar, which insinuates Hagar was hers to give. Hagar probably managed the household

---

[201] Johnson, Ken. *Ancient Book of Jasher* (p. 36). Kindle Edition.

affairs since she was of a higher station. As the daughter of Pharoah, she was likely trained to handle the demands of a house of great wealth. In more relatable terms, Hagar was a lady-in-waiting. Her service was one of assisting, not of performing unskilled tasks.

Regarding this, note Paul's teaching to the Galatians, Chapter 4:23-31, *"For it is written that Abraham had two sons,* **one by the slave woman and** *the other* **by the free woman**. *His son by the slave woman was* **born in the ordinary way,** *but* **his son by the freewoman was born due to a promise**. *These things may be taken* **figuratively,** *for the women represent two covenants. One covenant is from Mount Sinai and bears children who are to be slaves: This is Hagar. Now* **Hagar stands for Mount Sinai in Arabia and corresponds to the present city of Jerusalem because she is in slavery with her children**. *But the* **Jerusalem that is above is free, and she is our mother**. *For it is written: 'Be glad, O barren woman, who bears no children; break forth and cry aloud, you who have no labor pains; because more are the children of the desolate woman than of her who has a husband.' Now you, brothers, like Isaac, are children of promise. At that time,* **the son born in the ordinary way persecuted the son born by the power of the Spirit**. *It is the same now. But what does the Scripture say? 'Get rid of the slave woman and her son, for the slave woman's son will never share in the inheritance with the free woman's son.' Therefore, brothers, we are not children of the slave woman but of the freewoman."* (NIV emphasis added).

Paul noted the symbolic meaning of this story. So should we. And we begin with the question: Why compare Hagar to a slave if she was the daughter of Pharaoh? First, Hagar was a gift; she wasn't captured, then bought and sold. However, she wasn't free. For Hagar, leaving Sarai's service would have dishonored Pharaoh.

Since she was a gift, the only one who could release Hagar from servitude was Sarai. Yet, Sarai did not set Hagar free because Sarai was also honor-bound. It was now her responsibility to care for Hagar and to release her would have been cruel. Left on her own, without protection, Hagar would have starved or been enslaved in the truest sense.

Hagar was obliged to fulfill the desire of Sarai, which made her obligated to give a child to Sarai.

Women and marriage were viewed differently in that day. Marriages between royal houses were arranged. Primarily to form pacts or treaties. Marriages were made to ally enemies or unite the military forces of tribes. These arrangements were covenants made purposefully to add land or value of some manner to a kingdom and its court. That arrangement also provided a means by which surrogates were accepted legally. Surrogates existed in the household only to gain heirs. This practice was often stipulated in or conditioned by the writing of formal marriage documents. Providing a "wife" proxy in a marriage allowed the "bride" to maintain a girlish figure. In some instances, a royal wife of noble blood could refrain from "wifely" duties altogether if those assignments were allocated to a surrogate/concubine.

Women or wives were often viewed as trophies and put on display. Their sole purpose was for social entertainment. They were obligated to give lavish parties and were paraded about as status symbols. Therefore, surrogates allowed the wife to forego any confinement associated with childbearing.

Additionally, consigning concubines as surrogates also eliminated the physical discomfort of giving birth. If a wife opted to use a surrogate, then a child born to the surrogate was recorded as hers. However, in the strictest sense, the child belonged to the father.

Yet, another concern was the birth mother's legal status. Was she a concubine, a slave, or perhaps a second wife whose bloodline was void of nobility? The legal standing of the birth mother determined the child's future and inheritance.

If for some reason, the child was not acknowledged as belonging to a wife, then the child would be a slave if the birth mother were one. Slaves remained slaves unless the master or the legal wife of the house decided otherwise. If the mother and child were slaves, each had to be set free separately. Once the child was freed, the father could legally adopt the child.

To record a surrogate's child as the wife required a formal agreement between the wife and the husband. Once that pact was finalized, the adoption proceedings began.

Usually, the birth mother was the child's wetnurse. Therefore, a deeper relationship evolved between wife and surrogate as time passed. It was typical for the constraints of slavery to be removed, causing the wife to promote the surrogate to concubine status. This usually occurred if the wife wanted additional children by the same surrogate.

Concubines were the property of the "house" and obtained for the master's entertainment. They were given rights only if the master of the house agreed to allow them certain freedoms. In rare cases, a concubine could rise in status and become a "second wife."

A second wife was inferior to the first. Even so, she would have a great deal more freedom and luxury than that given to a concubine or to a slave surrogate.

So, you can see how different their culture was from the one we have today. It was common for a man of wealth and status to have more than one wife or a wife to insist upon house concubines. That Sarai said, *"See now, Yahweh has restrained me from bearing children. Please, go into my maid; perhaps I shall obtain children by her,"* was not bizarre. Neither was it strange that Abram agreed – it was acceptable behavior.

Sarai had tried and failed for ten years to give Abram what Yahweh had promised. Ten is the number of completion of divine order. However, Sarai believed Yahweh had closed her womb, thus, keeping her from conceiving. In other words, like Eve, Sarai viewed herself as inferior because, like Eve, she believed Yahweh was withholding something from her. (Wonder who was whispering in Sarai's ear, "you need to eat from the tree of knowledge"? An adversarial god, perhaps?) Like Eve, Sarai believed the deception. Consequently, she repeated it to Abram. Abram, like Adam, listened to his wife.

As Paul so aptly said, Abram had a son *"by the slave woman, born in the ordinary way."* Just as Eve gave Adam the fruit, Sarai gave Hagar to Abram in that same sense. Abram took the Egyptian maiden. Legally, in human terms, Abram had the right. His act was not illegal, given the culture of his day. But, in Yahweh's eyes, it was not obedience. Using Hagar to fulfill "all righteousness" was ordinary, not based upon Yahweh's promise to give him an heir who would inherit Eden.

Then, *"when she saw that she had conceived, I became despised in her eyes,"* Genesis 15:14. "And when Hagar saw that she had conceived she rejoiced greatly, and her mistress was despised in her eyes, and (Hagar) said within herself, 'This can only be that I am better before God than Sarai, my mistress, for all the days that my mistress has been with my lord, she did not conceive, but me the Lord has caused in so short a time to conceive by him.'"[202]

Hagar, controlled by pride, taunted Sarai. As I thought about this, I wondered what Hagar said to Sarai. Perhaps she simply compared herself to Sarai as a woman, pointing out that she was favored, whereas Sarai was not. Maybe she demanded to be promoted to wife. It's also possible Hagar wanted the child to be considered hers, not Sarai's. Whatever was said, Sarai felt maltreated (*chamac*) and wronged. When Sarai could no longer stomach the sneers, she went to Abram. She demanded that Abram consult Yahweh, saying, *"let him judge between you and me."*

In other words, Sarai wanted a judgment concerning the child. She wanted to know to whom did the child belong. Apparently, Abram did not seek Yahweh. Instead, he answered, *"Sarai, 'Indeed your maid is in your hand* (under your authority); *do to her as you please.' And when Sarai dealt harshly* (chasten Hagar by answering her taunts), *she* (Hagar) *fled from her presence."*

Now the Angel of the Lord (the Messenger of Yahweh) found her (Hagar) by a spring of water in the wilderness, by the spring on the way to Shur. And he said, *"Hagar, Sarai's maid, where have you come from, and where are you going?"* This question was put to her by design and demanded a verbal answer. The Angel of Yahweh wanted her to speak aloud so that she would hear herself admit that Sarai was her mistress. Until she did, the Angel of Yahweh was restrained from helping her. Hagar needed to submit appropriately to authority.

Hagar answered, *"I am fleeing from the presence of my mistress Sarai."* Notice that after Hagar submitted, she received a promise. Her descendants would be multiplied. The Angel of Yahweh (who I believe was the pre-Incarnate Yeshua) instructed, *"Return to your mistress and submit yourself to her. I will multiply your descendants exceedingly so that they shall not be counted for multitude. You are with child, and you shall bear a son. You shall call his name Ishmael (God will hear) because Yahweh has heard your affliction. He (Ishmael) shall be a wild man; his hand shall be against every man, and every man's hand against him. And he shall dwell in the presence of all his brethren."*

Hagar then called the name of the One who spoke to her, "You-Are-the-God-Who-Sees." This indicates Hagar was less than familiar with Yahweh.

She asked, *"Have I also seen Him who sees me here?"* That is why the well (the spring) where she rested is called *Beer Lahai Roi* – which means "Well of the One Who Lives and Sees." That spring was between Kadesh and Bered.

---

[202] Ibid

Genesis Seventeen

Genesis 17: *When Abram was ninety-nine years old, the Lord appeared to Abram and said to him, "I am Almighty God; walk before me and be blameless. And I will make my covenant between you and me and will multiply you exceedingly." Then Abram fell on his face, and God talked with him, saying: "As for me, behold, my covenant is with you, and you shall be a father of many nations. No longer shall your name be called Abram, but your name shall be Abraham, for I have made you a father of many nations. I will make you exceedingly fruitful, and I will make nations of you. Kings shall come from you. I will establish my covenant between you and me and your descendants after you in their generations, for an everlasting covenant, to be God to you and your descendants after you. Also, I give to you, and your descendants after you, the land in which you are a stranger, all the land of Canaan as an everlasting possession. I will be their God." And God said to Abraham: "As for you, you shall keep my covenant, you and your descendants after you throughout their generations. This is my covenant which you shall keep, between you and me and your descendants after you: Every male child among you shall be circumcised. You shall be circumcised in the flesh of your foreskins, and it shall be a sign of the covenant between you and me. He who is eight days old among you shall be circumcised, every male child in your generations, he who is born in your house or bought with money from any foreigner who is not your descendant. He who is born in your house and bought with your money must be circumcised. My covenant shall be in your flesh for an everlasting covenant. And the uncircumcised male child, who is not circumcised in the flesh of his foreskin, that person shall be cut off from his people; he has broken my covenant." Then God said to Abraham, "As for Sarai, your wife, you shall not call her name Sarai, but Sarah shall be her name. And I will bless her and give you a son by her; then I will bless her, and she shall be a mother of nations; kings of peoples shall be from her." Then Abraham fell on his face and laughed and said in his heart, "Shall a child be born to a man who is one hundred years old? And shall Sarah, who is ninety years old, bear a child?" And Abraham said to God, "Oh, that Ishmael might live before You!" Then God said: "No, Sarah, your wife shall bear you a son, and you shall call his name Isaac; I will establish My covenant with him for an everlasting covenant, and with his descendants after him. And as for Ishmael, I have heard you. Behold, I have blessed him, and will make him fruitful, and will multiply him exceedingly. He shall beget twelve princes, and I will make him a great nation. But My covenant I will establish with Isaac, whom Sarah shall bear to you at this set time next year." Then He finished talking with him, and God went up from Abraham. Abraham took Ishmael and all the males (born to his house or bought with his money) and circumcised the flesh of their foreskins that very same day Yahweh had commanded to do so. Abraham was ninety-nine years old when he was circumcised in the flesh of his foreskin. And Ishmael, his son, was thirteen years old. That very same day, Abraham was circumcised, and his son Ishmael; and all the men of his house, born in the house or bought with money from a foreigner, were circumcised with him.*

"Therefore, the One whom you worship without knowing, Him I proclaim to you. God, who made the world and everything in it, does not dwell in temples made with hands since He is Lord of heaven and earth. Nor is He worshiped with men's hands, as though He needed anything since He gives to all life, breath, and all things. And has made from one blood every nation of men to dwell on all the face of the earth. He determined their pre-appointed times and the boundaries of their dwellings so that they should seek Yahweh in the hope that they find Him. He is not far from each one of us, for in Him we live and move and have *our being, as also some of your own poets have said, 'For we are also His offspring.' Therefore, since* **we are the offspring of God**, we ought not to think that Divine Nature is like gold or silver or stone, something shaped by art and man's devising. *In these times of ignorance, God overlooks (and foregoes punishment). Yet, He commands all men everywhere to repent because* **He has appointed a day in which the world will be judged according to the righteousness of the Man (Yeshua) whom (Yahweh) ordained. He (Yahweh) has given assurance of this by raising Him (Yeshua) from the dead,**" Acts 17:23-31 (emphasis added).

Luke 8:10, *And He said, "To you, it has been given to know the mysteries of the kingdom of God, but to the rest, it is given in parables, that 'Seeing they may not see, and hearing they may not understand.'"* One of these mysteries is the purpose of seed/Seed. It was a "mystery kept secret since the world began."[203]

The keeping of that secret was one of the reasons heaven was disconnected, dimensionally, from the earth. *'Erets* needed to receive seed/Seed. Yet, that also meant physical *'erets* would need to be reinstated - to "merge" with the spirit realm. But only after the choice of good and evil was forever settled.

For that reason, Yahweh used his enemies. He allows them to "test" mankind so that every human would be called upon to make a choice: To *"love the Lord your God with all your heart."*

"What shall we say then? Is there unrighteousness with God? Certainly not! For He says to Moses, 'I will have mercy on whomever I will have mercy, and I will have compassion on whomever I will have compassion.' So, it is not of him who wills, nor of him who runs, but of God who shows mercy. For the Scripture says to the Pharaoh, 'For this very purpose I have raised you up, that I may show My power in you, and that My name may be declared in all the earth.' Therefore, He has mercy on whom He wills and whom He wills He hardens. You will say to me then, 'Why does He still find fault? For who has resisted His will?' But indeed, O man, who are you to reply against God? Will the thing formed say to him who formed it, 'Why have you made me like this?' Does not the potter have power over the clay, from the same lump to make one vessel for honor and another for dishonor? What if God, wanting to show His wrath and to make His power known, endured with much longsuffering the vessels of wrath prepared for destruction, and that He might make known the riches of His glory on the vessels of mercy, which He had prepared beforehand for glory," Romans 9:14-24.

After he sinned, Adam had to find a replacement for himself. His death was warranted and inevitable. But how? Who? Perhaps, Yahweh had a heart-to-heart talk with his son and explained the "birds and the bees," but Adam already knew what was expected. After all, he had named the birds and the bees. Instead, I imagine Yahweh explained the need for the Firstborn Priesthood and the requirements demanded of every Firstborn.

Adam to Noah was ten generations. During those ten generations, the *elohim* came. Divine rebellious celestials traveled back and forth, in and out of the realms between heaven, the netherworld, and *'erets*. They attacked the Melchizedek's kingdom, deceiving who and wherever possible. They inflicted havoc, chaos, and destruction. The Melchizedek Kingdom grew weaker as the years passed, and evil became more pervasive. Adam, and those who served following his reign, failed Yahweh. They could not harness chaos or stand

---

[203] Romans 16:25

against the wickedness of the gods.

Perhaps it would be more merciful to say that those who served as regents to the Melchizedek Kingdom lacked revelation. Only Enoch "walked" with Yahweh. Seemingly only he knew how to stand against the wickedness. Yet, that was part of the Divine Plan, but no one knew. And as the gods began to think they had solved the mystery of what Yahweh planned, they attempted to unlock the purpose of the seed. They realized DNA held secrets. So, they began manifesting in various forms to manipulate human DNA for their purpose. As a result, the gods fathered offspring that were a mixture of terrestrial and celestial DNA.

Yahweh quickly ruled that the offspring of the "fallen ones" were illegally gotten. An order went out that the offspring of the Watchers were to be removed from the earth. Meanwhile, Noah was commanded to build an ARK! That ark represented Yahweh's provision for preserving seed – and for the resurrection of life illegally stolen. It symbolized – Covenant. It revealed Yeshua - the Promised Seed!

You know the adage, "there are two sides to every coin." Well, there were two consequences to the flood. Noah emerged to view the cleansed earth – the fallen gods viewed a destroyed sphere. Noah was kept safe because he was a Melchizedek Regent, hidden in the ARK of Yeshua. Yet, at the same time, judgment fell upon the unrighteous. But why was Yahweh protecting Noah and his family? The simple answer: Noah and Shem were Seed/seed carriers.

After the flood, evil returned. The fallen gods were angry, even more determined to spoil human DNA as retribution. It didn't take them long to discover how to "dis" mantle the Melchizedek regency. Essentially, the fallen gods worked until the earth was divided. They handed their portion to Nimrod (rebellion).

No, Noah did not willingly hand over the reins to *'erets*. Even so, that was the effect. As the eighth temporary Melchizedek, Noah allowed Nimrod to usurp his God-given authority. As a result, this world's government (kingdoms) was handed over to the adversaries of the Eternal Melchizedek. Even that transference of power was rooted in the "need" to control the "seed." More precisely, the fallen gods seemingly controlled the "narrative."

Yet, Yahweh was never caught off-guard. He purposefully allowed the enemy to think they had won. That through the gentile nations, they controlled the world. Quietly and calmly, Yahweh called on Abram. He assigned the task of cleansing Eden for the sake of the Eternal Melchizedek. While Yahweh would work through Abraham, Isaac, and Jacob, His end goal was to restore the world and convert the "gentiles" into Hebrews. That was the mystery of the Kingdom. It would be accomplished through faith, not through works.

"When Abram was ninety-nine years old, the Lord appeared to Abram and said to him, 'I am Almighty God; walk before Me and be blameless," Genesis 17:1. Twenty-four years after he built the altar at Shechem when he was ninety-nine, Yahweh appeared to Abram and revealed himself as *El Shaddai*. First, note ninety and nine are symbolized by *tsahdee* and the *tet* – pictographically ⚬⊗ - **"surround the harvest."**

Genesis 17:1 is the Bible's first use for the epithet, *El Shaddai*. Strong's Concordance and Dictionary defines

El Shaddai as "the all-powerful God, the One who destroys his enemies and avenges those who are his." Scholars of ancient Semitic languages suggest *El Shaddai* should be translated as "God of the Mountains." The conclusion is that *shaddu* or *shadda* refers to "mountain-dwellers," and in that "the gods" dwelled on mountains, the assumption is *shadda* was merely another term to denote "*el*." Also, as used in this context, mountains suggest strongholds and positions of power.

Abram was told to "**walk** and be **blameless**" - "*halak*" and "*tamiym*." The best explanation I can offer is to point you to Enoch. He walked as a friend with Yahweh and became *tamiym* (perfected). Genesis 5:24, "*Enoch walked with the Elohiym (Yahweh), and he was not, for the elohim took him.*" Enoch was a Firstborn and served Yahweh as a priest. Later, as an anointed king/high priest, he served only a short time in *'erets* before being translated to *shamayim* to become a witness for the Melchizedek Kingdom. Even though he ceased to "live" in the realm of *'erets*, he did not stop walking with the *elohim*. Enoch's relationship with *Elohiym*, the Supreme Judge, grew to such perfection that he was safeguarded from the adversarial system and hid where the Spirit of Death could not take him. So, in essence, Yahweh was saying, "Abram, walk with me. I will add you as a beneficiary to my covenant if you remain righteous. The agreement you witnessed shall establish your offspring as Melchizedek royalty. We shall increase their number until they are a great harvest. Your walk shall perfect your offspring, spiritually."

The *Book of Jasher* stated that Abram was a member of Noah's household until age fifty. Abram knew firsthand the responsibilities of the "temporal" Melchizedek and the duties of the Firstborn, though he was neither. So, how did Yahweh legally bring Abram's Seed into the Melchizedek succession? Well, first, Abram had to leave his natural birthright behind him. Then be "born-again" in Eden. Strictly speaking, Abram needed to be "adopted" into the Divine Royal family.

Yahweh renewed the covenant between Himself and the Eternal King. God (Yahweh-Yeshua) allowed Abram to witness their agreement. Furthermore, they marked Abram as their legal representative when they ordained Abram as "the" Melchizedek Prophet to Eden (Genesis 15). If called upon, Abram could give testimony as to the legalities of the Melchizedek Covenant since he had witnessed it firsthand. He could testify to the Divine Council that the conditions of that all-important cosmic covenant were met and ratified. This meant that he and his descendants were under the protection of that covenant. Therefore, Abram was acting in obedience to occupy Eden. And since that covenant was everlasting, Abram and his offspring had an endless right to occupy Eden.[204]

Years came and went. Still, Abram had no heir. Sarai grew weary; I'm sure that Abram did too. He fathered a son by Hagar though she was not Abram's "legal" wife. When viewed from the spirit realm, Ishmael was a product of works and not born of faith. So, Ishmael resulted from Abram's carnal flesh. Ishmael was produced from an unsanctioned mixture of DNA (Abram's and Hagar's).

Changing Abram and Sarai's identities was mandated. Circumcision was important. Yet, there was more at work in these two things than we might initially imagine. So, let's dig in and see what happened.

---

[204] Walking between the animal pieces ratified the covenant.

Thirteen years after Ishmael's birth, Yahweh again appeared to Abram and, at that time, said, *"My covenant is with you… **you shall be the father of many nations*** (goy). *No longer shall your name be called Abram, but **your name shall be Abraham**, for I have made you a father of many nations. I will make you exceedingly fruitful, and I will make nations of you, and kings shall come from you. And I will establish My covenant between you and Me and your descendants* (seed) *after you in their generations* (time), *for an everlasting covenant, to be God to you and your descendants* (seed) *after you. Also, I give you and your descendants after you the land in which you are a stranger, all the land of Canaan, as an everlasting possession. I will be their God,"* Genesis 17:4-8 (emphasis added).

"Behold my (*Aleph-Tav*- Melchizedek royal) covenant exists. Father, many nations! No longer call your name Abram; you shall be Abraham. (This renaming was the proclamation of adoption. Yet, it was performed as a bride taking the name of the groom.). You are appointed fruitful, exceedingly, as the father of many. I assign to you a nation of kings. (This statement marked Abram as divine royalty.) I will establish my covenant with your Seed – properly in time – as an everlasting covenant to exist for the purpose of the *Elohiym* Seed. Hereafter. I grant your seed after you the *(Aleph-Tav)* land (currently known as) Canaan for an everlasting possession. I exist as *Elohiym* (marking this decree as an official cosmic command)."[205]

"And God (Elohiym) *said to Abraham: 'As for you, you shall keep My covenant, you, and your descendants **(seed)** after you throughout their generations. Every male child shall be circumcised, and you shall be circumcised in the flesh of your foreskins. It shall be a sign of the covenant between you and Me. He who is eight days old among you shall be circumcised, every male child in your generations, he who is born in your house or bought with money from any foreigner who is not your descendant* **(seed)**. *He who is born in your house. He who is bought with your money must be circumcised. (The sign of) My covenant shall be in your flesh for an everlasting covenant. And the uncircumcised male child, who is not circumcised in the flesh of his foreskin, that person shall be cut off from his people; he has broken* (violated) *My covenant,"* Genesis 17:9-14 (emphasis added).

For a few moments, let's focus on the heart of this matter, that the promises made in Genesis 12, 13, 15, and 17 focused on "Seed." Note Paul's teaching: *"Now to Abraham **and his Seed were the promises made**. He does not say, 'And to seeds,' as of many, but as of one, 'And to your Seed,' who is Christ. And this I say that the law, which was four hundred and thirty years later, cannot annul the covenant that was confirmed before by God in Christ, that it should make the promise of no effect. **If the inheritance is of the law, it is no longer a commitment; God gave it to Abraham by promise**,"* Galatians 3:16-18. These things are noteworthy because Yeshua would need to prove his lineage, that he was "human" royalty.

*Now Jesus Himself began His ministry at about thirty years of age, being **(as was supposed)** the son of Joseph, the son of Heli, the son of Matthat, the son of Levi, the son of Melchi, the son of Janna, the son of Joseph, the son of Mattathiah, the son of Amos, the son of Nahum, the son of Esli, the son of Naggai, the son of Maath, the son of Mattathiah, the son of Semei, the son of Joseph, the son of Judah, the son of Joannas, the son of Rhesa, the son of Zerubbabel, the son of Shealtiel, the son of Neri, the son of Melchi, the son of Addi, the son of Cosam, the son of Elmodam, the son of Er, the son of Jose, the son of*

---

[205] Genesis 17:4-8 modified by the author.

Eliezer, the son of Jorim, the son of Matthat, the son of Levi, the son of Simeon, the son of Judah, the son of Joseph, the son of Jonan, the son of Eliakim, the son of Melea, the son of Menan, the son of Mattathah, **the son of Nathan, the son of David,** *the son of Jesse, the son of Obed, the son of Boaz, the son of Salmon, the son of Nahshon, the son of Amminadab, the son of Ram, the son of Hezron, the son of Perez,* **the son of Judah, the son of Jacob, the son of Isaac, the son of Abraham,** *the son of Terah, the son of Nahor, the son of Serug, the son of Reu, the son of Peleg, the son of Eber, the son of Shelah, the son of Cainan, the son of Arphaxad, the son of Shem, the son of Noah, the son of Lamech, the son of Methuselah, the son of Enoch, the son of Jared, the son of Mahalalel, the son of Cainan, the son of Enosh, the son of Seth, the son of* **Adam, the son of God,"** *Luke 3:23-38* (emphasis added).

Luke's gospel presents Mary's lineage. Four names of significance must be examined. They are **Nathan, Judah, Abraham**, and **Adam**.

Note the path that follows back from Judah to Abraham. Abraham was born Abram. The way his name was changed was essential an adoption into the Adamic stream of Firstborns. This seems complicated. However, since Adam was a " son of God," Abraham needed to be also.

From Adam to Eber, the succession was passed from Firstborn to Firstborn. But then the earth was divided, and the line waited at Eber until Abraham was adopted. It continued through Isaac until it was hidden in Judah.

Then concerning Judah, the path provided for the Melchizedek bloodline had to remain righteous. The first three of Jacob's twelve sons were deemed unsuitable. They had committed unrighteous acts prohibiting them from passing "righteous" DNA. Therefore, Jacob hid the "scepter" of the Melchizedek Kingdom in Judah. That scepter stayed hidden until Yeshua.

Yet, David, like Abram, was given a promise. The commitment made to David was that his offspring would rule forever as king/high priest. David served as king over Israel, legally. Yet, he was not a priest – of any priesthood, nor was David a Firstborn. To further complicate the matter, not all King David's sons were righteous. Therefore, some were unsuitable pathways for David's "anointed" DNA to pass through the generations to Yeshua. Such as Solomon's son Jeconiah since God had placed a blood curse upon Jeconiah. But we note Mary descended from David's son Nathan, not from Solomon.

Adam's DNA was unique. Only he was created as a divine royal spirit housed in human flesh. And only he was divinely appointed to act as Regent! Everyone that served as Regent had done so in Adam's stead.

Yeshua was considered the "second Adam." Or the second "created" man - "birthed" to inherit the Melchizedek Kingdom. Still, regarding this matter, there were two requirements placed upon Yeshua. He needed a legal bloodline that tied him to Adam to remove the penalty Adam owed. That is to say that Yeshua had to show he was "like" Adam – and thus the Son of Man.

As the Son of God, Yeshua was to inherit the cosmic kingdom. Therefore, he had to be both Son of God and Son of Man.

Matthew presented Joseph's lineage. Although Matthew focused on Abraham and King David, the bloodline of Joseph was flawed due to Jeconiah. Yeshua did not carry Joseph's DNA. Even so, according to Roman law, Yeshua was the son of Joseph. Therefore, Yeshua could lawfully claim the title, Son of Man, through Joseph. Still, Yeshua's matrilineal descent determined his right to the "throne" of David and the right to the Melchizedek Priesthood through Jacob, Isaac, Abraham, and so on to Adam.

*"The book of the **genealogy of Jesus Christ, the Son of David, the Son of Abraham**: Abraham begot Isaac, Isaac begot Jacob, and Jacob begot Judah and his brothers. Judah begot Perez and Zerah by Tamar, Perez begot Hezron, and Hezron begot Ram. Ram begot Amminadab, Amminadab begot Nahshon, and Nahshon begot Salmon. Salmon begot Boaz by Rahab, Boaz begot Obed by Ruth, Obed begot Jesse, and Jesse **begot David, the king. David, the king**, begot Solomon by her, who had been the wife of Uriah. Solomon begot Rehoboam, Rehoboam begot Abijah, and Abijah begot Asa. Asa begot Jehoshaphat, Jehoshaphat begot Joram, and Joram begot Uzziah. Uzziah begot Jotham, Jotham begot Ahaz, and Ahaz begot Hezekiah. Hezekiah begot Manasseh, Manasseh begot Amon, and Amon begot Josiah. Josiah begot **Jeconiah** and his brothers about the time they were carried away to Babylon. And after they were brought to Babylon, Jeconiah begot Shealtiel, and Shealtiel begot Zerubbabel. Zerubbabel begot Abiud, Abiud begot Eliakim, and Eliakim begot Azor. Azor begot Zadok, Zadok begot Achim, and Achim begot Eliud. Eliud begot Eleazar, Eleazar begot Matthan, and Matthan begot Jacob. And Jacob begot Joseph the husband of Mary, of whom was born Jesus who is called Christ. **So, all the generations from Abraham to David are fourteen generations, from David until the captivity in Babylon are fourteen generations, and from the captivity, in Babylon, until the Christ are fourteen generations**,"* Matthew 1:1-17 (emphasis added).

Yeshua's legal ancestors, reckoned by Jewish law, can be traced to Abraham. Therefore, Yeshua came into the world as Abraham's Seed. Hence, Abraham was not only the father of many; he was the Exalted Father of a Divine King!

Abram needed a name change. He also needed to circumcise his flesh. He needed to be marked as righteous.

Circumcision was a sign, a seal of righteousness, of faith. How was circumcision a sign? Romans 4:9-12, *"For we say that faith was accounted to Abraham for righteousness. How then was it accounted? While he was circumcised or uncircumcised? Not while circumcised, but while uncircumcised. And **he received the sign of circumcision, a seal of the righteousness** of the faith which he had while still uncircumcised, that he might be the father of all those who believe, though they are uncircumcised, **that righteousness might be imputed to them also**, and the father of circumcision to those who not only are of the circumcision **but who also walk in the steps of the faith which our father Abraham had while still uncircumcised."***

Muwl, circumcise, is defined by Strong's OT#4135 as a primitive root that means to cut short, curtail (circumcise) by implication; figuratively, to destroy.

Circumcision marked Abraham as righteous and also the males of his house likewise. However, only Abram had witnessed the Yahweh-Yeshua Melchizedek Covenant. So, only Abraham was sealed by circumcision unto righteousness because of faith. Those in his camp were marked sealed. Not due to their faith or righteousness, but according to their obedience to Abraham. That indicated Abraham would function within his house as a priest and the Melchizedek Prophet unto the whole of Eden.

Circumcision destroyed the fleshy covering of the male genitalia. Metaphorically, circumcision represented the cutting away of the foreskin of the human heart. Deuteronomy 10:6, *"Circumcise therefore the foreskin of your heart, and no longer be stubborn."*

Abram submitted in absolute reverence, falling on his face when *El Shaddai* (the God of the Mountain) began speaking. Overwhelmed by the holiness that accompanies *El Shaddai*, Abram could not remain upright while listening to the command, "be blameless and **passionately** multiply." I imagine the tone of that command came similarly to the one given Adam, *"Be fruitful and multiply."*[206] In fact, the Hebrew word spoken in Genesis 17:2 (*rabah*) was first said to Adam in Genesis 1:22. *Rabah* means to increase with abundance. The significance is that when Yahweh commands a thing to be accomplished, He enables it. So, Abram both heard and felt that command.

Abram fell on his face, sensing the Word, the power that holds all things together. Though his flesh was weak, his spirit was willing. He surrendered. He fell, becoming a ready vessel to receive. Yahweh immediately filled him with His Spirit and with His Word. (One of the markings of a Melchizedek was the infilling of Yahweh's Spirit. Yahweh breathed into Adam, and he became a living soul. That was when Adam was filled with God's Spirit. After that, at the anointing ceremony of each Firstborn, they were embodied with Yahweh's Spirit. That is why the Dove rested on Yeshua's shoulder when John the Baptist immersed Yeshua in the River Jordan.)

But going back to Abram, he was born anew at that moment – his DNA changed. Whether it was a sudden epiphany or a realization that had matured with the past thirteen years, Abram suddenly knew he needed help. At that point, he realized his impotence. How could Abram replicate himself into a multitude of people, let alone into many kings, without Divine assistance? If Abram's offspring was to be a great nation,[207] a multitude as numerous as "the dust of the earth,"[208] he needed a miracle. His flesh was indeed weak. So, Abram submitted to Yahweh, and Yahweh filled him with Divine power so that he could do as commanded. In fact, I would venture to say that Yahweh also filled Abram with "seed" by planting His Word in Abraham! (Selah!) That, my friend, is why Abraham is the king of the Third Day!

"No longer shall your name be called Abram, but your name shall be Abraham, for I have made you a father of many nations" Genesis 17:5-6.

→ Strong's OT# 87 אברם Abram translates as high (head) father.

→ Strong's OT#85 אברהם Abraham translates as a father of a multitude.

---

206 Genesis 1:22
207 Genesis 12:2
208 Genesis 13:16

The difference between the spelling of the two names is the addition of the *hei*. The ancient symbol representing the *hei* was drawn to symbolize a man with his hands lifted ⚐. Once Abram had surrendered, Yahweh breathed upon him and revealed Abram's heart. The *hei* is the fifth letter of the Hebrew alphabet. It can mean to behold or to cry aloud with passion. When a *hei* is inserted into the middle of a word, as with Abraham, the *hei* symbolizes "the revealing of the heart." Abraham's name was given to reveal to all who spoke his name that his heart belonged to Yahweh. The term also marked him as the first (head) father of faith. Additionally, the first father of a royal family.

However, hidden in Abraham's name was Yeshua, the revealing of Father's heart. The understanding of that concept was missed by the unseen realm. Although the name change did cause the spirit realm to see Abraham in a new light, it was made clear Abraham was to "be the father of many." Even so, no one caught on to the double entendre, seed/Seed – that through the many would "One" come!

Circumcision also marked Abraham, but that marking was intimate. It existed as a reminder to Abraham that his seed/Seed belonged to Yahweh.

Not until it was revealed to Paul, who in turn wrote about the revelation, did the New Testament believer understand the importance of Abraham. (Excuse me for being skeptical, but I am not entirely persuaded that today's church understands Paul's revelation more than the Second Temple rabbis did. Or, for that matter, the spirit world in Abraham's day.)

So, to open our understanding, let's go down another path for a few moments. Hopefully, it will shed more light on what I am striving to communicate.

Mantle[209] —

> (1) *'addereth,* a large over-garment. This word is used concerning Elijah's mantle, which was probably a sheepskin. It appears to have been the only garment he wore. He bound it with a strip of skin or leather around his loins, which kept the garment in place. *'Addereth* occurs twice with the epithet 'hairy.'
>
> (2) *me'il,* frequently applied to the 'robe of the ephod,' a splendid undertunic of blue that touched just below the knees. It was woven without a seam. It had to be pulled over the head to wear it. The *me'il* was worn not only by priests but by kings, prophets, and rich men. Samuel's mother brought a 'little coat' from year to year to Shiloh; it was a miniature *me'il.*
>
> (3) *Semikah,* 'a rug,' the garment Jael threw as a covering over Sisera. *Semikah* occurs nowhere else in Scripture.
>
> (4) *Maataphoth,* plural, found only in Isaiah 3:22, denoting an oversized exterior tunic worn by females.

Essentially, the garments Yahweh provided Adam and Eve were mantles - *'addereth.* Those *'addereths* covered Adam's nakedness (his shame of failure) and symbolized Yahweh's forgiveness. Adam's *'addereth* also served as his Melchizedek's *me'il.* As time passed and civilization progressed, mantles represented a person's power

---

[209] *Easton's Bible Dictionary,* PC Study Bible formatted electronic database Copyright © 2003, 2006 Biblesoft, Inc. All rights reserved.

and/or authority. A mantle's color, attached emblems, or shape indicated that a person was military, held a political post, or perhaps a ruler or priest. In other words, mantles and their insignia were outward signs affording each individual their due respect according to that outer garment.

When wearing his mantle, Adam stood before Yahweh as righteous. The Courts of *Shamayim* were obliged to uphold his words because he was the Melchizedek Regent, and outwardly, Adam manifested purity. That was also true of all the Melchizedeks from Adam to Noah. But then that mantle was stolen. It was taken from Noah as he slept, drunk in his tent. Metaphorically, Noah became intoxicated with his own works, the fruit of his labor. And as he slept, the adversary of Yahweh stole the Melchizedek mantle, which had been handed down to him from Adam. The bottom line, Noah lost Adam's cover. After that, the regent's authority was not recognized globally. Even more notably, the gods mocked the Melchizedek Kingdom as weak and ineffectual. Those same gods encroached upon Yahweh's territory. They incited men to build altars on the mountains that belonged to Yahweh. Those altars were not erected to worship Yahweh but to venerate the dead, the *Rephaim*.

So, Yahweh changed the marking of His kingdom's authority. Instead of a mantle, Yahweh gave the sign of the Cross. Righteousness would no longer be attributed to a Melchizedek Regent because he wore a mantle or according to his works. Beginning with Abraham, all who approached Yahweh would need to show faith. A person's heart had to be circumcised. The flesh of it had to be removed. Abram fathered this change when he believed Yahweh and, in his heart, determined to faithfully perform his duties as Yahweh executed all He promised.

Discovering his weakness, that he could not do all that was required of him, Abram fell upon his face. At ninety-nine, Abram realized he could not produce a "harvest." Spiritually, Abram cut away the flesh of his heart. That is why Yahweh gave him the command to circumcise his flesh. Circumcision became Abraham's spiritual mantle, a mantle that could be seen only by Yahweh. When He looked at Abraham, God saw the "sign of the covenant" – x – a tiny scar on Abraham's flesh that pointed to the Cross of Yeshua. But going beyond that, the Eternal God saw Abraham spiritually through the work of the Cross. Being eternal, Yahweh could see Abraham, his Seed, and his seed at the Cross. Oh! The faithfulness of Yah!

Abraham was grafted into the Melchizedek Covenant because his heart was right. Consequently, Yahweh needed the seed of Abraham to pass "through" the sign of the Cross – a tiny scar that signified the most crucial covenant ever made – so that seed would become fruitful.

Let's look at the implications of Sarai becoming Sarah. A *hei* was also added to her name. For Sarah, the *hei* caused her to be fruitful. Only after she was named Sarah by Yahweh did she conceive. Rabbinical teachings hold that by adding the *hei*, Sarai was promoted to a Matriarch, the mother of a people.

Strong's Bible Dictionary indicates that the original *yod* was removed, and a *hei* took its place. A *yod* can symbolize "works." Adding a *hei* as a postfix completes the word by adding the phrase, "what comes from." *Hei* or "breath" would come from Sarah because Yahweh would "bless her."

"Bless" is *barak* –indicating that because Yahweh blessed her, she would produce a son and be a mother of nations and kings. *Barak* was used when Yahweh first told Abram his name would be great; see Genesis 12:2. Strong's Hebrew Dictionary defines *barak* as "to kneel." Yahweh didn't kneel in Genesis 12; neither did He in Genesis 17. So, what was Yahweh doing? Mainly, Yahweh caused Abraham to kneel.

Let me explain by paraphrasing what Yahweh said: "I shall breathe on Sarai, your wife. She shall give you a son after she becomes Sarah and, ultimately, the mother of kings and of nations." Again, Abraham fell upon his face to worship. Although the NKJV implies Abraham laughed as to scorn, I don't think that was the case. Primarily, I find it hard to accept that a righteous person would scorn Yahweh, even in thought, especially in Yahweh's presence as Abraham was. Look ahead to Genesis 21:6-7, *"And Sarah said, God hath made me laugh so that all that hear will laugh with me"* KJV. That statement is not disrespectful or scornful. I am persuaded Abraham fell on his face under the "power" of God. He did not mock or even question Yahweh as to doubt, instead wondered how it could be.

Here is my opinion. Abraham fell upon his face and laughed outwardly as Holy Spirit entered his being. Giddy with joy, he thought, "Is it possible that a man who is one hundred and a woman of ninety can conceive a child?" Then remembering Ishmael, he said to *Elohiym*, *"Oh, that Ishmael might be permitted to live before your Face!"*

I suggest Abraham wondered how God would bring to pass what was promised, and as he questioned the "how," he remembered the son he loved. Did you notice Abraham petitioned *Elohiym?* That implies the Divine Council heard Yahweh's decrees. I suspect Abraham knew they were there and hoped to gain a place before the Council for his son, Ishmael.

Okay, let me say this outright: Yahweh, as *El Shaddai* appeared, but so did the Divine Council. Genesis 17 provides the account of what could be viewed as a Holy Conclave. The attendees were Yahweh, the Divine Council, and Abram. Abram's name was changed, and he was empowered to complete his assignment. And Yahweh made sure that it went into the record book that Sarai was Sarah and that she, like Abram, was an instrument of His making. Effectually, Yahweh adopted Abraham and Sarah and brought both into His House. Then Yahweh named their son, who, by the way, would be a Melchizedek, Isaac.

Why was Isaac given a name that means "laughter," *Yitschaq?* The laughter of Yahweh empowered Abraham and Sarah to be fruitful. And quite frankly, Yahweh laughed at the gods, appreciating the irony of what Genesis 17 represents, which is the "seeding" of HIS Kingdom. Psalms 2:4, *"He who sits in the heavens shall laugh* (yischaq).*"*

Genesis 17 is an exchange of names, the marking of the covenant, and the empowerment to do all that is commanded. Like Genesis 15, these are explained in greater depth in *Survey Two*. There was an additional exchange to occur, that of Firstborns.

Genesis Eighteen

Then the Lord appeared to him by the terebinth trees of Mamre as he was sitting in the tent door in the heat of the day. So, he lifted his eyes and looked, and behold, three men were standing by him. When he saw them, he ran from the tent door to meet them, and bowed himself to the ground, and said, "My Lord, if I have now found favor in Your sight, do not pass on by Your servant. Please let a little water be brought, wash your feet, and rest yourselves under the tree. And I will bring a morsel of bread that you may refresh your hearts. After that, you may pass by since you have come to your servant." They said, "Do as you have said." So, Abraham hurried into the tent to Sarah and said, "Quickly, make ready three measures of fine meal; knead it and make cakes." And Abraham ran to the herd, took a tender and good calf, gave it to a young man, and hastened to prepare it. So, he took butter and milk and the calf which he had prepared and set it before them, and he stood by them under the tree as they ate. Then they said to him, "Where is Sarah, your wife?" So, he said, "Here, in the tent." And He said, "I will certainly return to you according to the time of life, and behold, Sarah, your wife shall have a son." Sarah was listening in the tent door behind him. Now Abraham and Sarah were old, well advanced in age, and Sarah had passed childbearing age. Therefore, Sarah laughed within herself, saying, "After I have grown old, shall I have pleasure, my lord being old also?" And the Lord said to Abraham, "Why did Sarah laugh, saying, 'Shall I surely bear a child, since I am old?' Is anything too hard for the Lord? At the appointed time, I will return to you, according to the time of life, and Sarah shall have a son." But Sarah denied it, saying, "I did not laugh," for she was afraid. And He said, "No, but you did laugh!"

Genesis 18:1-15

We begin by noting that Yahweh, accompanied by two other entities, approached Abraham. These two were celestial envoys sent to the domain of 'erets to administer judgment. Their mission, however, was not made known to Abraham until it was time for them to depart.

Most translations state Abraham was sitting at the door of his tent. Since the Hebrew word used for sitting is *"yashab,"* most likely Abraham was seated at the entrance of his camp, officiating as the judge over the doings there. That thought is consistent with the word *"pethach,"* translated as "door." *Pethach* can mean either entrance or gate, implying a larger area than a door.

Recall that I speculated in a previous chapter that Mamre might have switched his allegiance to Yahweh. Abraham might have convinced him that Yahweh was the one true God. If I am correct, then after his conversion, Mamre's garden (trees) served as a portal between the upper cosmic dimensions and those of 'erets. Whereas, before his switch, Mamre's altar, as a portal, opened into the lower dimensions. This is speculation but a reasonable assumption since the "trees" of Mamre was intentionally referenced in the text. Even so, Abraham built an altar to Yahweh near those same trees. So, perhaps Yahweh used Abraham's altar as a portal. Additionally, I assume it was Mamre's garden that Yahweh and his companions came through because of the mission of the two envoys. I think that Yahweh wanted the fallen realm to know of his anger.

Whichever the portal Yahweh opened was either "in" or "near" the *"trees of Mamre."* And Abraham was seated nearby, guarding that entrance into Eden. Yahweh, I believe, also chose that moment and that spot because he came to speak to Judge Abraham.

"In the heat of the day" is an idiom referring to the time when the sun is directly overhead. Abraham lifted his eyes; he looked up and saw three men standing nearby and ran to them. Most translations state he ran from the door of the "tent" – *ohel*. However, *ohel* can also mean "booth."

Abraham bowed to the ground and said, "Adonai, if I have found favor in your sight, I pray that you do not pass on. Let me bring water to wash your feet. Come and rest under the tree. I will have bread brought that you might refresh your hearts."

Initially, I thought it odd that Abraham said, "refresh your hearts." Come to find out, the ancients believed the whole person was refreshed when they ate. Food fuels the body. Silly me, nothing was strange in that. Abraham was gracious, extending a warm welcome,[210] not wanting the three to travel past without affording them every measure of hospitality, especially since it was the "heat" of the day. The three visitors responded to his welcome by saying, *"Do as you have said."* Abraham hurriedly found Sarah. He ordered bread and then ran to the herd. He gave orders for a young calf to be butchered and prepared. That took time. Probably several hours.

When the beef and bread were ready, Abraham carried the meal to the three strangers. Abraham, having great wealth and prestige, viewed himself as "a servant" of his guests. He stood nearby, watching as they ate because it was customary not to "sit" as guests ate. Especially if the guest outranked the host.

The meal consisted of the meat from a young calf, bread made from a fine meal baked on a hearth, curds, and milk. The meal was a feast fit for royalty. The young calf served represented substitution, fine flour would later be offered by the poor as a sin-offering, and milk represented blessings and luxury. Abraham would have provided curds, not butter. Curds, made from either sheep or goat's milk, were a refreshing milk by-product considered a delicacy and typically reserved for important guests.

Genesis 18:9, *"Then they said to him, 'Where is Sarah, your wife?'"* Likely, it was Yahweh who asked the question. God has a way of asking questions, so we will focus on a matter. I love that the question zoomed in on Sarah being Abraham's wife, his helpmate. The nuance in Hebrew suggests that Abraham answered, "There," and pointed "to the tent." The NET Bible hints Abraham was uncertain to whom he spoke initially. However, what was said next removed any doubt. Yahweh merely continued His prior declaration. Compare Genesis 18:11, *"I will surely return to you when the season comes round again, and your wife Sarah will have a son!"* with Genesis 17:21. *"But My covenant I will establish with Isaac, whom Sarah shall bear to you at this set time next year."*

Sarah didn't overhear; she listened carefully, indicating her tent was close. *"Abraham and Sarah were old, well advanced in age, and Sarah had passed the age of childbearing."*[211] That she could no longer conceive indicates she

---

210 Hebrews 13:2 supports this conclusion.

was not capable of getting pregnant. This is true of women once they have passed menopause; they no longer ovulate. For a woman to become pregnant after menopause requires a donated egg. Thus, it is essential to note that Holy Spirit said of her that *"the way of women hath ceased to be to Sarah."*[212]

*"**Sarah laughed** (tsachaq) within herself, saying, 'After I have grown old, shall I have pleasure, my lord being old also?' And **Yahweh** said to Abraham, 'Why did Sarah laugh (tsachaq), saying, 'Shall I surely bear a child, since I am old?' Is anything too hard for **Yahweh**? At the appointed time, I will return to you, according to the time of life, and Sarah shall have a son.' But Sarah denied it, saying, 'I did not laugh (tsachaq),' for she was afraid. And He said, 'No, but you did laugh (tsachaq)!'"* Genesis 18:12-15 (emphasis added).

For centuries, the Church has misunderstood what transpired between Yahweh and Sarah. So, let's put the scene into its proper context. Sarah laughed, yes. Hearing her husband chat with his guests, Sarah heard one of them say to Abraham, "I will return to you when the season comes again. Your wife Sarah will have a son!" Post-menopausal Sarah thought, "Now that I'm worn out, will I conceive? Especially now when my husband is old too?" The construction of the Hebrew text causes her question to be, "Indeed, truly, will I have a child?" **Then she laughed.** You see, this little word "*achar*" in Hebrew means "after." Sarah laughed "after," she thought about being too old. Laughter came upon her – just as it had with Abraham. After she "heard" Yahweh, she was overcome with supernatural giddiness. In other words, Holy Spirit fell upon Sarah.

Hearing her thoughts, Yahweh responded to Abraham. Still, his reaction was directed to Sarah, "Why did Sarah laugh and think, Will I really have a child, now that I am old?' Is anything too extraordinary for Yahweh? I will return when the season comes again, and Sarah will have a son." Yahweh's response was weighty; it was a spiritual decree, which could be interpreted as, "Oh, but Laughter has fallen on you!"

Not only were her thoughts overheard, but Sarah realized that their guests were more than guests of immense importance; they were supernatural. So, with reverential fear, she said aloud, "I did not laugh." But again, hearing her, Yahweh responded, "Oh, but you did!" That is to say, "Oh, but Holy Spirit got ya! Don't deny it!"

While Yahweh had come to see Judge Abraham, He also came to bring "laughter" to Sarah. Yahweh brought purpose to more than one dimension. He spoke to the future while speaking to Sarah for her benefit by empowering her through laughter to conceive Isaac (laughter) because she laughed. Yahweh had already planted "seed" in Abraham with laughter. It was time for Sarah to receive. She needed to laugh also. Her body had to undergo a transformation so that she might conceive laughter. God was not offended by Sarah's laughter. He needed it!

Isaac (laughter) was a Divine "gift." Laughter, Yahweh's laughter, was a creative tool. (Don't you just love Holy Spirit's wordplay?)

---

[211] Genesis 18:11, NKJV
[212] Genesis 18:12 YLT

> *Then the men rose from there and looked toward Sodom, and Abraham went with them to send them on the way. And the Lord said, "Shall I hide from Abraham what I am doing, since Abraham shall surely become a great and mighty nation, and all the nations of the earth shall be blessed in him? For I have known him, in order that he may command his children and his household after him, that they keep the way of the Lord, to do righteousness and justice, that the Lord may bring to Abraham what He has spoken to him." And the Lord said, "Because the outcry against Sodom and Gomorrah is great, and because their sin is very grave, I will go down now and see whether they have done altogether according to the outcry against it that has come to Me; and if not, I will know." Then the men turned away from there and went toward Sodom, but Abraham still stood before the Lord. And Abraham came near and said, "Would You also destroy the righteous with the wicked? Suppose there were fifty righteous within the city; would You also destroy the place and not spare it for the fifty righteous that were in it? Far be it from You to do such a thing as this, to slay the righteous with the wicked, so that the righteous should be as the wicked; far be it from You! Shall not the Judge of all the earth do, right?" So, the Lord said, "If I find in Sodom fifty righteous within the city, then I will spare all the place for their sakes." Then Abraham answered and said, "Indeed now, I who am but dust and ashes have taken it upon myself to speak to the Lord. Suppose there were five less than the fifty righteous; would You destroy all of the city for lack of five?" So, He said, "If I find there forty-five, I will not destroy it." And he spoke to Him yet again and said, "Suppose there should be forty found there?" So, He said, "I will not do it for the sake of forty." Then he said, "Let not the Lord be angry, and I will speak: Suppose thirty should be found there?" So, He said, "I will not do it if I find thirty there." And he said, "Indeed now, I have taken it upon myself to speak to the Lord: Suppose twenty should be found there?" So, He said, "I will not destroy it for the sake of twenty." Then he said, "Let not the Lord be angry, and I will speak but once more: Suppose ten should be found there?" And He said, "I will not destroy it for the sake of ten." So, the Lord went His way as soon as He had finished speaking with Abraham, and Abraham returned to his place.* Genesis 18:16-33

Genesis 18:16-33 is a conversation between the second Yahweh-power of heaven, King Yeshua, and Judge Abraham. Yeshua is God, but he serves the Eternal Kingdom as Eternal King, under the name of Yahweh, the Eternal God.

The Eternal Melchizedek met with his '*erets*-based partner. Since he was to occupy Eden for Yahweh, the judgment against Sodom and her sister cities needed to be discussed with Abraham. Consequently, a mutual determination had to be reached before any execution could be administered.

Before we unpack the negotiations, let's examine a few facts. Look at Ezekiel 16:49-50: *"Look, this was the iniquity of your sister Sodom: She and her daughter* [Gomorrah] *had **pride, the fullness of food**, and **abundance of idleness**; neither did she strengthen the hand of the poor and needy. And they were **haughty and committed abomination before Me**; therefore, I took them away as I saw fit."*

Ezekiel listed three sins that Yahweh hates:
- → **Pride** – Proverbs 8:13, *"Pride and arrogance and the evil way, the perverse mouth I hate."*
- → **Failure to help the needy**- Psalms 82:3-4, *"Defend the poor and fatherless; do justice to the afflicted and*

needy. Deliver the poor and needy. Free them from the hand of the wicked."

→ **Abomination-** Jeremiah 23:14, *"They commit adultery and walk in lies, they also strengthen the hands of evildoers, so that no one turns back from his wickedness. All of them are like Sodom to Me, and her inhabitants like Gomorrah."*

These three sins are the result of chaos. Pride leads to arrogance, breeds wickedness, and wickedness becomes an outrage that enrages Yahweh's sense of justice. Sodom's sins went way beyond being "merely" of a sexual nature. The social elites of Sodom, Gomorrah, and the other cities of the Jordan River plain were greedy tyrants. The wealthy and influential brutalized[213] the poor and ordinary by handing them over to the gods in exchange for power and increase.

Jude 6-7, *"And the angels who did not keep their proper domain, but left their own abode, He has reserved in everlasting chains under darkness for the judgment of the great day;* **as Sodom and Gomorrah, and the cities around them in a similar manner to these, having given themselves over to sexual immorality** (sexual acts that were more than sodomy – they were perverse beyond measure) **and gone after strange flesh** (they sought to have sex with the fallen gods, including the Rephaim), **are set forth as an example,** *suffering the vengeance of eternal fire"* (emphasis added).

Jude used the term "strange flesh," implying that the mystical dark practices of the pre-flood era had reappeared in Sodom and Gomorrah. Contained in those cultic practices were perverse sexual acts. However, when those acts began to include using the innocent[214] as sacrifices upon altars dedicated to the gods, Yahweh viewed them as an abomination.

The poor and needy were handed to the gods as favors; no one spoke against that sin. Nevertheless, the outcry of the blood of those sacrificed was great. Yahweh heard, and because the situation was so grave, he came to Abraham.

(One of the duties of a wealthy man was to sit as a judge over his household, to arbitrate any matter concerning members of his house. A prophet was to sit in judgment concerning the sins of the people to whom he was called. Abraham was named as a Prophet to Eden. Sodom and Gomorrah were within the territory of Eden. Lot, his brother's son, lived in Sodom.)

Abraham's three guests rose to leave, and as they did, they looked out toward the Jordan and these cities east of the river, toward Sodom. Abraham went with them. I suspect he was accompanying them to the gate of his camp as any good host might. Verse seventeen provides insights into Yahweh's thoughts. Though it is likely, that he was speaking telepathically to his two celestial companions.

Yahweh asked, "Shall I hide the thing I do from Abraham? After all, Abraham will be a noble nation of powerful people. All nations on the earth will be blessed because I have recognized and chosen him. His

---

213 People were murdered, raped, and tortured.
214 The poor and needy were sacrificed. Children were sacrificed. It is in that regard that the word innocent is used.

household and his children after him will keep the ways of Yahweh. They will do what is right and just. Yahweh will give what was promised to him."

If we follow the progression of thought, the Eternal King stated why he would linger with Abraham as his two companions went to Sodom. Essentially, it was because he needed to speak with Abraham privately.

"Shall I hide from Abraham the thing I do?" was a rhetorical question. Note, Yahweh continued by saying Abraham would become a "*gadol 'atsuwm*" nation. Those terms are usually translated as "great and mighty." However, it is also possible to translate them as "a nation noble and strong." The key to unlocking these verses is found in the phrase "find blessing." That phrase refers to Genesis 12:2-3. God blessed Abraham, and others "find" or receive blessing through him.

James 2:23, "*And the scripture was fulfilled which saith, Abraham believed God, and it was **imputed unto him for righteousness**: and he was called the Friend of God.*"

Romans 4:11, "***that he might be the father of all of them that believe**, though they are not circumcised; **that righteousness might be imputed unto them also***" (KJV emphasis added).

Hebrews 1:8, "*But to the Son, He says: 'Your throne, O God, is forever and ever. **A scepter of righteousness is the scepter of Your kingdom**"* (emphasis added).

The King of Righteousness holds a scepter of righteousness. He administers justice with that scepter. Yahweh wanted Abraham to know the judgment against Sodom **before** it was executed. Why? Because Abraham had a voice (vote) as to who was righteous. This story proves that Abraham was held in high esteem and was more than just "received" into the Eternal Kingdom because of his faith. He was marked as royal and thus had a say in the government. Appointed because he was adopted as royalty, Abraham held the position of Judge (priest) and Prophet. And like all the prophets who would follow him, Abraham was told in advance of the coming judgment.

Overhearing Yahweh speaking with his companions - "*Abraham came near and said, 'Would You also destroy the righteous with the wicked? Suppose there were fifty righteous within the city; would You also destroy the place and not spare it for the fifty righteous that were in it? Far be it from You to do such a thing as this, to slay the righteous with the wicked, so that the righteous should be as the wicked; far be it from You! **Shall not the Judge of all the earth do, right?**'"* Genesis 18:23-25 (emphasis added).

Abraham realized he stood before the Eternal Melchizedek. That is why he referred to Yahweh as "*ha'shaphat* of *'erets*," a phrase that means "ruler of *'erets*." Also, we should note Abraham invoked the term "righteousness." Essentially, Abraham was saying, "You are the Eternal King of Righteousness. Would you destroy the righteous along with the wicked? What if there were fifty righteous souls in Sodom? Would you kill them? That is the same as equating righteousness with wickedness."

Yahweh answered, "If I find fifty righteous in the city of Sodom, I will spare the whole region for their sake." Why the number fifty? While no one can be certain regarding Sodom's population, I have read estimations that it exceeded 100,000. So, perhaps Abraham was inquiring, "If less than a tithe exists, will you not spare the area from destruction?"

"So, Yahweh said, 'If I find in Sodom fifty righteous within the city, then I will spare all the place for their sakes'" Genesis 18:26. Abraham rebutted, "Since I have spoken so boldly, Adonai (though I am dust and ash), what if there are forty-five? Will you destroy the whole because five are lacking?"

Yahweh replied, "I will not destroy if I find forty-five." Abraham again spoke, "Please, my Adonai, don't be angry. What if there are thirty?"

Yahweh replied, "I will not destroy if I find thirty." Abraham spoke again, "What if only twenty are found?"

Again, Yahweh replied, "I will not destroy for the sake of twenty righteous souls." Finally, Abraham asked, "May Adonai permit me once more. What if there are ten?" Yahweh answered, "If I find ten, I will not destroy for the sake of those ten."

Then Yahweh left; the negotiating was over, and the matter was settled. Abraham returned home. Probably to the altar he had erected nearby, where he waited and prayed.

Genesis Nineteen

Genesis 19:1-29, *Now, the two angels came to Sodom in the evening, and* **Lot was sitting at the gate of Sodom.** *When Lot saw them, he rose to meet them, and he bowed himself with his face toward the ground. And he said, "Here now, my lords, please turn in to your servant's house and spend the night and wash your feet; then you may rise early and go on your way." And they said, "No, but we will spend the night in the open square." But he insisted strongly, so they turned in to him and entered his house. Then he made them a feast* (mishteh) *and baked unleavened bread* (matstsah), *and they ate. Before they lay down, the men of the city, the men of Sodom, both old and young, all the people from every quarter, surrounded the house. And they called Lot and said to him, "Where are the men who came to you tonight? Bring them out to us that we may know them carnally." So, Lot went out to them through the doorway, shut the door behind him, and said, "Please, my brethren, do not do so wickedly! See now, I have two daughters who have not known a man; please, let me bring them out to you, and you may do to them as you wish; only do nothing to these men since this is the reason they have come under the shadow of my roof." And they said, "Stand back!" Then they said, "This one came in to stay here,* **and he keeps acting as a judge;** *now we will deal worse with you than with them." So, they pressed hard against the man Lot and came near to break down the door. But the men reached out their hands, pulled Lot into the house with them, and shut the door. And they struck the men who were at the doorway of the house with blindness, both small and great, so that they became weary trying to find the door. Then the men said to Lot, "Have you anyone else here? Son-in-law, your sons, daughters, and whomever you have in the city — take them out of this place! For we will destroy this place because the outcry against them has grown great before the face of the Lord (Yahweh), and the Lord (Yahweh) has sent us to destroy it." So, Lot went out and spoke to his sons-in-law, who had married his daughters, and said, "Get up, get out of this place; for the Lord will destroy this city!" But to his sons-in-law, he seemed to be joking. When the morning dawned, the angels urged Lot to hurry, saying, "Arise, take your wife and your two daughters who are here, lest you be consumed in the punishment of the city." And while he lingered, the men took hold of his hand, his wife's hand, and the hands of his two daughters, the Lord being merciful to him, and they brought him out and set him outside the city. So, it came to pass when they had brought them outside that he said, "Escape for your life! Do not look behind you nor stay anywhere in the plain. Escape to the mountains, lest you be destroyed." Then Lot said to them, "Please, no, my lords! Indeed now, your servant has found favor in your sight, and you have increased your mercy which you have shown me by saving my life. Still, I cannot escape to the mountains, lest some evil overtakes me, and I die. See now, this city is near enough to flee to, and it is a little one; please let me escape there (is it not a little one?), and my soul shall live." And he said to him, "See, I have favored you concerning this thing also, in that I will not overthrow this city for which you have spoken. Hurry, escape there.* **For I cannot do anything until you arrive there."** *Therefore, the name of the city was called Zoar* (little). *The sun had risen upon the earth when Lot entered Zoar. Then the Lord rained brimstone* (gophriyt) *and fire on Sodom and Gomorrah, from the Lord out of the heavens. So, He overthrew those cities, the plain, the inhabitants of the cities, and what grew on the ground. But his wife looked back behind him, and she became* **a pillar** (netsiyb -something stationary) **of salt** (melach – a powder easily dissolved). *And Abraham went early in the morning to the place where he had stood before the Lord. Then* **he looked toward Sodom and Gomorrah,** *and toward all the land of the plain; and he* *saw, and behold, the smoke of the land which went up like the smoke of a furnace. And it came to pass, when God destroyed the cities of the plain, God remembered Abraham and sent Lot out of the midst of the overthrow and overthrew the cities in which Lot had dwelt* (emphasis added).

Yahweh's companions, who I suggest were *Malakim*, went on to Sodom. Most Bible translations state that they were angels. But to be more specific, the *Malakim* are assigned to assist the *Malak* (king). Typically, they are dispensed into *'erets* as messengers carrying throne messages; still, they are capable destroyers. By that, I mean they are powerful, thus, able to administer judgments. When manifesting to interact with humans, they appear as men, not as winged angels. So, Lot, upon initially spotting them, would not have been able to detect anything unusual. As they approached him at the gate of Sodom, he would have thought them men of authority. He might have even thought they were royalty due to their demeanor and attire. If that were the case, it explains why he rose to greet them; he realized these two were important guests to the city.

Like Abraham in the previous chapter, Lot sat at the gate as a judge. Note the following from 2 Samuel 19:8, *"Then the king arose and sat in the gate. And they told all the people, saying, 'There is the king, sitting in the gate.' So, all the people came before the king."*

In that era, judges, kings, and even priests sat at a walled city's gates since that was where city matters were determined. Judges primarily negotiated with caravan merchants or dignitaries at the city gates to establish whether they and their wares were welcomed or, if warranted, denied entrance into the city. Typically, the position of "judge" was appointed to those having extreme wealth or power, which amounted to being the same. Obviously, Lot was selected because he was wealthy or because Abram had rescued the people from Chedorlaomer.

Lot saw the *Malakim*, rose from his "seat," and went to meet them. Bowing low, he said, *"Here now, my lords, please turn in to your servant's house and spend the night, wash your feet, then you may rise early and be on your way."* The text suggests that Lot recognized that the two "men" were influential, but unclear if he realized they were celestials. I don't think that initially, he did. Nevertheless, he extended to them the use of his home, which was most likely near the entrance into the city. They responded, *"No, we will spend the night in the open square."* Lot insisted. He knew they needed the protection of his home. This causes me to believe Lot was aware of the evil that ran amuck in Sodom.

The two celestials went with Lot to his house and ate the feast prepared in their honor. But before the two could ready themselves for the night, the men of Sodom surrounded the house. The Hebrew text of verse four stresses that young and old men from every corner of the city surrounded Lot's house. They began to shout to Lot, "Where are the men who entered your house? Bring them out so that we can take them. To know them."

"To know" is a euphemism, a delicate way of saying "to have sex." Considering the context of this verse and the others that mention the sins of Sodom, "to know" in this case was more than mere intercourse of a sexual nature. It expressed the intent to molest with force. Realizing the implications of the demand, Lot went outside to the men and closed the door behind him. That door was probably a large wooden gate that closed off an enclosed courtyard. Lot said to those outside his house, "I beg you, my brothers, do not act wickedly. I have two daughters who are yet virgins. Let me bring them to you. Do with them as you please. Only do not molest these two who have entered the protection of my house."

The crowd of men commanded Lot to "Stand back!" They then began to murmur among themselves by saying, "Lot came to us to stay here; he keeps acting as a judge. We will deal with him worse than we deal with the two inside." The men of the city pressed hard against Lot. According to the story, they pressed Lot up against the gate. Then pushed with the intent to break through into the courtyard. But the two *Malakim*, from inside, extended their hands and pulled Lot back into the yard. They then shut the gate, but not before they struck those at the entrance with blindness. Unable to find the gate, the men outside grew weary and left.

Once Lot was inside, the two visitors asked, "Who else is here? Do you have sons-in-law, sons, daughters, or other relatives? If so, get them out of this place. We are going to destroy it! The cry against this city is great! Yahweh has sent us to destroy it."

At that point, Lot knew his visitors were not of this world. He slipped out of his house and went to the homes of his future sons-in-law and said to them, "Get out of this city; Yahweh is about to destroy it!" But his sons-in-law did not believe him. Instead, they thought he was joking and making "sport" of them.

When the sun broke on the morn, the *Malakim* hurried Lot by saying, "Get going! Take your wife and two daughters and flee, or else you too will be destroyed by the coming judgment!" Lot hesitated. So, the *Malakim* grabbed Lot by the hand and hurried him out of the city. They also took Lot's wife and two daughters.

When Lot and his family were outside the city, the celestials commanded them, saying, "Run for your lives! Don't look back or stop at any juncture until you reach the mountains! Or you will die!"

"No, please, my lords!" Lot, past the age of ninety, pleaded, "since your servant has found favor, and you have shown me great kindness, understand I physically cannot run to the mountains. This disaster will overtake me, and I'll die. Look, that town over there is close. Can we not escape to it? It's just a little one. Let us go there. It's just a little place, isn't it? Then we'll survive."

"Alright," the *Malakim* agreed, "We will not overthrow that town. But run to it quickly, for we cannot do anything until you are safely there."

The sun was over the land when Lot reached Zoar when Yahweh rained down brimstone and fire on Sodom and Gomorrah. Upon Yahweh's command, disaster fell from the sky, and the cities, inhabitants, and vegetation were destroyed. Sadly, Lot's wife looked back and was dissolved into a pile of substance, a powder-like material that resembled salt.

That's the story according to Scripture. Now, let's go outside the four corners of the Bible and look at additional information. Mainly, let's focus on the discoveries made at Tall el-Hamman.

On the northeast corner of the Dead Sea, Tall el-Hamman sits on the rift of the Jordan River Valley. This archaeological site in Jordan was recently accepted academically as the ruins of ancient Sodom.

The Jordan River Rift is an elongated geological depression following the river's length, including the mountains north of the Sea of Galilee (Mount Hermon), continuing south through the Dead Sea (the planet's lowest elevation) to the Red Sea. From the summit of Tall el-Hammam, facing east, Jericho is at 12 on a clock, Jerusalem at 11, and Hebron at 9. From Bethel (Genesis 13), Lot could look due east and see Sodom in the distance. Not only the green of the valley but the walls of the city.

The city being unearthed at Tall el-Hamman (Sodom) dominated the southern Jordan Valley during the Bronze Age. It was a massive socio-political center, a kingdom unto itself. Its territory spread into the hills east and south, and southwest to the Dead Sea. From its western citadel, the city's king could view virtually all of his domain, estimated to have been approximately 200 square kilometers.[215]

Sodom was a fortified city. Its walls were eighteen feet thick and forty feet in height. The wall encircled the municipal area, with several towers and multiple gates. Around the perimeter was a vast, packed earth/clay road perfect for traveling and moving goods in and out of the city. Within Sodom proper were palaces, temples, markets, and administrative complexes. It is estimated that, at a minimum, the city was fifty or more acres in size. There were larger Canaanite cities in Abraham's day, but very few.

The main gate of Sodom had a central gatehouse. So perhaps, Lot lived in a gatehouse. He likely lived nearby in one of the many dwellings unearthed that had open-air courtyards. Those yards served as cooking areas, having enclosed ovens and open firepits. A brick or stone wall would have retained the courtyard, making it a vital part of the house.

The area surrounding the city was much like the Nile Delta. The Jordan River flooded similarly to the Nile, bringing fresh alluvial silt with its floodwaters. Additionally, the area had many springs of freshwater, which brought prosperity to the valley and caused it to be *"well-watered, like the garden of Yahweh, like Egypt."*[216] And in turn, giving the region upward of three harvests each year, it had a sub-tropical climate at that time.

Salem, Bethel, Hebron, and the cities west of the Jordan River continued into the Late Bronze Age and beyond. The city buried beneath Tall el-Hamman did not. It was destroyed, and its destruction caused the area to remain unoccupied for five to seven hundred years.

Dolmens are stone structures erected as monuments to venerate or bury the dead. They are table-like in appearance because dolmen-stones are slab-shaped. Presently, it is thought the dolmens of Tall el-Hamman were built and maintained by families. Not as a cemetery but as sacred monument gardens serving as meeting places for ritual gatherings. Researchers have "documented the precision of the astronomical alignments of these dolmens, which were arranged to designate equinoxes and solstices marking the southern and northern drifts of the sun as it hits the earth."[217]

---

215 https://tallelhammam.com/discoveries retrieved August 7, 2021
216 Genesis 13:10

The city-dwelling tribes of the Transjordan were Amorite, but as noted previously, these tribes originated in Sumer. They worshipped and revered the *Rephaim*.

Rephaim refers to 1) "spirits" of deceased humans or 2) spirits of dead Nephilim. Amorites, the city dwellers of Mesopotamia, worshipped both types of *Rephaim* by summoning them through necromancy rituals. In the Bronze Age, venerating the dead was a vital part of the culture throughout the Middle East. The ancients thought that the quality of one's existence in the afterlife depends upon descendants. Descendants worshipped the gods, which appeased them, making the ancestors' existence in the netherworld more bearable.

Additionally, without the help of ancestors to keep the gods in the underworld appeased, the descendant would be tormented by angry spirits. So, specific rituals were performed to honor the dead, to keep them happy. These rituals were usually performed (celebrated) every month.

"The standard practice in the ancient Near East was to perform the *kispum* rite twice a month for kings, usually on the 15th and 30th. As with the family *kispum*, long-dead rulers had to be called to the meal by name. Forgetting the dead meant their spirits were unsettled and thus unpredictable. Proper performance of the ritual was key to maintaining the health and stability of the realm." [218]

Sodomites worshipped the dead by incantations that produced the effect of opening the portals to the underworld. Thereby welcoming these spirits into *'erets*. And for that reason, Yahweh removed Sodom's inhabitants from the face of *'erets*. Take note of Genesis 13:13, "*The men of Sodom were exceedingly wicked and sinful against Yahweh.*" The Hebrew text suggests they were "vehemently" wicked against Yahweh. I believe the "men" of Sodom petitioned the fallen gods to release demonic hordes into *'erets* while performing aberrant sexual acts. Note Deuteronomy 32:31-33, "*For their rock is not like our Rock, even our enemies themselves being judges. For their vine is of the vine of Sodom and the fields of Gomorrah; their grapes are grapes of gall, their clusters are bitter.* **Their wine is the poison of serpents and the cruel venom of cobras.**" And the preceding verse, 32:17. "**They sacrificed to demons, not to God, to gods they did not know, to new gods, new arrivals that your fathers did not fear**" (emphasis added).

The language used in these verses is more than just hyperbolic. It is metaphoric language to impart a serious message. Deuteronomy 32 reminded the children of Abraham why Yahweh decreed judgments. Yahweh views the worship of, thus, the alliance with fallen gods as an abomination!

"Skeletal remains lie as they fell, wrench, and contorted. There's human bone-scatter all through the final-day ash; human beings who blew apart before they fell."[219]

---

[217] *Discovering the City of Sodom: The Fascinating, True Account of the Discovery of the Old Testament's Most Infamous City*, Collins, Steven, and Scott, Latayne. p. 50

[218] It is not possible to discuss all the necromancy rituals in this writing. I highly recommend Derek and Sharon Gilbert's book, *Veneration*, if you want to know more regarding this subject. Gilbert, Sharon K.; Gilbert, Derek P. *Veneration: Unveiling the Ancient Realms of Demonic Kings and Satan's Battle Plan for Armageddon* (p. 24). Defender. Kindle Edition.

[219] *Discovering the City of Sodom: The Fascinating, True Account of the Discovery of the Old Testament's Most Infamous City*, Collins, Steven, and Scott, Latayne. p. 60

"Abraham went early in the morning to the place where he had stood before the Lord. Then he looked toward Sodom and Gomorrah, and toward all the land of the plain; and he saw, and behold, the smoke of the land which went up like the smoke of a furnace. And it came to pass, when God destroyed the cities of the plain, God remembered Abraham and sent Lot out of the midst of the overthrow and overthrew the cities in which Lot had dwelt" Genesis 19:27-29.

Hebron, west of the Dead Sea, has a higher elevation than the Jordan River plain. Abraham could see the far eastern horizon. He saw the smoke rising upward, dissipating into the upper atmosphere. It is estimated that the smoke was visible even farther away than the forty-five miles separating Hebron and Sodom.

The entire civilization of the plain ended abruptly, leaving behind what has been described as a "grisly scene. It is destruction, literally, of biblical proportions."[220] During excavations of Tall el-Hamman, weapons, jewelry, vessels of alabaster, and of course, pottery has been unearthed, all buried under multiple layers of ash. The human remains thus far discovered attest to "extreme trauma."

A substance like trinitite has been identified at Tall el-Hamman. Trinitite is a glass-like material, olive green in color, formed from sand melted by the heat of a nuclear blast. This glass-like substance is also called "impact glass." It can be produced by meteors, asteroids, or atomic detonations. After analyzing the impact glass found at Tall el-Hammam, it was estimated the heat of whatever hit the city reached upward of two thousand degrees Fahrenheit.

Furthermore, it is believed that whatever happened was instantaneous. It came from the sky and destroyed everything, including vegetation. And not only did it fall with a tremendous impact, it also sucked all breathable air from the atmosphere. Animals and humans were vaporized; others were asphyxiated from the smoke and superheated air. To make matters worse, the concussion that resulted from the impact disintegrated nearly every object for miles.

The prevalent theory is it was superheated molecular debris from a meteor that formed a fireball. If that is true, Abraham likely felt the fireball's wind and thundering sound as it traveled across the sky to Sodom.[221]

Genesis 19:30-38, *"Then Lot went up out of Zoar and dwelt in the mountains, and his two daughters were with him; for he was afraid to dwell in Zoar. And he and his two daughters dwelt in a cave. Now the firstborn said to the younger, 'Our father is old, and there is no man on the earth to come into us as is the custom of all the earth. Come, let us make our father drink wine, and we will lie with him that we may preserve the lineage of our father.' So, they made their father drink wine that night. And the firstborn went in and lay with her father, and he did not know when she lay down or when she arose. It happened the next day that the firstborn said to the younger, 'Indeed I lay with my father last night; let us make him drink wine tonight also, and you go in and lie with him, that we may preserve the lineage of our father.' Then they made their father drink wine that night also. And the younger arose and lay with him, and he did not know when she lay down or when she arose. Thus, both the daughters of Lot were*

---

[220] Ibid, p. 228
[221] I highly recommended reading *Discovering the City of Sodom: The Fascinating, True Account of the Discovery of the Old Testament's Most Infamous City.*

> *with child by their father. The firstborn bore a son and called his name* **Moab**; *he is the father of the Moabites to this day. And the younger, she also bore a son and called his name Ben-Ammi; he is the father of the people of* **Ammon** *to this day"* (emphasis added).

The meaning of these verses is clear. I feel confident you understand what happened between Lot and his two daughters. Moab means "from father." Ammon [Ben Ammi] means "son of my people."

Numbers 21:29, *"Woe to you, Moab! You have perished, O people of Chemosh!"* 1 Kings 11:33, *"Chemosh the god of the Moabites, and Milcom, the god of the people of Ammon…."* The Moabites venerated Chemosh as their patron deity, viewing him as one of the "creator gods" – Milcom was seen as a gatekeeper to the underworld. Both were worshiped similarly as "chief" gods, often by sacrificial funerary rituals.

The Moabites and Ammonites dwelt on the "other side" of the Jordan, the east side.

"But on Sodom there are areas that tell a remarkable story. There are places on the mound where no one ever rebuilt after a catastrophic event destroyed it. Not in the Iron Age, not later, not ever. The soil is powdery, nasty with burnt things in it. Sometimes you can smell ash still, thousands of years later."

— from *Discovering the City of Sodom: The Fascinating, Tr... by Steven Collins*

Genesis Twenty

Genesis 20: *Abraham journeyed from there to the south, dwelt between Kadesh and Shur, and stayed in Gerar. Now Abraham said of Sarah, his wife, "She is my sister." And Abimelech, king of Gerar, sent and took Sarah. But God came to Abimelech in a dream by night and said to him, "Indeed you are a dead man because of the woman whom you have taken, for she is a man's wife." But Abimelech had not come near her, and he said, "Lord, will You slay a righteous nation also? Did he not say to me, 'She is my sister?' And she, even she said, 'He is my brother.' In the integrity of my heart and innocence of my hands, I have done this." And God said to him in a dream, "Yes, I know that you did this in the integrity of your heart. For I also withheld you from sinning against Me; therefore, I did not let you touch her. Now, therefore,* **restore the man's wife; for he is a prophet, and he will pray for you, and you shall live**. *But if you do not restore her, know that you shall surely die, you and all who are yours." So, Abimelech rose early in the morning, called all his servants, and told all these things in their hearing, and the men were very much afraid. And Abimelech called Abraham and said to him, "What have you done to us? How have I offended you that you have brought on me and on my kingdom a great sin? You have done deeds to me that ought not to be done." Then Abimelech said to Abraham, "What did you have in view that you have done this thing?" And Abraham said, "Because I thought, surely the fear of God is not in this place, and they will kill me on account of my wife. But indeed, she is truly my sister. She is the daughter of my father, but not the daughter of my mother, and she became my wife. And it came to pass when God caused me to wander from my father's house, that I said to her, 'This is the kindness that you should do for me in every place, wherever we go, say of me, "He is my brother."' Then Abimelech took sheep, oxen, and male and female servants and gave them to Abraham, and he restored Sarah, his wife, to him. And Abimelech said, "See, my land is before you; dwell where it pleases you." Then to Sarah, he said, "Behold, I have given your brother a thousand pieces of silver; indeed,* **this vindicates you before all who are with you and before everybody."** *Thus, she was rebuked. So, Abraham prayed to God, and God healed Abimelech, his wife, and his female servants. Then they bore children, for the Lord had closed all the wombs of the house of Abimelech because of Sarah, Abraham's wife* (emphasis added).

Scripture is unclear why Abraham left Hebron and his alliance with Mamre to live in Gerar. Nevertheless, he did by moving into the territory of Abimelech. That was not an easy undertaking. As mentioned, the "company" belonging to Abraham was extensive. Pulling up stakes and moving across the street would have been a daunting task, let alone moving from Hebron to Gerar.

And at that time, Abraham journeyed from the plain of Mamre, and he went to the land of the Philistines, and he dwelt in Gerar....[222]

So, let's set the stage by establishing that Abraham was sort of a "warlord." After all, he had over three hundred men in his camp who were military types. That was a sizable army for a nomadic herdsman,

---

[222] Johnson, Ken. *Ancient Book of Jasher* (p. 42) Kindle Edition.

although Abraham was more than a nomad with a tent or two. Genesis 13 confirms Abraham's herds and flocks were vast. There were herdsmen and shepherds, men who worked in the camp proper, wives, and families; thus, it would have been impossible to move such a large company in secret.

Though we don't know for sure, it's highly conceivable Abraham was seeking better pastures. For that reason, he trekked south from Hebron to Gerar. Probably because the hills of Gerar are rolling hills. Less treacherous than those of Hebron, making pasture for his herds and flocks more accessible.

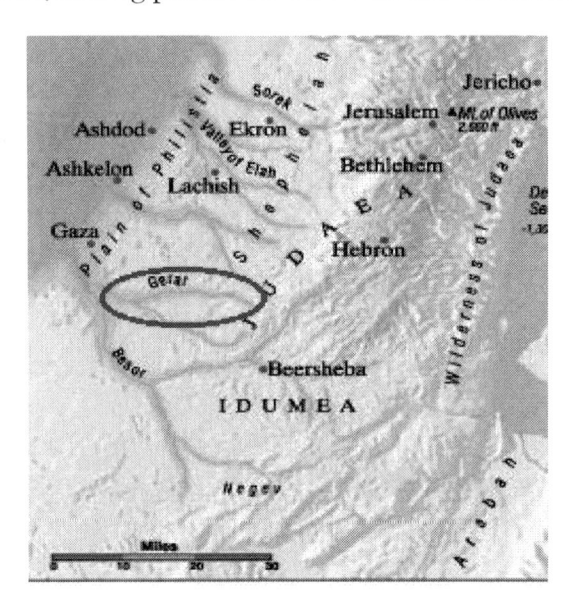

Abraham did not enter this territory unaware of his surrounding, that is to say, the political environment of the area. He was aware he needed to seek permission to graze his herds. Hoping favor would be extended, Abraham again asked Sarah to tell the Abimelech and his court she was his sister.

Abimelech is a title, not a name. Although there are various interpretations, "father-king" or "my father is king" are the two most accepted. Philistines, like the Canaanites, descended from Ham. The first of their tribe was a disinherited son of a Pharaoh. Hence, why the ruler was called "*Ab-i-Melek.*"

There was no way Abimelech or his captain would have allowed Abraham's company to enter Gerar without investigating the purpose. They likely had been spying on Abraham long before he entered Gerar. And I'm sure that Abraham knew his moves were being watched. That was why he reminded Sarah – "tell them when they come, you are my sister." Apparently, Abraham was doing what he thought best to avoid confrontation. The servants of Abimelech, king of the Philistines, saw that Sarah was exceedingly beautiful, and they asked Abraham concerning her, and he said, "She is my sister." And the servants of Abimelech went to Abimelech, saying, "A man from the land of Canaan is come to dwell in the land, and he has a sister that is exceeding fair." And Abimelech heard the words of his servants who praised Sarah to him, and Abimelech sent his officers, and they brought Sarah to the king.[223]

---

223 Ibid.

Thinking Abraham's sister was unmarried, not bound by an existing treaty, Abimelech sent for her. Like his Egyptian "cousin," Abimelech wanted to see her for himself. When she entered his court, Sarah was beautiful; she pleased him. He said, "What is that man to you? The one with whom you came to my land? Sarah answered, "He is my brother, and we came from Canaan to dwell where we could find a place (pasture).[224]

And Abimelech said to Sarah, "Behold, my land is before you; place your brother in any part of the land that pleases him. It will be our duty to exalt and elevate him above all the people of my land since he is your brother." And Abimelech sent for Abraham, and Abraham came. Abimelech said to Abraham, "Behold, I have given orders that you shall be honored on account of your sister, Sarah." Abraham went from the king, but the king's (men) followed him.[225]

Next, we note from the *Book of Jasher*: As at evening time, before men lie down to rest, the king was sitting upon his throne. A deep sleep fell upon him…, he dreamed an angel (*elohim*) of (Yahweh) came to him with a drawn sword…, the angel stood over Abimelech (as to) slay him…, terrified (by) his dream…, (he asked) "In what have I sinned…? The angel answered…, "on account of the woman (you brought into your) house…, she is a married woman, the wife of Abraham…, return (to) that man his wife…,"[226]

Abimelech had not come near her, and he said, "Lord, will You slay a righteous nation also? Did he (Abraham) *not say to me, 'She is my sister?' And she, even she said, 'He is my brother.' In the integrity of my heart and innocence of my hands, I have done this." And* (Elohiym) *said to him in a dream, "Yes, I know that you did this in the integrity of your heart. For I also withheld you from sinning against Me; therefore, I did not let you touch her. Now, therefore, restore the man's wife; for* **he is a prophet, and he will pray for you, and you shall live.** *But if you do not restore her, know that you shall surely die, you and all who are yours"* Genesis 20:4-6 (emphasis added).

Yahweh told Abimelech that Abraham was a "*nabiy*" – a prophet or inspired man. A prophet carries the "word" of Yahweh as His mouthpiece to the living.

This incident sites the Bible's first use of the term *nabiy*. Abraham is the first to be called a Prophet.

Notice that Yahweh not only called Abraham a prophet but also linked the position with intercession. This verse is our evidence that Yahweh considered Abraham to be a member of the Melchizedek Priesthood. Which was the only sanctioned priesthood within '*erets*. The only viable way for Abraham to be appointed and anointed as a Melchizedek priest was that he was adopted as a Firstborn. That is to say, Yahweh had personally intervened to make this happen.

Abimelech summoned his advisors the following morning and told them about his dream; they were afraid. The king then called for Abraham to be brought to him and demanded why Abraham had said Sarah was his sister. Notice Abraham's answer: "You do not fear my *Elohiym*, Yahweh. You did not understand that my God will kill you if you kill me." Of course, I'm paraphrasing his words. Yet that is their inference.

Abraham understood that his marriage covenant with Sarah meant nothing to Abimelech but everything to

---

224 Ibid.
225 Ibid. p 42 Kindle Edition. (Modified by the author to enhance the ease of reading)
226 Ibid. p 42 Kindle Edition. (Modified by the author to enhance the ease of reading)

him and, thus, to Yahweh. Nor had he forgotten the promises of Yahweh: Sarah would give him a son.

Abraham desired that his presence in the land be viewed as friendly, not mistaken for an invasion. Furthermore, because he was confident Yahweh was on his side, Abraham told Abimelech of the pact he and Sarah made not to speak of their marriage. Unless they were satisfied, no harm would befall him.

Simply put, Abraham stated that he and Sarah had not lied but that Abimelech acted aggressively. That seemingly, he thought, because he was king, he could take. So, it happened as Abraham had suspected. Abimelech took Sarah.

Remember Abimelech had "sent his officers" for her! We must also consider that Abraham knew who the Philistines worshipped, understanding that their gods would work against him, inciting Abimelech to do as he did.

It is also significant that Abraham had not at that time built an altar or made any outward move to invite Yahweh to "interfere." While none of what I am suggesting is explicitly noted in Scripture, Abraham was not naïve. He knew the pagan beliefs of the Amorites, Canaanites, and the Philistines – he was very aware their gods hated Yahweh.

Keep in mind this incident followed immediately after the destruction of Sodom and Gomorrah, occurring less than 90 days later. Naturally, the fallen gods were angry. They wanted retribution and sought a way to damage Yahweh's kingdom. The quickest and most certain way to accomplish their goal, harm Abraham or Sarah. The adversarial gods, aware Sarah was to give Abraham a male heir, probably thought, what better way to have revenge than to arrange for that promise to be obstructed by Abimelech.

If any man had been intimate or violated Sarah, the lineage of Isaac would forever be in question. Remember Yahweh had prepared her womb, but she had yet to conceive. Sarah carried the "word" given to her like an egg, literally and figuratively. Yet, the timing for the fertilization of "who" she carried had not come.

It is necessary to understand Yahweh planned Isaac. Nothing about him was circumstantial; every generation, from Isaac to Mary and Joseph, was designed. God is that detailed and that concerned with DNA. Meticulously, Yahweh protected the name and honor of Sarah, not allowing a human or an entity to thwart the timing or purpose of His Word.

Abimelech, seeking to appease Abraham, gave sheep, oxen, and servants. Then made a pact with Abraham before returning to Sarah, "See, my land is before you; dwell where it pleases you." Then to Sarah, Abimelech said, "I gave your brother a thousand pieces of silver. This vindicates you."

The King James Version continues Genesis 20:16 with, "behold he is to thee a covering of the eyes," – that rendering is incorrect. Abraham was not a covering over 'her eyes.' Sarah's eyes did not need a cover. The point: Sarah was not "rebuked" – she was redeemed! She typifies the redeemed Bride.

One thousand pieces of silver was a considerable fortune. It's estimated the weight of the silver was twenty-five pounds. And note what Abimelech said: "I gave a fortune to your brother because of you. You told me that he was your brother. Therefore, the silver I gave to him redeems you to your brother. Others witnessed the taking of you from him. They will now know I have not touched you. The value I placed upon you indicates that you are untouched. If I had touched you, you would not be returned with that much silver. The excessiveness of the silver means your value has not decreased but increased."

Abraham prayed to Yahweh. Abimelech, his wife, and his female servants were healed. They again conceived children. Yahweh had closed their wombs because of Sarah. But when Abraham prophesied over Abimelech's household, God removed the curse.

Barrenness, the very thing that plagued Abraham and Sarah for years, is what God used against Abimelech's household. So, when Abraham prayed against the barrenness of Abimelech's house, Yahweh also broke the curse over Abraham and Sarah. Abraham's prayers were a double-edged sword; they cut the curse as it ran in both directions. In a matter of weeks, Abraham and Sarah conceived Isaac.

Genesis Twenty-One

*And the Lord (Yahweh) visited Sarah as He had said, and the Lord (Yahweh) did for Sarah as He had spoken. For Sarah conceived and bore Abraham a son in his old age, at the set time of which God (Elohiym) had spoken to him. And Abraham called the name of his son who was born to him — whom Sarah bore to him — Isaac. Then Abraham circumcised his son Isaac when he was **eight days** old, as God (Elohiym) had commanded him. Now Abraham was **one hundred** years old when his son Isaac was born to him. And Sarah said, "God (Elohiym) has made me laugh, and all who hear will laugh with me." She also said, "Who would have said to Abraham that Sarah would nurse children? For I have borne him a son in his old age"* Genesis 21:1-7 (emphasis added).

Yahweh "visited" Sarah. The Hebrew verb "visit" (*paqad*) depicts divine intervention as an appointment to bestow providence. This type of visit might be a blessing or a curse. A *paqad* should be viewed as "special" attention. In this case, the "visit" caused her to conceive the promise. The specifics of that visit are left to our imagination. However, it is reasonable to assume Yahweh simply said, "it is time."

Why wait eight days before circumcision? The primary reason, the optimal time after birth for blood to clot is not reached until the eighth day. To develop clotted blood, both vitamin K and Prothrombin must be present. He would bleed to death if vitamin K were absent in the blood when the infant is circumcised. Vitamin K usually starts forming between 5 and 7 days after birth. Prothrombin begins developing on day three to peak on day eight at 110% before it drops to normal at 100%.

Abraham was *"me'ah"* – one hundred. He was the last of the "ancient" way, the first of the "new." He symbolized the ק – the end of a cycle. With Abraham, Yahweh began administering justice according to faith. Previously, divine justice was granted if a person was in allegiance with the temporal Melchizedek. But no one was righteous if the Melchizedek was not.

The Melchizedekian Regents had ceased to evangelize the world on behalf of Yahweh. And they had ceased to function as global judges. Therefore, the people perished - due to a lack of knowledge. Job 9:32-33, *"For He (God) is not a man, as I am, that I may answer Him, and that we should go to court together. **Nor is there any mediator between us,** who may lay his hand on us both"* (emphasis added).

Abraham was born under the old system. Isaac, however, had come to the new. Consequently, he was called "Laughter!" God, henceforth, pronounced righteousness according to the heart; the measure of faith exhibited by whomsoever willed. Job 8:19-21, *"Behold, this is the joy of His way, and out of the earth, others will grow. Behold, God will not cast away the blameless, nor will He uphold the evildoers. He will yet fill your mouth with laughter and your lips with rejoicing."*

> *"So, the child grew and was weaned. And Abraham made a great feast on the same day that Isaac was* ***weaned****. And Sarah saw the son of Hagar the Egyptian, whom she had borne to Abraham,* ***scoffing****. Therefore, she said to Abraham, 'Cast out this bondwoman and her son; for the son of this bondwoman shall not be heir with my son, namely with Isaac.' And the matter was very displeasing in Abraham's sight because of his son. But God said to Abraham, 'Do not let it be displeasing in your sight because of the lad or because of your bondwoman. Whatever Sarah has said to you, listen to her voice,* **for in Isaac, your seed shall be called***. Yet I will also make a nation of the son of the bondwoman* **because he is your seed***.' So, Abraham rose early in the morning and took bread and a skin of water; and putting it on her shoulder, he gave it and the boy to Hagar and sent her away. Then she departed and wandered in the* ***Wilderness of Beersheba****. And the water in the skin was used up, and she placed the boy under one of the shrubs. Then she went and sat down across from him at a distance of about a bowshot, for she said to herself, 'Let me not see the death of the boy.' So, she sat opposite him, and lifted her voice, and wept. And* ***God heard the voice of the lad****. Then the angel of God called Hagar out of heaven and said to her, 'What ails you, Hagar? Fear not, for God has heard the voice of the lad where he is. Arise, lift up the lad and hold him with your hand, for I will make him a great nation.' Then God opened her eyes, and* ***she saw a well of water****. And she went and filled the skin with water and gave the lad a drink. So, God was with the lad, and he grew and dwelt in the wilderness and became an* ***archer****. He dwelt in the* ***Wilderness of Paran****, and his mother took a* ***wife for him from the land of Egypt****" Genesis 21:8-21 (emphasis added).*

In ancient times, infant mortality rates were high; most children did not live to adulthood. Therefore, in ancient Mesopotamia, children were not generally weaned until the age of three, or in some cases, not until five. If the child survived infancy, which was thought to be the most challenging stage of childhood, the occasion was marked by a grand celebration.

And the child grew up, and he was weaned, and Abraham made a great feast upon the day that Isaac was weaned. And Shem and Eber and all the great people of the land, and Abimelech king of the Philistines, and his servants, and Phichol, the captain of his host, came to eat and drink and rejoice at the feast which Abraham made upon the day of his son Isaac's being weaned. Also, Terah, the father of Abraham, and Nahor, his brother, came from Haran, they and all belonging to them, for they greatly rejoiced on hearing that a son had been born to Sarah. And they came to Abraham, and they ate and drank at the feast which Abraham made upon the day of Isaac's being weaned. And Terah and Nahor rejoiced with Abraham, and they remained with him many days in the land of the Philistines.[227]

Ishmael was fourteen when Isaac was born. That would mean that Ishmael was probably seventeen or older when Isaac was weaned. Indeed, old enough to know not to "scoff" at the younger Isaac. Mock is the word the KJV used; however, the Hebrew word is *"tsachaq"* – "to laugh outright." *Tsachaq* is the root of *Yitschaq* (Isaac). The Septuagint translated verse nine as, *"And Sarrha having seen the son of Agar the Egyptian who was born to Abraam, sporting with Isaac, her son."*[228]

---

[227] Johnson, Ken. *Ancient Book of Jasher* (p. 43). Kindle Edition.
[228] Septuagint with Apocrypha: English, Brenton, Lancelot C.L., 1851

The Book of Jasher has Ishmael attempting to shoot Isaac with an arrow. Paul wrote that Ishmael *"dioko"* (pursued) the younger child. *"Now we, brethren, as Isaac was, are children of promise. But, as he who was born according to the flesh then **persecuted** him who was born according to the Spirit, even so, it is now. Nevertheless, what does the Scripture say? 'Cast out the bondwoman and her son, for the son of the bondwoman shall not be heir with the son of the freewoman.' So, then, brethren, we are not children of the bondwoman but of the free,"* Galatians 4:28-31.

Why would a seventeen-year-old chase a three-year-old, mock and scoff, or shoot an arrow at him unless he intended to harm? Holy Spirit, however, didn't think it necessary that we know the details, but whatever happened, Sarah was perturbed. She demanded that Abraham remove that "bondwoman and her son." She wanted them *"garash,"* which means she wanted Abraham to divorce himself from the *'amah* and **her** *ben*. Sarah said, "Divorce the servant and **her** son by expelling them from your tent. He shall not be your heir with **my** son." Yahweh agreed with Sarah.

"The physical atomic form of the current homo sapien-2 species is easily influenced and vulnerable to sound frequencies since our original cosmic form is built upon infrasound. Therefore, specific sound frequencies can assist the human body for self-healing or nefariously cause disease and even death. Specific words, sounds, and images unequivocally can alter our consciousness, either raising or lowering it. Sound is more powerful than light as language is utilized as an energetic carrier for certain frequency tones that activate elements that affect the chemicals in our body, which in turn affects the DNA. One must be able to sense the energetic encryption behind sound and language if one is to know the difference between harmful or beneficial intentions and frequencies."[229]

The promises concerning Abraham's seed were to be fulfilled through Isaac, not realized through Ishmael. Isaac was a gift, a creative miracle that Sarah conceived because she received a divinely structured egg. This was not the case with Ishmael.

Sarah's egg contained twenty-six appointed chromosomes. Those combined with the twenty-six selected from Abraham made more than one generation. Isaac's DNA also included all the generations Yahweh wanted, down to the end of time.

Abraham is the father of all, who shall receive the kingdom by faith. Therefore, if we are in the Melchizedek Kingdom, we came because Abraham and Sarah birthed *Yitschaq*. That is factual, regardless of ethnicity, gender, or any other marker we as humans might attribute to the flesh.

We also must consider that Abraham's prophetic prayer broke the curse of barrenness the adversarial system attempted to place upon him and his offspring. The spiritual richness of God's wisdom is so deep and vast – I am constantly in awe.

Note that the name Ishmael was not spoken. Not by Sarah nor by Yahweh. Or even by the "angel" who spoke to Hagar. For a good reason, he was not the work of faith, of grace. *"Do not be entangled again with a* **yoke of bondage***. Indeed I, Paul, say to you that if you become circumcised, Christ (the* **Anointed One)** *will profit you nothing. And I testify again to every man* **who becomes circumcised** *that he is a debtor to keep the whole law. You have*

---

[229] https://www.ijser.org/researchpaper/The-Language-of-Our-DNA-Scalar-Energy.pdf retrieved August 12, 2021

become estranged from Christ, you who attempt to be justified by law; **you have fallen from grace***. For we through the Spirit eagerly wait for the hope of* **righteousness by faith***. For in Christ Jesus, neither circumcision nor uncircumcision avails anything* **but faith working through love***"* Galatians 5:1-6 (emphasis added).

Ishmael equates with Adam as the son not born to the covenant of faith. Isaac equates to Yeshua.

Ishmael is like the Book of the Law. Isaac is like the Book of Covenant.

Ishmael, born of the flesh, though circumcised, fell from grace. Whose grace? Yahweh's! Why? He did not have the right spirit; he did not love Isaac as he should have. Yet God promised Abraham Ishmael would be a great nation. Although implied in the promise was a warning, Ishmael was the by-product of bondage from the bondwoman. His offspring would be held in servitude to cruel "taskmasters," the fallen gods.

Ishmael's God was the Creator and Supreme Judge of the Cosmos, *Elohiym*. That was why it is noted that *Elohiyim* spoke. Ishmael did not have a personal relationship with Yahweh. But Isaac did.

Later, as a grown man, Ishmael would dwell in the desert, married to a pagan.

Be'er Sheba, an oasis in the area dominated by the Philistines, was also known as the Well of Oath. However, to Hagar and her son, it was a wilderness – a place of dryness. And because she could not locate water without divine help, they wandered aimlessly. Hagar wept. However, *Elohiym* heard the voice of the lad. The text does not state Ishmael cried, only that Hagar did. Seemingly she cried uncontrollably. But God heard Ishmael's voice, which I venture to say sounded like Abraham's voice to heaven.

Consequently, the *"mal'ak"* of *Elohiym* spoke to Hagar from the realm of heaven, saying, "What is the matter? Don't be afraid; the *elohim* have heard the voice of the lad." Hagar's eyes were opened, and she saw the well. Despite that, they did not remain there. Hagar and the lad moved further into Paran. Paran is the east-central region of the Sinai Peninsula. It is desert, although its name means foliage as an embellishment of green.

> *"And it came to pass at that time that Abimelech and Phichol, the commander of his army, spoke to Abraham, saying, 'God is with you in all that you do. Now, therefore, swear to me by God that you will not deal falsely with me,* **with my offspring, or with my posterity***; but that according to the kindness that I have done to you, you will do to me and to the land in which you have dwelt.' And Abraham said, 'I will swear.' Then Abraham rebuked Abimelech because of a well of water that Abimelech's servants had seized. And Abimelech said, 'I do not know who has done this thing; you did not tell me, nor had I heard of it until today.' So, Abraham took sheep and oxen and gave them to Abimelech, and the two of them made a covenant. And Abraham set seven ewe lambs of the flock by themselves. Then Abimelech asked Abraham,* **'What is the meaning of these seven ewe lambs, which you have set by themselves?'** *And he said, 'You will take these seven ewe lambs from my hand, that they may be my witness that I have dug this well.' Therefore, he called that place* **Beersheba because the two of them swore an oath there***. Thus, they made a covenant at Beersheba. So, Abimelech rose with Phichol, the commander of his army, and they returned to the land of*

the Philistines. **Then Abraham planted a tamarisk tree in Beersheba and there called on the name of the Lord, the Everlasting God.** *And Abraham stayed in the land of the Philistines many days"* Genesis 21:22-34 (emphasis added).

Wells were necessary for survival. Successful herdsmen and shepherds needed them for their animals. If a well fell into disrepair and the owner did nothing, the one who restored the well gained the right to possess the well. Maintaining a well on unoccupied land established a right of possession to the oasis and surrounding land.

While Captain Phichol worried about the number of men obligated to Abraham for their well-being, Abimelech noted Abraham grew in riches. Abraham, although wealthy, increased in wealth as the size of his herds and flocks increased. So, the two men went to Abraham to make a peace covenant. Phichol wanted to bind Abraham to a pact of peace. He wanted one that would last to the second generations and beyond. Apparently, Abimelech wanted a share in Abraham's riches.

Abimelech began the negotiation by reminding Abraham of "the kindness I have done to you." He returned Sarah and granted Abraham the right to dwell wherever he desired. Returning the civility, Abraham swore to not deal falsely with either Abimelech or his offspring. However, he also rebuked Abimelech. A well he had dug had been seized by the king's servants.

Abimelech, of course, denied knowledge of the injustice. So, after agreeing upon the terms of a peace covenant and exchanging oaths, Abraham gave Abimelech seven ewe lambs. These were in addition to the sheep and oxen provided for the covenant ritual. Abimelech questioned Abraham about the seven lambs. Abraham explained they were his witnesses that his men had dug the well in question. In other words, these lambs, valuable animals, were given to redeem the well. Abraham would have never placed such a gift before Abimelech without a worthy cause. That was the meaning of the phrase, "they may be my witness."

Abimelech returned to Gerar. Abraham took possession of the oasis, which he promptly named Be'er Sheba (well of the oath).

Abraham then planted a grove at Be'er Sheba and called on the name of Yahweh. The well was his, so he planted a "garden," which made it a monument. *"And called there on the name of Yahweh, El 'Olam."* An expression that means Abraham worshiped Yahweh as the Eternal God, though he "sojourn" in a land not his, as a temporary resident. (Sojourn, *"guwr,"* means to dwell or lodge in a place as a guest.)

Genesis Twenty-Two

> Genesis 22:1-2 *"**Now it came to pass after these things** that **God tested** Abraham and said to him, "Abraham!" And he said, "Here I am." Then He said, 'Take now your son, your only son Isaac, whom you love, and go to the **land of Moriah**, and offer him there as a burnt offering on one of the mountains of which I shall tell you"* (emphasis added).

Chapter 22 is so significant I almost don't know which treasure to unpack first. So, let's start with the phrase, "now it came to pass, after." After what? Going back to the last sentence of the previous chapter, we note, *"Then he (Abraham) planted a tamarisk tree in Beersheba and there called (addressed Yahweh as)* **the Everlasting God,** *and Abraham stayed in the land of the Philistines many days."* So, the "after" must have been the "after" Abraham planted the tree and called out to his *Elohiym* that "*El* tested" Abraham.

Let's reconstruct what happened. 1) Abraham gained the right to "the Well of Oath" from an Amorite king. 2) He did not build an altar and call on Yahweh until he had the right to do so. 3) Abraham had invoked the name of Yahweh many times. However, on that occasion at Beersheba, Abraham addressed Yahweh by another title, which brought about the testing.

God tested Abraham, not as Yahweh, but as *Elohiym*, the Supreme God, the Superior Judge over the Divine Council. The test was not to prove Abraham for Himself but for the benefit of the lesser gods. I suggest the reason is two-fold. Mainly, Yahweh was foreshadowing the Cross of Yeshua. Secondly, He was exchanging Firstborns.

Whether Abraham planted a "tree" or a grove of trees is incidental to this story. That he "planted" means he created a *gan* (a garden.) Why? To build an altar, to call on Yahweh.

Oasis Beersheba was legally Abraham's possession for as long as he "sojourned" and maintained it. He had purchased that right from Abimelech. Still, should Abraham cease to "sojourn" at Beersheba, he would, in effect, relinquish any right of possession he held. The oasis would subsequently return to Abimelech. Which basically defines "to sojourn." Only Abimelech owned the land; he leased it out. Therefore, all who lived in his domain sojourned.

Remember that the Amorites were the Semitic-speaking people of the known world and inhabited the lands west of the Euphrates and beyond the Nile, even dwelling in Egypt. It could be said that the Philistines of Abraham's day were Amorites because they, like the Canaanites, were incorporated into the pagan culture initiated by the Sumerians. The more pertinent fact is that they were *goy*.

After he built the altar at Beersheba, Abraham addressed Yahweh as "the Eternal God." At that time, the epithet "Eternal God" was associated with the Amorite/Canaanite god, *El*. The Babylonians called this same god *Enlil*, the Greeks Kronos, and the Romans Saturn. And the correlation?

The Canaanite *El* demanded human sacrifice. We can only speculate as to why. However, I'm convinced because "life" is found in the blood. Blood has a voice. Remember Abel's blood cried out from the ground.

So, is it possible that vengeful Watchers and/or the demon spirits of their dead children, the Rephaim/Nephilim, lured the pagan nations of the ancient world into burning their sons and daughters as sacrificial offerings to gods of the dead?[230]

Leviticus 18:21-22, *"And you shall not let any of your descendants pass through the fire to Molech, nor shall you profane the name of your God: I am the Lord."*

Molech was an Ammonite god that tracks back to **Rapi'u,** the **"king of eternity,"** who was also believed to be the lord (*bēl*) of the underworld and king of the Rephaim. Bottom-line, the spirits of the offspring of the fallen Watchers, as the Rephaim, roamed the Jordan River Rift, down from Mount Hermon to the Dead Sea and beyond. They lied, deceived, and killed the *goyim* (people) of the upper world, *'erets*.

The Amorites dominated the world of Abraham, Isaac, and Jacob. They founded Babylon and its occult system, which was condemned in the Bible by everyone from Moses to John the Revelator. And their kings claimed to be descended from the Titans.[231]

Genesis 15:13-16 is crucial to Chapter 22. *"Then He* (Yahweh) *said to* **Abram,** *'Know certainly* **that your descendants will be strangers in a land that is not theirs** *and will serve them, and they will* **afflict them four hundred years.** *And, the nation they serve, I will judge; afterward, they shall come out with great possessions. Now, as for you, you shall go to your fathers in peace; you shall be buried at a good old age. But in the* **fourth generation,** *they shall return here,* **for the iniquity of the Amorites is not yet complete"** (emphasis added).

Abraham and his descendants wandered (sojourned) in Eden (Canaan) without citizenship rights. Then in a land, which was not theirs, they served another people (Egypt) for four generations before the "iniquity" of the Amorites would be dealt with. Thus, the Amorites would be allowed to pervert the truth for another four hundred years. Then, when their sin reached its tipping point, judgment would fall.

As a way of explaining the symbolism, allow me to point out that Adam and Noah wandered in Eden for 1,656 years. Then Yahweh sent a flood to cleanse Eden of the offspring of the fallen Watchers. Then 337 years later, Yahweh came down again. This time to confuse the languages of mankind and quash the Tower of Babel. (1656 + 337 = 1993 that is 7 years shy of 2000)

Three times in the first two thousand years following the Creation of Genesis 1, Yahweh had to personally deal with the fallen gods.

- Yahweh cast down the satan who deceived Eve (Isaiah 14:12)[232]
- Yahweh bound the fallen Watchers in Tartarus (2 Peter 2:4).[233]

---

230 Gilbert, Derek P. *Last Clash of the Titans: The Second Coming of Hercules, Leviathan, and the Prophesied War Between Jesus Christ and the Gods of Antiquity* (p. 44). Defender Publishing. Kindle Edition.
231 Ibid, p. 70.
232 *"How you are cut down to the ground, you who weakened the nations!"* NKJV

- Yahweh brought down the Tower of Babel (Genesis 11:7-8).

Essentially every maneuver the fallen gods attempted, Yahweh refuted. Psalms 2 – *"Why do the nations rage, and the people plot in vain? The* **kings of the earth** *set themselves, and* **the rulers take counsel together against the Lord and against his Anointed,** *saying, "Let us burst their bonds apart and cast away their cords from us." He who sits in the heavens laughs;* **Yahweh** *holds them in derision. Then he will speak to them in his wrath and terrify them in his fury, saying, "As for me, I have* **set my King on Zion, my holy hill***." I will tell of the decree: Yahweh said to me, "You are my Son; today I have begotten you. Ask of me, and I will make the nations your heritage and the ends of the earth your possession. You shall break them with a rod of iron and dash them in pieces like a potter's vessel." Now, therefore,* **O kings, be wise; be warned, O rulers of the earth.** *Serve the Lord with fear and rejoice with trembling.* **Kiss the Son***, lest he is angry, and you perish in the way, for his wrath is quickly kindled. Blessed are all who take refuge in him"* (ESV emphasis added).

1 Enoch, Chapter 19:1, "And Uriel said to me: 'Here shall stand the angels (Watchers) who have connected themselves with women, and their spirits assuming many different forms are defiling mankind and shall lead them astray into sacrificing to demons as gods, (here shall they stand,) **till the day of the great judgment** in which they shall be judged **till they are made an end of.**"[234]

Psalms 82: *"God (Elohiym) stands in the congregation of the mighty (gods); He judges among the gods (elohim). How long will you judge unjustly and show partiality to the wicked? Selah - Defend the poor and fatherless; do justice to the afflicted and needy. Deliver the poor and needy; Free them from the hand of the wicked. They do not know, nor do they understand; they walk about in darkness; all the foundations of the earth are unstable. I said,* **'You are gods (elohim), and all of you are children of the Most High. But you shall die like men and fall like one of the princes (Watchers).'** *Arise, O God (Elohiym), judge the earth for You shall inherit all nations (goyim)"* (emphasis added).

By the time of Abraham, the first 2,000 years of human history had elapsed. Those years were ruled by the Melchizedek Regency of Adam and Noah. The next 2,000 years would belong to Abraham's "physical" offspring. The final 2,000 to his spiritual Seed/seed. Then the last 1,000 years shall be ruled by the Eternal Melchizedek.

"…it still does contain commentary about the ages as taught by the School of Elijah. The epistle taught that human history would be divided into four "ages." The first age was called the Age of Chaos and was a period of two thousand years. It started with Creation and ended with the call of Abraham. According to Jasher, God called Abraham in the year 2000 AM. The second age was also to last two thousand years. It was called the Age of Torah and was supposed to exist from the call of Abraham to the first coming of the Messiah. When Messiah came, it would start the third age, which was called the Age of Grace. This Age of Grace was also called the temporary messianic period. We are not told why in the commentary, but the Essenes believed it was because the Messiah would die for our sins at his First Coming and rule as king at his Second Coming. The third age was to last for two thousand years.

---

[233] "*For if God messengers who sinned did not spare, but with chains of thick gloom, having cast* [them] *down to Tartarus.*" YLT
[234] *Old Testament Pseudepigrapha: Book of Enoch,* PC Study Bible formatted electronic database Copyright © 2003, 2006 by Biblesoft, Inc. All rights reserved.

After the Age of Grace, there would be a Messianic Kingdom which would last for one thousand years.[235]

The Essenes held that the Age of Chaos began with Creation. Thus, Chaos and Adam-Noah reigned concurrently. This simply means that the kingdom of darkness and the Kingdom of Light co-existed throughout *'erets*. The next four thousand years were given to determine the "fullness of the Gentiles," which would co-exist with the seed/Seed of Abraham. But at the end of the six thousand years, the Gentiles are cut-off, and the Eternal Melchizedek effectively shuts down the kingdom of darkness. The last enemy, Chaos (Death), shall be destroyed at the end of the seven thousand years.

Yahweh speaks on many levels and still hides the truth in plain view, as Genesis 15 reveals. *"Your descendants will be strangers in a land that is not theirs and will serve them, and they will **afflict them four hundred years.**"* In a prophetic sense, that weighty pronouncement correlates to the four thousand years allotted to Abraham's "seed."

While the enemy works, so does Yahweh. Yet Yahweh is always - several millennia ahead of the adversary.

Before the flood, the fallen realm began to structure itself as an assembly (pantheon), countering Yahweh's Divine Council. After the flood, they regrouped as Enlil, El, Kronos, Saturn, and so on. Later, those personas were replaced with Bel, Marduk, Baal, Zeus, and Jupiter. But their iniquity was not yet complete. The truth is the fallen gods[236] simply created new masks. Same gods, same tactics, merely different names.

When Yahweh called Abraham, He was restructuring also. Through Abraham, Yahweh renewed His covenant with the Eternal Melchizedek. And through Abraham, the Eternal Melchizedek would "sit" as King of Zion on Yahweh's holy hill. The fallen realm did not understand the significance of Abraham, or for that matter, Isaac. They would be even more confused by Jacob, whose story is another book altogether.

Why did Yahweh ask Abraham to sacrifice his son? The same reason Yahweh sacrificed His only begotten Son. To express love for all of humanity. Yet, what was being required was an exchange – of Firstborns.

Abraham would give his Firstborn to Yahweh, and Yahweh, in return, provided Abraham His!

To the fallen realm, this transaction was seen as a sacrifice. And indeed it was – just not the way it was witnessed by the fallen gods.

The fallen gods held the souls of mankind in the pit; Yahweh wanted His sons returned. To "get" what He desired, He had to give His only begotten Son!

> Genesis 22:1-8, *After these things, God tested Abraham and said to him, "Abraham!" And he said, "Here I am." He said, "Take your son, **your only son Isaac, whom you love**, and go to the **land of Moriah, and offer him there as a burnt offering** on one of the mountains of which I*

---

235 Johnson, Ken. *The Ancient Dead Sea Scroll Calendar: And the Prophecies it Reveals* (p. 74). Kindle Edition
236 These gods were the Titans – they reformed as the gods of Olympia before the flood. Afterward, as the Anu of the Sumerians. I have used Greek terms because they are the most familiar.

> *shall tell you." So, Abraham rose early in the morning,* **saddled his donkey**, *and took* **two** *of his young men with him and his son Isaac. And he cut the wood for the burnt offering and arose and went to the place of which God had told him. On the* **third day***, Abraham lifted up his eyes and* **saw the place from afar**. *Then Abraham said to his young men, "Stay here with the donkey; the boy and I will go over there and worship and come again to you." And Abraham took the wood of the burnt offering and laid it on Isaac, his son. And he took in his hand the fire and the knife. So, they went both of them together. And Isaac said to his father Abraham, "My father!" And he said, "Here I am, my son." He said, "Behold, the fire and the wood, but where is the lamb for a burnt offering?" Abraham said,* **"God will provide for Himself the lamb for a burnt offering***, my son." So, they went both of them together* (ESV emphasis added).

"Take your only son." Yahweh knew Abraham had fathered Ishmael. However, Ishmael was begotten before the *hei* (the breath of Yahweh) was added to Abram's name. (Exchange One)

The Hebrew text reads, *"Take your one son, whom you passionately love, Isaac."* The Septuagint – *"Take thy son, the beloved one, who thou hast loved – Isaac."* Abraham loved Ishmael, but his passion and heart wrapped around Isaac. Isaac was his joy, his miracle, a gift from Yahweh that was his inheritance and the keeper of his name. Through Isaac, Abraham would be eternally remembered. The Septuagint continues, *"Go into the high land, and offer him there for a whole-burnt-offering on one of the mountains which I will tell thee of."*

- The "high-land" - is "the land of Moriah." Strong's Concordance offers the Hebrew as *'erets ha moriyah*, which means the "land seen by Yah."
- "Whole-burnt-offering" - Burnt-offering is *'olah*, meaning to ascend. Whole-burnt-offering signifies a complete surrender and complete acceptance.
- "The mountain I will tell you of" - "*echad har 'ahser 'amar 'el*," translates as "a mountain that I appoint you to go up."

2 Chronicles 3:1-2 offers more insight as to where these mountains were located. *"Now Solomon began to build the* **house of the Lord at Jerusalem on Mount Moriah***, where the Lord had appeared to his father David, at the place that David had prepared on the threshing floor of Ornan the Jebusite"* (emphasis added).

Elohiym instructed Abraham to go to the "high places" at Salem, the mountains of Yah. This was also the same area of Eden's "*gan*." Which made it the location where the Divine Council assembled. In other words, Moriah was the physical location of Yah's cosmic high place. Additionally, it was where David would build his Jerusalem. And where Yahweh shall install His King, Yeshua. Scripture is replete with references that tie the area to Zion and Jeru(Salem).

Abraham clearly understood one specific mountain would be appointed for worship once he arrived in Salem's hills and would know which mountain when he saw it. Genesis 22:3, *"Early in the morning, Abraham got up and saddled his donkey. He took two of his young servants with him, along with his son Isaac. When he had cut the wood for the burnt offering, he started out for the place God had spoken to him about,"* The NET Bible.

Abraham rode a donkey. Donkeys were considered symbols of peace; horses were used only in battle. Abraham approached Yah's High Place in peace. Zechariah 9:9, *"Rejoice greatly, O daughter of Zion! Shout, O daughter of Jerusalem! Behold, your King is coming to you; He is just and having salvation, lowly and riding on a donkey,"*

"On the third day, Abraham looked up and saw the place in the distance." Abraham saw the place on the third day, making the third day Abraham's day! And again, dear Reader, I remind you that the third day signifies the "planting of the seed." Genesis 1:12-13, *"and the tree that yields fruit, whose seed is in itself according to its kind. And God saw that it was good. So, the evening and the morning were the third day."*

Note Abraham saw the place "afar," *rachoq*, literally and figuratively, a place or time from afar or long ago. I suggest Abraham saw the temple of Yahweh outside of time. In other words, he saw a "city not built with hands," the Garden of Yahweh as it existed in Eden. You see, Abraham brought Isaac, as commanded to *Elohiym*, and before the Divine Council, that they might witness Yahweh as the righteous, Eternal God, exchange Firstborns with Abraham.

Hebrews 11:8-10, *"By faith, Abraham obeyed when he was called to go out to the place which he would receive as an inheritance. And he went out, not knowing where he was going. By faith, he dwelt in the land of promise as in a foreign country, dwelling in tents with Isaac and Jacob, the heirs with him of the same promise; for he* **waited for the city which has foundations, whose builder and maker is God,***"* (emphasis added).

Abraham also supplied the wood for the sacrifice. He gathered the wood from the trees near his dwelling. "Wood," or *'ets*, translates as a tree or sticks of wood. John 19:17, *"bearing His cross, went out to a place called the Place of a Skull, which is called in Hebrew Golgotha."*

Why take two servants? Abraham needed two witnesses to establish that he and Isaac went into the hills to worship Yahweh. Deuteronomy 19:15, *"at the mouth of two witnesses, or at the mouth of three witnesses, shall the matter be established,"* KJV.

Abraham believed Isaac was dead. From the moment he submitted to the will of God, Isaac was no longer his son; Isaac was Yahweh's. Abraham fully intended to place Isaac on the altar, sacrifice him to *Elohiym*, and leave him there. Hebrews 11:17-20, *"By faith Abraham, when he was tested,* **offered up Isaac** *(past-tense). He had received the promises, yet he was ready to offer up his only son. God had told him, 'Through Isaac, descendants will carry on your name,' and* **he reasoned that God could even raise him from the dead, and in a sense, he received him back from there***"* (The NET Bible emphasis added). Because he trusted Yahweh, he obeyed. So, with confidence, Abraham instructed his servants, *"wait here with the donkey. My son and I will go on, and <u>after we worship, we shall return to you.</u>"*

God was foreshadowing the fulfillment of the mission[237] assigned to Yeshua. However, no one saw the correlation. Abraham didn't. Neither did the Divine Council, only Yahweh.

Yahweh was not installing Abraham or Isaac as Melchizedek but instead proving their obedience to the

---

[237] The Melchizedek had to prove his righteousness through obedience.

Divine Council. And in a sense, Yahweh – Yeshua were signing the Marriage Covenant, the Ketubah. That Abraham and Isaac were there doing their part also implies that they signed the Ketubah. Then there were the witnesses, the celestials, the terrestrials, and the Holy Spirit. The Bride had yet to be born. However, Abraham signed for her. (Abraham would not be alive when the Ketubah was handed to the Bride by Moses. These negotiations and exchanges had to be made with him. He is the Bride's father. [That he would father two Brides was also hidden.])

Abraham's heart must have hurt, heavy with grief. I can only imagine the pain. Yet, after receiving the command to offer Isaac, he rose the following morning, cut the wood, saddled the donkey, then set forth for the hills of Salem, nearly 40-50 miles away.

Since they arrived at the hills of Salem on day three, the journey took two full days, representing the age of Torah, according to ancient rabbinical manuscripts. "According to these numbers, our forefather Isaac was 37 years old when Father Abraham bound him to the altar."

	A.M. Birth/Yr.	A. M. Yr/Death	Lived Yrs.		Age @ Isaac's Birth
Terah	1878	2083	205	*	170
Abraham	1948	2123	175	***	100
Sarah	1958	2085	127	**	90
Isaac	2048	2228	180	****	

* Genesis 11:32, *"So, the days of Terah were two hundred and five years."*
** Genesis 23:1 *"Sarah lived one hundred and twenty-seven years."*
*** Genesis 25:7, *"This is the sum of the years of Abraham's life…,*
        one hundred and seventy-five."
**** Genesis 35:28, *"Now the days of Isaac were one hundred and eighty years."*

"And Abraham sojourned in the Philistines' land many days." Genesis 21:34. The "many days" lasted longer than the years he dwelt at Hebron. He lived in Hebron for 25 years and in the Philistines' land for 26 years. During that time, Rebecca was born. Isaac married Rebecca when she was 14 years old. Our forefather Abraham buried his father Terah two years before Sarah died.[238] This quote from the *Ancient Sedar of Olam* agrees with the previous excerpt from the *Book of Jasher*. The number 37 was calculated using the lifespans of Terah and Sarah.

Sarah died after Abraham offered Isaac on Mount Moriah. Biblical scholars suggest her death came immediately afterward. If so, Isaac was thirty-seven when he was placed on the altar. But whether he was thirty-seven or younger, he was a grown man, fully aware and committed to his father.

Abraham laid the wood (tree) on Isaac, and he carried the torch and knife. The two went up the mountain together. As they climbed, Isaac asked, "Where is the lamb for the offering?" Abraham responded, *"Elohiym* will appear to have a lamb to offer." Genesis 22:8, *"And Abraham said, 'God will provide himself a sheep for a*

---

[238] Johnson, Ken. *Ancient Seder Olam* (p. 14). Biblefacts.org. Kindle Edition.

whole-burnt-offering, my son,'" Septuagint: Brenton Edition.

Abraham built an altar, laid the wood upon it, then bound the feet of Isaac.

> Genesis 22:9-12, *"Then they came to the place of which God (Elohiym) had told him. And Abraham built an altar there and placed the wood in order;* ***and he bound Isaac his son and laid him on the altar, upon the wood.*** *And Abraham stretched out his hand and took the knife to slay his son. But the* ***Angel of the Lord called to him from heaven and said, 'Abraham, Abraham!'*** *So, he said, 'Here I am.' And He said, 'Do not lay your hand on the lad, or do anything to him;* ***for now, I know that you fear God since you have not withheld your son, your only son, from Me"*** (emphasis added).

Abraham bound Isaac's feet using a cord and laid him on the wood upon the altar. This scene depicts what happened at Calvary. Yahweh laid His only begotten Son on the Cross. And what is even more impressive, Isaac (Yeshua) didn't protest but obeyed. That's worship. That's a whole-burnt-offering, a sacrifice made complete and utterly received – that's love!

Remember, the Divine Council was watching; they saw it all. I imagine just as Abraham drew back the knife, Yeshua jumped to his feet and cried out, "Abraham, Abraham! Do not lay your hand on my servant. Do him no harm. I know you fear *Elohiym* since you have not withheld your son, your Melchizedek-son, from me."

> Genesis 22:13-14, *"Then Abraham lifted his eyes and looked, and there behind him was a ram caught in a thicket by its horns. So, Abraham went and took the ram and offered it up for a burnt offering instead of his son. And Abraham called the name of the place,* **Yahweh**-*Will-Provide; as it is said to this day, 'In the Mount of* **Yahweh** *it shall be provided"* (emphasis added).

Abraham answered, "I see you!" He lifted his eyes and looked. Coming "after his time" was a "ram" (a chief Deity) caught in a thicket (the twisted branches of humanity) by his horns (the strength of his royal position). So, Abraham (Exalted Father of Nations) took the mighty Prince and offered it (Him) instead of Isaac.

> Genesis 22:15-19, *"Then* **(Yahweh)** *called to Abraham a second time out of heaven, and said: 'By Myself, I have sworn, because you have done this thing, and have not withheld your son, your only son — blessing I will bless you, and multiplying I will multiply your descendants as the stars of the heaven and as the sand which is on the seashore, and* ***your (Seed) shall possess the <u>gate</u> of (his) enemies.*** *In your Seed, all the nations of the earth shall be blessed because you have obeyed My voice.' So, Abraham returned to his young men, and they rose and went together to Beersheba. Abraham dwelt at Beersheba* (modified by the author to align with the Hebrew text).

The cosmic war would be won through Abraham's Seed. Accordingly, it would be his Seed who took the keys to the gates of Hades. *"I am the First (Aleph) and the Last (Tav). I am He who lives, and was dead, and behold, I am alive forevermore. Amen. And **I have the keys of Hades and of Death**,"* Revelation 1:17-18, (emphasis added). Genesis 22:17 is the second time the word *"sha'ar"* (gate; portal; opening; door) is used. The first time was, *"and Lot sat in the gate of Sodom,"* Genesis 19:1 KJV. The first use typified the gate to the underworld, and so did the second use of *"sha'ar."* It would be the gate that Yeshua gained possession of upon his death.

Previously, when Yahweh promised to bless Abraham's seed, the gate of "his enemies" was not mentioned (see Genesis 12). The Melchizedek blessed Abram saying, *"El Elyon has delivered your enemies into your hand"* (see Genesis 14). The point is this: Abraham's obedience foreshadowed Yeshua's - and released an authority that had not previously been released. The gate to the underworld would submit to the Melchizedek Kingdom because of the exchange of Issac with Yeshua.

Yahweh, as *Elohiym* proved Abraham and Isaac's obedience, they were worthy to represent the Melchizedek Kingdom. They were righteous.

Yahweh also proved His righteousness – He provided a Lamb! Yahweh was not a God asking for human sacrifice – He was the God who became the Sacrifice for humanity.

Isaiah 53: *Who has believed our report? And to whom has the arm of the Lord been revealed? For He shall grow up before Him as a tender plant and a root out of the dry ground. He has no form or comeliness, and when we see Him, there is no beauty that we should desire Him. He is despised and rejected by men, a man of sorrows and acquainted with grief. And we hid, as it were, our faces from Him; He was despised, and we did not esteem Him. Surely, He has borne our griefs and carried our sorrows; Yet we esteemed Him stricken, smitten by God, and afflicted. But He was wounded for our transgressions. He was bruised for our iniquities. The chastisement for our peace was upon Him, and by His stripes, we are healed. All we like sheep have gone astray; we have turned, everyone, to his own way; <u>and the Lord has laid on Him the iniquity of us all</u>. He was oppressed, and He was afflicted, yet <u>He opened not His mouth. He was led as a lamb to the slaughter</u>, and as a sheep, before its shearers is silent, So He opened not His mouth. He was taken from prison and from judgment, and who will declare His generation? For He was cut off from the land of the living for the transgressions of My people. He was stricken, and they made His grave with the wicked — but with the rich at His death because <u>He had done no violence, nor was any deceit in His mouth. Yet it pleased the Lord to bruise Him; He has put Him to grief. When You make His soul an offering for sin, He shall see His seed</u>, He shall prolong His days, and the pleasure of the Lord shall prosper in His hand. He shall see the labor of His soul and be satisfied. By His knowledge, My righteous Servant shall justify many, for He shall bear their iniquities. Therefore, I will divide Him a portion with the great. He shall divide the spoil with the strong because He poured out His soul unto death and numbered with the transgressors. He bore the sin of many and made intercession for the transgressors* (emphasis added).

Genesis Twenty-Three

> Genesis 22:20-24, *"Now it came to pass after these things that it was told Abraham, saying, 'Indeed* **Milcah** *also has borne children to your brother* **Nahor***: Huz his firstborn, Buz his brother, Kemuel the father of Aram, Chesed, Hazo, Pildash, Jidlaph, and* **Bethuel.***' And* **Bethuel begot Rebekah***. These eight Milcah bore to Nahor, Abraham's brother. His concubine, whose name was Reumah, also bore Tebah, Gaham, Thahash, and Maachah"* (emphasis added).

§1:51 Now, Abram had two brethren, Nahor and Haran. Haran left a son, Lot, and Sarai and Milcah, his daughters, and died among the Chaldeans in a city of the Chaldeans, called Ur, and his monument is shown to this day. These married their nieces. Nahor married Milcah, and Abram married Sarai.[239]

§1:153 Now Nahor had eight sons by Milcah: Uz and Buz, Kemuel, Chesed, Azau, Pheldas, Jadelph, and Bethuel. These were all the genuine sons of Nahor; for Teba and Gaam, and Tachas, and Maaca, were born of Reuma, his concubine; but Bethuel had a daughter, Rebecca, --and a son, Laban.[240]

Milcah means queen. She was both Abraham's niece and sister-in-law.

Milcah had a son with Nahor, who they named Bethuel. According to Easton's Bible Dictionary, Bethuel means "house of God." Bethuel begot Rebekah – and the purpose for placing these five verses as an opening to Genesis 23 was that as Sarah departed from Isaac's life, Rebekah was entering. We shall look closer at Rebekah in the following chapter; however, we now turn our attention to Sarah.

> Genesis 23, *"Sarah lived one hundred and twenty-seven years; these were the years of the life of Sarah. So, Sarah died in* **Kirjath Arba (that is, Hebron) in the land of Canaan***, and Abraham came to mourn for Sarah and to weep for her. Then Abraham stood up from before his dead and spoke to the sons of* **Heth***, saying, 'I am a foreigner and a visitor among you. Give me property for a burial place among you, that* **I may bury my dead out of my sight.***' And the sons of Heth answered Abraham, saying to him, 'Hear us, my lord: You are a mighty prince among us; bury your dead in the choicest of our burial places. None of us will withhold from you his burial place that you may bury your dead.' Then Abraham stood up and bowed himself to the people of the land, the sons of Heth. And he spoke with them, saying,* **'If it is your wish that I bury my dead out of my sight, hear me, and meet with Ephron the son of Zohar for me, that he may give me the cave of Machpelah which he has, which is at the end of his field.** *Let him give it to me at the* **full price** *as property for a burial place among you.' Now Ephron dwelt among the sons of Heth; and* **Ephron the Hittite** *answered Abraham in the presence of the sons of Heth, all who entered* **at the**

---

[239] Josephus: *Antiquities of the Jews* [Greek Text], PC Study Bible formatted electronic database Copyright © 2014 by Biblesoft, Inc. All rights reserved.
[240] Ibid. 1:153

gate of his city, saying, 'No, my lord, hear me: **I give you the field and the cave that is in it; I give it to you in the presence of the sons of my people. I give it to you. Bury your dead!'** *Then Abraham bowed himself down before the people of the land, and he spoke to Ephron in the hearing of the people of the land, saying, 'If you will give it, please hear me.* **I will give you money for the field;** *take it from me, and I will bury my dead there.' And Ephron answered Abraham, saying to him, 'My lord, listen to me; the land is worth* **four hundred shekels of silver.** *What is that between you and me? So, bury your dead.' And Abraham listened to Ephron; and Abraham weighed out the silver for Ephron, which he had named in the hearing of the sons of Heth, four hundred shekels of silver, the currency of the merchants.* **So, the field of Ephron, which was in Machpelah, which was before Mamre, the field and the cave, which was in it, and all the trees that were in the field, which were within all the surrounding borders, were deeded to Abraham as a possession in the presence of the sons of Heth, before all who went in at the gate of his city.** *And after this, Abraham buried Sarah, his wife, in the cave of the field of Machpelah, before Mamre (that is, Hebron) in the land of Canaan. So, the field and the cave that is in it were deeded to Abraham by the sons of Heth as property for a burial place"*
(emphasis added.).

Sarah died in *Kirjath Arba* (Hebron) in the land of Canaan. Why use the term *Kirjath Arba* and then say it is the same as Hebron in the land of Canaan? Why was she not in Beersheba with Abraham? (Just two of the questions that popped into my mind when I began studying Chapter 23.)

Interestingly, *Kirjath Arba* is also spelled *Qiryath `Arba`* (keer-yath' ar-bah). With the article interposed, *Qiryath ha 'Arba'* translates as *Arba,* the **city of the four (giants).**

Arba means four, but also, it was the name of a giant, the father of Anak. Joshua 14:15, *"Hebron used to be called Kiriath Arba after Arba, who was the greatest* (mighty) *man among the Anakites,"* NIV.

"Hebron would appear to have been the original name of the city, and it was not till after Abraham's stay there that it received the name Kirjath-Arba, who [i.e., Arba] was not the founder but the conqueror of the city, having led thither the tribe of the Anakim, to which he belonged. It retained this name till it came into the possession of Caleb when the Israelites restored the original name, Hebron."[241]

Jubilees 19:1-8, "Abraham returned and dwelt opposite Hebron that is Kirjath Arba…, the days of the life of Sarah were accomplished, and she died in Hebron. And Abraham went to mourn over her and bury her…., he conversed with the children of Heth to the intent that they should give him a place in which to bury his dead. And the Lord gave him grace before all who saw him, and he sought in gentleness the sons of Heth, and they gave him the land of the double cave over against Mamre, that is Hebron, for four hundred pieces of silver. And they sought him saying, we shall give it to thee for nothing, but he would not take it from their hands for nothing, for he gave the price of the place, the money in full, and bowed down before them twice. After this, he buried his dead in the double cave. And all the days of the life of Sarah were one hundred and twenty-seven years, that is, two jubilees and four weeks and one year: these are the days of the years of the life of Sarah."[242]

---

241 *Easton's Bible Dictionary*, PC Study Bible formatted electronic database Copyright © 2003, 2006 Biblesoft, Inc. All rights reserved.

The *Book of Jasher* tells the same story but slightly different. From *Jasher's* perspective, the story is long, so for the sake of brevity, here's the condensed version: Abraham informed Sarah that he and Isaac were going north to the hills of Salem. He offered her the justification by saying he was taking their son to Shem, that Isaac might learn "the ways of Yahweh." She agreed. After Abraham and Isaac departed, Satan approached Sarah and told her that Abraham sacrificed Isaac on an altar. "She afterward rose up and went about making inquiries till she came to Hebron, and she inquired of all those whom she met walking in the road, and no one could tell her what had happened to her son. And she came with her maidservants and menservants to Kireath-Arba, which is Hebron, and she asked concerning her son, and she remained there while she sent some of her servants to seek where Abraham had gone with Isaac; they went to seek him in the house of Shem and Eber, and they could not find him, and they sought throughout the land, and he was not there."[243]

"And behold, Satan came to Sarah in the shape of an old man, and he came and stood before her. He said unto her, I spoke falsely unto thee, for Abraham did not kill his son and he is not dead; and when she heard the word, her joy was so exceedingly violent on account of her son that her soul went out through joy; she died and was gathered to her people. And when Abraham…, returned with his son Isaac to…, Beersheba…, Abraham sought for Sarah, and could not find her, and he made inquiries concerning her, and they said unto him, she went as far as Hebron to seek you both where you had gone, for thus was she informed. And Abraham and Isaac went to her to Hebron, and when they found that she was dead, they lifted up their voices and wept bitterly over her…."[244]

Let's unpack the story. First, push aside the incidental information. The bottom line is Sarah died in Hebron (while in the land of the four giants), meaning she passed into the afterlife while away from Beersheba (the well of the Oath), where she lived.

Abraham no longer owned property in Hebron. He had no place to bury his wife, and it was necessary to bury the dead as quickly as possible. Transporting her body back the twenty-plus miles to Beersheba was not an option.

It was not unusual to bury the dead in caves. Openings or crevices in hills or mountains were often used as tombs, and when used as graves, caves became sacred sites, for they were thought of as doorways to the netherworld.

The story, as written in Genesis 23, is straightforward. Yet, hidden within it is a surprising allegory that connects with Galatians 4:23-26. *"But he who was of the bondwoman was born according to the flesh, and he of the freewoman through promise, which things are symbolic. For these are the two covenants: the one from Mount Sinai which gives birth to bondage, which is Hagar — for this Hagar is Mount Sinai in Arabia, and **corresponds to Jerusalem** which **now is**, and is in bondage with her children — but the **Jerusalem above is free**, which is **the mother of us all**"* (emphasis added).

As has been pointed out numerous times, Jerusalem is Yah's dwelling place of Peace! Symbolically, Sarah

---

[242] *Old Testament Pseudepigrapha: Book of Jubilees*, PC Study Bible formatted electronic database © 2007 by Biblesoft, Inc. All rights reserved.
[243] Johnson, Ken. *Ancient Book of Jasher* (p. 51). Kindle Edition.
[244] Ibid. p 51

equates with Jerusalem. And in the allegory of Genesis 23, Abraham correlates with the Second Power of Yahweh, the "Exalted Father of Nations" – the Eternal King. Isaac parallels the Promised Son, who shall be the Eternal King. Heth equates to the god of Dread, the son of Terror. Zohar means the dazzling one. Hittite means to terrorize by confusion and fear.

Now, let's put those representations into the story: Jerusalem (Yah's Mountain, the Bride of Yeshua) ceased existing in *Kirjath Arba* (formally, the place of alliance between God and man). She became Canaan (humiliated) and was taken to the netherworld as dead.[245] The Exalted Father came to mourn for his bride. He stood in the place of the dead and, speaking to the sons of Dread, said, "I am an alien, a visitor to this place of the dead. Give me a portion of this abyss for a burial place where I may hide my dead while they are out of sight." The sons of Dread answered the Exalted Father, saying, "Hear us, our Lord. You are the Prince of the Elohim. Bury your dead in the choicest place of our burial places. None of us will withhold from you a burial place; you may bury your dead."

Exalted Father stood and bowed to the residences of the Pit, to the sons of Dread. Speaking again, He said, "If your leader is to inter my dead out of my sight, you must mediate for me with the one who is cursed as dust. You know, the one who dazzles you. He must give me a place where my dead may rest until they can be resurrected at the end of time. He has such a place at the end of his time. It is in the field. Let him give it to me at the full price as property for a burial place for my Beloved."

Now, the cursed one from Eden, who dwelt among the sons of Dread, who was also begotten by Terror, stepped forward and answered in the presence of the sons of Heth and all who enter through the gate of the Watchers of Hermon by saying, "No, my Lord, I give you the field and the cave that is in it. I give it to you in the presence of the sons of my kind. I give it to you. Bury your dead!"

Father bowed graciously before those who dwelt in the Pit as He spoke to the Shiny One, saying, "If you do this, I will give you value for the field and the cave. Take it from me, so I can bury my dead." A price was agreed upon. Exalted Father gave the Cursed One the price he asked for in the currency of his merchants. The price requested was the release of four Travelers.

This allegory I have presented depicts Yahweh negotiating with the *nachash* of Eden, who I suggest is the Spirit of Death. Yahweh's goal was to keep the righteous dead apart from the unrighteous. Yahweh had to negotiate with the gods of the underworld. Desiring a place for the righteous to rest in peace, where they would not be terrorized but cared for by His ministering spirits, He had to approach them in their domain.

Luke 16:22-23, *"So it was that the beggar died, and was carried by the angels to Abraham's bosom. The rich man also died and was buried. And being in torments in Hades, he lifted up his eyes and saw Abraham afar off, and Lazarus in his bosom."*

Isaiah 57:1-2, *"See how the just man has perished, and no one lays it to heart: and righteous men are taken away, and no one considers: for the righteous has been removed out of the way of injustice. His burial shall be in peace; he has been removed out of the way."*[246]

---

[245] See Revelation 21:9-13 the bride is a people.
[246] *Greek-English Septuagint: Brenton Edition.* Biblesoft Formatted Electronic Database. Copyright © 2020 by Biblesoft, Inc. All rights reserved.

"Abraham's Bosom is a unique phrase found in a parable of Jesus describing the place where Lazarus went after death (Luke 16:19-31). It is a figurative phrase that appears to have been drawn from a widely held belief that the righteous would rest by Abraham's side. This was an opinion described in Jewish literature at the time of Christ. The word *kolpos* literally refers to the side or lap of a person. Figuratively, as in this case, it refers to a place of honor reserved for a special guest, like its usage in John 13:23. In the case of Lazarus, the reserved place is special because it is beside Abraham, the father of all the righteous. The phrase may be synonymous to the paradise promised to the thief on the cross (Luke 23:43). Together, these passages support the conviction that a believer enjoys immediate bliss at the moment of physical death."[247]

Paradise is a loanword borrowed from the Persians. It means "an area enclosed by a wall or garden." From the beginning, it was taught that Yahweh provided a "paradise" for the righteous dead. However, that paradise was in the underworld. That is why Yeshua promised the penitent thief, *"Today you will be with me in Paradise."*[248] Yeshua was not speaking of heaven but of the paradise in Hades.

This teaching is ancient but lost to the modern church. It involves more than what we can unpack in this present discussion, including the promise of redemption and resurrection. Yet, it must be understood that the Spirit of Death was permitted to hold captive the spirit of Adam and Adam's seed as the penalty for Adam's sin. The best and shortest explanation I can offer is - seed belongs with its "kind." These matters are legal, but the focus here involves human existence, apportioned to Adam. Humans are Adam's offspring and thus subject to the sin he committed and the penalty he owed.

Yeshua descended into the lower parts of the earth – before he ascended to take his seat at the right hand of the Ancient of Days.[249] Yeshua took from Death and Hades the keys to the netherworld. These ancient fallen gods can no longer hold the righteous captive – Adam's penalty was paid, and Adam was redeemed, along with his righteous seed.

Oh, and don't forget, all who believe in Yeshua are born again. That means they have the right to take on his DNA and become his seed, conformed to his image!

Philippians 3:20-21, *"For our citizenship is in heaven, from which we also eagerly wait for the Savior, the Lord Jesus Christ, who will transform our lowly body that it may be conformed to His glorious body, according to the working by which He is able even to subdue all things to Himself."*

1 Peter 1:22-23, *"Since you have purified your souls in obeying the truth through the Spirit in sincere love of the brethren, love one another fervently with a pure heart, having been born again, not of corruptible seed but incorruptible, through the word of God which lives and abides forever."*

Through this story in Genesis 23, Holy Spirit indicated that Yahweh bargained for a peaceful existence for the righteous until they could be redeemed!

---

[247] *Evangelical Dictionary of Biblical Theology*. Copyright © 1996 by Baker Books. All rights reserved. Used by permission
[248] Luke 23:43
[249] See Ephesians 4:9

*"Daniel spoke, saying, 'I saw in my vision by night, and behold, the four winds of heaven were stirring up the Great Sea. And **four** great beasts came up from the sea, each different from the other,"* Daniel 7:2-3.

Could the four beasts of Daniel merely be a different manifestation of the four giants of *Qiryath 'Arba*? Or perhaps, the four horsemen of Revelation? *"And I saw and behold a white horse: and he that sat on him had a bow, and a crown was given unto him: and he went forth conquering, and to conquer. And when he had opened the second seal, I heard the second beast say, Come and see. And there went out another red horse, and power was given to him that sat thereon to take peace from the earth, and that they should kill one another: and there was given unto him a great sword. And when he had opened the third seal, I heard the third beast say, Come and see. And I beheld, and lo a black horse, and he that sat on him had a pair of balances in his hand. And I heard a voice among the four beasts say, A measure of wheat for a penny, and three measures of barley for a penny; and see thou hurt not the oil and the wine. And when he had opened the fourth seal, I heard the voice of the fourth beast say, Come and see. And I looked, and behold a pale horse, and his name that sat on him was Death, and Hell followed with him. And power was given unto them over the fourth part of the earth, to kill with sword, and with hunger, and with death, and with the beasts of the earth,"* Revelation 6:2-8 KJV.

War has been present for a long time. Peace has not existed since before Cain slew Abel. Poverty and lack have also been around for a long time. Without a doubt, Death and Hades have been riding since Cain slew Abel. So, what I am suggesting is Yahweh allowed these gods to attempt to steal, kill, and destroy for a season of six thousand years. They had already rebelled. The Ancient of Days had already passed sentence upon them. Still, during those same six thousand years, Yahweh wanted a peaceful rest for His Beloved.

The abyss, the pit, hades, or whatever term is used, is inhabited by the fallen entities who hate humans. It belongs to Death. I'm not convinced that the netherworld was created by Yahweh as much as it was formed by the workings of the fallen god, Chaos.

Please understand the story of Abraham and Sarah occurred as written. However, this story is similar to what I imagine happened in the unseen realm when Yahweh demanded that the righteous dead not be terrorized. Due to Adam's sin, all the dead were taken by Death into the abyss, whether righteous or unrighteous. That is until the penalty owed by Adam could be paid. That penalty was not settled until the Eternal Melchizedek died on the Cross.

I'm sure you are ahead of me by now. While it is true that Yahweh's authority supersedes all others, that isn't what we are discussing. In this instance, the matter concerns territorial rights. The altar at Moriah needed to come first because the Eternal King, Yeshua, could not go into Hades and take from them their authority without legal cause. So, to complete this picture of redemption, Isaac had to representationally "die" on the altar and then be received again by his father, and then, days later, he and his father secured the field of Ephron (who represents the Canaanites – humiliation).

These things parallel, or type, the work of Yeshua. Yeshua demanded the keys to death, hell, and the grave. He had the right; he was transported by the fallen realm into Hades illegally. Now that we have this understanding, we can see the significance of the promise, "your Descendent shall possess the gates of His enemies."[250] Genesis 23:17-20, *"So Abraham secured Ephron's field in Machpelah, next to Mamre, including the field, the cave that was in it, and all the trees that were in the field and all around its border, as his property in the presence of the sons of Heth before all who entered the gate of Ephron's city. After this, Abraham buried his wife Sarah in the cave in the field of Machpelah next to Mamre (that is, Hebron) in the land of Canaan. So, Abraham secured the field and the cave that was in it as a burial site from the sons of Heth,"* The NET Bible.

Abraham did not want others to trample on Sarah's burial place. For that reason, the cave and the field surrounding it had to belong to him, legally.

Reading in between the lines and the Hebrew of the text. Since the property was next to Mamre, Abraham purchased it because it was where he had lived. I am convinced this was where he had built his altar to Yahweh and where Yahweh had appeared to him. It was a sacred place, therefore, a fitting resting place for Sarah.

Perhaps I have left you with more questions than I have answered. But here is the bottom line: Everything that Yahweh does is LEGAL.

250 Genesis 22:17

Genesis Twenty-Four

Genesis 24:1-9, *Now Abraham was old, well advanced in age; and the Lord had blessed Abraham in all things. So Abraham said to the oldest servant of his house, who ruled over all that he had, 'Please,* **put your hand under my thigh,** *and I will make you swear by the Lord, the God of heaven and the God of the earth, that* **you will not take a wife for my son from the daughters of the Canaanites,** *among whom I dwell; but you shall go to my country and to my family, and take a wife for my son Isaac.' And the servant said to him, "Perhaps the woman will not be willing to follow me to this land. Must I take your son back to the land from which you came?" But Abraham said to him, 'Beware that you do not take my son back there. The Lord God of heaven, who took me from my father's house and from the land of my family, and who spoke to me and swore to me, saying, "To your descendants, I give this land," He will send His angel before you. You shall take a wife for my son from there. And if the woman is not willing to follow you, then you will be released from this oath*; **only do not take my son back there.**' *So, the servant put his hand under the thigh of Abraham, his master, and swore to him concerning this matter"* (emphasis added).

Abraham remarried and started another family, and Isaac, according to the *Book of Jasher*, went to live with Shem. Isaac needed to learn the ways of Yahweh and how to be Melchizedek. However, Abraham grew old, and it came time to hand over to Isaac the family "company," but first, Isaac needed a bride.

In that era, the father was responsible for arranging the marriages of his children. This was especially true for the son who would inherit the father's portion. That son would be the overseer of the extended family, including their inheritance. That son received a "double portion" of the estate so that he might provide adequately for the family. He was the firstborn of the family. And like the generational Firstborn of the Melchizedek, he was his father's choice, not necessarily the son born first.

Isaac was well past the age of thirty (according to the *Book of Jasher*, he was forty). However, he had been busy preparing to be the next Melchizedek. That meant Isaac first needed to serve in the priesthood and be appointed in his generation as Firstborn.

If the *Book of Jasher* is correct, then Shem was alive. In fact, Shem lived for another seventy years. Shem and his great-grandson, Eber, lived in Salem; they would also train Jacob.

Shem, Eber, and Isaac were all that was left of the Melchizedek Priesthood system. As of this writing, I have not found an account of Shem's son, Arphaxad, and Selah (grandson) serving as Melchizedeks or Firstborn Priests. Arphaxad would pass in ten years after this story, and Selah in less than forty. All of Eber's sons had already died; his sole surviving "son"[251] was Abraham. That meant Isaac was "solely" the future of the Melchizedekian Order.

---

251 Abraham was Eber's great-great-great-great grandson.

That aside, it was time for Isaac to have a wife and produce sons. So, Abraham called for the servant who had been with him the longest, the one he trusted. Genesis 24 doesn't name the servant, but the *Book of Jasher* nonetheless proclaims him to be Eliezer.

And Abraham called for Eliezer, his head servant, to give him orders concerning his house, and he came and stood before him. And Abraham said to him, "Behold, I am old, I do not know the day of my death; for I am advanced in days; now, therefore, rise up, go forth and do not take a wife for my son from this place and from this land, from the daughters of the Canaanites amongst whom we dwell. But go to my land and to my birthplace, and take from thence a wife for my son, and the Lord God of Heaven and earth who took me from my father's house and brought me to this place, and said unto me, 'To thy seed will I give this land for an inheritance forever,' he will send his angel before thee and prosper thy way, that thou mayest obtain a wife for my son from my family and from my father's house."[252]

Abraham placed two demands on his servant, asking him to swear by oath not to choose a Canaanite woman or take Isaac to search for a bride. Instead, the servant was to select a bride for Isaac from Terah's family. This was extremely important for several reasons, but primarily because Abraham knew the "ancestors" of his family. He knew they did not worship Yahweh as he did, but to his knowledge, none were spawned from the fallen gods. The same could not be said of Canaanite women.

Abraham bound his servant by oath before Yahweh, the *Elohiym*. "An oath is always sworn in the name of a god. This places a heavy responsibility on the one who swears such an oath to carry out its stipulations since he would be liable to the divine as well as human retribution if he did not. Sometimes, as in this case, a gesture is added to the oath. The gesture usually is symbolic of the task to be performed by the oath-taker. For instance, by placing his hand inside Abraham's thigh (in the vicinity of or on the genitals), the servant ties his oath of obedience to the acquisition of a wife for Isaac and thus the perpetuation of Abraham's line."[253]

The practice of marrying within one's own tribe or family is called endogamy. Endogamy could be the result of religious, social, or ethnic concerns. In this text, it appears to be ethnic in that there are no suggestions that the family of Laban, Rebekah, and Rachel shares the religious beliefs of Abraham and his family. Likewise, social standing is usually an issue only when nobility and commoners are involved, or certain classes of urban society are seen as necessarily distinct. Ethnic concerns usually center around clan traditions or family landholdings. At times they represent long-established hostilities between two groups. In this text, the endogamy seems motivated by the covenant that seeks to prevent Abraham and his family from simply being assimilated into the ethnic melting pot in Canaan.[254]

> Genesis 24:10-14, *"Then the servant took **ten** of his master's **camels** and departed, for all his **master's goods were in his hand**. And he arose and went to **Mesopotamia, to the city of Nahor**. And he made his camels kneel outside the city by a **well of water at evening time**, the*

---

[252] Johnson, Ken. *Ancient Book of Jasher* (pp. 52-53). Kindle Edition.
[253] *IVP Bible Background Commentary: Old Testament*, Copyright © 2000 by John H. Walton, Victor H. Matthews, and Mark W. Chavalas. Published by InterVarsity Press. All rights reserved.
[254] Ibid. Gen. 24:4

time when women go out to draw water. Then he said, **'O Lord God of my master Abraham,** *please give me success this day, and show kindness to my master Abraham. Behold, here I stand by the well of water, and the daughters of the men of the city are coming out to draw water. Now let it be that the young woman to whom I say, "Please let down your pitcher that I may drink," and she says,* **"Drink, and I will also give your camels a drink"** — *let her be the one You have appointed for Your servant Isaac. And by this, I will know that You have shown kindness to my master"'* (emphasis added).

The occasional reference to camels in Genesis is authenticated by evidence found in Ugarit texts from the early second millennium. Although their use for transporting goods was not commonly accepted until about 1200 B.C. It was known that a camel could carry heavy loads through hostile desert terrains. Still, the means to domesticate these animals was limited. The domestication of camels parallels the development of saddles. Accordingly, to own a camel and a saddle was a sign of wealth. To own ten such animals spoke of extreme wealth.

Mesopotamia (between the rivers) was the Greek term applied to the entire region between the Euphrates and Tigris Rivers. In the text, "Mesopotamia" is the translation for the Hebrew expression *"Aram naharayim,"* meaning *"Aram* of the two rivers," a term that denotes more precisely only the northwestern part of Mesopotamia. Nahor, probably should be identified with Nakhur (which is mentioned in ancient texts recovered from Mari on the Euphrates), was located near Haran in northern Mesopotamia. "Nahor" is also the name of Terah's father and Abraham's brother. The use of the same name for both a city and a person is not unusual; settlements were sometimes named after people, and people were sometimes named after places.[255]

Communal wells, or water springs, were usually located outside a town's main gate if the city was walled. If not, then very close to the city proper as possible. Depending on the water source, the well might be below ground level. If that were the case, the well could be difficult to reach. Young maidens were typically assigned the task of drawing water for the family. Primarily because they were the most physically fit for such a demanding chore. For safety's sake, they mainly went to the communal well in groups, generally in the cool of the early morning and evening.

Merchants traveled in caravans. Those caravans would seek water for their animals and, of course, their weary travelers. It was customary for travelers to rest at the well before entering the town proper. This was especially true if the city, like Nahor, was on one of the major trade routes. However, politeness demanded that one seek permission to draw "water" for themselves or their animals. Yet, on the other hand, hospitality compelled to offer the traveler a drink. But a young maiden was not obligated to also draw water for a visitor's animals. That Rebekah extended this courtesy to Abraham's servant indicated that she had uncommon grace, which made her suitable as a king's bride. So, to Abraham's servant, this act answered his prayer, which was prayed to Yahweh *Elohiym*, asking that a maid give him water to drink and also for his

---

[255] ESV Study Bible, English Standard Version® [ESV®], Copyright © 2008 by Crossway Bibles, a publishing ministry of Good News Publishers. All rights reserved. Study Notes edition arranged for PC Study Bible, © Biblesoft, Inc

camels. He bargained that if a maid did, he would receive her as Isaac's appointed bride.

The request the servant made was considerable since there were ten camels. To fulfill his request, Rebekah had to draw water ten times for each camel. A thirsty camel can drink more than twenty-five gallons of water; the jug she would have carried held no more than three gallons. Watering the camels would have taken considerable time and left her exhausted.

According to the text, the well at Nahor was below ground. Rebekah had to go down to draw water, then climb back up. Though the task was grueling, she did so without complaint. Abraham's servant was astonished (wondering) at her graciousness. In fact, he was stunned to silence. He, however, wanted one more sign from Yahweh to know for sure she was indeed the one appointed unto Isaac. She had to be from Abraham's family.

Genesis 24:15-28: *"And it happened, before he had finished speaking, behold, Rebekah, who was born to Bethuel, son of Milcah, the wife of Nahor, Abraham's brother, came out with her pitcher on her shoulder. Now, the young woman was very beautiful to behold, a virgin; no man had known her. And she* **went down to the well, filled her pitcher, and came up.** *And the servant ran to meet her and said, 'Please let me drink a little water from your pitcher.' So, she said, 'Drink, my lord.' Then she quickly let her pitcher down to her hand and gave him a drink. And when she had finished giving him a drink, she said, 'I will draw water for your camels also until they have finished drinking.'* **Then she quickly emptied her pitcher into the trough, ran back to the well to draw water, and drew for all his camels. And the man, wondering at her,** *remained silent to know whether the Lord had made his journey prosperous or not. So, it was when the camels had finished drinking that the man took a* **golden nose ring weighing half a shekel and two bracelets for her wrists weighing ten shekels of gold** *and said, 'Whose daughter are you? Tell me, please, is there room in your father's house for us to lodge?' So, she said to him, 'I am the daughter of Bethuel, Milcah's son, whom she bore to Nahor.' Moreover, she said, 'We have both straw and feed enough and room to lodge.' Then the man bowed down his head and worshiped (Yahweh). And he said, 'Blessed be the (Yahweh Elohiym) of my master Abraham, who has not forsaken His mercy and His truth toward my master. As for me, being on the way,* **Yahweh led me to the house of my master's brethren.'** *So, the young woman ran and told her mother's household these things"* (emphasis added).

Nose rings were trendy during the Bronze and Iron Ages. Most were made of silver, bronze, or gold. They were often tubular with two ends for placing in the nostril, and some included a tiny pendant. The bracelets were worn around the wrist as bangles. The gold the servant gave Rebekah was considerable since a ten-shekel bracelet weighed about four ounces. A half-shekel measure of weight equaled one-fifth of an ounce. The servant gave Rebekah far more than her service necessitated, for a laborer of that period, if blessed, might expect ten shekels per year.

The servant's gifts and questions ("Whose daughter are you? Is there room in your father's house?") clued Rebekah to his intent: a marriage proposal was in the offering. And because Rebekah perceived his purpose, she ran to tell her mother of "these things."

> Genesis 24:29-49, *"Now Rebekah had a brother whose name was **Laban, and Laban ran out to the man by the well.** So, it came to pass when he saw the nose ring and the bracelets on his sister's wrists, and when he heard the words of his sister Rebekah, saying, 'Thus the man spoke to me,' that he went to the man. And there he stood by the camels at the well. And **he said, 'Come in, O blessed of Yahweh!** Why do you stand outside? For I have prepared the house and a place for the camels.' Then the man came to the house. And he unloaded the camels and provided straw and feed for the camels and water to wash his feet and the feet of the men who were with him. Food was set before him to eat, but he said, **'I will not eat until I have told about my errand.'** And he said, 'Speak on.' So, he said, 'I am Abraham's servant. Yahweh has blessed my master greatly, and he has become great; and He has given him flocks and herds, silver and gold, male and female servants, and camels and donkeys. And Sarah, my master's wife, bore a son to my master when she was old; and **to him, he has given all that he has.** Now my master made me swear, saying, "You shall not take a wife for my son from the daughters of the Canaanites, in whose land I dwell; but you shall **go to my father's house and to my family,** and take a wife for my son." And I said to my master, "Perhaps the woman will not follow me." But he said to me, "Yahweh, before whom I walk, will send His angel with you and prosper your way; and you shall take a wife for my son from my family and from my father's house. You will be clear from this oath when you arrive among my family, for if they do not give her to you, then you will be released from my oath." And this day, I came to the well. I said, "O Yahweh God of my master Abraham, if You will now prosper the way in which I go, behold, I stand by the well of water; and it shall come to pass that when the virgin comes out to draw water, and I say to her, 'Please give me a little water from your pitcher to drink,' and she says to me, 'Drink, and I will draw for your camels also,' — let her be the woman whom the Lord has appointed for my master's son." **But before I had finished speaking in my heart, there was Rebekah,** coming out with her pitcher on her shoulder; and she went down to the well and drew water. And I said to her, "Please let me drink." And she made haste and let her pitcher down from her shoulder and said, "Drink, and I will give your camels a drink also." So, I drank, and she gave the camels a drink also. Then I asked her and said, "Whose daughter are you?" And she said, "The daughter of Bethuel, Nahor's son, whom Milcah bore to him." **So, I put the nose ring on her nose and the bracelets on her wrists.** And I bowed my head and worshiped the Lord, and blessed the Lord God of my master Abraham, **who had led me in the way of truth to take the daughter of my master's brother for his son.** Now, if you will deal kindly and truly with my master, tell me. And if not, tell me that I may turn to the right hand or to the left"* (emphasis added).

The literal meaning of this story is transparent. We shall examine its symbolism shortly. But first, note that Rebekah's brother, Laban, is the same person Jacob would go to for sanctuary later in Genesis. Then note that Abraham's servant would not rest until he was sure Laban understood why he had come to Nahor. The servant would not partake of wine or food until all the terms of the marriage proposal were met.

Additionally, the jewelry he gave to Rebekah was a token guaranteeing his sincerity. Rebekah was his choice for Isaac, but he acted upon Abraham's behalf, not on his own. So, the servant asked, "Will you bargain with me,[256] or do I go on to look for another?"

> Genesis 24:50-61, *"Then Laban and Bethuel answered, and they said, **'The matter has gone out from Yahweh;** we are not able to speak bad or good to you. Here is Rebekah before you. Take her and go; let her be a wife for the son of your master as Yahweh has spoken.' And it happened that when the servant of Abraham heard their words, he bowed down to the ground to Yahweh. And the **servant brought out silver jewelry, gold jewelry, and garments, and he gave them to Rebekah. And he gave precious gifts to her brother and to her mother**. And he and the men who were with him ate and drank, and they spent the night. And they got up in the morning, and he said, 'Let me go to my master.' And her brother and her mother said, 'Let the girl remain with us ten days or so; after that, she may go.' And he said to them, 'Do not delay me. Now, Yahweh has made my journey successful. Let me go. I must go to my master.' And they said, 'Let us call the girl and ask her opinion.' And they called Rebekah and said to her, 'Will you go with this man?" And she said, **'I will go.'** So, they sent Rebekah, their sister, her nurse, and the servant of Abraham and his men. And they blessed Rebekah and said to her, 'You are our sister; may you become countless thousands; **and may your offspring take possession of the gate of his enemies.'** And Rebekah and her maidservants arose, and they mounted the camels and followed the man. And the servant took Rebekah and left."* (The Lexham English Bible emphasis added).

Laban knew Abraham, if not personally; he knew of him through his father and grandfather, Bethel and Nahor. So, when Abraham's servant asked to enter their house as a Matchmaker, Laban accepted the servant. First, however, there needed to be an agreement that this marriage between the two families benefited both. Which gives meaning to Laban's statement: "The matter has gone out from Yahweh." Laban was stating he agreed - Yahweh had brought the servant to Nahor.

Next, there had to be an exchange of value for the bride. Only after an exchange of value was realized was a marriage legal. Rebekah's family was in no regard as wealthy as Abraham. She would not have been drawing water at the well if they were. A servant would have gone in her stead. Hence, due to the family's standing, the proper protocol was to offer her family a bridal payment, a *mohar*. This would compensate her family for the loss of her labor.

Abraham's servant had come with ten camels laden with *mohar* and *mattan*. The bride received the *mattan*. A gift typically used to prepare her for marriage. The *mohar* and the *mattan* could be offered in currency, but it was also acceptable to give valuables instead. Gifts given to the bride by her family were *shiluhim*, parting gifts. Rebekah's "nurse" was the parting gift her family gave to her. A dowry was commonly thought of as the bride's inheritance. Her share of her father's possessions. That is why the dowry or *shiluhim* was hers, not her groom's.

---

256 A formal agreement needed to be negotiated.

Once a marriage contract was agreed upon, the marriage was finalized, except for the act of consummation. However, coupling was not what made the agreement final or legal. The exchange of the *mohar* and *mattan* "sealed the deal" and why Abraham's servant would sit at Laban's table only after all terms were met.

Usually, the time between signing the agreement and its completion would take months. But, in this case, Abraham's servant was anxious to return to his master. Since the distance between Nahor and Beersheba was great, the trek would require many weeks. Although her family asked for more time, the servant refused to grant their wish. So, the family asked Rebekah if she was willing to leave immediately. She was. Rebekah was ready to go, demonstrating her acceptance of Isaac, sight unseen. She considered herself married to him and her obligation to her mother's house complete.

The family blessed Rebekah, "may your offspring take possession of the gate of **his** enemies." That blessing was royal – literally and typically spoken over rulers.

> Genesis 24:62-67, *"Now Isaac came from the way of **Beer Lahai Roi**, for he dwelt in the South. And Isaac went out to meditate in the field in the evening, and he lifted his eyes and looked, and there, the camels were coming. Then Rebekah lifted her eyes, and when she saw Isaac, she dismounted from her camel, for she had said to the servant, 'Who is this man walking in the field to meet us?' The servant said, 'It is my master.' So, **she took a veil and covered herself.** And the servant told Isaac all the things that he had done. Then Isaac brought her **into his mother Sarah's tent**, and he took Rebekah, and **she became his wife**, and he loved her. So, Isaac was **comforted** after his mother's death"* (emphasis added).

Beer Lahai Roi means "well of the Living One who sees me." That oasis was southwest of Hebron in the desert of Negev. You might recall that it was the well that was named by Hagar. Scripture is not clear if Isaac lived there or if he was visiting. Nonetheless, it was there at that oasis where Isaac first saw Rebekah, and she saw Isaac. How appropriate.

To "lift up one's eyes" is an idiom that underscores a close examination of someone or thing. Isaac lifted his eyes and saw the caravan of camels as it approached. At the same time, Rebekah lifted her eyes and saw Isaac. Rebekah then dismounted to inquire who he was. As soon as she knew it was Isaac, she veiled her face.

While in the groom's presence, a bride's face was veiled, that is, until the marriage was consummated.

Rebekah had traveled from Nahor without a veil. That she veiled herself suggests she showed respect and submission to Isaac as his bride.

Once Isaac was told all that happened, he accepted the servant's choice. He took Rebekah to his mother's tent, another biblical idiom that indicates Isaac received Rebekah as his wife. He made her the mistress of his house, establishing her with all rights and honors as his wife.

Genesis, Chapter 24 is the last chapter of Volume One. As we have progressed through Genesis, I have attempted to present the text's literal meaning. However, if we fail to look at the symbolism, the spiritual depth of Moses' writing, which was inspired by God, is missed.

John 4:24, *"God is Spirit* (pneuma), *and those who worship Him must worship in spirit* (pneuma) *and truth* (aletheia).*" Pneuma*, as used in this context, means "rational soul." *Aletheia* means "not ignorant." Thus, those who worship Yahweh must not be ignorant but rationalize why they pay homage to Him. The meaning of John 4:24 is simple. It doesn't matter where you are when you acknowledge Yahweh. When you do, however, recognize Yahweh because He is a loving Father. He gives good gifts, meant to prepare humans for eternity, as the Bride of Christ.

"But when the Helper comes, whom I shall send to you from the Father, the Spirit of truth who proceeds from the Father, He will testify of Me. And you also will bear witness because you have been with Me from the beginning."[257]

The name Eliezer means – Help of my God or God's help. So, with that in mind, let's look at the symbolism.

I imagine that the Ancient of Days sat with Holy Spirit and discussed Yeshua's bride at some point in the past. Father might have said to Holy Spirit, "Please, put your hand under my thigh. Swear that there will be no evil in her. She must be pure. Her garments must not have spots or wrinkles. She must be family."

"If I go to *'erets* and find her, what shall I do if she is unwilling to conform?" asked Holy Spirit. Ancient of Days shook His head, "You may not take my Son back there, but you will find her by testifying His works. You are released from this oath if none are willing to follow you. Just do not take Yeshua back there. Instead, unite them only when she is made ready."

"When the Day of Pentecost had fully come, they were all with one accord in one place. And suddenly, there came a sound from heaven, as of a mighty rushing wind, and it filled the whole house where they were sitting. Then there appeared to them divided tongues, as of fire and sat upon each of them. And they were all filled with the Holy Spirit and began to speak with other tongues, as the Spirit gave them utterance."[258]

The disciples went down to the Well of Oath and filled their pitchers, and when they came up, a crowd outside heard the strange sound they made. "Whatever can this mean?" asked those standing nearby. Someone answered, "They are full of new wine." Peter raised his voice and said to the crowd, "All who dwell in Jerusalem, let this be known to you, and heed my words. These are not drunk, as you suppose, since it is only the third hour of the day. But this is what was spoken by the prophet Joel - it shall come to pass I will pour out on all flesh My Spirit. Drink and be filled."

Those who drank the new wine of Holy Spirit became the Church, betrothed to Yeshua. *"For I am jealous for you with godly jealousy. For I have betrothed you to one husband, that I may present you as a chaste virgin to Christ."*[259]

---

[257] John 15:26-27
[258] Acts 2:1-4
[259] 2 Corinthians 11:2-3,

"There are different kinds of gifts, but the same Spirit…, to each one, the manifestation of the Spirit is given for the common good. To one there is given through the Spirit the message of wisdom, to another the message of knowledge by means of the same Spirit, to another faith by the same Spirit, to another gift of healing by that one Spirit, to another miraculous power, to another prophecy, to another distinguishing between spirits, to another speaking in different kinds of tongues, and to still another the interpretation of tongues. All these are the work of one and the same Spirit, and he gives them to each one, just as he determines" 1 Corinthians 12:4-11 NIV.

Holy Spirit came to *'erets* bearing gifts to prepare the House of Israel for her marriage. He brought her oil for her lamp. And strength to overcome her sensual nature.

"Listen, O daughter, consider and incline your ear; forget your own people also, and your father's house so the King will greatly desire your beauty because He is your Lord, worship Him." [260]

"You were bought at a price; do not become slaves of men." [261]

"For you were bought at a price; therefore, glorify God in your body and in your spirit, which are God's." [262]

"Then I heard a loud voice saying in heaven, 'Now salvation, and strength, and the kingdom of our God, and the power of His Christ have come, for the accuser of our brethren, who accused them before our God, day, and night has been cast down. And they overcame him by the blood of the Lamb and by the word of their testimony, and they did not love their lives to the death." [263]

"Come, I will show you the bride, the Lamb's wife." And he carried me away in the Spirit to a great and high mountain. He showed me the great city, the holy Jerusalem, descending out of heaven from God, having the glory of God. Her light was like a most precious stone, like a jasper stone, clear as crystal." [264]

2 Thessalonians 2:13-14, *"But we are bound to give thanks to God always for you, brethren beloved by the Lord because God from the beginning chose you for salvation through sanctification by the Spirit and belief in the truth."*

Ephesians 1:4-6, *"He chose us in Him before the foundation of the world, that we should be holy and without blame before Him in love, having predestined us to adoption as sons by Jesus Christ to Himself, according to the good pleasure of His will, to the praise of the glory of His grace, by which He made us accepted in the Beloved."*

---

[260] Psalms 45:10-11
[261] 1 Corinthians 7:23-24
[262] 1 Corinthians 6:20
[263] Revelation 12:10-12
[264] Revelation 21:9-111

Source Material

Barnhouse, D. G. (1965). *The Invisible War*. Grand Rapids, Michigan: Zondervan.

Bullinger, R. E. (1893). *The Witness of the Stars*. London, England.

Cepher Publishing. (2016). *Cepher*. Dexter, Michigan: Thomson-Shore Co.

Charles, R. H. (1913). *The Book of Jubilees*. Oxford: Clarendon Press.

Charles, R. (n.d.). *The Book of Enoch*.

Collins, S., & Scott, L. (2020). *Discovering the City of Sodom*. Howard Books.

Cross, F. M. (1973). *Canaanite Myth and Hebrew Epic*. Cambridge, Massachusetts: Harvard University Press.

Davis, J. J. (1968). *Biblical Numerology*. Grand Rapids, Michigan: Baker Book House.

Flynn, D. (2012). *Temple at the Center of Time*. Crane, Missouri: Defense Publishing.

Gilbert, D. P. (2018). *Last Clash of the Titans*. Crane, Missouri: Defender Publishing.

Gilbert, S. K. (2019). *Veneration: Unveiling the Ancient Realms of Demonic Kings and Satan's Battle Plan for Armageddon*. Defender Publishing.

Ginzberg, L. (n.d.). *The Legends of the Jews - Volume One*.

Hamp, D. (2011). *Corrupting the Image*. Defender Publishing, LLC.

Hamp, D. (2021). *Corrupting the Image II*. Eskaton Media Group.

Heiser, M. S. (2015). *Supernatural*. Bellingham, Washington: Lexham Press.

Heiser, M. S. (2015). *The Unseen Realm*. Bellingham, Washington: Lexham Press.

Heiser, M. S. (2017). *Reversing Hermon*. Defender Publishing.

Heiser, M. S. (2018). *Angels, What the Bible Really Says About God's Heavenly Host*. Bellingham, Washington: Lexham Press.

Johnson, K. (2013). *Ancient Book of Jasher*. Biblefacts Annotated Edition.

Josephus, F. (n.d.). *The Complete Works of Josephus*. Grand Rapids, Michigan: Kregel Publications.

Ken Johnson, T. (2006). *Ancient Sedar Olam*.

Ken Johnson, T. (2010). *Ancient Post-Flood History*.

Ken Johnson, T. (2020). *The Ancient Dead Sea Scroll Calendar*.

Ken Johnson, T. (n.d.). *Ancient Book of Enoch*.

Missler, C. (2014). *Signs in the Heavens*. Coeur d'Alene, Indiania: Koinonia House.

Munk, R. M. (1983). *The Wisdom in the Hebrew Alphabet*. Brooklyn, New York: Mesorah Publications, Ltd.

Segal, A. F. (1945). *Two Powers in Heaven*. Baylor University Press.

Seiss, J. A. (1884). *The Gospel in the Stars*.

Glossary

Adam [Hebrew] – the name given to the first human who was created by God. The term *adam* first appears in Genesis 1:26 when, *"God said, 'Let us make man (adam) in our image.'"* However, as a proper name, it was first used in Genesis 2:19. *"Out of the ground, the Lord God formed every beast of the field, and every fowl of the air and brought them unto Adam…."* When used as a noun but not a proper name, *adam* means showing blood as flushed or blush, particularly on the face. Biblically, *adam* often refers to the human species.

Anoint - the application of oil poured upon a designate during the ceremonial rites of ordination. Ancient ceremonies were extensive, involving a considerable amount of dedicated oil poured upon the head of the postulate and allowed to flow until it reached his feet. Only when drenched with oil was the new priest or king truly anointed. An anointing ceremony provided the outward exhibition of an inward consecration. *Mashach* [Hebrew] and *Christos* [Greek] refer to the consecrated individual who had undergone such an anointing ceremony. Messiah is the English pronunciation of *Mashach*. New Testament Christians used *Christos* (Christ) to refer to Jesus, whereas the Jews used *Mashach*. Regarding the Melchizedek Kingdom and the anointing ceremony, the oil represented the empowerment of the Holy Spirit and an outward indicator that the king/priest embodied the Holy Spirit.

Apocrypha [Latin]– Plural in form but used as a singular verb, referred to the fourteen books in the Septuagint. These fourteen, which were not canonized as being inspired, were considered valuable sources of historical information. Various portions were proposed as additions to the New Testament but were rejected by the Church Fathers as not inspired. The Protestants felt these scrolls were non-canonical because they were not a part of the original Hebrew Scriptures. Therefore, they omitted them from their Bible. Yet, on the other hand, they were included in the Vulgate. Eleven, in fact, were accepted and placed in the Roman Catholic canon.

Appointed – simply means "to be selected," or designated for the priesthood of the Melchizedek Priesthood as a Firstborn. A Firstborn was selected by his father, then tested. If he met all the qualifying requirements, only then was he approved. Once approved, the Firstborn was ceremoniously anointed and publically proclaimed by his father with the words, "This is my beloved son, in whom I am well pleased."

Bene' elohim [Hebrew] – an ancient Sematic term typically used to identify certain divine beings, primarily those of high rank, since the phrase means "sons of God."

Canaan [Hebrew] - *Kená'an* was a Sematic-speaking civilization in the region of the ancient Levant. The Ancient Greeks referred to this civilization as the Phoenicians. *Genesis* chronicles Canaan as the grandson of Noah. And also, as the progenitor of those who occupied the Promised Land, before and after, the Israelites made their exodus from Egypt.

Celestial – an adjective that pertains to the sky, to the heavens. When used as a suggestive of heaven, the term relates to spiritual entities. Celestial is Latin, meaning "of the sky."

Cosmos – the present-day understanding of this word was derived from the Greek term "*kosmos*," which initially meant the orderly arrangement of the universe. Over time the term came to be understood as the opposite of chaos. However, it was also used to denote the world, or earth, mainly when translating the New Testament from Greek to English. Yet, the ancients associated cosmos with all existence - heaven, earth, and the underworld.

Curse – *qalal* [Hebrew] means to show contempt; despise; to make small or of no value.

Death – *muwth* [Hebrew] meaning to die; to cease to exist in the physical world; the process of a spirit departing the body.

Dimension – the measurement of something, usually referring to the length, width, height, or depth. The number of elements or magnitude of size. A dimension is a range or degree to which something exists. A fundamental unit of measurement.

Divine Council – the Divine Council is an assembly of superior beings that sit in heaven's "high" court as judges over the cosmos.

Domain – a territory or land that a ruler governs: an area of knowledge or activity.

Dominion – the power to rule; the control (authority) over a territory; sovereignty.

Earth/*erets* – the abode of the living embodied human souls. Symbolically, '*erets* is the field of Yah.

Eden – depending upon how the word is placed in a sentence, may refer to the territory assigned to Adam as his original home or to a place of spontaneous pleasure. If the first definition is the intent, then Eden is viewed as having a masculine tense. If the latter meaning is the intent, then the tense is feminine and not capitalized. Eden, as a metaphor, refers to Yah's cosmic domain, which houses His celestial "high place," His Gan (garden), the heavenly Jerusalem.

Elohim – *Elohiym* [Hebrew], the plural form of *Eloah*. In the ordinary sense, *elohim* should be translated as gods. However, when specifically used in the plural form, especially if "the" is the precedent article, *elohim* is almost always translated as the Supreme God. In nearly all regards, *elohim* equates to *allah* [Aramaic], for both words denote the divine; or the deities that came from the higher dimensional spirit world. The singular root of *elohim* is *el*. *El* can either be translated as a god or as "God." When understood properly, *elohim* signifies residency, and *elohim*, when used in the collective sense, should be viewed as "those who are from the spiritual world." *Elohim* can literally be translated as the "gods of, or from, there."

Firstborn – the son who was chosen by his father, the Melchizedek, to represent the generation of his birth. This term did not signify a birth order. Instead, indicated a particular generation. The Firstborn was the "first of his generation." In other words, he was the priest "over" his generation. He served as such within the Melchizedek Priesthood because he was chosen and approved as righteous.

Hades – [Greek] is the underworld or netherworld and the name of its chief god. As a place, this sphere of existence was assigned to the divine beings who sin against Yahweh. However, its god (king) was also called *Apollyon* [Greek], *Abaddon* [Hebrew]. The Israelites used *Sheol* [Hebrew] to refer to the netherworld.

Heaven – *shamayim* [Hebrew] is the realm of the righteous, the present abode of Yahweh.

Holy – *Kodesh* [Hebrew] means to be set apart for, or unto, righteousness for the purposes of Yahweh.

Jurisdiction - a formal state or a domain such as a kingdom.

Kingdom – a territory governed by a king.

Melchizedek – the term Melchizedek was never a name but a declaration that stated, "my king is the righteous king." *Malk-i-zedek* is a construct phrase that translates as "my King is Righteous."

Nephilim is associated with the hybrid offspring of the Watchers of Genesis 6. There is compelling evidence that this term was misspelled in the original translated texts. The correct spelling renders the word *naphiyla*, which links the Watchers with the Mesopotamian *apkallus* (the sky-gods) and their offspring, who were giants.

Nimrod – the progenitor of the Assyrians and Babylonians. *Nimrod* means - "shall revolt."

Realm – a kingdom; a sphere of influence; a domain.

Rephaim [Hebrew] – Originally referred to a people who were giants. Over time this term was assigned to the dead warrior-kings that were either the Nephilim or their celestial fathers, the Watchers of Mount Hermon. These kings, when they lived, were treated as gods. When they died, they became the "shades" of the underworld, a metaphor suggesting spirit entities. The Rephaim were primarily Canaanite and revered as "the mighty men of old," empowered by a patron god known as *Rpu* or *Rapha*.

Satan [Hebrew] – translates as an adversary or challenger; it carries a legal connotation of being a prosecutor.

Serpent –*Nachash* is Hebrew for "serpent." The deciding factor as to how this word is defined is dependent upon which vowels are inserted into *n-ch-sh*. *Nochesh* – n. the diviner; *Nachash* – adj. denotes shiny or bright like copper. An image depicting a serpent was familiar to the ancients, mainly associated with the deities, the royal court, or both.

Sheol [Hebrew] - the underworld, the abode of the dead. Synonyms: the netherworld, the land/abode of the dead, the infernal regions, the abyss, the residence of the damned, perdition, hellfire, fire and brimstone, *Gehenna, Tophet, Abaddon, Hades, Tartarus*, the pit.

Spirit – *ruach* [Hebrew] translates as breath. *Ruach* is the unseen force of life.

Terrestrial – relates to earth; an inhabitant of *'erets*. A Latin term that means "of the earth."

Torah [Hebrew] – when translated as "teaching," the root means throwing or shooting an arrow. *Torah*, or Pentateuch, is the first five books: Genesis, Exodus, Leviticus, Numbers, and Deuteronomy. The Mosaic Law is *Torah*.

Yahweh [Hebrew] - derived from the Tetragrammaton *yod-heh-vav-heh* to represent the God of Abraham, Isaac, and Jacob. Creator of the Cosmos; Supreme God; Ancient of Days; God the Father; Giver of Life.

Yeshua [Hebrew] - a verb that means "to rescue" or "to deliver." Yeshua is transliterated from *Yehosua* (Joshua). Jesus is the Latin derivate of the Greek *Iesous*.

Made in the USA
Columbia, SC
14 August 2022